COACHING VOLLEYBALL

AMERICAN VOLLEYBALL COACHES ASSOCIATION

Edited By Kinda S. Asher

MASTERS PRESS

ssociation.

ISBN 1-57028-124-6
1. Volleyball—Coaching.   I. American Volleyball Coaches Association.
GV1015.5.C63C64   1997
796.325—dc21

97-2296
CIP

Published by Masters Press
A division of NTC/Contemporary Publishing Group, Inc.
4255 West Touhy Avenue, Lincolnwood (Chicago), Illinois 60646-1975 U.S.A.
Copyright © 1997 by American Volleyball Coaches Association
Printed in the United States of America
International Standard Book Number: 1-57028-124-6

18   17   16   15   14   13   12   11   10   9   8   7   6

Contents

ACKNOWLEDGMENTS

In today's world of increasingly sophisticated electronic gadgets, including the Internet, video conferencing, pagers and cellular phones, one might imagine the written word would experience a massive decline. However, experts agree that books remain one of the most tried-and-true methods of education available. This editor agrees and is happy to present *Coaching Volleyball* to its readers — those who still believe learning is an ongoing, ever-changing, hands-on experience.

Of course, the written word does not magically appear. It takes countless hours of time and effort on behalf of scads of people all with the same goal in mind — to provide a quality product. Those who have aided me in the process of seeing this publication come to fruition have that goal in mind.

First of all, I must thank Sandy Vivas, AVCA executive director, for her endless support and foresight to realize that coaches are always hungry for new volleyball knowledge. It is our job to provide it — and I believe we have served the reader well. To Tom Bast, publisher, and Heather Lowhorn, editor, both of whom represent Masters Press, this project is the direct result of your hard work.

The ones I truly have to thank, however, are the people who were willing to share their insight into this fast-developing sport. Volleyball is growing by leaps and bounds and it takes a truly dedicated individual to keep up. The authors of the chapters in this publication should be duly commended for their adherence to the principles of sound education for coaches. Their authorship, editing and, in some cases, second and third editing efforts, have not gone unnoticed. In addition, I took advantage of the members of the USA Volleyball Sports Medicine and Performance Commission (SMPC) to provide expert insight into a number of the book's chapters, as well as Ken Kontor, president of Conditioning Press and publisher of *Performance Conditioning for Volleyball*, who so graciously allowed us to reprint a number of offerings from his publication in an effort to promote coaching education in volleyball. Many thanks are extended to Dan Houser, whose eye through the photographic lens conceived many of the wonderful photos displayed in the book. Finally, I would be remiss if I failed to thank Bob Bertucci who edited *The AVCA Volleyball Handbook*, the original publication from which this book stems. Without the foundation he provided, this book would not have been possible.

Kinda S. Asher
AVCA Director of Publications
May 1997

PREFACE

More than 100 years have passed since the invention of the game of volleyball in Springfield, Mass., in 1895. The sport, from its humble beginnings at the YMCA in Springfield to one of the most watched competitions at the Olympic Games in Atlanta, has literally exploded onto the international sports scene. With the portentous growth of the game, however, comes unenviable responsibility on the part of those who teach the game. The volleyball coaches have a duty to themselves and to their players to provide the most comprehensive, safe and up-to-date training available. *Coaching Volleyball* is here to aid in that process.

The American Volleyball Coaches Association (AVCA) has the mission to educate volleyball coaches of all levels. It is one of the most comprehensive professional coaches' organizations in the world and continually strives to bring cutting edge material to the masses. With the help of Masters Press, that goal has been attained. *Coaching Volleyball* is one of the most sweeping publications catering to the sport of volleyball on the market today. It includes ideas, techniques and strategies from the top collegiate coaches in the country, as well as unmatched expertise from sports scientists and sports medicine professionals from around the country. The publication focuses on three elements of the game: basic (individual skills), advanced (team play) and related (program development), yet it also provides expert insight into injury prevention, statistics, nutrition and conditioning. Most importantly, however, is the foray into coaching philosophy and coaching ethics, two often-overlooked areas in instructional endeavors.

The book contains a myriad of visual references to educate and encourage the reader, from excellent photos and illustrations to the most informative diagrams. *Coaching Volleyball* is truly one-stop-shopping for the volleyball professional who is concerned with being the finest coach possible.

Kinda S. Asher

Credits:
General Editor: Kinda S. Asher, Director of Publications, American Volleyball Coaches Association
Copy Editor: Sandra L. Vivas, Executive Director, American Volleyball Coaches Association
Cover design by Suzanne Lincoln
Cover photographers: Dan Houser and Randy Nolen

CONTRIBUTORS

Andy Banachowski, head women's volleyball coach, UCLA

Doug Beal, head coach, 1984 U.S. men's Olympic gold medal team, current U.S. men's national team

Jacqueline Berning, Ph.D., R.D., assistant professor, Biology Department, University of Colorado, Colorado Springs

Laurel Brassey Iversen, head women's coach, University of New Mexico

Greg Brislin, M.S., C.S.C.S., USAV/AVCA Sports Medicine and Performance Commission

Jay Coakley, Ph.D., sociology professor, University of Colorado, Colorado Springs

Jim Coleman, director, National Teams Training Center

Frances Compton, assistant women's volleyball coach, Louisiana State University

*****Terry Condon**, assistant athletic director, UCLA

*****Tony Crabb**, staff member, U.S. men's national team

Barbara Day, M.S., R.D., C.N.

Linda Delk, head women's volleyball coach, University of Northern Colorado

Randy Dolson, head women's volleyball coach, University of Dubuque

*****Vanessa Draper**, graduate teaching associate, University of Tennessee

Reid P. Elam, Ph.D., A.T.,C., C.S.C.S., Washington State University

*****Cheryl Fuller**, certified athletic trainer, HealthSouth Sports Medicine and Rehabilitation Center, Birmingham, Ala.

Bob Gambardella, director of youth development and programs, USA Volleyball

Vern Gambetta, conditioning coach, Chicago White Sox

Kathy Gregory, head women's volleyball coach, University of California, Santa Barbara

Mick Haley, head coach, U.S. women's national team

Michael Harnden, girls' volleyball coach, Nazareth Academy, Rochester, N.Y.

Berkley Laite, librarian, head women's volleyball coach, Shippensburg University

Terry Lawton, Ph.D., nationally ranked official for the National Association for Girls and Women in Sport and USA Volleyball

Terry Liskevych, former head coach, U.S. women's national team

*****Sandy Lynn**, head women's volleyball coach, University of Tennessee

Len Marquart, Ph.D., Cornell University Cooperative Extension

M. Eileen Mathews, volleyball coach, East Valley School District, Yakima, Wash.

Dan McDonough, A.T.,C., former USA Volleyball national team conditioning coach

*****Lois Mueller**, associate professor, Concordia University

Marilyn Nolen, head women's volleyball coach, Saint Louis University

*****Ruth Nelson**, director of international volleyball for the Special Olympics

Author's position at the time the chapter was originally written

Bill Neville, head women's volleyball coach, University of Washington

Geri Polvino, Ph.D., head women's volleyball coach, Eastern Kentucky University

*Ian Pyka, strength training director, University of Massachusetts

Stephanie Schleuder, former head women's volleyball coach, University of Minnesota

Dave Shoji, head women's volleyball coach, University of Hawaii

Patti Stanton, girls' volleyball coach, Bryan Station High School, Lexington, Ky.

Rosie Wegrich, head women's volleyball coach, Cal Poly Pomona

*Craig Wrisberg, professor of sports psychology, University of Tennessee

Nate Zinsser, Ph. D. Sport psychologist, Performance Enhancement Center, United States Military Academy

The History of Volleyball

The world was a drastically different place in 1895, especially in a still-wet-behind-the-ears country called the United States of America. The unrest of the Civil War was but a 30-year-old memory and the citizens of this country were ready to take on the challenges the 20th century were sure to bring.

Indeed, 1895 was a year chock full of historic events for America. Stephen Crane's *The Red Badge of Courage*, a novel of impressionistic realism set on a Civil War battlefield, was published. President Grover Cleveland was in the White House just beginning his second term and was concerned with the assertion of U.S. hegemony in Latin America, bolstered by the auspices of the Monroe Doctrine. Despite a brilliant defense by none other than Clarence Darrow, Eugene Debs was convicted and imprisoned for leading a shutdown in the servicing of Pullman cars in Chicago. And William G. Morgan invented the game of volleyball at the Young Men's Christian Association (YMCA) in Holyoke, Mass.

Today, which of these landmark historical events still has a major influence over people? Considering the fact that volleyball is played by millions of people in the world and nobody even remembers Cleveland was the 22nd and 24th president of the United States, one could assume volleyball wins hands down!

The Birth of Volleyball

In 1895, William G. Morgan was the physical director of the YMCA in Holyoke, Mass., in charge of developing activities for the reams of local businessmen who would frequent the establishment in search of physical fitness. The sport of basketball had been invented four years earlier, yet many businessmen found the game too physically taxing. As a result, Morgan invented a game known as mintonette, which incorporated aspects of badminton (the net), basketball (the ball), baseball (the game was originally played in innings) and handball (the hands were used to hit the ball over the net).

"The objective was to hit the ball back and forth with the hands. Each team, having any number of players, was permitted three outs before the team forfeited the ball" (Kluka/Dunn, 7).

The game grew quite popular with the Holyoke businessmen in a very short time. Yet, the name "mintonette" did not seem to fit.

"Several months after the introduction of mintonette, Springfield College Professor Alfred T. Halstead convinced Mr. Morgan to change the name to volleyball because it was more descriptive and marketable to a sports-minded public" (Neville, 3).

By 1912, "the YMCA formed a special committee and developed major rule modifications, including standardizing ball handling. The court was enlarged to 35' x 60'; the net was raised to 7'6"; serve rotation of players was incorporated, as well as the establishment of the two-out-of-three game match. In 1916, the YMCA, in conjunction with the National Collegiate Athletic Association (NCAA), published men's rules. The net was elevated to 8' and the game was concluded at 15 points" (Kluka/Dunn, 7). Volleyball as we know it today had begun.

Governance of a Growing Sport

Undeniably, the game of volleyball spread like wildfire in the early part of the 20th century. U.S. missionaries introduced the game into Asia and Russia, while in 1918-19, U.S. armed forces brought volleyball to Europe. Worldwide growth of the sport then took place during World War II, resulting from American armed forces stationed in Europe once again. The popularity of the sport invited the formation of the United States Volleyball Association (USVBA) in 1928. In that year, the Volleyball Rules Committee of the YMCA was reorganized to become the USVBA, "whose purposes were to coordinate the volleyball rules on a national level and to create a national open tournament. The rules of the game, as well as information on various volleyball activities such as tournament standards and qualifying officials, have been published annually by the USVBA since its inception" (Haley, 2).

By 1948, it soon became evident that an international governing body was needed to oversee the sport on such a huge scale. As a result, the United States and 12 other nations joined together to form the FIVB. The first World Championships (for men) followed immediately in 1949 and were held in Prague, Czechoslovakia (the women first participated in the World Championships in 1952).

"Buoyed by the general public's acceptance of the game, the FIVB began lobbying to add volleyball to the Olympic Games, a dream that came true in Tokyo, Japan, 15 years later (1964)" (Olympics Factbook, 557).

Into the Future

The game of volleyball in the U.S. and around the world today is fast-paced, incredibly athletic and most of all, varied. Enthusiasts from all walks of life can enjoy the game year-round, indoors or out, using two, three, four or six players, on coed or single-sex teams. As a result, participation numbers have exploded. In addition, the U.S. men's and women's teams have enjoyed brilliant success internationally since the 1984 Olympic Games, garnering two golds, one silver and one bronze (men), along with one silver and one bronze (women).

Unique Features

Traditional indoor volleyball has several unique features. There are 12 players on the court — six per side — in a very small area. Each player must cover approximately 14 sq. m (150 sq. ft.) of the court. Players must play all positions and each position has different physical and technical demands. Legal contact with the ball is very limited in both time and distance, making precise movement prior to touching the ball extremely important. Volleyball is also the only sport in which a player's maximum force is typically applied while the body is unsupported (in the air). The game is characterized by short, high energy bursts and periods of rest. Unlike most other sports, volleyball games are most often determined by negative play — for example, a team failing to control the ball. The volleyball playing environment quickly and constantly changes because of the movement of the players, the speed of the ball, the variety of formations and movements of the two teams and the relationship of the ball to the players on both sides. The movements required of each player change at an extremely fast speed and the great variety of offensive and defensive maneuvers (for individuals or for whole teams) makes the environment even more changeable. Volleyball also requires a great deal of planned deception on the part of two highly trained teams. Thus, volleyball players require a wide range of abilities and volleyball training must be broad-based.

The Court

Volleyball is played on a court 18 m long by 9 m wide (59 ft. by 29.6 ft.). The court is defined by markings called boundary lines, attack lines and the center line. Boundary lines consist of the baselines (at each end of the court) and the sidelines (perpendicular to the net). Attack lines are used as guides for the hitters and are located where the hitter's approach to the ball begins. Extending indefinitely beyond the side lines, these lines are 3 meters from the center line on each side and parallel to it. The center line lies directly under the net and divides the playing area into two equal parts. Its 5 cm (2 in.) width was developed after the discovery that opposing players' feet went under the net and injuries occurred. The entire court is surrounded by boundary lines that are 5 cm (2 in.) wide and at least 2 m (6 ft. 6 ins.) from all obstructions. The height of the net measured from the center of the court is 2.43 m (7 ft. 11 5/8 ins.) for the men and 2.24 m (7 ft. 4 1/8 ins.) for women and children.

The Players

Volleyball is played with six players per team on the court at a time. Even though a team is allowed only six people on the court, it usually has 12 people on its roster, especially in international competition. Players start the game in the right, center and left front positions and the right, center and left back positions. Each player has a special task. On every team there are one or two setters whose primary responsibilities are to select a teammate who will attack the ball and to direct the ball to that attacker. Attackers (hitters) are players who focus on directing the ball into the opponent's court.

These two main positions — setter and attacker — can be further broken down. Besides setters, there are off-setters, players who usually play the right front position, where they are effective as either setters or hitters. Attackers can be divided into outside hitters and middle blockers. Outside hitters are usually strong, powerful players who can effectively hit a variety of shots around the block posed by the defenders' raised hands. Middle blockers utilize quick, deceptive movements to the set and hit with more finesse than raw force.

Players can also be front- or back-court specialists who play either the three front-court or the three back-court positions and then substitute out. Players are used on the substitution principle that pertains to that type of competition.

Equipment

Playing volleyball requires special equipment. The constant jumping involved in playing makes wearing proper footwear extremely important. Most people use lightweight footwear with strong ankle and arch support, as well as good shock absorption. Because volleyball players are constantly falling or diving on the floor, knee pads are essential. Clothing varies greatly in volleyball — players wear anything from long-sleeved to short-sleeved T-shirts, shorts or cycling shorts.

The Ball

A standard volleyball has a circumference of 65 to 67 cm (25 1/2 to 27 ins.) and weighs 260 to 280 g (9 to 10 oz.). The inflation pressure is stated on the ball and should be strictly observed in order to ensure normal feel and ball life expectancy. The pressure should be between 0.30 and 0.325 kg per cm2 (between 4.3 and 4.6 lbs. per square inch). The players should become familiar with the feel of a properly inflated ball and should strive to maintain that correct pressure. The referee must check the ball before and during the match to be sure it has not become wet or slippery.

The type of ball to select is determined by the type of use expected. Although a rubber ball will outlast even the toughest leather one, players may experience pain and a general loss of feeling in the forearms when using a rubber ball. Consequently, several manufacturers have produced relatively inexpensive, amazingly durable leather balls which prove to be much better than rubber ones.

The Officials

A match is conducted by a first and second referee, a scorer and two or four linespersons. The first referee is responsible for the correct conduct of the match. With the blow of the whistle, the first referee begins each play and signals service to begin. Each action is considered to be finished when the first referee blows the whistle. The first referee has authority over all players and officials throughout the match, including any periods during which the match may be temporarily interrupted. Generally speaking, first referees should only interrupt play when they are sure that a fault has been committed, and they should not blow the whistle if there is any doubt. The first referee has the power to settle all questions, including those not specifically covered in the rules. Furthermore, the first referee may overrule decisions of other officials when, in the first referee's opinion, they have made errors.

The official next in line is the second referee. The second referee's position is on the side of the court opposite and facing the referee. Like the first referee, the second referee has many responsibilities. At the beginning of the game, the second referee must verify that the positions of the players of both teams correspond with the serving orders listed on the score sheet and with the line-ups as given to the scorer. At the time of service, the second referee must supervise the rotation order and positions of the receiving team. The second referee makes calls pertaining to violations at the center line and the attack lines. The second referee also signals any ball contact with the antenna or a ball crossing the net not entirely between the antennae. In addition, the second referee must judge player contact with the net. With the assistance of the scorer at the scoretable, the second referee must keep track of the number and length of time-outs, supervise the conduct of the coaches and substitutes on the bench, and authorize substitutions requested by captains or coaches of the teams.

Unlike the first and second referees, the scorer has no first-hand control of the match. The scorer may stop play because of a rotation or point problem, but must do so through the first referee. Before the match begins, the scorer records the number of players on the score sheet. As the match progresses, the scorer records the scores, carefully noting the number of time-outs and substitutions. The scorer must also make sure that the serving and rotation orders of players are followed correctly.

The Play

The Serve. A volleyball match begins with a coin toss. The team winning the toss picks either first serve or the side of the court they would like. The game begins with the serve: The right back player hits the ball into the opponent's court. If the serve is good, an ace or a point for the serving team may result. If the player serves the ball into the net, a side out occurs and the service goes to the opposing team. The first service alternates with each game. If play goes into a deciding game, a second coin toss determines who will serve.

Defense. The most basic defensive movement in volleyball is the underhand pass, or dig, in which the ball is contacted with the upper surface of the forearm. The player receives the serve in the defensive position, then digs the ball toward the setter. The setter passes the ball overhand to the hitter. The setter also has the option of passing the ball backward (a back set) or executing a set while airborne (a jump set).

Offense. There are many ways for hitters to get the ball into the opponent's court. The hitter may direct the ball diagonally, inside the blocking team's hands and toward the far sideline of the court, resulting in a cross-court spike. In a line spike, the hitter directs the ball outside the blocker's hands and down the near sideline of the court. The spiker could also make a wipe-off spike by intentionally directing the ball to rebound off the defender's block and fly out of

bounds. Another trick is changing the speed at which the ball is contacted. For example, the spiker might either hit a half-speed shot or tip the ball. A tip is an attack shot that lobs the ball over the net into a vulnerable area of the defending team's court. Any time the defending team is unable to return any type of a spike or tip, a kill is recorded in the statistics.

Blocks. The first line of defense against a hitter is the block. One or more front line players jump and reach above the net, intercepting the attack by deflecting the ball into the opponent's court. Blockers may block solo, in pairs and even in threes. When setting up the block, players may intentionally position themselves to take away certain areas of the court, as in line blocks (the blockers attempt to stop all shots down the line) or cross-court blocks.

Rallies. During a volleyball rally, each team is allowed a maximum of three successive contacts of the ball in order to return to the ball to the opponent's side. The ball is out of play when it touches the ground, goes out of bounds or contacts the net or the antenna on either side of the net. Many rule infractions can occur during a rally which also terminate play. The ball may not be held too long and it may not be played by two players at the same time. Also, the ball cannot make a double contact with any player's body or be unnaturally lifted or thrown in any way. During play, no one is allowed to cross over the center line. Furthermore, servers are not allowed to step over the service line when serving. Finally, no back-row player is allowed to hit the ball in front of the attack line. If any of these rules are violated, play is stopped and a side out is rewarded to the opposing team.

References

Connors, Martin, Diane L. Dupuis and Brad Morgan (1992). *The Olympics Factbook*. Detroit, MI: Visible Ink Press.

Kluka, Darlene A. and Peter J. Dunn (1989). *Volleyball*. Dubuque, IA: William C. Brown Publishers.

Neville, William (1994). *Serve It Up: Volleyball For Life*. Mountain View, CA: Mayfield Publishing Co.

Plant, Gayle, ed. (1992). *Legacy of Gold*. Colorado Springs, CO: United States Olympic Committee.

Stokes, Roberta and Mick Haley (1992). *Volleyball Everyone*. Hunter Textbooks, Inc.

THE HISTORY OF THE AVCA

The mission of the American Volleyball Coaches Association is to advance the development of the sport of volleyball by providing coaches with educational programs, a forum for opinion exchange and recognition opportunities. Member participation is vital to the association accomplishing this mission.

The following principles guide the AVCA in the attainment of its goals: To maintain a membership group representative of all levels of competition; to promote the game of volleyball within the general philosophical framework of education; to encourage participation within the highest standards of competition; and to develop greater interest, understanding and support of the sport.

History of the AVCA

In 1981, the AVCA was incorporated as a private non-profit 501-(c)-3 educational corporation. The original Board of Directors consisted of eight NCAA Division I collegiate coaches. A part-time executive director administered the programs.

As the AVCA began to grow and diversify, a full-time executive director was hired in July 1983. An associate director was hired in April 1986 and an administrative assistant in September 1988.

In August 1992, the association moved from San Mateo, Calif., to Colorado Springs, Colo. The staff has increased to the following positions: executive director, director of membership services, assistant director of membership services, director of sports information, assistant director of sports information, director of publishing and part-time accountant. In addition, the association employs interns and other part-time people.

In 1986, the Board was increased to 13 members, and in 1987 and 1989, the Board was increased to enfranchise first the high school and then the junior community.

Membership increased steadily from 1981 through 1987 (about 150 new members per year), followed by a 106 percent boom in 1988. Since 1986, high school membership has more than tripled. High school coaches from 46 states and the District of Columbia are members. At the collegiate level, all major NCAA conferences are represented and membership among the club coaches has risen dramatically.

The original members of the AVCA were all intercollegiate coaches who joined together to unite this particular coaching body. They have been the backbone of the association's existence and a united voice determining volleyball's future.

Perhaps the most significant decision was made at the San Francisco convention in 1986, however, when the membership recognized the growing and developing high school and club communities. The name of the association was changed to reflect these growing constituencies. From the original Collegiate Volleyball Coaches Association, the American Volleyball Coaches Association was born with the intent of responding to and serving all volleyball coaches.

Service Functions

The AVCA services its members through many varied functions. The AVCA only involves itself with activities that best exemplify the image of amateur athletics. Its ultimate mission is to enhance the image and increase awareness for the sport of volleyball. Listed below are summaries of just some of the many AVCA activities:

1. The AVCA serves as the main liaison between its members and the NCAA for sport legislation. This role is vital in that the AVCA communicates members' beliefs and opinions on issues affecting volleyball and its participants.

2. The AVCA prepares, edits and distributes 12 monthly newsletters and six professional journals to all of its members. Associate members receive 12 newsletters/drill bulletins that deal with issues affecting high school and juniors coaches. College members receive a weekly publication during the season that covers the ongoing results and activities of teams around the country.

3. The AVCA orchestrates a series of awards programs which recognize the competitive efforts of over 325 student-athletes and coaches. These programs include acknowledging athletes at the regional/district level as well as on the national level. These programs are for all Division levels and are as listed:

For NCAA Division I
Eight All-District Teams - 1st and 2nd: 12 members each
For NCAA Division II
Eight All-Region Teams - 1st and 2nd: 12 members each
For NCAA Division III
Eight All-Region Teams - 1st and 2nd: 12 members each
For NCAA Divisions I, II, III, NAIA & JC/community college:
All-AmerIca Teams - 24 recipients each
National "Player of the Year" - 5 recipients
Coaches "Victory Club" Award
National "Coach of the Year" - 5 recipients
Region "Coach of the Year" - 8 (Div 11), 8 (Div 111), 9 (NAIA), 8 (JC/CC)
District "Coach of the Year" - 8 (Div 1)
For Men
All-AmericaTeams - 18 recipients
National "Player of the Year"
Coaches "Victory Club" Award
National "Coach of the Year"

4. The AVCA organizes and conducts an annual convention and clinic for all its membership in conjunction with the NCAA Division I Women's Championship.

5. The AVCA actively prepares and develops clinics, seminars and workshops for the professional development of its constituency. In particular, AVCA works with the Coaches Accreditation Program (CAP) of USA Volleyball to ensure quality of programming.

6. The AVCA promotes and increases the media exposure of volleyball. The founding of the U.S. Volleyball Media Association in cooperation with USA Volleyball is a mayor step towards involving media in their own network. In addition, the AVCA is a member of the College Sports Information Directors of America and delivers presentations to that group. AVCA reports weekly results for all divisions and writes a weekly update during the season (Facts on File) that provides coaches and the media with information about the current season.

7. The AVCA has written a National Volleyball Statistics Manual and Video and has been the primary force in developing a consistent method of compiling volleyball statistics.

8. Until 1994, the AVCA compiled and publicized all individual and team statistical information for every Division I school on a weekly basis and monthly for every Division II, III and NAIA school throughout the women's season. Upon compilation of statistics by the NCAA in 1994, the AVCA ceased this activity except for the NA1A.

9. The AVCA coordinates the polling of coaches weekly for ranking of the Top 25 teams in Division I, sponsored by USA Today; the Top 25 in Division 11, the Top 15 in Division III and Division I men's and the Top 10 in Division III men's volleyball. The Division I men's and women's polls are carried by USA Today. The other polls are carried by the AP Sports Stats Wire and major papers.

10. The AVCA, in conJunction with USA Volleyball, operates Volleyball Informational Products (VIP). This department develops new and existing educational products for sale to the volleyball community and general public. In addition, VIP assists in marketing the AVCA and USAV logos on educational products.

11. In 1997, the AVCA and USA Volleyball joined together to operate the Molten Division III Men's Invitational Volleyball Championship. This is a season-ending national championship tournament for NCAA teams competing in Division III men's volleyball. It was started due to the fact that no Division III institution has had an opportunity to participate in a national championship.

Part 1

DEVELOPING A COACHING PHILOSOPHY

Chapter 1

COACHES CODE OF ETHICS AND CONDUCT

AMERICAN VOLLEYBALL COACHES ASSOCIATION PRINCIPLE — PROLOGUE/CREED

As a member of the American Volleyball Coaches Association (AVCA), I am committed to sound educational processes, establishing traditions and promoting values for my volleyball community. I am dedicated to advancing the welfare of those who seek my assistance and to the maintenance of high standards of professional conduct and competence. I am accountable for all of my actions and to this Code of Ethics, and my acceptance of this fiduciary responsibility is expressed in all of my personal and professional relationships in that coaching may involve my direction of youth, adolescent or adult teams. I will follow these principles in all environments and abide by them completely when coaching.

PRINCIPLE I — PROFESSIONAL PRACTICES

I pledge to maintain practices that protect the public and advance my profession; I will:

    A. Maintain responsible association with USA Volleyball, its national programs and member organizations.

    B. Continue personal and professional growth, remaining current on new developments in the field through continuing education.

    C. Use my knowledge and professional association(s) for the benefit of the people I serve.

    D. Always strive to be truthful and put colleagues or other professionals in a positive light.

    E. Avoid discrimination in all of its forms.

PRINCIPLE II — COACH/ATHLETE RELATIONSHIPS

I pledge to maintain relationships with athletes on a professional basis; I will:

    A. Conduct all my relationships from a perspective of dignity and sound educational and scientific foundation to:

        1. Direct comments or criticism relative to the performance, not the athlete.

        2. Ensure that all activities are suitable for the age, experience and ability of the athletes.

        3. Educate athletes as to their responsibilities in contributing to a safe environment, and to do my best to ensure that all facilities and equipment meet safety standards and that they are age/ability appropriate.

        4. Consider the athlete's future health and well-being as foremost when making decisions regarding an injured athlete's ability to continue competing or training, and seek professional medical opinions

to serve as a basis for my decisions.

5. Be aware of academic responsibilities; conduct practices and match schedules in a manner so as not to unduly interfere with academic success. Never encourage, condone, or require any behavior that threatens an athlete's high school, USA Volleyball, collegiate eligibility or amateur status.

6. Comply with regulations and ethical guidelines for recruiting practices as defined by governing sport organizations.

7. Strive to develop individual and team respect for the ability of opponents.

8. Prioritize being present at all practices and competitions and, when unable to, assure knowledgeable and safe supervision.

B. Work with and strive to develop every member of the team.

C. Show sensitive regard for the moral, social, religious and sexual orientations of others and communities. I will not impose my beliefs on others.

D. Recognize the trust placed in, and the unique power of, the coach and athlete relationship. I will not exploit the dependency of athletes and will avoid dual relationships (e.g., business or close personal relationships) which could impair my professional judgment, compromise the integrity of the process and/or take advantage of the relationship for my own gain.

E. While serving in a professional capacity or as a role model, avoid any drug, tobacco or alcohol use while in the presence of athletes. I will discourage by way of education any consumption of these substances by minors and will remain at all times within the limits of the law with regard to legal substances. I will avoid illegal ones entirely.

F. Not engage in physical, verbal or emotional harassment, abusive words or actions, or exploitative coercion of current or former athletes. I will report any suspected cases of abuse to the appropriate authorities immediately.

G. Recognize that all forms of sexual abuse, assault or harassment with athletes are illegal and unethical, even when an athlete invites or consents to such behavior or involvement. Sexual abuse and harassment is defined as, but not limited to, repeated comments, gestures or physical contacts of a sexual nature. I will report all suspected cases of sexual assault or abuse to law enforcement as required by law.

PRINCIPLE III — CONFIDENTIALITY

I will respect the integrity and protect the welfare of all persons with whom I am working and pledge to safeguard information about them that has been learned or obtained during the coaching relationship, including performance reviews, statistics and all personal confidences. Further, I will obtain permission from athletes before sharing videotape recordings or other data of them with anyone excepting the recognized coaching staff; when current or former athletes are referred to in a publication, while teaching or in a public presentation that is not laudatory, their identity will be thoroughly disguised. The only exception to this will be that I will not use these standards of confidentiality to avoid intervention when it is necessary (e.g., when there is evidence of physical or psychological abuse of minors, or legal issues).

PRINCIPLE IV — STAFF/EMPLOYEE RELATIONSHIPS

All relationships with employees and staff will be maintained on a professional and confidential basis, and I will avoid exploiting their trust and dependency.

The Code of Ethics is a condition of membership in the AVCA.

Photo by Dan Houser

Chapter 2

ETHICS IN COACHING
CHILD DEVELOPMENT OR CHILD ABUSE?
Jay Coakley, Ph.D.

> **"If** coaches are concerned with maintaining the intimacy and privacy of the lockerroom, then they should treat their players with respect and dignity. In other words, as human beings. This will uphold the integrity of the lockerroom because student-athletes would have no reason to protest or speak out about the behavior of their coach."
>
> *Keith McDermott*

I have no problems talking about ethics in coaching because I define ethics as rules of respect for human rights; ethics encompass guidelines for being sensitive to the needs of other human beings. Social existence depends on "codes of ethics." This is not a new thing. However, formalizing and enforcing those codes of ethics in formal ways is new for many groups.

When we think about formalizing a code of ethics, it gives us the opportunity to examine critically what we are doing and the kinds of things we expect from ourselves in relation to other people. Coaches should do this more because in the last 15 years, I have seen expectations for coaches go right through the roof. Many people expect coaches to do absolutely everything for young people when it comes to performance issues, developmental issues and all sorts of things. I think that when we get together to talk about a code of conduct or a code of ethics for coaches, one of the things that we are doing is trying to clarify for other people what they can expect from us as we work with young people.

Developing a code of ethics provides a good opportunity to clarify what we expect to happen to young people in sport. For example, if you buy into the "sport as war" metaphor, that creates a whole framework for considering ethical issues. In war, killing is ethical. But if you do not define sport as war, and you define it as being about growth and development, then that will set up a different ethical framework for you.

When I talk about abuse, I have to be careful because in addition to not wanting to create a lot of defensiveness on the part of coaches, I do not want to create a moral panic. I have seen how destructive moral panics can be; they can lead to people being accused for things that in many cases they are not guilty of — and lives can be ruined. I am really sensitive to the fact that when we are talking about abuse, we are dealing with a legal issue and I want coaches to keep that in mind, too, and be very cautious when using the term abuse.

First, I am going to tell you that coaches are certainly on the right track in dealing with the issue of a code of conduct. I am going to talk about children in particular now (using the United Nation's Convention on Children's Rights definition of a child — anyone under the age of 18). I am also going to give some guidelines to consider when thinking about the characteristics of a coach's code of conduct.

A coach's code of conduct or a code of ethics should be based on 1) what we know about the social and physical development of young people and 2) what outcomes we think should be associated with sports participation. In other words, what are the social and developmental consequences that we want to be associated with sport participation? Do not expect from sport more than it can deliver. Sport can deliver all sorts of things, but not without hard work and thoughtful strategies. Be cautious about what it is you really expect. Do not base a code on mythical ideas about sport automatically building character and force yourself to use unrealistic standards to evaluate your own behaviors. Also, a coach's code of conduct should be included as a mandatory part of the education and credentialing program developed by NGBs under the general guidelines of the USOC (this is just one possibility). Other sport organizations could do this as well, as in the case of high school sports, intercollegiate sports and so on. A coach's code of conduct should be enforced by state-based or sport-based "child athlete advocacy committees" — there has to be some way of enforcing standards. I think what we need are formally designated child advocates around the U.S. Finally, the code of conduct should be systematically and assertively publicized to all athletes and their families. It should be on locker-room and club walls and coaches' office walls. Coaches are always putting little hints about performance on lockerroom walls. I think athletes should put these little reminders on coaches' walls, letting them know that they as athletes are aware of ethical expectations for coaches.

When I first considered this idea of a code of ethics for coaches, I thought, "Well, maybe we are being a little alarmist here," but then I remembered the origins of child labor laws in this country and the special laws regulating the conditions surrounding child performers in the entertainment industry. I began to think about how some child athletes in high performance sports are similar to child entertainers. After all, we have rules that protect children from being used as laborers for the pleasure and benefit of adults in the entertainment business. So, maybe we ought to look at child labor laws and see how they might apply to young athletes in some of our youth sport programs. The thought is ironic because child labor laws were passed in this country to free children of adult control over things other than the growth and development of young people. Laws were designed to give children free time. That opened up the door for them to play sports. But now, some sports have become so work-like that we need laws to protect children from the adults who control children's "free" time.

Some of the things going on in certain youth sport programs today resemble things that led to the passage of child labor laws. Also, if we take a look at entertainment, we see laws passed back in the 1950s because some adults had exploited or abused some child actors in the 1940s and early '50s. The "child-entertainer" laws generally limit the number of hours and days that children can work or rehearse; they set minimum times between performances; they safeguard personal income; and they bring work conditions in line with national health and safety regulations. There are some sport organizations that have rules in these particular areas, but the only area that amateur sports laws cover across-the-board is the third one: safeguarding personal income (putting athlete income in trusts). The interesting thing is that the basis of these rules about income does not have a thing to do with an interest in protecting the welfare of children in sport itself. All they do is perpetuate the illusion of amateurism. So, I think that just like child entertainers have rules safeguarding their physical and social well-being, we now need similar kinds of rules for child athletes, especially in high performance sports.

Things are considerably different in the sports world, but I think there are enough similarities to use these child actor laws as a guide. The NCAA has passed rules about the number of hours college athletes can practice per week and there are similar rules in high school, but we need a concerted, overall consistent approach to setting certain limits on what coaches can demand from child athletes in sports. What we know about child development should guide the setting of these limits.

Why is a Code Needed Now?

Why is a coach's code of conduct needed right now, at this particular point in time? It is because things have changed relating to children's sport participation over the past 10-20 years and there have not been corresponding changes in the rules that regulate the connections between adults and child athletes. Unlike the past, there are many adults now whose livelihoods, careers and reputations depend on the performances of child athletes in their camps, academies, schools or training programs. The livelihoods of adults now depend on children winning medals. When you have the bread and butter of adults riding on the shoulders of children between the ages of 8 and 18, we have a new situation that encourages abuse. It is a situation we must be aware of with respect to a code of conduct.

Another new situation is that there are parents who have actually quit their jobs or only work part-time now because they manage their child's sport career. This is not happening in all cases, but it does happen and it is something new. When it occurs, it puts pressure on children. The livelihoods of families now depend on that athletes' performances — and not just the performances in particular events, but commitments to sports for the next 10-15 years! Such commitments are too much to expect from 13-year-olds.

In addition, in the 1990s, we have many children making uninformed choices about their sport participation and sport lives. Young people are making decisions to dedicate exclusive, full-time attention to achievements in sports that are organized, controlled, and coached by adults. These children often see their goals and performances in very serious terms because they realize that the adults around them are depending on what they do as athletes. Children in this type of situation quickly learn that when times get tough, they must suck it up — because adults depend on them. Is that the kind of expectations we want to impose upon young children? My point is that kids get caught up in this very easily. They make

these decisions to win a gold medal or be on a national team. Then, adults take advantage of the fact that this child has made an uninformed decision (basically, what this child has just done is make a commitment for the next five to 15 years of his or her life). Children do not realize the nature of that commitment. But adults hold them to it and they say, "You made this commitment and if you want to achieve your goals, then this is what you have to do."

A German sports sociologist who was thinking about these issues in 1985, said after his own research that, "Children would never think of their own accord of subjecting themselves to an organized form of sport aimed at long-term performance and to organization of their daily, weekly and yearly schedules as required by the preparations to achieve top performance." This is something that adults orchestrate. It is something to be sensitive to as we think about a code of ethics for coaches. To what extent are children making informed choices about sports? One of the questions that I would like to see coaches ask is, "How do you make distinctions between motivating children and taking advantage of uninformed choices on the part of children?" My question is: do we want to define abuse to include situations when coaches do not help young athletes set limits on training in a world where the rewards of high performance sport are hyped to such an extent by the media and that kids buy into them without question? Is it the job of coaches to help kids set limits and raise questions about uninformed decisions they have made? Or should coaches and parents take advantage of the hype that the media has created and kids have naively accepted, then force kids to honor the commitments that they made on the basis of that hype?

Another reason we need a code of conduct now is that corporate sponsors often control part of the conditions of children's sport participation. I know that there are some nice corporations out there, but I know that most of them do not give their highest priority to what goes on in the lives of 12-year-old athletes. Whenever I see coaches and corporations getting together to arrange things that affect the lives of children, I always wonder about what the outcome will be and whether it will reflect primarily the interests and needs of children or corporations.

One of the biggest reasons we need a code of conduct for coaches is because people in this culture have always looked at coaches through special "moral lenses;" in other words, most people have not had the same kinds of expectations for coaches they have for teachers or other adults who work with children. In many cases, excessive control of a child's life by a coach, even to the point of using particular types of treatment that in other settings would be defined as abusive, are defined as legitimate if it is done on the athletic field. If you were the parent of a 15-year-old boy and you found out that the social studies teacher dragged him by his coat to the principal's office, you (and many other parents) would hire a lawyer. But, what if that same 15-year-old came home and told his father that his coach came up to him and grabbed him by the face mask on his helmet and pulled him around the football field and got him on his knees and told him he was "playing like a girl"? Often times, even in the case of grabbing the face mask, fathers do not say, "That's not right" but instead say, "You deserved it, son. That is the way we build character on the athletic field." It is interesting that we often apply a different ethical code for coaches than for other adults working with children.

Many people believe that coaches should push and drive people to achieve. Young people often buy into this belief. When this occurs, you end up with young people who will not identify the things that coaches do as abusive because they have a mindset that leads them to conclude that they have to be driven and pushed by coaches. So we have many young athletes who believe that the use of coercive tactics by coaches is a "normal" phenomenon. In fact, young athletes often brag to each other by telling "macho stories" about how much abuse they have endured from their coaches.

One of the problems faced when setting standards for coaches has been illustrated when I ask my students if coaches can be democratic. Many (athletes and non-athletes) say, "No." These students earlier in my course said that one of the great things about sports is that they prepare young people to live as citizens in a democracy. Then they tell me that they basically expect coaches to be autocratic. The reasons they give are 1) "coaches have more experience and know more about sport than athletes do so they have to make all of the decisions;" or 2) "athletes cannot be trusted to make responsible decisions and coaches must make decisions if they are to be respected; 3) If athletes make decisions, it would destroy the basis for discipline and authority on teams;" or 4) "athletes look to coaches for answers and decisions, and

coaches have a right to make these decisions because their jobs depend on it." When people believe democracy has no place in sports, the door is opened for possible abuse.

The financial and emotional stake that adults have in the performances of child athletes has never been greater than it is today. Therefore, there is a need to intervene with a coach's code of ethics. I could give you examples of 10-year-old hockey players who play 90 games in a year, 13-year-old figure skaters who train 60 hours a week to prepare for national competitions or coaches who use punishment in the form of physical abuse or coercion to extract maximal performance out of child athletes. If you ask young athletes about the need for setting limits, in some cases, they are the first ones to object. This is similar to the young boys who worked in the mines around the turn of the century before child labor laws. They were the first to say, "The government cannot pass those labor laws; they are restricting our right to work." Now child athletes have learned to live with such rigid controls over their lives that they, too, accept them as "normal."

Regulating Adult Control of Child Athletes

The question remains, how much adult control is too much? When does adult control interfere with the overall development of young people? When does it contribute to burnout? When does it contribute to binge deviance (a phenomenon that sometimes occurs when adults have so totally and completely controlled young athletes that once that control is withdrawn, those athletes sniff, drink and inject anything that is not nailed down)? Episodes of binge deviance have included wrecking hotel rooms, throwing TVs out of windows, engaging in assault, etc. How do systems of autocratic adult control affect these young athletes once the systems are taken away? When does adult control create unhealthy dependence among athletes, where instead of learning to control their own lives, they look more and more completely to the coach to control their lives? Sometimes dependency relationships with coaches are so complete that young athletes will do anything for their coaches. When does this "connection" with a coach become unhealthy?

These are issues most common in high performance sport. I know that I am talking about things from the perspective of athletes right now, but I have also studied coaches and I know that coaches experience considerable conflict and role strain. One of the biggest sources of role strain for coaches is that they must live up to the expectations of a diverse set of others in their lives, and the only thing that will make all of them happy is if you win all of your games, meets, matches or events. This creates excessive pressure on coaches and leads to tremendous turnover (especially among high school coaches). I would argue that if high school coaches had a clearly written code of conduct in their hands, they could give it to these people and say, "This is what you can expect of me; evaluate me in terms of this code." This could help control role strain in coaches' lives. As it turns out, coaches get hung up with control issues. Coaches must remember that the outcome of games, meets and matches are often affected by factors not subject to their control. A code of conduct would possibly help them set some parameters that would be realistic when it comes to control-related issues with their players.

The last issue I want to address is one that coaches should have already thought about — that is, the issue of sexual abuse and harassment in the coach-athlete relationship. This is a tricky issue to deal with when you talk about a coach's code of conduct. It is difficult to get data from people who have actually experienced harassment and abuse. We are dealing with some complex social dynamics when it comes to sexual abuse and harassment, so it is easy to ignore this problem. There are enough data on coaches who marry their athletes and coaches who date their athletes and marry their former athletes to raise concern and there are also some women coming forward now who describe past abuse by coaches. Over the next couple of years, this is going to be a major issue that will get national coverage. What we need in our ethical codes are rules that prohibit coach-athlete dating.

Am I being prudish? If we are talking about a masters level women's swimmer who goes out and hires a coach and then chooses to have a sexual relationship based on mutual consent, then I wish them all the luck in the world. But, in the case of a coach who controls the training, the competition and a good part of the life of a woman who is in college or under age 18, there are good reasons for rules that prohibit dating, especially if you know about the dynamics of power relationships. Sexual feelings can and do exist in the case of some coach-athlete relationships. And, I would argue that this is not abnormal. But, it is the expression of these feelings that is the issue; expression is inappropriate.

We need coaches to learn about power, dependence and love. Some men get carried away when they have control and power over women and the women look to them for approval and would do anything for them. These men can mistakenly believe that it is really their own innate attractiveness that is causing this "attachment." Instead, the woman's feelings of attachment and attraction are a result of the power the coach has over her. Male coaches need "awareness training" to understand and deal with these issues and dynamics.

Also, coaches need more information about controlling women's bodies. Between 20 percent and 33 percent of all young women involved in high performance sport have pathogenic eating behaviors. I am not saying that these behaviors are all caused by coaches. But coaches need to know about what special issues there are when it comes to controlling and disciplining a young woman's body. Coaches also need information about controlling young men's bodies by threatening their masculinity. If a coach tries to motivate young men by calling them "ladies" or "fags" and takes advantage of the homophobia among many young men, is that a violation of ethical standards? Should it be? Should we raise questions about coaches using language that would lead young male athletes to believe that it is only through their performance that they can prove their manhood? I think so. And that is a good place to stop and let you ask questions and discuss the need for a coaches' code of conduct.

The preceding was transcribed from a presentation given at the 1993 United State Olympic Committee Coaching Symposium, Sept 16-18, 1993.

Photo by Mark Philbrick

Chapter 3

A Sense Of Dignity

Kinda S. Asher

> "...from a legislative standpoint, the concept of sexual harassment has only been critically reviewed in the workplace setting. Coaches and athletic administrators are not exempt from scrutiny in the gym, and neither are other players."

Perception is a nebulous term. Confusion often results from the diverse interpretations of the surroundings our senses provide at any given moment. Indeed, one person's perceived ideas about a particular situation can vary greatly from someone else's. This is the inherent problem with defining and legislating sexual harassment. A person's perception, rather than the behavior itself, is often the determining factor of whether or not actions are assessed as sexual harassment. However, one thing is certain — whether male or female, the right to respect and dignity — in the workplace or in the sports arena — is inalienable. Sexual harassment, like any other verbal or physical abuse, undercuts a person's dignity.

The Definition

Sexual harassment (verbal abuse or physical abuse) in any setting, whether it be in the office, on the court or out in public, is defined as "A continuing pattern of unwelcome sexual overtures, requests for sexual favors, or other conduct of a sexual nature when 1) a person must submit to such conduct to keep a job or position; or 2) submission to or rejection of such conduct is used as a basis for employment or promotion decisions about you; or 3) such conduct has the purpose or effect of substantially interfering with your work performance, or is offensive or objectionable to you, causes you discomfort, or creates a hostile atmosphere for you. This type of conduct may be considered sexual harassment whether it is initiated by a manager, supervisor, co-worker, or third party with whom you interact in the course of business, such as a customer, vendor or subcontractor" (Coleman 1993).

Bear in mind that from a legislative standpoint, the concept of sexual harassment has only been critically reviewed in the workplace setting. Coaches and athletic administrators are not exempt from scrutiny in the gym, and neither are other players.

Especially in athletics, sexual harassment assumes many forms. According to Helen Lenskyj, associate professor at the Ontario Institute for Studies in Education, sexual harassment and violence are endemic to athletics. "The woman-centered analysis of male violence against women developed by Elizabeth Stanko (1985) puts forward the concept of a continuum of violent behavior ranging from the "everyday" kinds of leering and whistling directed at women on the street, to sexual assault and date rape. Men's aggression toward women is explained as an act of power which takes a sexual form, and not simply a sexually motivated act. For example, a male coach has power over a young female athlete through his status, his gender and his age, and there is the potential for abuse of power and for sexual harassment in the male coach/female athlete relationship.

Sport has retained its historical legacy as a highly competitive activity organized by and for men, and girls and women cannot be blamed for holding different values, interests and perspectives" (Lenskyj 1992). In addition, "any discussion of sexual harassment in sport needs to include the problem of homophobic harassment of women; that is, harassment based on fear and violence toward lesbians. Female participation in the traditionally male domain of sport has, for many decades, given rise to allegations of lesbianism directed at all sportswomen, regardless of their sexuality" (Lenskyj 1986). "Allegations of lesbianism directed at female athletes deter many women from rejecting unwanted sexual attention from men, or reporting instances of sexual harassment, since they fear that such actions will confirm that they are not sexually interested in men, and therefore lesbian" (Lenskyj 1992).

Finally, sexual harassment extends to derogatory remarks about an athlete's body. "Women engaged in activities that by their nature attract the male gaze are particularly vulnerable to harassment in relation to diet and body size. The young women who participate in aesthetic sports such as gymnastics, figure skating and synchronized swimming are subject to ongoing scrutiny. Their performance is evaluated on artistic as well as technical merit, and an ultra thin body is seen as a prerequisite for physical attractiveness, and hence for artistic merit. In the growing body of literature on eating disorders among female athletes, sexually harassing and psychologically abusive behavior on the part of male coaches in relation to

female athlete's body size and shape is well-documented" (Lenskyj 1992).

A Look at the Numbers

A 1992 survey in the United States of 25,000 federal employees produced a remarkable response rate. Results showed that 42 percent of women (and 14 percent of men) had experienced some form of uninvited and unwanted sexual attention at work (Forster 1992). (No such survey was found regarding athletes and coaches in the sports arena.) Decidedly, even though sexual harassment is also experienced by both straight and gay men, the vast majority of victims are indeed women.

The Law and Sexual Harassment

Perhaps the most hyped case of sexual harassment in recent history is the 1992 case of Anita Hill and U.S. Supreme Court Justice Clarence Thomas. All eyes were focused on CNN during the congressional hearings and everyone seemed to have an opinion. In actuality, sexual harassment came to the forefront a number of years ago in the Supreme Court's 1986 decision in *Meritor Savings Bank v Vinson*. The decision upheld the Equal Employment Opportunity Commission's (EEOC) expanded interpretation of sex discrimination under Title VII of the Civil Rights Law of 1964. The 1964 Act, originally construed as a quid pro quo exchange of promotions or benefits for sexual favors, has given way to a much more broad legal definition.

In 1986, once and for all, the law made it crystal clear that all employers "had an affirmative duty to provide a workplace free from a sexually hostile, abusive or offensive atmosphere, and that employees were protected under the law from unwelcome sexual advances" (Coleman 1993).

The Civil Rights Act of 1991, signed into law in November of that year, "provides remedies to compensate employees who are victims of intentional sex discrimination, including sexual harassment. The new law permits women or men to sue for compensatory damages — which can cover medical bills and other costs resulting from the harassment — as well as punitive damages" (Turnquist 1992).

Education and Training

As with most controversial subjects or ideas, education can go a long way in resolving some of the inherent problems related to sexual harassment. Indeed, the more coaches and athletes alike are aware of the basics about sexual harassment, the better off everyone will be in the long run.

"Education and legislation are needed to propel true equality between the sexes. Like rape, sexual harassment is not about lust. Both are about power, domination and control, expressed sexually" (Turnquist 1992).

"And that," says psychologist Bob Weinrich of the Men's Resource Center in Southeast Portland, "is another manifestation of the imbalance of power between the genders" (Turnquist 1992). Proactive steps on the part of both men and women need to be taken in order to terminate the perpetuation of sexual harassment in any domain. However, in a sport-specific arena, Helen Lenskyj provides the following recommendations to educate everyone about the problem.

Recommendations

- All national sports organizations should develop, publicize and implement zero tolerance sexual harassment policies.

- Coaching certification programs should include information and awareness-raising sessions for all coaches on the issue of sexual and homophobic harassment.

- Coaching certification programs should include thorough coverage of eating disorders, including guidelines for coaches.

- Mandatory workshops on these issues should be provided for coaches who are already certified.

- Professional journals should publish special issues on sexual harassment and eating disorders.

- Women's committees within national sports organizations should develop support networks for girls and women who have experienced harassment.

Conclusion

Sexual harassment, along with verbal abuse and unmitigated physical abuse, are not to be tolerated in any workplace. The intensity of competition and the stakes people play for in sports offer a number of opportunities for abuse to occur. However, as professionals, coaches must maintain a sense of dignity on the court at all times for all involved-including themselves.

References

Coleman, F. (1993). Creating a workplace free of sexual harassment. *Association Management*, 69-75.

Forster, P. (1992). Sexual harassment at work. *British Medical Journal*, 305, 944.

Lenskyj, H. (1992). Sexual harassment: Female athlete's experiences and coaches' responsibilities. *Science Periodical on Research and Technology in Sport*, 16.

Turnquist, K. No more secrets. *Oregonian*, Dec. 6, 1992, pp. L1+.

Photo by Dan Houser

Chapter 4

PRINCIPLE CENTERED COACHING

Patti Stanton

You may make a favorable first impression through charm; you may win through intimidation. But secondary personality traits alone have no permanent worth in long-term relationships. If there is not deep integrity and fundamental character strength, true motives will eventually surface and human relationships will fail.

(Covey, 1991)

Current trends in business management are moving away from traditional hierarchical structures. As we learn more about the dynamics of working with people, we find that people who are empowered and feel a sense of ownership invest more of themselves and their energies into their work. The results are greater productivity at less expense. Can we apply this to coaching volleyball? Definitely.

To be successful coaches, we must continually sharpen our management skills. There are many resources available to aid in this process. Two books by the same author, Stephen R. Covey, stand out as complementary of the principles and standards espoused by the USA Volleyball Coaching Code of Ethics. First, *The Seven Habits of Highly Effective People* is a guide to developing personal skills in dealing with people. Second, *Principle Centered Leadership* describes a leadership style that will produce greater motivation within those with whom we work.

The old idea of authoritarian (and sometimes tyrannical) coaching is already being replaced by the cooperative style. In the National Federation Interscholastic Coaches Education Program text, *Successful Coaching*, Rainer Martens stresses the benefits of this more positive approach. The text should be read by all who coach volleyball at any level. The best way to be exposed to the information, however, would be to attend USA Volleyball's CAP I course, which includes a glimpse into the American Sport Education Program (ASEP) and Martens' text.

Successful coaching begins within the coach.

Whether we want to admit it or not, we are, to a large degree, a product of the influences of our parents, teachers and coaches. How we reacted to those influences shaped and may still be shaping our behavior as adults. Some of our responses to our players may stem more from our background than from actual interaction with the players themselves. Our attitudes toward people are shaped early in life. It is crucial to examine these attitudes honestly to see what influence they may have on coaching style.

What do we believe about our players? Is it based on real knowledge of them as individuals or an attitude we possess? Do we have any racial and/or gender biases that may affect the way we perceive them and their actions? Be careful not to dismiss the idea too quickly. Being politically correct outwardly does not completely relieve us of the responsibility to ourselves and our teams to examine our inner attitudes and work to correct those that are negative.

Covey's *Seven Habits* is a step-by-step guide to improving our people skills. It is much more than an "instant success" book. We explore the way we see ourselves and others and the effect it has on our relationships. We are then presented with an inside-out approach to developing habits that apply not only to management and/or coaching, but to every aspect of our lives. We come out with a simple way to apply common sense principles to our personal and professional lives.

As an example, one of the habits is to "begin with the end in mind." Applied to coaching, one might evaluate current methods by looking ahead to the desired end. How do we want to be remembered by our players and colleagues? What influence do we hope to have on our players' lives? With those questions answered, we can check ourselves to see if what we are now doing moves us toward or away from those results.

In *Principle Centered Leadership*, Covey helps us develop an alternative style, either to being too hard or too soft. Using principles as guidelines, it allows us to maintain control, yet empowers the team, developing the players' internal motivation to succeed.

Principles, according to Covey, work like a compass. They are objective and external like natural laws such as gravity. Values, however, are subjective. "Principles are not values. The German Nazis...shared values, but violated basic principles" (Covey, 95). One of the fundamental principles of the ASEP course is, "Athletes first, winning second." Operating on principles like this, applying them to our coaching style and communicating them to our teams can develop a high level of trust and cooperation between coaches and players.

How do we empower our teams? We can begin by including them in goal setting and the development of team rules. We can also educate them on different playing systems and why we use the ones we do. The more the players know, the more intelligent choices they can make on the court. They may also come up with their own ways to improve on the system. The more they feel that they are truly involved, the more importance they will place on the success of the team.

Finally, athletes today need positive role models. Too many of our highly skilled professional athletes exhibit many negative character traits. We need to be people whom our athletes can believe in. We certainly cannot be perfect, but we can make an effort to be the kind of people they can look up to. Without integrity we will fall short.

The most productive atmosphere we can have on our teams is one of high trust. Business management and coaching have a common resource — people. The more we understand what motivates them, the more successful we will be as leaders. Our level of success will depend greatly on our willingness to examine our own character honestly and make any necessary changes.

References

Covey, Stephen R. (1989). *The Seven Habits of Highly Effective People.* New York: Simon and Schuster.

Covey, Stephen R. (1991). *Principle Centered Leadership.* New York: Simon and Schuster.

Martens, R. (1990). *Successful Coaching.* Champaign, IL: Leisure Press.

Photo by Dan Houser

Chapter 5

THE GIVE AND TAKE OF RESPECT IN COACHING

Michael Harnden

Coaches are generally accorded something that usually takes time and hard work to acquire. It is something that, if built upon, can foster teamwork and success. Left to wither, it can create disharmony and a poor learning environment. This important thing is respect.

There is an obvious reason that a coach needs respect from the athletes. The coach is the final authority, a decision maker, a leader. If a team loses respect for its coach, it will begin to lose faith in the coach's decisions and abilities. The players will begin to second-guess every decision, every action of the coach. They will start to make judgments. In doing so, they will also lose focus of teamwork. People also tend not to put forth 100 percent effort when they do not believe in what they have been told to do.

A more subtle, but equally important, aspect of the loss of respect involves the teaching process. Coaching is teaching and for something to be taught, something must be learned. Learning new physical skills and concepts invariably requires failure. Few are the natural athletes who get it right the first time and require only refinement of skills. The ability to fail and learn from it requires a great deal of self-confidence. Self-confidence is not a trait a lot of beginning athletes — or adolescents in general — possess. The need for self-confidence can be largely circumvented if the individual trusts and respects the person who asks them to take the risk of failure. Being unable to risk failure stagnates the learning curve of the individual and, in turn, that of the team.

As aforementioned, a coach is given a certain level of respect simply due to the position as coach. The coach is supposed to know more and be able to teach the skills required for successful participation in sport. This level of respect is fairly easy to maintain even for the moderately dedicated coach. The most simple way is by knowing the game. By staying abreast of changes and evolving with the sport, a coach will maintain and build a good working knowledge of the game. This can be done in numerous ways, including attending clinics, reading books and viewing instructional videotapes. This level of respect, however, is not enough.

The level of respect a coach needs for an athlete to go through the proverbial wall must be earned. The coach, in order to earn this respect, must realize that respect is a two-way street. It must be given to be earned. The easiest way to do this is to make the players feel that they are a contributing part of the organization — contributing not just to the actual on-court performance, but to everything leading up to it. The coach has to be open to and solicit input from the players.

The lines of communication should be open right from the beginning of the season. Goals need to be set, team rules created. This must be a democratic and cooperative effort. Both the athletes and the coach must become aware of what the priorities of the other are. With this understanding, the two sides much reach a common ground of priorities and goals. Athletes do not always understand why a coach does not want them to miss the practice before a match or how being five minutes late upsets a practice plan. A coach can lose sight that their athletes may live non-athletic lives the 20 hours a day that they are not in the gym. Common goal setting is important due to the need to have everyone working toward common goals. This will lessen confusion and the resentment that can arise if the coach and the athletes are pulling in opposite directions.

As the season progresses, there are many ways for a coach to keep the athletes involved. The coach can ask for their input in practice planning. Even the trained eye of a coach is not always 20/20. Who better to include in the planning process than those involved? Asking the simple question, "What do you feel we need to work on?" can give the coach interesting and enlightening feedback. Empower the athletes to be involved in the communications process with the outside interests that involve the team. Have the athletes go over the ground rules with the referees, voice team concerns to the athletic director, help arrange fund-raisers and concessions with the booster club. It is important in all of these situations that the people are aware the athletes are speaking for the team with the coach's consent. The coach needs to be careful not to abuse the delegation of tasks. Assigning others to do everything can create the impression of a dictatorship, leaving the athletes to feel taken advantage of.

Finally, the coach must care about the athletes. The coaches must be aware of how they perceive their players. Does the coach view the athletes as tools or resources? Are the athletes people who exist for four hours every day in the gym or are they people who happen to participate in athletics? By taking the time to talk to each individual every day, the coach can get to know each player. Listening to the players affords the coach the opportunity to learn what makes each player tick. This knowledge will help a coach to motivate and teach individuals in the best way. Taking the time to recognize the individual gives the athlete the feeling that not only are their athletic abilities valued, but their personal contributions are important, as well.

Indeed, the most technically sound coach will fail to achieve the maximum from a team if the players have no respect. It is far too easy given the coach's position of being the final authority to drift toward a know-it-all attitude. The age and experience difference between coach and players, especially at the high school level and below, can add to this sense of "knowing it all" and needing to do it personally for it to be done correctly. By following and believing in a plan designed to gain the players confidence and respect, a coach will afford himself/herself the best opportunity to develop a successful program — a successful program that develops both competent athletes and well-rounded individuals.

Photo by Dan Houser

Chapter 6

INTERACTIVE BEHAVIOR BETWEEN OFFICIAL AND COACH

Terry Lawton, Ph.D., and Geri Polvino, Ph.D.

> **It** is not the coach's job to evaluate the officiating in the middle of the match any more than it is the official's job to evaluate the coaching of the team.

There are numerous debates concerning effective interactive behaviors between coaches and officials during competition which have the potential to influence the progress of the match. These behaviors combine for performance enhancement and match facilitation.

The best officials in any sport have achieved skill and rank over years of training, practice and study of the game. During that time, they develop a sense of professionalism that conforms to the ethical standards of sport.

- Officials are expected to conform to specific standards for behavior, attire and promptness.

- Officials are expected to be friendly and courteous but never to the point of potential charges of bias or aloofness.
- The official may smile and even laugh but may never give anyone the impression that this is not a serious situation or is only a hobby or part-time job.
- Officials are expected never to lose their control or concentration, regardless of the intensity of the match or how they feel physically.
- Should the match deteriorate and problems develop, the official never responds verbally and must withdraw from all unofficial dialogue, and above all, remain fair and enforce the rules of the game.

The professional official protects the integrity of the sport to benefit the players and ensures that both teams are provided with an equal opportunity to win the match.

The coach also maintains professional standards defined by the profession. Victory is crucial to the success of any program. Skill development, teamwork, cohesiveness and personal growth are also very important factors to the coach and team. The coach is responsible for providing opportunities for the team to win.

During each match, the coach uses many techniques to influence the momentum to the advantage of his/her team. The coach is expected not to dishonor or embarrass the team, the university, the sport, or the profession, and is responsible for performance stabilization at a high level which, in part, is achieved by focusing attention on the significant aspects of the match. The coach assists the athlete in the processing of information leading to performance enhancement and stabilization at a high level. When both coach and athlete lose concentration, that performance breaks down.

Pre-Match Interactive Behaviors Between Official and Coach

Often the coach can influence the officiating subtly before the match begins by making sure that the official is greeted at courtside. The official wants to greet the coach (protocol) but does not like to interrupt the pre-match routine. If the coach is aware that the officials have entered the gym, then it is easier to approach the official as soon as possible. Conversation need not be lengthy or involved, but should be sincere and professional. It is often at this time that the coach might subtly ask, "Are you the first referee?" Then the coach responds, "Good," if the official says, "Yes," or "Too bad," if the answer is, "No." Regardless, the official is unconsciously complimented and walks away with a more receptive attitude. The coach might also compliment the official on a previous match and gain similar results.

Another tactic during this prematch conversation might involve asking a simple rule interpretation question. The rule may involve an area of officiating that the coach was previously unhappy about or an area that the coach wants to prepare the official to respond to in a specific way in the future. The official will not particularly change the interpretation to match that of the coach, but will probably investigate the rule and give the interpretation additional thought. The official may even realize that the coach was correct and may increase the number of non-calls that are made during the match. The coach might also help the official by pointing out that during the last match against their opponent, player No. 3 consistently came under the net, "almost" causing potential danger to the outside blocker. The official will certainly be more careful to stay at the net when player No. 3 can possibly be involved in an "under the net call." The officials will be meeting their job responsibilities, and the coach has influenced the official, if only to be more vigilant at the net.

Coach-to-official communication might also include helping out with overlap calls during the game. All second referees are aware of the assistant coach who yells at the three hitters on the opponent's team. The official will be better able to make a questionable out-of-position call when he/she is sure of the rotation order of the opponents. This is a much more effective tactic than simply yelling that "they are overlapping." Therefore, the coach mentions that the opponents often overlap in a specific rotation and then makes sure that the assistant coach points out that position each time it occurs on the court. Eventually, if the out-of-position players are really obvious, the official will probably make the call sometime during the match.

The coach can also choose to make no effort to communicate with the official at all. The coach can always seem busy and at the far end of the gym in conversation with someone. This form of nonverbal communication is at best neutral and is possibly the most appropriate if there are serious problems between the coach and the specific official. The official will not be anxious to confront the coach before the match and will maintain a certain distance, as well. Negative non-communicative behaviors are counterproductive to all concerned and should be eliminated. Negative non-verbal encounters between the official and coach are definitely not desirable and are best eliminated if the official does not accept the assignment because of these encounters. This is difficult for the official if the coach is employed at the best school in the area, yet this is the most professional approach to the situation.

Interactive Behaviors Between Official and Coach During A Match

When the match begins, the referees concentrate on the tasks defined by their respective assignments. Further verbal communication with coaches is restricted by protocol and the rules of the game. However, the coach has ample opportunity to attempt to influence the officiating during the match with controlled and specific body language.

Minor actions like shaking the head, putting both hands up in the air in a pleading motion, or even suddenly sitting back in surprise will often draw an official's attention to the coach and the apparent displeasure. Similar actions can be used to express satisfaction with a call. Even without "rabbit ears," most officials will hear the occasional "good call, ref" comment from the bench. These actions may not influence the match officiating but will serve to distract the official from the current play. More serious non-verbal actions should elicit a sanction from the official, especially if they concern a judgment call. The sanction should be looked at as a response to a specific action of the coach that is covered within the rules. Most officials realize that the coach will often seek a card in order to change the momentum of the game or inspire the team to increase intensity. The official should not deprive the coach of this tool by withholding sanction.

Many conference coaches are now being required to complete official evaluation forms after each match. The general response seems to be that coaches are concerned about match control and want the official to control the match. The official has to decide how to define what this means: does it mean prevent all and any stalling tactics; make consistent call; police participant behavior? Sometimes it is difficult to determine whether the coach refers to both sides of the net or just for the opponents. Officials often receive feedback that coaches no longer fear the individual yellow card and are prepared to receive as many as one per game if it increases the opportunity for winning. An individual yellow card is merely a warning regarding the limits of acceptable behavior.

Also, during a match, an official observes various coaching behaviors that demonstrate coaching frustrations and efforts to influence the officiating of the match. The obvious result of these behaviors might appear to be the "reversal" of some decision by the official. However, it is a rare situation when an official is inclined to reverse a decision, and then usually only when the first referee is "certain" that a misinterpretation of a rule has actually occurred. Therefore, the coach is really trying to influence future decisions of the first referee during the match rather than obtain a "mind change."

The official's response to these coaching behaviors could occur in any number of ways. The most desirable professional and ethical response would be not to respond or allow any obvious effect at all. However, the outburst of behavior from the coach usually causes a temporary break in concentration. The more secure, confident and experienced official allows only a momentary break and will quickly regain total concentration with no effect on the flow of the game.

Other potential responses by the official would be to make calls against the opposing team. This scenario would be as unlikely as the official making calls against the coach's team as a result of the outburst. Officials remain vigilant about their ability to handle tough, stressful game situations and maintain their integrity, objectivity (rational thought vs. automatic thought triggered by anger), and concentration. Officials quickly lose credibility and respect when any hint of bias is linked to their officiating.

A lot is known about attention behavior and information processing which affects competitive outcomes. This can be applied to the interaction of the official, coach and athletes. More elite performers discard information which does not have a positive effect on the match. It is not uncommon to see less-experienced performers focus on behaviors distracting in nature or on momentum shifts; thus, attention to significant match information is lost. More elite performers will also plan ahead for situations which are likely to occur, matching the appropriate plan to the occurrence. Attention behaviors are critical to performance stabilization and enhancement.

The Non-Call Situation

Officials use several tricks to maintain their concentration after the coach attempts to influence their judgment with certain behaviors. One technique simply is to concentrate totally on the ball. The official actually watches the ball hit the arms, follows it during the path of the pass to the setter's hand, and then upward during the set to the hitter, etc. This total focus of concentration on the ball restricts the ability to focus on the distracting actions of the coach. The use of this tactic partially explains the official's tendency to turn from the coach, quickly initiating play, which provides the opportunity to focus as soon as possible and prevents notice of any further distracting behavior of the coach. A second method involves the use of visualization as the official imagines a sound-proof glass enclosure surrounding the volleyball court. The players and officials are inside this enclosure while the coaches and fans are outside. The official is protected and can concentrate solely on the game in progress. (Often, the official adds to this visualization wild lions which are allowed to roam freely among the coaches and fans, bringing a quiet sense of controlled revenge to the image and projecting a peaceful, smiling countenance.)

Officials tend to become overcautious about responding to coaching behavior and may overreact and over-deliberate, which results in the "non-call" situation. It would be interesting to research the occurrence of the "non-call" versus a "call" after a coaching outburst. The official in the "non-call" situation would not whistle a questionable contact, thus allowing the ball to remain in play. It would appear that the best the coach should hope for would be the "non-call" situation which, in essence, removes the official from any immediate influence on the play. This would be especially important at a crucial point in the match when the coach's team would be negatively affected by a call. The "non-call," at least, results in continued play, and the point is either won or lost by the players later in the rally.

It is important to note that this response is within the cognitive control of most officials. In an effort to be non-biased, the official takes a little longer to consider the situation rather than reacting immediately to the "visual" illegal contact which is often questionable to begin with. Each official sets the level of play for a match and tries to maintain that level throughout the match. If the level of officiating changes, it must not be the result of an emotional response to any coaching behavior. The change would be reflected in more "non-calls" and the coach might conclude that the official became more consistent and "let them play."

Replacing the automatic response with more situational information is a positive behavior, influencing the quality of the match. The current USA rule on multiple first contacts (not the current NAGWS rule) requires a highly developed ability in this aspect of judgment. The official must be able to react to the multiple contact when players use their hands (finger action) differently on first and second contacts. A horrible, mangled, mishandled first contact is allowed while a definite, slow and comparably minor (second contact) set must be called, presenting an interesting demand on the ability of the official to maintain consistency and respond to the ball contact on the basis of situation information. The "non-call" is evidence that this process is taking place. Less experienced officials and coaches tend to replace rational responses with increases in automatic responses stemming from frustration or anger. Rational responses are part of the information processing necessary to enhance the quality of competition.

Thinking skills are developed through rational response behavior. Competitive outburst behaviors interrupt the decision mechanism of the information processing system. Performance is information processing, a cognitive function. Facilitation of this process eliminates hesitation, which may compromise confidence, not rational response. The system runs smoothly and the quality of the match is enhanced.

Coaching behaviors are divided into levels by virtue of their sanctions; however, often many behaviors are tolerated at early stages in the match without sanction. Typically, examples of these behaviors include small but visible hand signals, uncontrolled and accidental moans/groans and other miscellaneous minor physical reactions. These behaviors indicate a minor annoyance with the call or non-call and serve notice that displeasure has been recorded on the coach's rating sheet. At this time, the official should respond quickly without emotion with a yellow card to indicate that displeasure has been noted, but that any further behavior of this type will not be acceptable. This quick response by the official to the coaching behavior should be interpreted as the first step in Canter's method of "assertive discipline." It is a specifically defined response to a specific unacceptable behavior demonstrated by the coach, regardless of the purpose. The purpose is always generalized to "a coach can do whatever is necessary to win, but it will elicit specific responses." The official who responds in this manner can quickly move on to concentrate on the following play and does not have to worry about whether the coach was correctly evaluating the officiating or not. It is not the coach's job to evaluate the officiating in the middle of the match any more than it is the official's job to evaluate the coaching of the team. The official knows that a coach does not have the right to question judgment calls, and when it happens, a sanction is required. The official can now release his/her focus on the past play and concentrate on future action.

When the coach does question a judgment call, the percentage of occasions when the coach is correct will vary with three major factors. These factors are: the level of ability of the official, the level of ability of the player and the view of the observer. A less-experienced official will demonstrate much greater variability during a match in making ball-handling decisions. A less-skilled player will attempt to play balls more frequently with incorrect techniques or from difficult body positions, resulting in questionable contacts. The position or location of the player on the court provides the major observers (officials and coaches) distinctly different views of the ball contact. For example, a setter facing the first referee provides an ideal view of a double contact but a poor view of the held/lifted ball. The opposing coach, however, has the perfect location to see the length of time and distance that the hands were in contact with the ball. If the setter presents a side view to the first referee, the "one-two" double contact will be obscured from view by the ball. The opposing coach, again, will have the ideal view. Since the official is only to call what is "actually seen at the moment of contact," the call will be missed. The referee is very aware of these situations and how they influence consistency. A missed call due to visibility will not prevent a later ball-handling call of equal severity from being called. The official merely makes the calls that are visible in relationship to position and/or speed of movement.

The coach does not have the right to question a judgment call but does have the right to lodge a formal protest before continuing the match concerning rule interpretation or application. The match is then continued, and the rules interpreter reviews and investigates the protest. If the protest is upheld, the conference decides how to handle the match management and results. Sue Lemaire, former NAGWS rules interpreter, "estimates that more than half of the protests that were brought to her attention over the last few years were denied because the correct protest procedures were not followed, and that less than one-half of the protests would have been upheld even if they had been filed correctly."

There are occasions when the official feels the need

Revisualization

Situation: A back-row setter jumps so that the hand is raised higher than the top of the net in order to save a bad pass from a teammate. As the setter redirects the ball, which was traveling toward the net, the opposing middle blocker reaches over to block the ball back into the setter's upraised hand.

In slow motion, the first referee revisualizes the action and makes decisions in a sequential fashion:

1. The ball was traveling toward the net.
2. The ball was still on the attacker's side of the net.
3. The back-row setter still has the right to make a play on the ball.
4. The setter was not attempting to send the ball across the net.
5. Therefore, the blocker must wait for the ball to penetrate the plane of the net.
6. The back-row setter is not a back-row attacker until the ball totally crosses the net or is legally blocked.
7. The ball was legally contacted by the setter.
8. The ball was not legally contacted by the blocker and is "dead" upon contact, which eliminates a back-row blocker call.
9. The correct call is "reaching over the net."

---

to review a quick play at the net to ensure that the proper interpretation was made. The first referee will often take a few seconds mentally to "rewind and replay" the mental video tape of the rally in slow motion. During this momentary pause, the referee is concentrating on revisualizing the sequence of events and the decision. Excessive verbalization by a player or coach actually hinders this process. Coaches aware of this "revisualization process" often wait a few seconds and then calmly request an explanation of the ruling. The official is now able to explain with an equally calm response and will often award a replay (if an improper ruling has been made) without losing self-confidence. Excessively verbal coaches hinder the entire process and are often met with only a firm warning glance or stare as the referee looks away to begin the next play quickly. The first referee may have never been given the opportunity to review the action as the priority now becomes one of controlling the behavior of the coach. Behavior earning sanctions hinders this process and mind changes or replays are rarely awarded.

Occasionally, coaches will become so angry at an official that they lose control during the match. Typically, the coach stands at the sideline and verbally expresses anger before requesting a time-out. (The time between games is also used to express frustrations directed toward the officials.) The coach should use this time to calm the players while redirecting the focus to positive actions, changing or diffusing any momentum obtained by the opposition. Continued demonstrations of anger with the officiating are easily transferred to the players. This transference of anger is often the turning point in the match because the anger and frustration are detrimental to motor performance. As this negative impact increases, the team makes additional and costly errors that may result in losing the match. Great efforts should be made to see that behaviors that are detrimental to performance and the game are not professionally acceptable. (Loss of control by a coach has been met with suspension by an institution or conference if deemed a "serious breach of professionalism.")

At the same time, recognizing behavior by the coach which is strategic (e.g. going after a card in order to motivate a complacent team) versus behavior which is emotionally out of control is critical.

Post-Match Interactive Behavior Between Official and Coach

Currently, the relationship between the coach and official is controlled by conference rules in an effort to prevent post-match outbursts. The officials now have the "toot and scoot" rule that does not require that they approach the table at the end of the match but leave the gym immediately. This rule is intended to remove the official from the immediate proximity of coach and fans after an unusually difficult match. Institutions have a responsibility to ensure the safety of the officials and the event manager or security should escort the officials from the court.

It is never appropriate for either the coach or the official to discuss the difficult match in the media. This situation, it is hoped, rarely occurs. The normal situation after a match would involve a simple handshake and "thank you-good match" exchange between coach and official. This simple courtesy would help to promote positive feelings between official and coach for the next encounter. Even a "thank you" from the assistant coach or team captain will demonstrate to the official that their efforts were

appreciated. This is a strategically sound behavior on the part of the coach. Most officials do not officiate for the financial rewards but work because of the internal satisfaction they earn from doing a good job. Coaches' opinions are crucial to the officiating assignments during future seasons, and the coach should use every means available to maintain positive relationships with the officials.

Interactive behaviors between coaches and officials can also occur during the off-season at times unrelated to a scheduled match. Officials may respond to personalized communication from the coach during the off-season in a more receptive manner. Conversation that is objective and carried on in a non-emotional and non-threatening manner would allow the official and coach an opportunity to reflect on specific situations and go beyond automatic response behavior to rational response behavior.

As the official listens to the calm and logical explanation of the coach (and vice versa) concerning the rule interpretation or ball-handling call, new insight or understanding may occur for each. The official and coach may decide to research the situation and react differently during the next season. The coach may make various statements that will influence the official in other ways. A subtle statement concerning the coach's perception that "certain officials often call ball-handling tighter in specific situations" may act like a post-hypnotic suggestion triggering a "non-call" in that exact situation during a future match. The official may not even be consciously aware that the "non-call" was the result of the conversation with the coach. There is the outside chance the coach will gain new insights regarding these situations, thus reducing the frustrations in future matches.

When people feel they are being judged, their thinking behavior may shut down and more automatic responses occur. Their responses may replace rational responses which influence changes in behavior. More rational dialogue must take place between coach and official. This will lead to a higher quality of competition as information pools become more similar than different. Processing of situational information is enhanced.

Summary

Positive interactive behaviors between the coach and official enhance the quality of competition. Understanding the information process, performance and cognitive behaviors helps access systems without compromising confidence or concentration. The goal is for two professionals, the official and the coach, to come together and use their expertise to guarantee the athlete the best of competitive situations.

References

Canter, L. (1976). *Assertive Discipline: A Take Charge Approach for Today's Educator*. Los Angeles: Lee Canter & Associates.

Lemaire, S. (1991, December). *Personal Communication*.

Schmidt, R. A. (1988). *Motor Control and Learning*. Champaign, IL: Human Kinetics.

Sparks, D. (1990, Spring). Cognitive coaching: an interview with Robert Gormston. *The Journal of Staff Development*, 12-15.

Webster's New Collegiate Dictionary. (1991). New York: Random House.

Photo courtesy of Ball State University

Chapter 7

STUDENTS OF THE GAME

Randy Dolson

There are many instances in which players will be asked to perform certain tasks or skills. As coaches, we give them direction or demonstrate what we wish them to perform -- but many times forget to explain why they must perform in this manner. It is this simple concept of letting your players become more aware of what it takes to be successful; in other words, coaches must help them understand the game by explaining the "whys" of techniques, plays, strategies and philosophies. Doing this will increase a player's performance to higher levels of play. When players understand why we ask them to perform in a certain way at specific times, they will have a better understanding of the game and will perform better at crucial and stressful moments.

As coaches we spend a tremendous amount of time coaching fundamentals, conditioning and strategies, but spend little time (or limited amounts of time) on mental aspects. John Wooden, who is considered to be one of the greatest coaching minds of all time, explains in his book, *The Wooden-Sharman Method*, that "conditioning is not only physical, but mental, as well. It means curbing your temper and your selfish tendencies and not letting anger get the best of you. By curbing these emotions, you develop poise and self-control and that means you will not only be able to perform better physically, but you can also prevent unnecessary pressure mistakes" (Wooden, et. al., 104). How many times have we witnessed players lose control of their emotions in the pressure of big moments and watch their physical game deteriorate because of it? Conditioning players' emotions and mental toughness comes through not only developing their skill levels and confidence, but by becoming students of the game and realizing that what they

have control over on the court will enhance their performance, as well.

However, it goes beyond using mental conditioning just for those so-called pressure moments. Ultimately, it is those moments when it may bring about the most noticeable results; letting your players become aware of some of the following examples increases their knowledge of the game and helps them understand why we do the things we do.

Philosophy

Explain your coaching philosophy to your players early on. Although the players will most likely find out what you are all about eventually, let them know your make-up from the start. Also, help them believe in your philosophy by explaining and giving examples of how and why it works. Hopefully this will develop their understanding of your program and how they fit into your scheme. This not only will heighten their awareness of the game, but may also alleviate any guessing they may have of you and your philosophy. This is the first step on a new awareness for many players. Just having the knowledge of what to expect from the coach will help create a better atmosphere among the players.

The Volleyball Pyramid

Understanding the volleyball pyramid will help your players understand the importance of the various steps it takes to make a successful team, or as Terry Pettit of Nebraska may state, "Why one team is more successful than another in the realm of volleyball" (Pettit, 1995). On the base of the pyramid are the athletes themselves for the foundation. The next step of the pyramid is the mastery of fundamentals. If teams are equal in talent, the team that has the mastery of fundamentals will overcome the other. The next step of the pyramid includes the system design. Again, if both teams are equal up to this point, the team with the greater system design will endure. The next level includes conditioning. The team equal to the other with talent, fundamentals and systems that will overcome the other will now be the team that is in greater condition -- both mentally and physically. On top of the pyramid is the ability to adjust. The team that will now have success when equal in all other facets will be the team that can adjust to what is happening on the court, both defensively and offensively (Pettit, 1995). Your team must understand and believe the importance of all of these levels of the pyramid. If your team is aware of these steps, it will help them understand your coaching methods better and will be ready to climb the pyramid to success.

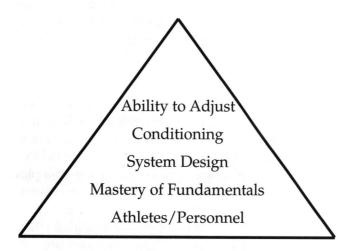

Ability to Adjust

Conditioning

System Design

Mastery of Fundamentals

Athletes/Personnel

Understanding How to Score

Many times, I ask prospective student-athletes and incoming freshmen to list the four ways to score in volleyball. It may seem easy enough, but many players simply play the game without realizing the various ways they can score. Most answer service aces and kills, but many forget about the other two ways of scoring: blocks and opponent errors. Not only should players know that to be successful on the court is to score more points than the opponent, but they should also know the various ways to score and create scoring opportunities. At every level you should become aware of the percentages of each scoring method. For example, at the high school level, almost

45 percent of all points are scored from opponent errors, 20 percent from the serve, 10 percent from blocking and 20 percent from offensive attacks. At the collegiate level, approximately 32 percent of points are scored from the attack and opponent error and 16 percent from both the serve and block (Pettit, 1995). From this information, a coach may wish to develop the understanding among players of the style you wish to play and let your players set goals from these standards.

Emotion

Your players must be aware of the role emotion and momentum play in volleyball. All things considered, 50 to 75 percent of a game can and will be decided on emotion and momentum. When two highly competitive teams are matched against one another, the game is usually won by the team that makes a run. Runs are fueled more from opponent errors than by kills and blocks; however, consistently strong serving, attacking and blocking will create an atmosphere that promotes your opponents making errors. When the momentum comes, our emotion will help fuel the fire of success. It again is up to your players to understand they must keep their emotional level strong through every point and be mentally prepared for every play. This can carry you through to success.

Again, introduce your players to your philosophy of player reaction on the court; practicing these emotional levels during practices and scrimmages will affect them positively on the court.

The Golden Zone — GZ

There are probably many names for this area on the court, but whatever the name, we know if we pass the ball more frequently into this area than our opponent, we will probably be more successful in winning the match. Therefore, create an understanding among your players that the way to be successful is not to allow the other team to make easy passes into this area. How? By serving tough, using effective downball placement, not giving easy freeballs and simply attacking smartly and in a tough manner. Hit the weak links and lanes created by your opponent. Just seeing this simple diagram can help your players visualize just how important it is to try to keep your opponents out of this zone. On the other hand, it is also easier to see why your team must pass into this zone and just how important it is to practice directing balls into this area with high consistency.

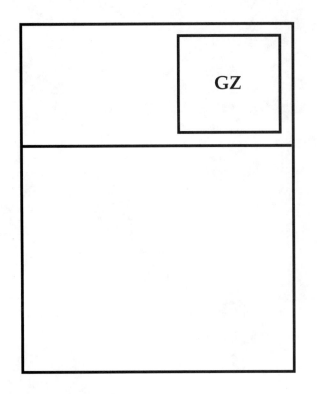

Individual Roles

Be honest with your players in understanding their roles. Most coaching staffs have developed certain strategies that enable every person to have a role, whether it be a starter or sub, server or defensive specialist. If players understand their roles and why they have those roles, it will help create the understanding it takes to achieve a total team effort for success.

Once an understanding of these facets of the game is obtained, practices containing game-like situations are critical. As stated earlier, many coaches and their drills are directed to developing skills and plays in a controlled environment. Although there are times when this can be helpful or useful, developing all aspects of player performance should be practiced in an open, uncontrolled environment. Truly, technical instruction and repetition are keys for success and it is within other key elements for which more practice time should be devoted. Creating random and unpredictable situations for players to develop their mental capacities and abilities to read cues given to them by their opponent are highly recommended. Situations should be developed in which players' reactions become reflexes and ball contacts can become more controlled.

Another aspect to developing players' mental capacity is to create stressful situations in practice. As Wooden suggests, not letting pressure situations get the best of your players will let them perform better. Practice scenarios in which players can become aware there are many things which are out of their control. For example, during scrimmages, make calls against your players which can test their mental toughness; make scoring changes for one team or another; make extensive time-outs as if there were a scoring table mistake/discussion. Discuss these situations during practice and at team meetings. Make players accountable for situations by quizzing them on or off the court. All of these situations can help your players understand the importance of staying mentally tough.

These areas of mental work are a major part of what is necessary for success. Each area will help the player become a student of the game. The environment you create in practices will encourage your players not only to perform better in game-like situations, but should also help them understand the situations and the strategies that will make them better all-around players.

Photo courtesy of the University of Alabama

VOLLEYBALL AND ACADEMIC SUCCESS

Berkley Laite

College athletes and their classroom performance is probably one of the most controversial topics in academia today. Faculty discuss it at the lunch table, articles are written in the academic press and the admissions office issues warnings about academically weak recruits. Even librarians talk about student-athletes and worry about their academic performance: An article in the *Journal of Academic Librarianship* titled "Scoring: Bibliographic Instruction Helps Freshmen Athletes Compete in the Academic League," describes how the University of Florida instituted a special library instruction program for student-athletes to help them succeed in college (Ruscella, 1993). The *NCAA Manual* contains almost 50 pages discussing athletes' academic eligibility, their grade-point averages, course loads, etc. Directors of athletics routinely issue reports of the grade-point average of their athletic squads.

In a study to see what effect, if any, intercollegiate sports had on a student-athletes' grades, Clemson University researched its intercollegiate athletic programs (Maloney, 1993), investigating 594 different student-athletes and their grades from 13,026 different courses. Researchers discovered that the average grade for the student-athletes was 2.379, which was lower by a statistically significant margin than the average grade for the overall student body, which was 2.681. In almost every case, the grades of student-athletes in each sport are lower than those of the overall student body. However, the researchers felt that the data did not tell whether the act of participating in athletics hurts or helps a student-

athlete's academic performance because there are too many other complicating factors: Student-athletes may major in harder or easier courses; they may come from weak or strong family backgrounds; they may enter the university with lower- or higher-than-average SAT scores; student-athletes with a natural advantage in academics may steer away from athletics and vice versa. To account for these factors, Clemson created a dummy variable for athletic participation to include the grade equation. After again examining the grades of student-athletes and the general student body, Clemson still found that student-athletes' grades were lower than ordinary students, other things being the same; however, the magnitude of the effect is quite small — about .02 of a grade point.

Indeed, this difference is not homogeneous across all sports. In fact, when the various sports are broken down, only the revenue sports — football and men's basketball — show significantly negative results. Grades of student-athletes in the non-revenue sports are almost identical to the rest of the student body relative to their background characteristics. Interestingly enough, one of the groups of athletes in the study — female volleyball players — made higher grades than the student body (2.885 compared to the average of 2.681).

Student-athletes in the revenue sports devoted greater amounts of time to their sport than the student-athletes in the non-revenue sports. It was also found that student-athletes in the non-revenue sports had higher grades in their off-season, whereas student-athletes in the non-revenue sports showed no grade differential between their on- and off-season. Researchers determined that coaches and university administrators do not put as much pressure on the non-revenue student-athletes to perform; as a result, they can thus put more emphasis on their studies.

Coaches can take a position on academics and athletics with their volleyball players that supports the findings of Clemson's research. When a coach recruits, he/she might recite a litany to any prospective student-athletes, "I am looking for a student first and a player second." Once on the team, players are told that academics are their first priority and volleyball their second. Coaches should insist that players maintain at least a 2.0 average or they are assigned to a supervised study hall in the library. Sometimes, coaches can take even stronger measure to reinforce the importance of academic achievement, e.g., suspending a player from practice and competition for a week if a mid-semester deficiency report is received.

Truly, none of this guarantees academic success, but it may help.

Regardless of how much a coach emphasizes the importance of good grades, a player may still have academic difficulty. Coaches constantly search for new and innovative ways to help players succeed in college. In 1992, the National Association of Secondary School Principals conducted a study to discover why some students fail (Motsinger, 1993). Is it the school's fault? Is it the teachers' fault? What makes the successful student behave differently than the student who seems to give up?

The NASSP researchers evaluated 417 high achievers, 105 dropouts who were enrolled in GED programs and 103 prison inmates. The study discovered many interesting differences between the groups that explained academic success and academic failure. Three common factors of high achievers are highlighted below.

The first factor which set the high achievers apart from their classmates was their family setting. Eighty-five percent of all high achievers lived with both parents (12 percent with their mother, two percent with their father and one percent with someone other than a parent), whereas only 46 percent of the GED students and inmates were from homes with both parents present. Thirty-five percent of the GED and 28 percent of the inmates lived with their mothers, 18 percent of the inmates and seven percent of the GED students lived with neither parent.

The second factor in this study that was noticeably different for the high achievers was their parents' parenting style. All of the students were asked to list the traits they like most in their parents. Three parental behaviors emerged: the ability to trust, listen and correct. Personal attention was the single most effective reward for student accomplishment. Parents of high achievers were aware of what their children were doing in school and consistently praised their children for doing well.

Finally, all of the students were asked about their parents' involvement in their school lives. All three groups recalled their parents attending teacher conferences in elementary school; however, GED students and inmates recalled parents coming to school to "clear up problems" while high achievers remembered their parents visiting their teachers to "see how much we had learned."

It can be concluded from this NASSP study that high achievers in high school tend to come from stable homes where the parents provided love and attention. These parents were aware of and involved in what their children were doing. These factors — love, attention and involvement — also apply to college students and their academic success. Parental attention and involvement are apparent when parents show up at a match to watch their children play, or talk to the coach after a match about their child, or send "goodies" home with their child on the bus. When parents are involved with their children like this, most often they are succeeding academically and are enjoying college life.

To increase this parental involvement, coaches may implement a parents' newsletter to keep them informed of the team's activities. Invite the parents to the end-of-the-season team banquet. Plan to have a parents' function such as a hospitality suite and get-together during an annual tournament. This attention toward the parents involves them even more in their childrens' activities and helps strengthen the sense of support for the player. It should also have the added benefit of making the players aware that the coach values their parents' support. As a coach, one of the responsibilities is to foster players' ties with their families; coaches are concerned not only with their players' success, but with their academic and social success, as well. Coaches are concerned with the whole person.

So, does playing collegiate volleyball interfere with academic success? Not if the student-athlete comes to college prepared academically, with a supportive family environment and encounters a coaching staff concerned with academic success. Players should know that a coach who is concerned about their academic success wants their parents also to be involved in their successes. Each player is still ultimately responsible for his/her own success, but each additional source of support makes that success more attainable.

As coaches, we must make it part of our job to know if our student-athletes are succeeding academically, as well as athletically. We must provide them with avenues of help if they are struggling academically. These avenues may range from scheduling tutoring sessions to withdrawing an athlete from participation in the sport. We must also foster a support system for our athletes by involving their parents in our athletic program. We must invite them to participate in their child's athletic life. We must create opportunities for parents to be involved. All of this takes time — time away from traditional coaching activities — but the rewards are well worth the effort. In the final analysis, the cap and gown are far more valuable than the briefs and jersey.

References

Motsinger, Hillery (1993). Recipe for success: factors that help students succeed. *NASSP Bulletin*, 77, 6-15.

Maloney, Michael T., and Robert E. McCormick (n.d.). An examination of the role that intercollegiate athletic participation plays in academic achievement: athletes' feats in the classroom. *The Journal of Human Resources*, 28, 555-570.

Ruscella, Phyllis L. (1993). Scoring: bibliographic instruction helps freshman athletes compete in the academic league. *Journal of Academic Librarianship*, 29, 232-36.

Part 2

BASIC ELEMENTS
INDIVIDUAL SKILLS

Photo by Dan Houser

Chapter 9

DIGGING

Kathy Gregory

Everyone familiar with volleyball knows that the best offense depends on a sound, consistent defense. After the initial attack — the spike or the service — defense is the first element involved in scoring points in volleyball. A team's desire to be fearless and tenacious on defense often makes the difference between winning and losing. Power volleyball can become a very one-sided affair unless each member of a team has this commitment to defense.

The underhand pass or dig is the most basic defensive movement in volleyball. Before delving into the essentials of digging — the various kinds of digs include the roll, dive and sprawl, as well as the common defensive situations — coaches must examine the mental and physical attributes of the athletes they teach these skills to. One basic physical drill in particular — the foot patter drill — unites both mental and physical training to ensure players remain injury-free and are more effective on the court.

MENTAL QUALITIES

Certain mental qualities are essential for an athlete to be a good defensive player. As coaches, we all recognize that teaching individual physical skills is an obvious part of our mission. But we also need to pay attention to the amount of motivation (in the form of desire and courage) we pass on to our players. A player with only average skill but intense motivation can play good defense. Another mental quality required for good defense is willingness — especially the willingness to overcome both the natural fear of falling and the natural tendency of ducking hard-hit balls. Look first for athletes with these mental qualities and then for the gifted volleyball player.

Good defensive players have to learn three lessons which call for instinctive behavior:

1. Always hustle after every ball; never give up on any ball.
2. Anticipate plays and move quickly; never hesitate. To execute a dig, you have less than half a second, which is half the time it takes to decide what to do. Thus, your responses must be pure reaction.
3. Go to the floor for a ball as naturally as you play any other phase of the game.

Practicing these and other fundamentals develops quickness, accuracy, smoothness and consistency.

Because time for decision making on defense is so limited, the players' responses need to be as nearly automatic as possible. Thus, athletes who excel at defense rely on following their coach's instructions to the letter. When the coach says a certain situation calls for a particular response, that situation should evoke that response automatically. There is too little time to decide what to do about an attacked ball.

The goal of techniques such as game-simulated training — making the practice drills resemble actual game situations as much as possible — is to train instinctive reactions. For example, athletes who automatically go for all balls in their area of responsibility (rather than thinking about it and going for some balls while letting others drop) not only play better defense, but also reduce their chances of injury. And the unthinking, instinctive dig and follow-through are automatically done with correct technique. Nearby teammates do not have to guess the instinctive defender's movements and coverage. Such spontaneity is found only in defensive players who have the right mental qualities: motivation to be intense on defense and willingness to retrain their instinctive reactions.

PHYSICAL QUALITIES

Using game-simulated training to convince the defense to react automatically provides a good bridge between mental and physical qualities. Players must be convinced that the physical skills the coach teaches them are important for both greater defensive effectiveness and greater safety. The goal is for the defensive players to react automatically — physically, as well as mentally. The key to good defense is reaction, not anticipation.

The Foot Patter Drill

The foot patter drill is just one example of how athletes can learn to respond to the opponent's action (based on instinct) rather than their own anticipation (based on thinking). Have you ever watched a good tennis player prepare to receive serve? The player does a little hop, or a side-to-side step followed by a hop, just as the opponent serves the ball. This movement, the foot patter or pre-hop, is designed to break the player's physical and mental inertia. The player crouches a little (with head and arms lifted, elbows relaxed) and lifts one foot, then the other — all without leaving a stationary position. The foot patter serves the same purpose in volleyball as in basketball and football warm-ups: it gets the athletes off their heels and ready to move to the ball.

Getting the athletes off their heels and ready to move is important because many players make the mistake of reaching with their arms on defense, rather than getting their bodies into position behind the ball. Usually this mistake happens because the athlete's body and mind have not been geared toward reaction. A player who lunges with the arms and body, rather than moving first with the feet, has less control of his or her center of gravity and hence less control of how and where the ball is struck. With the pre-hop, the player gets into position by moving the feet first and thus has center-of-gravity control, body control and ball control.

The following game-simulation drill teaches the foot patter. Have your players take their defensive positions and practice the foot patter. Then, to simulate the hitter's angles, stand on a chair or table on the other side of the net and follow these steps:

1. In rapid succession, alternate hitting harder, then softer balls at your athletes to help them break the habit of anticipating the speed of the ball.
2. Hit the balls higher, then lower to get the players used to adjusting their stances and the height of their crouches.
3. Keep surprising your players; do not let them think about what they are doing or start guessing what you are going to do next in these drills.

To re-emphasize, reaction — not anticipation — is the key to this and other game-simulation drills. Players need to react to the ball's height, its velocity, the hitter's arm angle and even the sound of the hitter's hand against the ball.

Practicing defense develops mental toughness, concentration and desire. It perfects footwork, improves speed and reflexes and establishes coordination with adjacent players on the court. These physical and mental attributes contribute not only to strong defense, but also to the offense. The remainder of this chapter covers basic elements of defense: the basic ready position; low, medium and high digs; the sprawl, roll, dive and running dive; and some important defensive situations and defensive tips.

BASIC READY POSITION

Defensive players always start in the basic ready position. Figures 9.1 and 9.2 show front and side views of the basic ready position. Note the elements of this position:

- Knees: slightly ahead of toes, bent at 100-120 degrees.
- Waist: bent forward, so that shoulders are in front of knees.
- Arms: relaxed, ready to come together to dig the ball.
- Head: up, eyes following the ball.
- Center of gravity: keep it low!

Figure 9.3 shows the forearms and hands in position to contact the ball. Note that for digging, the contact point on the forearm is lower than the contact point for passing: just above the wrist on the inside, soft tissue area of the forearm.

Reminder. Your players should listen to the sound of the ball and watch the attacker's armswing. They must see the ball and react. Do not let them plant their feet, even in this low position. Get them to use the patter or pre-hop instead. This low stance may

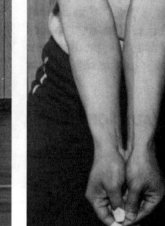

Fig. 9.1   Fig. 9.2   Fig. 9.3

All photos in this chapter courtesy of UCSB

be awkward initially, but make sure they crouch low and keep their heads up. Keep these points in mind:

- Body position must be kept low.
- Foot patter or pre-hop is the key to maintaining mobility.
- Wrist/hand/arm action must be strong and accurate.

DIGS: LOW, MEDIUM, AND HIGH

Players defend or dig the ball at three heights: low, medium, and high. There are recommended specific defensive techniques for each height.

Low Digs

Players execute 70 percent of the defense from the low position. Seven of every 10 balls will be received below the defender's knees and within 1 meter of the athlete's ready position.

Medium Digs

Balls received between the knees and the shoulders are in the medium range. These digs occur most often in the player-up defense in the mid-court area. Traditionally, players take the ball in front of their body, jumping so as to meet the ball on their forearms. I suggest a different technique: Train the athletes to move to the side of the ball and take it as shown in Figure 9.4.

High Digs

A few times during a match, the setters (and other players, as well) will get caught off balance behind the blockers. In these situations, they have to take the ball high above their shoulder — the high position — and use a "rebound" action. The thumbs should be "webbed" so they are out of the way. Figures 9.5 and 9.6 show the front and back views of the high dig. In this high position,

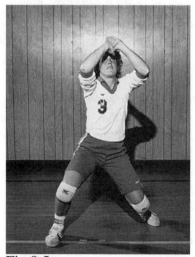

Fig 9.4   Fig 9.5   Fig 9.6

Fig. 9.7

Fig. 9.8

Fig. 9.9

Fig. 9.10

the elbows and wrists compress backward and downward upon impact to give better control, especially for harder hit balls. Although setters are the primary users of this once-outlawed technique, it is now common to see any player caught out of position using it.

LOW POSITION VARIATIONS: SPRAWL, ROLL, DIVE AND RUNNING DIVE

Because more than 70 percent of all attacked balls will be defended below the defender's knees, techniques for low position variations should be practiced much more than techniques for the other reception heights. First, take another look at the basic low position dig (Figure 9.7).

There are several techniques all power players must have in their defensive repertoires to use either after the dig or as part of it: the sprawl, roll, dive and running dive.

The Sprawl

The sprawl is perhaps the most widely used technique for digging low balls beyond the defensive player's one-step range. Proper execution of the dive (explained later in this chapter) takes much greater arm and shoulder strength than the sprawl. For a player who may not have quite so much upper body strength, the sprawl is far more comfortable both for digging and as a recovery move. Players should use two arms for harder hit balls and one for tips. The ball can be in front or to the side of the player. Changing directions in the sprawl is easy, making it especially effective.

Sprawl Progression. Figures 9.8, 9.9 and 9.10 show the sprawl progression. Use the sprawl when the ball is too low for a rolling recovery. Keep these points in mind:

- Do not let the feet leave the ground (as in diving).
- Try to use two hands on the ball.
- Shift the shoulders around the ball.
- Keep the shoulders relaxed to absorb the ball's impact.

Arm and Hand Action. In the sprawl (and the roll,

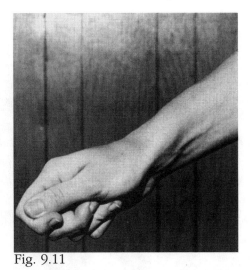

Fig. 9.11

Fig. 9.12

explained later), the hands have a unique function that may be new to many coaches. The defender can contact the ball very low to the floor with the soft tissue on the top of the fist (Figure 9.11). With the wrist flick, the wrist snaps upward and the sprawl (or roll) is executed (Figure 9.12).

Scoop. The scoop, in which the player uses the back of the hand as a scoop under the ball, is very popular, especially in combination with the dive. The wrist flick simply offers another option.

Barrel Roll. From the sprawl, the athlete may simply push up to his or her feet in a crouch position to get ready for the next movement, or barrel roll, to his or her feet. (Figure 9.13)

Remember, in the barrel roll the elbows and knees must be kept in such a position that the roll is done over the middle portion of the back. The barrel roll can be used as recovery after a dive, as well. It allows the player to stay focused on the ball after

executing the pick-up move, whether a wrist flick or a scoop.

The Roll

Since the Japanese introduced the roll in 1964, it has quickly become a standard element in volleyball defense worldwide. For medium- to low-hit balls that are to the side of the athlete, the roll is the most widely accepted technique for digging and recovering. The roll is also used for certain tips, deflections off the block and chasing down balls. Figures 9.14-9.17 show the roll in step-by-step progression.

Teaching the athletes to roll properly results in greater coverage of the defense area and less chance of injury once the defensive attempt has been executed. The properly executed roll allows the player to execute a defensive move and be ready immediately for the next demand. Whenever possible, athletes should use two arms with the roll for greater control and accuracy. Often, the roll only uses one arm. Remind your athletes to bend the elbow of the non-involved arm while rolling over the shoulder of that arm. These maneuvers will help prevent injury and aid in stability on recovery.

The Dive

Players use the dive to pick up tips and short hits in front of them. Mats and hip pads are highly recommended when this technique is first introduced. Take care to keep the chin high to avoid injury by contact with the floor. Figures 9.18-9.21 show the dive.

The Running Dive

The running dive allows the player to cover greater distance than the standard dive. The technique is popular with players who are capable of a move that

Fig. 9.13

Fig. 9.14

Fig. 9.15

Fig. 9.16

Fig. 9.17

takes great strength to execute. The athlete runs and leaps toward the ball, using the wrist flick to get under the ball with a clenched fist and recovers on the abdomen. The athlete slides, absorbing the shock after contacting the ball. For the most advanced players, the running dive could be a good emergency tool.

COMMON DEFENSIVE SITUATIONS: DEFENSIVE TIPS

Volleyball strategies in many textbooks assume the defensive player is behind a perfect two-person block. In reality, this degree of protection rarely occurs. This section outlines some of the common situations that face the defensive players (other than the blockers) and explains how each position responds. As these pointers illustrate, volleyball is a game of angles. The major point to note concerning adjustment to hitters is that defensive players must adjust to their own blockers' formation: Are there one, two or three blockers? Where are the holes in the block? A hole is created when blockers are late to their assignments at the net, leaving the left- or right-side blocker in a solo blocking position.

Trouble Sets

Trouble sets are situations in which the defense needs to recognize that because the ball has been set a certain way, a particular defensive reaction is immediately required. The following paragraphs describe some of the most common trouble sets and explain how the defense must react.

Down Balls. A down ball is one that is set off the net and thus usually hits with less velocity than a normal attack. The defensive player knows that the back court defense will usually be the first to handle the attack.

Trapped Sets. In a trapped set, the ball has been set very close to the net so that the hitter has little room to hit the ball with much control and effectiveness. These sets usually result in tips.

Sharp Cross-Court Sets. A ball set outside the antenna will usually result in a cross-court shot because of the angle needed to hit clear of the antenna.

Contact Height. The higher the attacker can contact the ball in the air, the greater the options for direction and velocity on the ball. The lower the ball is to the net, the fewer the options. Consider the advantage taller tennis players have when serving: Their angle of contact point relative to the net is higher than that of shorter players, increasing the options available with the serve.

Ball Direction. Teach your players to watch the attacker's approach angle and the position of the ball relative to the attacker's shoulder (Figures 9.22 and 9.23). The approach angle largely determines the ball's final destination. A 30-degree angle approach dictates a certain destination; a 90-degree angle suggests another. From the attacker's point of view, the 45-degree approach is most effective because it gives the most options for the ball's final destination. Similarly, the ball-to-shoulder proximity helps to determine the attacker's options of where the ball will go:

- Ball inside the shoulder: If the ball is contacted high, the attacker has the most options.
- Ball in line with the shoulder: The attacker still has some good options — though not as many — including good cross-court and line shots.
- Ball outside the shoulder: There are fewer options for the attacker, because the attacker will not cross the body with his or her shot.

Hitter's Tendencies. Many coaches chart the hitting tendencies of the opponents prior to competition. Consequently, defensive players should know their opponents' favorite and most effective shots.

Defensive Position Responsibilities

The traditional defensive alignment was predicated on a total contact allotment of three per side, including the block. As the rules evolved and three contacts were allowed after the block, the coverage possibilities and responsibilities changed accordingly. Figures 9.24 and 9.25 show the differences that have resulted and this section discusses these changing defensive responsibilities, position by position.

With the old style, deep tips and surprise shots over the heads of the defenders were unmanageable. The current style allows one player to back up another in whatever formation necessary to cover the hit.

Each player must know the specific responsibilities of each position for each attack possibility. Figures 9.26-9.30 show those responsibilities. Note first the numbering system for players on the court shown in Figure 9.26. Because positions 1 and 5 mirror each other, as do positions 2 and 4, these diagrams are combined.

In general, train your players to roll left and right. When playing a left-side position, the player should

Fig. 9.18

Fig. 9.19

Fig. 9.20

Fig. 9.21

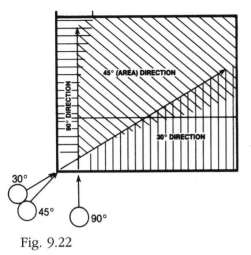

Fig. 9.22

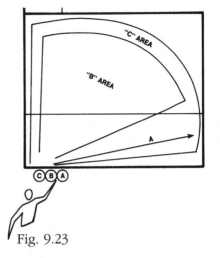

Fig. 9.23

have the left foot forward; vice versa on the right side. This foot position helps to square the shoulders to the ball, in effect creating a platform from which to keep the ball in the court. If your players start in the correct positions and roll left or right as needed, they will only be penalized during a game if they are not capable and confident of going to the floor for a ball.

Positions I and 5. The responsibilities for positions 1 and 5 are identical, but on opposite sides of the back court. Position 5 is the left back; position 1 is the right back. A special note about position 5 is warranted here. The majority of first attack hits come to this player and handling the initial attack is critical to success. Thus, a very good defensive player must be at this position. This player must be able to roll, dive and sprawl without stopping to think about these movements. Remember, the left side player has the left foot forward in the ready position and vice versa for the right side player (Figure 9.27: A, B, C).

A. Hard line spike or cross-court spike: The player should stand 1.5 m (5 ft.) from the endline and .3

m (1 ft.) from the sideline.

B. Middle attack: The player should stand 4.6 m (15 ft.) from the endline and .3 m (1 ft.) from the sideline.

C. After getting to the ball: The player will usually need to roll and to remember to stay low.

Positions 2 and 4. The responsibilities for positions 2 and 4 are identical, but on opposite ends of the net. Position 4 is the left front; position 2 is the right front. The players are primarily blockers, but when the ball is set to the end of the net opposite them, they pull off the net to help either behind the block or with sharp-angle hits in the front court (Figure 9.28: A, B, C).

A. The player starts at the net, but when the ball is set to the far end of the net away from this player, the role changes from blocker to defense player. The player backs off the net to spot A and waits to help with hits coming to that area, if necessary.

B. If player 2 or player 4 did not have time to get in position to block, they must move toward the attack

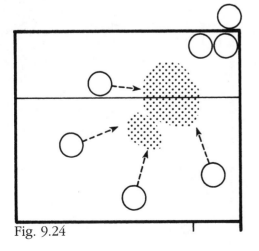

Fig. 9.24

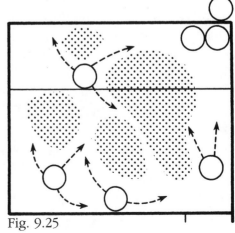

Fig. 9.25

line area in the middle to help with tips.

C. If there is a tip in the middle, the middle player must be able to roll or sprawl to recover after playing a ball in position C.

Position 3. Even the middle blocker has defense responsibilities to think about as an attacker is approaching to hit the ball. The middle blocker in position 3 must be one of the quickest and, if possible, most experienced players on the team. This player must be able to "read" the approaching offense and adjust quickly. He or she must move to help block with the left and right blockers, as well as cover the quick attack in the middle (Figure 9.29: A, B).

A. Block, then cover the tip behind, if necessary.

B. If late to move to assist the left or right blockers, this player covers the tip behind the block.

Position 6. The player in position 6 must be ready to move laterally (left and right), as well as forward. This player must be able to roll, dive and sprawl with equal ease. This position usually handles the most balls on defense and is considered to be the most critical position to staff. A coach will need an exceptional athlete to play this position well (Figure 9.30: A-D).

A. On the line spike, position 6 helps with the deep line.

B. On a cross-court shot, position 6 helps with position 5's responsibility deep.

C. If there is only one blocker at the net, position 6 cuts off the angle by moving up on the ball.

D. If there are no blockers at the net, position 6 moves up into the court for sharper angle hits.

CONCLUSION

Without defense, your team cannot score points in volleyball! Thus, volleyball begins with sound defense.

Every defensive player on the court has a responsibility for every situation. Situations arise so quickly and vary so greatly that there is too little time for complex decision making — players must simply react. If they have practiced and practiced, relearning the necessary responses to balls hit at them, they will know what to do.

Defensive techniques are complicated and possibly the most difficult aspect of volleyball to master. The ball must be defended within half a second of being hit and the defender must be quick and confident in order to meet the ball before it strikes the ground.

The athletes must understand that offense and defense are indistinguishable: A rally combines and interchanges them so that one is as important to the final outcome as the other.

Players will point out to coaches that practicing defense is not as much fun as practicing hitting. But defensive drills build more than good defensive techniques — they build the fight that excellent athletes need in order to win long rallies, as well. Practicing defense develops mental toughness, concentration, tenacity and desire. The physical benefits are countless: Footwork is perfected; speed and reflexes are improved; and coordination among adjacent players on the court is increased. All of these attributes carry over to the offense.

The women's game, in particular, uses a variety of shots combining skill and finesse, producing longer rallies than in the men's game. Longer rallies put a special emphasis on the ability to prolong a point with outstanding defense. But both men's and women's teams must train long and hard to be able to achieve the final result of entertaining, safe and competitive volleyball.

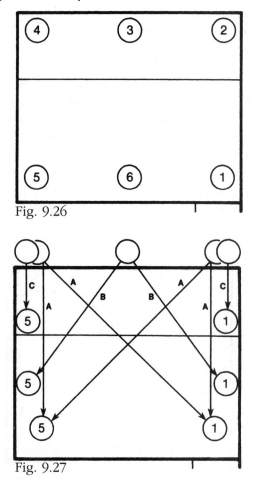

Fig. 9.26

Fig. 9.27

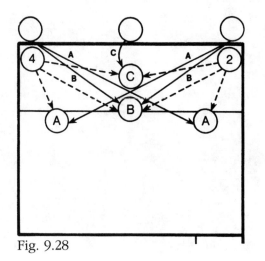

Fig. 9.28

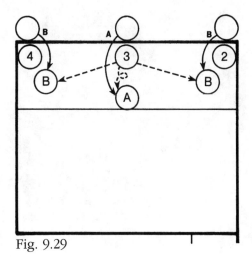

Fig. 9.29

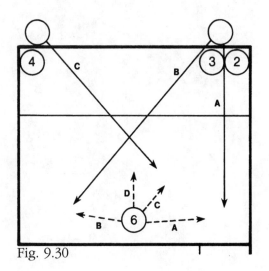

Fig. 9.30

Photo by Dan Houser

SETTING

Terry Condon and Sandy Lynn
Edited by Laurel Brassey Iversen

The setter is one of the most valuable assets any team can have. How a team performs usually depends on how well your setter performs. A good setter can convert a potentially precarious situation into a stable one; a weak setter cannot. Because setting must be decisive and accurate, the setter must be capable of reacting to situations that require speed, agility, coordination, intelligence and technique. Thus, for coaches, the development of the setter should be a priority.

There are many great setters with different styles and techniques. The techniques discussed in this chapter originate from a simple philosophy: A setter must be trained with solid fundamentals. As the setter gains experience, an individual style will inevitably develop.

As a coach, you must be willing to spend that extra time necessary to develop a setter. The minimum time per day specifically devoted to the setter (or setters) should be 30 minutes. If you can arrange an hour, the setter's progress will increase rapidly and so will the team's success. Neglecting the setter is neglecting the team. Results take time and repetition and the coach must initiate this directed workout.

IDENTIFICATION OF A SETTER

A coach's ability to place players in positions that enhance their talents is the first step toward a team's success. Even if a team is perfectly trained, how well a coach uses personnel on the court will determine the end result. Before you can begin to apply all of your knowledge to training a setter, you must have the right person. You may be choosing your setter from hundreds of players or from 15.

The following is a basic checklist for your initial search.

Physical Qualities

Height. Although there are many great small setters, height added to the qualities listed below is certainly an advantage.

Speed. The setter must have the ability to move the feet quickly, enabling him or her to get to the ball fast.

Eyes. The setter must demonstrate quick eye movement and good peripheral vision.

Ambidexterity. The setter must be able to hit the ball with either arm. This is a trainable skill if the player already has good upper body strength. A left-handed setter has an advantage.

Mental Qualities

Personality. If a player's off-court personality shows leadership, independence and self-motivation, then that player will probably demonstrate the same qualities on the court. A setter must be the kind of person who keeps his or her head when others are losing theirs.

Intelligence. Your setter should be able to make quick, smart decisions, always working with the hitters.

Responsibility. Because of a setter's leadership role,

the setter must be strong enough to accept more responsibility than any other player, even the responsibility of a loss.

TEACHING TECHNIQUE

Thorough instruction in correct methods is the most important factor in developing the setter's basic skills and in furthering the setter's progress. Consequently, setters need special attention during the initial stage of instruction, when mistakes can be corrected most easily. There are many different styles and techniques to setting. Following is a style to use to train a setter, which involves a traditional method for teaching body position and footwork. In the basic body position, the setter's shoulders, hips and toes face the target. The right foot should be slightly in front of the left, with the feet shoulder width apart. Ideally, the setter should move quickly, set the feet and square the shoulders to the target. No matter where the ball is passed, the setter's first priority is to beat the ball to position, square off and then set the ball. This one element of technique will take time and repetition to develop. The following sections explain other fundamentals in detail: movement, starting position, ball contact and hand position, releases, and integration of body and foot position.

Movement

It is immensely important to train setters in proper movement. The setter must be able to make all kinds of movements in all directions and at the same time get into proper position to set the ball. Patterns of movement encountered by a setter include the following:

Moving left and right, forward and back (Figure 10.1).
Turning left or right, 180 degrees (Figure 10.2).
Running, stopping, and jumping (Figure 10.3).
Moving and rolling to recover (Figure 10.4).

One of the most important movements of setters is the initial movement to the ball. They must first get to the proper position at the net and then adjust to the pass. The setter should be standing at the net waiting for the pass, then seeing and making a movement to the ball.

Starting Position

The starting position should be the same for all the sets so as not to advertise where the ball is going to

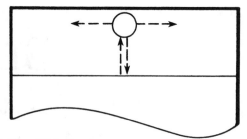

Fig. 10.1

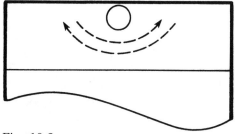

Fig. 10.2

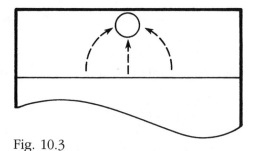

Fig. 10.3

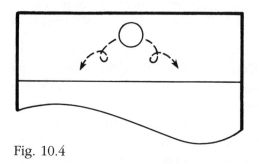

Fig. 10.4

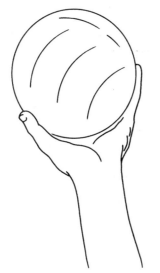

Fig. 10.5

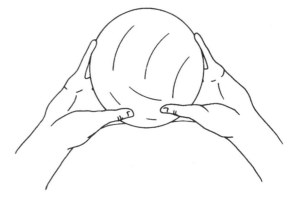

Fig. 10.6

Fig. 10.7   Fig. 10.8   Fig. 10.9

be set. For that same reason, the place of contact with the ball should be the same for every set. As the ball begins its descent, the player should assume a starting position with feet comfortably spread and body weight equally distributed. The knees are bent and ready to make minor adjustments as the ball approaches. The heels of the feet should not carry much weight. The wrists are cocked so that the angle between the forearms and hands is 135 degrees or less (Figure 10.5). The hands are cupped and relaxed. This relaxation is very essential to smooth setting.

Ball Contact and Hand Position

Ball contact is made above the face or forehead on the pads of the fingers. The ball is not batted, but it actually remains in contact with the hands for an instant. The fingers must form a cup between both hands. The thumbs are directed up and back, never forward and down. The greatest amount of contact is on the first three fingers, but some contact is made with all of the fingers (Figure 10.6). Most importantly, the ball should sink well into the hands.

A technique used to find the correct hand position

is to place the hands in a praying position at the forehead. The player opens the hands to form the correct position. Figure 10.7 shows the correct technique, while Figure 10.8 shows hand position too far from the forehead. The major force applied to the ball is not that of wrist snap, but more of a coordinated body action through the ball. The line of force extends from the feet (or trailing foot) through the center of gravity toward the ball. Neither the set nor the follow-through should be a quick, jerky motion; it should be one smooth, coordinated motion, with arms fully extended upon release (Figure 10.9). A flowing follow-through from ankles, legs and arms is very important to a smooth flight of the set. If the movement of the body is abrupt, then the flight of the ball will be uncertain, not deliberate.

Releases

The full-extension release is used for high (or long, distant) sets. The ball contact utilizes the same basic position — off the forehead — but the arms extend through the ball. This same technique will be used by all players when they set to a hitter. Figure 10.10 shows first contact; Figure 10.11 shows full extension.

The quick release is used in more advanced systems of play. Do not let the word "advanced" persuade you to eliminate this technique. This release is used for the shorter, quicker sets. The hands contact the ball at the forehead and return to the forehead with no extension, a technique that allows better ball control for the play sets. Figure 10.12 shows the first contact and Figure 10.13 shows the quick release.

Fig. 10.10

Fig. 10.11

Fig. 10.12

Fig. 10.13

Integration of Body and Foot Position

Integration of movement and footwork is fundamental to developing a setter. This integration normally involves the following sequence:

1. Movement to the estimated area of interception based on the flight of the ball.
2. Body alignment to intersect the path of the oncoming ball with the intended path of the set.
3. Orientation with intended target; foot positioning.
4. Final adjustments and execution.

REVIEW

Basically, the important fundamentals to be observed when setting the ball include the following:

- The midline of the body should correspond to the path of the ball and the desired direction of the pass; the feet should be in a front-back stride position to allow for weight transfer (see Figure 10.9).
- The longer the distance of the pass, the greater should be the force contributed by the legs.
- The hips should face in the direction of the pass and the body should follow through in the direction of the set.
- The setter should remember that passes made over a short distance require relatively minimal use of the entire body.
- The setter should move forward into the oncoming ball and never in a direction away from it.

TYPES OF SETS

There are many types of sets that may be used effectively in volleyball today. Discussed in the following sections are some of the most common: the back-court set, the back set, the play set, the save set, the forearm set and the jump set.

The Back-Court Set

Any ball set from behind the 3-meter line is designated a back-court set. The full-extension release will be necessary because the ball will be set higher and the distance of the set will be greater. The body position is the same as that explained previously. This set is one that all players should be able to perform with accuracy. Drill work and repetition are necessary to increase all players' consistency on the back-court set.

The Back Set

A back set occurs when you set the ball over your head to a spiker behind you. The beginning position for the back set is the same as in the front set. The hands are at the forehead with fingers spread. Immediately after the ball is contacted, the wrists rock back slightly. The amount of arm extension will depend on the distance and height of the set. The hips should be loose to push through the ball. The amount of hip thrust and arm extension will determine the height and distance of each set. As seen in Figures 10.14 and 10.15, it becomes important for the hand position to remain the same. If the hands reach above the head, the back set becomes less deceptive. Figure 10.14 shows the incorrect position; Figure 10.15 shows the correct one.

The back-set body position most common among setters is with the back squared off to the right front. The set is then sent directly overhead back to the right front position. The problem with this technique is that it alerts the blockers to where the ball will be set. Yet, many coaches still prefer to use this technique because it makes it easier for a setter to develop consistency.

A body position that can increase the deception of the back set is the one previously discussed as the basic body position. The back set does not change this position unless the ball is being set from an extreme back-court position. The setter should get to position quickly and set the feet with the hips, shoulders and toes facing the left front. The only motions that change are the extension of the arms and the follow-through. After the ball comes in contact with the hands, the hands and arms extend to the right and back to push the ball to the right front. Figures 10.16 and 10.17 depict the two back sets: 10.16 (the traditional back set) and 10.17 (the deceptive back set). Note that the direction of a set should not affect the change of the body position unless the set is from a deep back-court position.

The Play Set

It is important to use the quick release on all play sets to establish consistency. The setter must be able to set a consistent ball to each offensive position. Many techniques are employed to designate the type of set. The setter may call out a number to each hitter or may give a one-hand signal which tells all hitters

Fig. 10.14

Fig. 10.15

Fig. 10.16

Fig. 10.17

Fig. 10.18

Fig. 10.19

Fig. 10.20

what set they will hit. Since this chapter does not deal with offensive systems, you only need to know that your setter must be able to set all sets consistently.

The Save Set

The save set is used when the setter is unable to get the correct body position to the ball. This incorrect position could result from an off-dig or a deep pass. In this instance, the setter must be flexible and acrobatic in order to get hands on the ball and set a nice, high set. The most effective method is the set with a half roll, which allows the setter to get underneath the ball with hands at the forehead and set with a full-extension release.

Figures 10.18 through 10.20 illustrate how to teach the set and half roll:

1. The knees should be in front of the ball, with the right foot forward.
2. The hands begin at the forehead.
3. After ball contact, the arms extend through the ball.
4. Momentum will push the body into a half roll.

The Forearm Set

When it is impossible for the setter to get hands on the ball, the setter must use the forearm set. The body must still be in the full squat position. When the ball is contacted, the arms will follow through and the player will return to an upright position. Figures 10.21 and 10.22 show this set.

The Jump Set

The jump set should be added for any advanced offense. It increases the setter's options, thereby increasing the hitter's options. The position of the hands and body is important in the effectiveness of this set. The body position is the same as with a regular set and the hand position remains the same as in all other sets. If the setter broad jumps through the ball, the hitter will have difficulty in his or her approach angles. It is very important to keep the hands at the forehead. The ball is contacted at the peak of the jump. The setter jumps, hangs in the air and sets the ball. Figure 10.23 illustrates the jump set.

SECOND-BALL PLAY

Setters must be able to hit and tip the second ball, preferably with either hand. They must also be able to make split-second decisions on when and when not to tip or hit the second ball. In any hitting or tipping situation, it is the setter's responsibility to know what the blockers are doing. If the setter is blindly hitting away or tipping, the options will not be as effective. Figures 10.24, 10.25, and 10.26 show the left-handed tip, right-handed tip and left-handed hit, respectively.

The Tip or Dump

The tip (or dump) may be used with a jump set or from a regular standing position. The setter's hand position is the same as for a regular set. Only one

Fig. 10.21

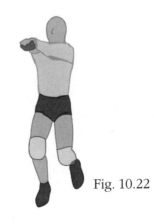

Fig. 10.22

Fig. 10.23

Fig. 10.24

Fig. 10.25

Fig. 10.26

hand contacts the ball. Use a left-handed tip when you want the ball to be placed off the net. If you want to tip the ball close to the net, the best method is to use the right hand, with the palm rotated back toward the face. Tight passes make this tip very effective. To make the tip more deceptive to the blockers, train your setter to keep both hands in the setting position.

Times to Tip

There are five situations in which it is appropriate to tip:

- When opponents are switching position during a rally.

- After a long rally.
- When a weak spot in the defense has been determined.
- When the left back player is serving. (Many times teams do not cover this position and the server is slow in switching into position.)
- Against a player-back defense.

Hitting the Second Ball

If your setter is left-handed, then you are fortunate. If not, start training your setter to hit the second ball with either arm. If you run a 5-1 offense, such flexibility is a valuable tool when the setter is in the front row. The setter now has the option to jump set, jump tip or jump hit. A well-trained setter can keep the blockers guessing by using all three of these options. The best time to get a good swing at the ball is on a medium-high pass close to the net. Again, the setter must first put the hands into setting position as if preparing to jump and set the ball. Immediately, the non-hitting arm drops and the hitting arm swings.

EYE CHECKS

After training your setters in the proper techniques, you must not forget to train their eyes. The more comfortable and experienced the setter becomes with basic setting, the more he or she will be willing to look away from the ball and at the total court. Many setters focus their eyes only on the ball, unaware of what their opponents are doing. This one skill — being able to look away from the ball to see the entire court — takes many hours of practice through eye-movement drills. The more efficient the eye movement becomes, the more successful your setter will be in the total team effort. It will be easier to get one-on-one situations for your hitters or to tip and hit at the most opportune time if the setter has total-court awareness.

Eye checks may be incorporated into most of your setting drills after your setter becomes familiar with basic setting skills. The following eye check progression is taken after the pass and before the set:

Step 1: Eye check to the left front. This check will also help in preparing the body to square off toward the left front.

Step 2: Eye check to the opposing right front blocker.

Step 3: Eye check to the opposing middle blocker — this one is critical.

Step 4: Eye check to the right front hitter.

Step 5: Eye check to the opponent's back-court defense.

Training in each of these eye checks will prepare the setter for any given situation.

Peripheral vision also becomes important because there are many times when the setter needs to see the blocker — the middle blocker especially — immediately before setting the ball. For example: Your setter is jumping to tip or hit and a blocker jumps, also. With good peripheral vision, your setter can turn and set the ball. Consequently, you need to broaden your setter's court vision through eye training.

SETTER RESPONSIBILITIES

Here is a summary list of the setter's responsibilities:

1. Set the best possible ball in all situations.
2. Set the most desired set according to each hitter. (Know your hitters.)
3. Take responsibility for hitting errors.
4. Make all passes look good.
5. Know your opponents! Be able to make the best possible choices.
6. Know the high-percentage and low-percentage sets.
7. Be able to recognize a "hot" hitter.
8. Keep a cool head and be a good leader.
9. Be aware of weak blockers and gaps in the defense.
10. Be in control of the game's rhythm.
11. Take responsibility to make things happen on the court!

TRAINING THE SETTER

Great setters are few and far between, usually because of inadequate coaching. A setter is like a quarterback on a football team or a director of an athletic department — no one could be successful in these positions without proper training and experience. Put in the time to provide the direction necessary to mold your setter into the director of your team. A setter's technical development requires time, patience, organization and effort. Following is a guideline for this development.

Mobility and Technique

Work with your setter on:

- speed, agility, coordination
- types of footwork
- posture
- basic overhand pass: technique

Sets from the Back Court

Your setter needs practice on:

- set after moving forward
- set after moving to the side
- set after moving backward
- set from a jump

Sets from the Near Net

Your setter needs to practice these basic sets:

1. The Basic High Set

- set after moving forward

- set after moving to the side
- set after moving backward
- set from neutral position
- set with forearms
- set with jump

2. The Back Set
- set after moving to net
- set after moving away from net
- set after moving forward or backward
- set from a jump

3. The Jump Set
- set after moving in different directions

4. The Quick Set
- set after moving in different directions
- set from different positions after moving
- set from a jump after moving

5. The Side Set
- set while facing the net
- set while back is to the net (jump set only)
- set from a jump while facing the net
- set after moving different directions while facing the net
- set from a jump while facing the net after moving in different directions

6. The Shoot Set
- set after moving
- set from a jump after moving

7. The Play Set
- set after moving
- set from different positions and postures

8. The One-Hand Set
- set from a jump after moving

DRILLS
Hand Position Drills

Following are some drills for teaching your setter(s) proper hand position:

1. Toss the ball to self 2 to 3 m straight up (6 ft. 6 ins. to 9 ft. 10 ins.) and catch it in front of the face, stressing proper hand position on the ball.
2. Same as No. 1, only increase the difficulty by making the player move before catching the ball. Toss the ball forward, to the sides and backward. Stress that the player must get under the ball. When the ball is low, the player must catch the ball by placing one foot in front of the other, bending the knees and dropping the hips below the knee of the lead foot.
3. Increase the difficulty of the ball/body orientation by having the player catch the ball in varying positions. Toss, then catch while kneeling, then while sitting. This forces the player to predict the path of the ball.
4. Toss the ball at the wall: Shift behind and under the ball and catch it in proper position; add movement.
5. Partners: A tosses, B catches in proper ball-body relationship with correct hand position.
6. Same as No. 4, only progress from no movement to movement: A tosses the ball so B has to shift forward, backward, left and right. As the player becomes proficient, vary the direction of the tosses from predictable to unpredictable.

Basic Back Set Drills
Following are basic back set drills to use when training your setter(s):

1. Toss and back set high in the air, follow through the ball in the direction opposite the set.
2. Pairs, one person passing to another: back set to the wall, catch and repeat.

Elementary Drills
The following drills can be used for either front or back setting. Jump setting can also be used for these elementary drills.

1. Partners, sitting on the floor 2 m (6 ft. 6 ins.) apart: Throw and catch the ball back and forth as quickly as possible.
2. Individual: Volley to self in different body positions — squatting, kneeling, sitting and standing.
3. Individual: Volley 3 to 5 m in the air (9 ft. 10 ins. to 16 ft. 5 ins.), let the ball bounce, move underneath the volley and set up again. Stress extending the legs so that the body is moving up into the ball.
4. Individual: Toss to self and volley at the wall. Stress movement into the ball and follow-through.
5. Individual: Volley at the wall, let the ball bounce and volley at the wall. Stress moving behind the ball before contact and moving forward into the ball prior to, during and after contact. This is a very difficult drill to perform correctly as it requires quick, continuous movement.
6. Partners: A tosses to B, B volleys to A, A catches the ball in proper position.

7. Partners: Continuous volleying, 1 m apart.
8. Partners: 3 to 5 m apart (9 ft. 10 ins. to 16 ft. 5 ins.), continuous volleying. A volleys to self, A volleys to B; B volleys to self, B volleys to A. Stress moving forward in direction of the pass while passing to partners.
9. Triangle: A passes to B, B passes to C, C passes to A; continuous volleying, both directions (Figure 10.27).
10. Triangle: Same as No. 9, only return the volley in the direction it came from and then pass to the next player (Figure 10.28).
11. Triangle, four players: Same as No. 9, only after making the pass, continue forward to replace the player who received the pass (Figure 10.29).
12. Square formation, five players: A volleys to B, then follows the pass to replace B after B volleys to D;

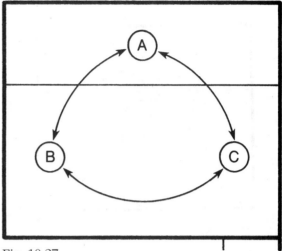

Fig. 10.27

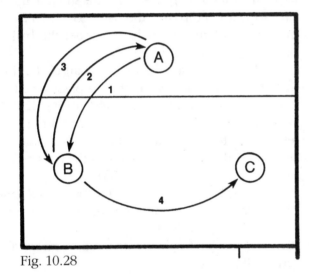

Fig. 10.28

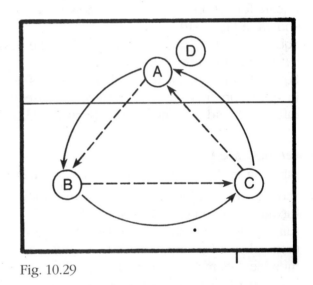

Fig. 10.29

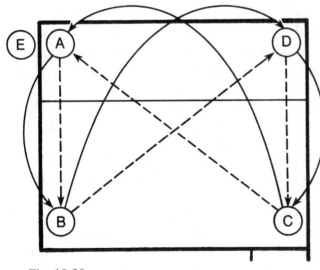

Fig. 10.30

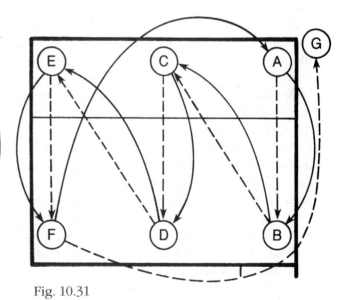

Fig. 10.31

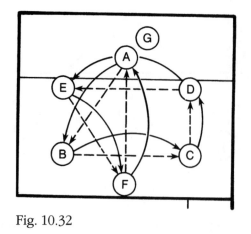

Fig. 10.32

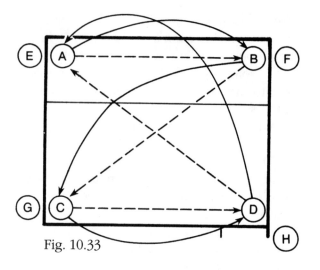

Fig. 10.33

D volleys to C, then C volleys to E (Figure 10.30).

13. Square formation, large group: Follow the pass as shown in Figure 10.31.

14. Square formation, group of seven: Follow the pass as shown in Figure 10.32.

15. Square formation, maximum of eight players, two in each corner. Follow your pass; increase the difficulty by adding another ball (Figure 10.33).

Intermediate Drills

Following are 14 intermediate drills for your setter(s):

1. Individual: Volley the ball straight up, volley it forward 3 to 4 m (9 ft. 10 ins. to 13 ft. 1 in.) and run forward under the ball; volley straight up and then volley it forward.

2. Individual: Same as number 1, only pass the ball backward, then straight up; sideways, then straight up.

3. Individual, 2 m (6 ft. 6 ins.) from wall: Continuous volleying at wall while shifting back and forth along the wall; also move closer to and further away from the wall.

4. Individual, 2 m (6 ft. 6 ins.) from wall: Volley the ball straight up, run and touch the wall and volley the ball straight up.

5. Partners: Each player volleys to self, then volleys to partner. Add movement which must be done during the time when the ball has been passed to partner: jump, turn 360 degrees, jump and turn, sit down, lie down on stomach, lie down on back, forward shoulder roll, backward shoulder roll, run up and touch partner's knee, run around partner, be parallel and near wall (2 m or 6 ft. 6 ins.) and run to touch it.

6. Partners: A and B stand 3 to 5 m apart (9 ft. 10 ins. to 16 ft. 5 ins.). A passes the ball straight up, B runs forward and passes the ball 3 to 5 m in front; meanwhile, A moves back and under the ball to pass straight up (Figure 10.34).

7. Partners: A and B stand 2 to 4 m apart (6 ft. 6 ins. to 13 ft. 1 in.), facing each other: A passes the ball 2 to 3 m (6 ft. 6 ins. to 9 ft. 10 ins.) to B's right, B shifts under the ball and passes it 2 to 3 m to A's left. Stress to your players that they should be stopped and facing the direction of the pass before making the volley (Figure 10.35).

8. Partners: Set moving forward and backward; one player advances and the other retreats to a spot, alternately (Figure 10.36).

9. Partners, consecutive sets with a roll: Partners take turns rolling and tossing.

10. A sets along the net and then retreats and sets again; consecutively performed by both partners (Figure 10.37).

11. Your setter is between two partners: The setter alternately moves from the attack line to the net and turns 90 degrees to set to partners (Figure 10.38).

12. Group of three, give and go: After passing, the players must run outside the sideline before making the next pass (Figure 10.40).

13. Partner, short then long: Partner at the net passes the ball short then long; B must move short then long (Figure 10.41).

14. Group of four: A passes to C, C passes to B, B passes to D, D passes to B, B passes to C, C passes to A. After passing, A and D run to the baseline and return to make the next pass, B and C only

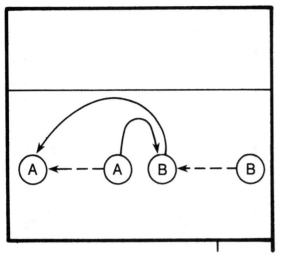

Fig. 10.34

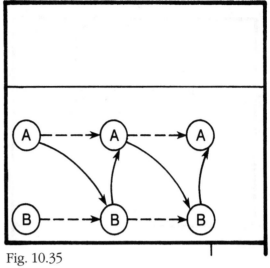

Fig. 10.35

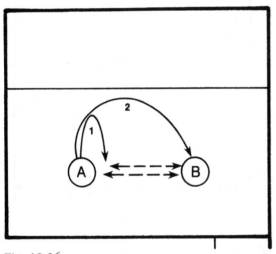

Fig. 10.36

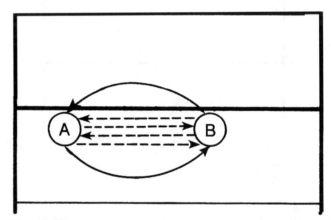

Fig. 10.37

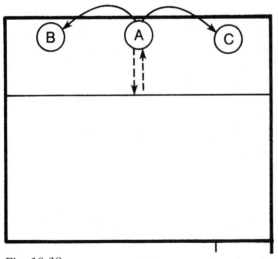

Fig. 10.38

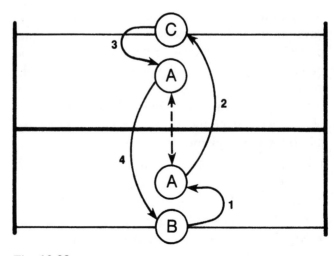

Fig. 10.39

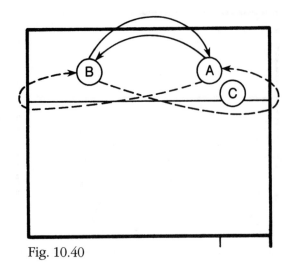

Fig. 10.40

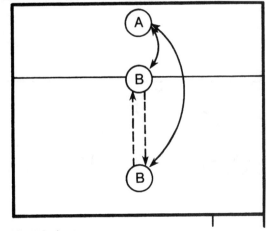

Fig. 10.41

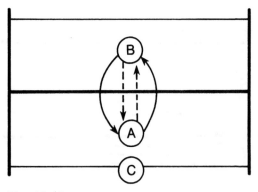

Fig. 10.42

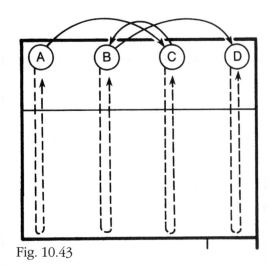

Fig. 10.43

run after passing to each other; then increase the difficulty (Figure 10.43).

Advanced Training

Players who have progressed to this point of training have mastered the individual techniques of overhand passing. These exercises are designed to orient your players to setting the ball along the net and to give your players experience in situations that demand ball control and mental discipline. Your setters should be able to execute the different sets and implement the following fundamental tactics:

1. Make pre-attack observations and be aware of the positions of attackers and opposing blockers.
2. Know who the strongest spikers are.
3. Know the types of sets each spiker prefers.
4. Know the types of sets each spiker prefers least and has the greatest difficulty with.

5. Direct the majority of the sets to the strongest spiker.
6. Be able to set deceptively; do not telegraph where the sets will be directed beforehand.
7. Recognize emergency situations and make the most appropriate set for that situation. For example, if a spiker digs the ball with a roll, your setter must see that and set one of the other hitters.
8. Be able to determine where the block is being set and direct the set to an area or position where a successful spike is more probable. For example, if the blocker is up for the one set in the middle, the setter must see that and set a different hitter.

Once players become familiar with the pattern of movement involved, the drill should become more goal-oriented. Some minimum standards of performance could be:

• Play the ball a certain number of times in succession.
• Play the ball from within the attack zone; players cannot touch the net or go over the center line.

- Keep the ball in play for a specific period of time.
- Require a proportion of the sets to be jump sets. For example, play the ball 30 times nonstop, of which 15 sets must be jump sets.

Setter Movement Drills. These drills are advanced and must be preceded by basic fundamentals. All tosses may vary in height and in placement on the court. The set direction can be predetermined by the coach. All sets — jump sets, tips, hits, set/half roll — can be implemented as any part of the drill. A heavier ball or a soccer ball may be used. The coach should move around and toss from every position on the court.

Note: Any time a chair appears in the following diagrams, it indicates a serve-reception drill. The coach slaps the ball, signaling for the setter to break to setting position. The toss is directed away from the setting position, which will require the setter to move, face the left front and set. A shagger is helpful in all drills and makes for a more efficient practice (Figures 10.44-10.66).

Setting Attackers. These drills are designed to improve your setter's accuracy and consistency in a game-like situation. It is also important for your setter to develop timing and rhythm with your team's attackers to enhance their effectiveness.

1. You toss the ball to the net. The setter runs in from the 3-meter line and you yell out a type of set to be set. The setter must wait for the call. For example, you toss the ball and the setter runs in, you yell "back," and your setter sets a back set. Then increase the difficulty. For example, the player must jump set every time (Figure 10.67).
2. You toss the ball at the net. The setter runs in from the 10-foot line. If the blocker jumps, the setter sets outside. If the blocker does not jump, the setter sets middle (Figure 10.68).
3. Sets with outside hitters: You toss a ball to the net and the setter runs in and sets the ball. Work on consistent sets: set forward and behind, short and deep, all varieties of sets. Penetrate from the middle and left positions (Figures 10.69 and 10.70).
4. Set with the middle hitters and vary the location of the toss along the net: The setter puts the ball the same distance in front of self; when the setter must go to the left of center court, the middle hitter comes behind for a back set (Figures 10.71-10.73).
5. Set with middle hitters: Similar series as No. 4, except the coach's pass is more than 2 m (6 ft. 6 ins.) back from the net.

6. Set with two or three hitters: You toss to the setter, who must now choose among three hitters (Figure 10.74).
7. Lob over an easy serve that one of the three passers receives. The setter sets; setters and hitters change positions each time (Figure 10.75).
8. Simulate a free ball: Bounce a ball on the floor, the players drop off the net and the setter penetrates. Underhand toss the ball over the net; set, hit, etc. (Figure 10.76).
9. Same as No. 8, except you add blockers. The setter should attempt to prevent a two-player block from forming (Figure 10.77).

When you are at the right stage of training for an advanced setter, change these drills by adding little items to make them more difficult. For example, the setter must jump set every ball, must look across the net before setting the ball and must know if the hitters are early or late. Most importantly, the setter must first get to the net, then react to the pass and/or situation and set the ball. Also, the position for each set, no matter what, must be the same each time so that no one will be able to determine where the ball is being set.

SUMMARY

The development of a setter must proceed according to sound teaching principles, starting with the basics and progressing systematically to the advanced techniques. Selection of a particular player to be trained as a setter should include the need for above-average athletic ability and intelligence. As the training process begins, the primary objective must be to develop superior execution of the overhand pass. The training sessions must emphasize correct hand position, body posture and technical performance. The setter in training must practice setting from two locations on the court: along the net and from the back court. Once the set is performed with relative consistency (75 percent accuracy), the training program can progress.

The need for repetition must be emphasized. An athlete training to become a setter must make many correct contacts with the ball, whether passing it alone to a wall, to targets or with a partner. There is no substitute for practice, and both the coach and the athlete must realize the importance of volume — the sheer number of repetitions. They must keep performing the skill over and over.

Ball

Chair

Coach

Setter

Fig. 10.44

Fig. 10.45

Fig. 10.46

Fig. 10.47

Fig. 10.48

Fig. 10.49

Fig. 10.50

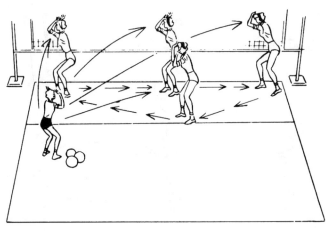

Fig. 10.51

Fig. 10.52

Fig. 10.53

Fig. 10.54

Fig. 10.55

Fig. 10.56

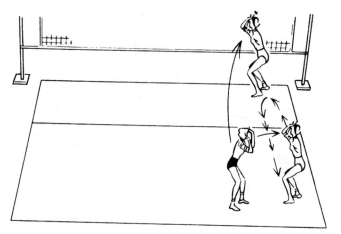

Fig. 10.57

Fig. 10.58

Fig. 10.59

Fig. 10.60

Fig. 10.61

Fig. 10.62

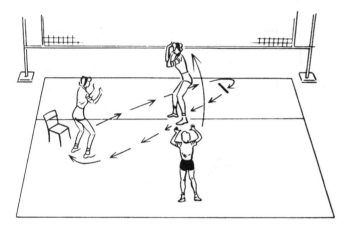

Fig. 10.63

Fig. 10.64

Fig. 10.65

Fig. 10.66

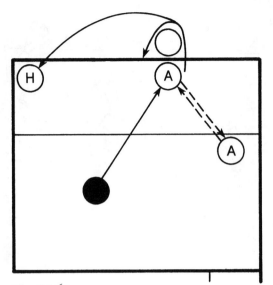

Fig. 10.67

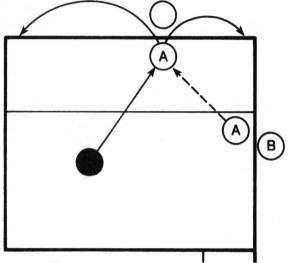

Fig. 10.68

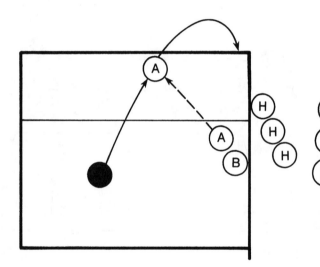

Fig. 10.69

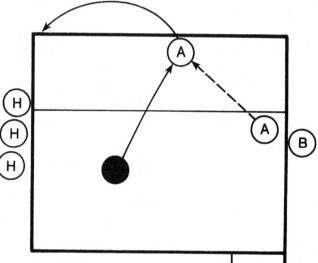

Fig. 10.70

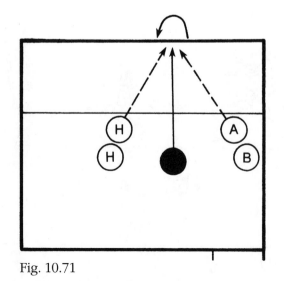

Fig. 10.71

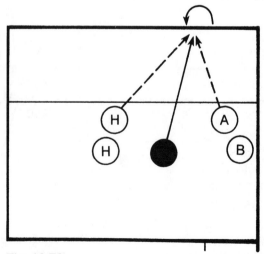

Fig. 10.72

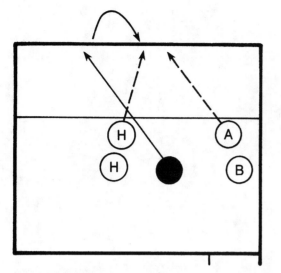

Fig. 10.73

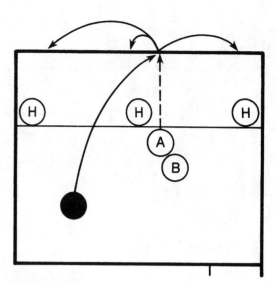

Fig. 10.74

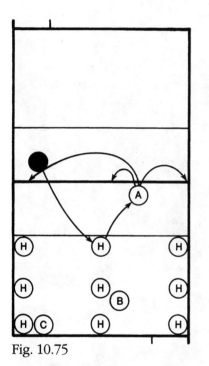

Fig. 10.75

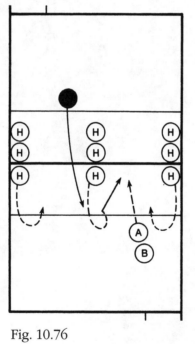

Fig. 10.76

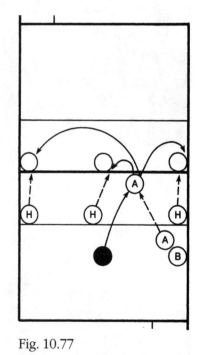

Fig. 10.77

REFERENCES

Canadian Volleyball Association. (1978). *Level I - Coaches Manual*. Dollco Printing.

—— *Level II - Coaches Manual*. (1979). Dollco Printing.

—— *Level III - Coaches Manual*. (1979). Dollco Printing.

Ejen, Miloslaz, Jaroslav Buchtel, and Karen Johnson. (1983). *Contemporary Volleyball*. Newport Beach: Volleyball Plus.

Gozansky, Sue. (1983). Championship Volleyball. *Techniques and Drills*. West Nyack: Parker Publishing Co..

FIVB Coach Training Course. (1971). *Textbook for Volleyball Coaches*.

Keller, Val. (1968). *Point, Game and Match*. Hollywood, California: Creative Sports Books.

Peppler, Mary Jo. (1986). *The Fifteen-Minute Setter*. Intervol Interprises.

Scates, Allen. (1969). *Power Volleyball*. Allyn and Bacon, Inc.

Selinger, Dr. Arie and Joan Ackermann-Blount. (1986). *Arie Selinger's Power Volleyball*. New York: St. Martin's Press.

Photo by Dan Houser

SPIKING

Mick Haley

A spike in volleyball is the act of hitting a set ball from above the level of the net into the opponent's court. It consists of an approach, jump, arm swing, follow-through and landing. Spiking is probably the most difficult individual skill to master in volleyball because it requires a great deal of body control and coordination while the spiker's body is airborne.

All of the spikers on a team should be able to hit the ball high and hard. They should also be able to hit with top spin at half to three-quarter speed or to open-hand tip — all at various positions on the court. This chapter presents the important basics of spiking: the approach, the jump, the spike and the landing. Also included are teaching techniques and general learning concepts.

THE APPROACH

The spiker begins an approach approximately 3 to 3.6 m (10 to 12 ft.) from the net. The exact approach distance will depend on each athlete's stride length. The angle of approach varies, depending on what the spiker wants to accomplish with the attack. Generally, the correct angle to the net will be between 45 and 60 degrees for a right-hander on the left side and between 60 and 90 degrees for a right-hander on the right side. For left-handers, the angles are reversed, as shown in Figure 11.1.

The speed of the approach should be from slow to fast, building momentum. The spiker should take at least three steps and probably no more than four. The approach begins with either the left or the right foot, depending on the number of steps in the approach and whether the player is right- or left-handed. Many right-handers start with the weight on the left foot for a four-step approach. Thus, the first step is taken forward with the right foot, followed by the left foot (sometimes called a directional step, since it is in the direction of the ball), then a right-left closing action (sometimes called a hop or step and close).

All of the foot movements must stay within 5 to 13 cm (2 to 5 ins.) of the floor, as opposed to a hopping action, where the feet go up in the air 30 cm or more (12 or more ins.), and then come down to the floor. Such a hopping action will disrupt the spiker's ability to accelerate during the approach.

Each foot should stay on the floor for as short a length of time as possible. Thus, the spiker's transfer of weight during the approach strides needs to be as efficient as possible. The center of gravity must move forward, not up and down, and must be low to the floor (so at the jump it only has to come up, not down and then up).

The length between steps depends on the kind of jump the spiker desires and the spiker's leg strength. The distance between each of the last steps is critical. In the traditional kind of approach jump, each step of the approach progresses in length and speed until

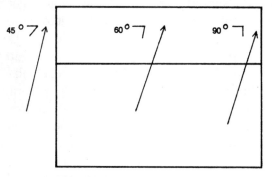

Fig. 11.1

the hop or step-close phase. The first step of the approach for right-handers in a four-step approach is taken with the right foot. The second step, the directional step, is taken with the left foot and should be twice as long and fast as the first step. The third step is taken with the right foot, twice as long and fast as the second step. To this point, the steps increase in distance and speed, increasing the spiker's momentum toward the ball. At this point, the traditional approach requires a great deal of strength, possibly limiting its effectiveness for some players. The last step of the traditional approach is taken with the left foot. It is a very short, quick step that plants the foot in a blocking action to stop forward momentum and convert it into a vertical jump. The combination of the plant of the right foot on the third step and the block by the fourth step is termed the step-close or hop step.

For the highest possible vertical jump, regardless of strength, the second of the four steps that most people take should be the longest. In this step the left foot goes forward and plants. Then the third or the next to the last step is taken with the right foot and is either as long as or shorter than the second step. For maximum vertical jump, the third step should be shorter than

feet are planted (a broad jump) as opposed to a point above where the feet are planted (a vertical jump). This broad jumping technique sacrifices a little height but allows the hitter to jump to the ball, thus creating various judgment and timing problems for the blockers. The ultimate broad jumping approach and the most radical change in the approach to spiking is the one-legged takeoff, like a lay-up in basketball. Common more than 30 years ago, this takeoff's recurrence has been made exclusively to increase broad jumping approach advantages. In contrast, a hitter who maximizes vertical jumping ability presents the blockers less difficulty in setting the block, but actually makes it harder for the blockers to contact the ball.

Many coaches recommend teaching the vertical jump style approach first. In the two vertical approach styles, the speed of the last step is critical. For maximum vertical height, the spiker's last two steps need to be such that the time both feet are on the floor is as short as possible. The last foot and the next-to-last foot go down simultaneously. The distance between the second and third steps may also be a key factor because it controls the distance the left foot has to travel. The longer that distance, the longer the right foot stays on

Fig 11.2

the second, but not so short that the momentum toward the net slows down. This slightly shorter length allows the last foot (the left) to get down and plant almost simultaneously with the right and the feet are on the floor the least amount of time. Using this foot position allows the body to rise upward for maximum height with minimal forward drift.

To travel a greater distance — to get the ball in a broad jumping kind of approach — the third step could be as long as the second. The last step is the step that makes the difference. It is not so short and quick as in the more vertical approach. The result is more forward momentum and a slight loss of vertical height. The transfer is toward a point out away from where the

the ground and the greater the loss of momentum and dissipation of forces.

The next-to-last foot planted should be the right foot and it should point toward the net at about a 45-degree angle. The last (left) foot planted should be somewhere between parallel and 45 degrees (Figure 11.2). One school of thought holds that rotating the toe at slightly more than a 45-degree angle will create a blocking action that transfers the weight quicker and forces the body to leave the floor quicker. This rotation will also stop some natural drifting common among younger players and it will open up the hitter's hips (make them more nearly perpendicular to the net) to increase power upon contact with the ball.

THE JUMP

During the approach, the hitter's arms should move the same way as if he or she were running or walking. At the third step, both arms should be behind the body, no more than 45 degrees back, and the upper torso should remain as nearly perpendicular to the floor as possible. If the arms are back more than 45 degrees, the upper torso bends too far forward at the waist, decreasing the efficiency of the jumping action. The spiker's arms should then be whipped forward so that they arrive at or above the top of the head before the feet leave the floor. This whipping movement starts with the arms being thrust straight below the waist, then up in front of the body with the elbows bent and next to the body so as to get them above the head quicker. This arm thrust is essential for assisting the jump; the key to the arm thrust is in the movement from the 45-degree back position to the front side of the body slightly above the waist. From there on it is a fight to get the arms above the head as quickly as possible and the arm action from that point on does not increase the hitter's jumping ability.

The hittter's hips and shoulders must be open (toward the setter) while leaving the floor. Although some people can jump strongly enough to be able to leave the floor with their shoulders and hips parallel to the net and still remain open and hit the ball, such jumping is not recommended either for younger players or for advanced players trying to maximize their efficiency.

As the body leaves the floor, the hitter's hitting arm is drawn into one of the two most widely used positions: one for maximum height and strength, the other for a little less height and more quickness.

Maximum Height

To achieve maximum height, as the arms ascend above the head, the hitting hand is drawn back with the elbow high toward the ceiling. The arm is drawn back, arching the back only slightly. This is a strength position and usually can be accomplished only if the armswing up to that point has been efficient. As the forward armswing begins, the player is simultaneously reaching for maximum height. Thus, the armswing must begin as the body is moving upward. Contact with the ball thus occurs at maximum height or just prior to it (Figure 11.3). If the arms do not get to

head height before the hitter leaves the ground, armswing problems usually result.

Fig. 11.3

Maximum Quickness

The other armswing is more like shooting a bow and arrow. The arms are not brought up as high — just somewhere near the top of the head — and the hitting hand is turned out to rotate the elbow high. The arm is drawn back as if drawing a bow, allowing for a much quicker, snapping action in the spike (Figure 11.4). The disadvantage is that many times the bow position does not allow a maximum reach upward to contact the ball, something that is especially a consideration for younger players.

Both arm swings serve a specific purpose. The high power position is a little bit more efficient and allows for maximum reach. The bow technique, for the most part, creates a faster armswing.

Fig. 11.4

THE SPIKE

Contact with the ball should be made in front of the hitter, preferably closer to the center of the top of the head, but at least somewhere in a position between the shoulder and the top of the head — not outside the line of the body. The hand should contact the ball slightly above center (Figure 11.3). Contact at this point gives a top spin. Contact above center and on the right side gives a right top spin; contact above center on the left gives a left top spin. If the ball lacks top spin, it usually means the spiker is not getting the wrists behind the elbow on the armswing. (This happens more with basketball players who are new to volleyball because of the elbow lead they use for the jump shot.) The wrist should snap upon contact. For less velocity and more control, attackers should open their hands more and spread their fingers slightly. For more velocity, they should bring their fingers closer together and slightly cup the hand. After contact, the hitting arm bends at the elbow and follows through, coming down toward the midline of the attacker's body. For a coach, the most important thing to watch is the elbow rotation or elbow snap — before, during and after the spike. Train yourself to look at each part of the hitter's movement and be especially sure that the elbow action is efficient.

For right-handers, the arm speed can be improved by lifting the left knee just prior to contact. This movement increases the speed of the arm action and allows the attacker to hit the ball with a slightly quicker arm speed. The opposite action works for left-handers.

THE LANDING

The attacker should land on both feet simultaneously whenever possible. The knees should be slightly flexed; the feet should be shoulder width apart; and the weight should be evenly distributed.

TEACHING TECHNIQUES

Make sure your teaching techniques are consistent with sound learning concepts. Try using only three or four key words to teach each skill and never change them. For example:

1. First keyword: "ready" or "ready position."
2. Second key word: "feet" or "feet to the ball."
3. Third keyword: "explode."
4. Fourth keyword: "swing" or "snap high."

Define the words at the beginning and do not add new ones. Do not become a sportscaster with your language and do not create situations that could disrupt the players' concentration.

Remember this learning sequence:

1. Picturing. The players need a positive picture of what they are supposed to do and they need to see it numerous times.
2. Trying. The players need to try the skill, then see it again, then try it again, over and over.
3. Evaluating. The players need to be evaluated on whether they are doing the skill properly. The evaluation should be short and quick.

The sequence outlined above is important in teaching any physical skill. Consistent with this sequence, following are some guidelines for teaching young players and beginners:

1. Provide a picture of the skill, with emphasis on just one point at a time. Do not confuse the mental process by giving too much information at once. And remember that for young players and especially for beginners, the attention span for learning new skills is usually no longer than 20 minutes.
2. Have the players repeatedly practice the skill.
3. Provide constant re-evaluation. Keep the evaluation brief. Be positive and make sure the players understand exactly what you want them to do.
4. Make sure that art of tossing the ball is done accurately and consistently. Tossing is a skill that must be practiced. During these drills it is important for players to learn to track and strike a moving ball. Stationary situations are not game-like and do not enhance players' abilities.

Providing plenty of positive examples is probably the most important key. Make sure the examples are mechanically efficient and technically correct, because new players may copy all of the wrong things. The most efficient process for teaching physical skills in this situation probably involves using key words, miming the skill and providing plenty of visual imagery.

Finally, organize your teaching so as to develop confidence and stimulate motivation in the players. For example, make sure that all training sessions end on a successful note, even if (especially with beginners) this means adjusting the situation by lowering the net and using foam balls or balloons.

SUMMARY

Spiking is one of the most difficult individual volleyball skills to master. In teaching the components of the spike, it is important to incorporate sound teaching principles, and to begin, the vertical jump style is a recommended technique. In order to learn the spike, players must work on their timing, footwork, and arm and body positioning, and they should pay particular attention to their elbow rotation. Coaches should teach the spike by helping players choose key words, mentally go through the learning sequence and practice. In addition, coaches must provide constant evaluation.

Photo by Dan Houser

BLOCKING

Doug Beal and Tony Crabb

Blocking is one of the necessary elements of winning volleyball. Blocking has two functions:

- To stop the ball from coming across the net (to block, roof or stuff the ball). This abrupt end to the action will result in a point or side-out for the blocking team.
- To deflect the ball up into the blocking team's court so that the three contacts can be used to mount an offensive strike.

As a preliminary overview, here is the sequence for your players to use when blocking:

1. Identify the attackers and their probable options.
2. Watch where the pass is going and assess the setter options.
3. Follow the person you are blocking and call out to teammates what that person is doing.
4. Get into position to block according to your assigned responsibility.
5. Jump while facing the net and scanning the attacker from shoulder to hand.
6. "Seal" the net with your arms on the way up and then extend as they penetrate over the net.
7. Just before the attacker hits the ball, press your midsection back. This action is sometimes called piking on the block because of the resulting body position or turning the ball into the court. Do not lock your elbows until after the attacker has committed to a direction of attack.

This chapter presents the basic elements of blocking in terms of the eight blocking skills, key transition ingredients and blocking principles. Each coach must carefully determine what role the block has for his or her team. Furthermore, the coach must determine how important blocking is at that team's level of competition. At the level of the USA men's or women's national teams, for example, blocking is critical.

BLOCKING SKILLS

Effective blocking depends on your players mastering the following eight skills:

- Recognition of when to block.
- Proper footwork.
- Correct body position.
- Correct hand and arm position.
- Reading visual keys.
- Good timing.
- Smooth coordination among multiple blockers.
- Careful study of the opposing spikers.

Recognition of When to Block

Players should block only when they can successfully perform one of the two blocking functions listed at the beginning of this chapter. Following are some keys for making that judgment:

- How well does the opponent handle the first ball? The worse the control of the first ball, the less the chance the setter has for accurately setting the second ball and thus the less need there will be for a block.
- Where is the attacker relative to the set? If the attacker is in poor position (for example, by being under the ball, too late to the ball or if the ball is coming from behind the attacker), then the blocker should give the unfortunate attacker the opportunity to make a spiking error rather than jumping up and presenting the attacker a potential tool (a target off of which to hit the ball).

Footwork

There are two types of footwork: the slide step and the cross step. The slide step should be used when the lateral distance to be covered is 1.8 m (6 ft.) or less, or when the ball is set high and there is plenty of time to get into position. The cross step is mainly used by the middle blocker to get to the outside in a hurry on a low set. A lateral move of more than 1.8 m (6 ft.) usually requires a cross step.

In the cross step, the weight is on the foot opposite to the intended direction. Step out with the foot on the side of the intended direction, cross step with the opposite foot in front of the body, plant that foot so that the toes point toward the opponent's court and swing the other foot around so the shoulders are squared to the net — then jump. If a high set comes to the outside, the block should be performed with care so that this footwork aligns you next to the outside blocker. For optimal body position, it is important that the toes be pointed toward the attacker and that the outside foot (the one on the side in the direction of the set) is well planted to be the base of the main force of the jump. An outside blocker should actually jump to the inside of the court.

Body Position

Eighty percent of all spikes are hit in the direction of the spiker's approach. Therefore, the blocker must first identify the spiker's angle of approach and the point where the spiker will intercept the ball, and second, get to the right spot on the continuation of the spiker's approach angle to block the shot. The blocker must have good balance and must be no more than 36 cm (14 ins.) from the net. The blocker must be able to jump with control, avoiding dismantling the net and always penetrating for the ball.

Hand and Arm Position

When the blocker is in the correct body position, the hands are above and in front of the shoulders. The jump rockets the blocker straight up and the hands penetrate the top of the net immediately. The jump must be straight up, not floating to the outside. The arms should not be fully extended until the spiker makes a final move. When the spiker's final move occurs, the blocker, stretching all the way up from the abdomen, extends arms, hands and fingers (thumbs pointing toward each other).

For outside blockers, the hands must not reach beyond the outside shoulder. Instead, the hands must be moving in. The blocking motion is pressing to the center of the back line, with the outside hand reaching over and out, across the net, perpendicular to the outside shoulder. Therefore, the blocker's outside arm and shoulder extend over the net slightly further than the other half of the body. Prior to contact, the blocker extends forward from the shoulders, with the deltoids touching the ears. The blocker seals the net with the triceps and pushes tension from the abdominals through the fingers upon contact with the ball.

Middle blockers use basically the same technique, with some minor adjustments for blocking the quick attack. The middle blocker positions with his or her head aligned with the extension of the quick attacker's arm. On the quick attack, the middle blocker jumps when the set occurs, not waiting for the hitter to hit the ball. The jump must be high enough for the middle blocker to place his or her hands on the ball. If possible, the middle blocker spreads the arms and then closes them after determining where the quick attack is going. Otherwise, the middle blocker should stay spread and cut off the angles. There is no chance for any pike action; the tension in this maneuver is primarily from the shoulders. The quick shot must be pressed back into the middle of the court. These same tips also apply to forming the block with the outside blocker outside on the high ball or slow play set.

Visual Keys

In order for the physical moves of blocking to be correct, continual practice in mastering the evaluation of information must be stressed. Following is the sequence of information to be given to the blocker:

1. Be aware of the score and game tempo. Since these factors will often indicate whom the setter will set, awareness of them is critical.
2. Review the tendencies of the spiker you must face.
3. Evaluate the quality of the service reception. How good or bad it is will affect where, what and how well the setter can set the ball.
4. Note what kind of set is on its way.
5. Watch the spiker's legs, determining the attack angle and what position the spiker is in to hit the ball.
6. Once the blocker has moved to cut off the attack angle, watch the spiker's hand and wrist. Then make the final hand adjustments to stuff the ball.

Timing

Other blocking skills become mere exercise if the timing is off. Here are two timing basics:

- If the ball is set within .5 m (1 ft. 8 ins.) of the net, then the blocker begins to jump as the attacker's hand is crossing in front of his or her face on the back swing.
- If the set is high and more than 1 meter off of the net, the blocker jumps as the attacker's hand is coming forward to contact the ball.

Blocking Responsibilities

The keys to successful blocking are always the same: talk-work hard-analyze-penetrate. The specific responsibilities for blocking change, depending on whether one is a right, left or middle blocker, or blocking the multiple attack.

Left Blocker. The left blocker plays the opponent's no. 2 position attacker (right front). The left blocker calls the offensive crossover or switch (against the crossing play or X) and helps on the quick attack if no. 2 runs the X play. The left blocker also takes the hitter if no. 2 flares out for a back set and sets the block for the middle person.

Right Blocker. The right blocker plays the opponent's no. 4 attacker (left front), takes the no. 2 opponent on the X play, takes the no. 4 attacker coming in for an inside set and sets the block for the middle person on the left side.

Middle Blocker. The middle blocker must block the quick hitter and always let the outside blockers know what to expect. The middle blocker must identify the attackers and get in on all blocks.

There are some slightly different responsibilities for blocking the multiple attack:

- Each blocker should block person-to-person, being responsible for the person directly across the net.
- The right blocker comes over to take the no 2 hitter, who is crossing when the left blocker calls the X. The right blocker always plays person-to-person and helps on the quick attack when possible.
- The middle blocker takes the quick hitter, then helps on the X.
- The left blocker helps on the X if that blocker's person is Xing. The left blocker calls the X if the left blocker's person is going, then calls "No!" if that person flares back. The left blocker must eliminate certain variables (especially against an

offensive system in which the no. 2 attacker calls where he or she is going to the setter) by intentionally overplaying and then coming back after that attacker.

If the left and middle blockers are on the X, they take away no. 5. If the middle and right blockers take away no. 1 they also need to cover tips.

Study of the Opposing Spikers

Here are the key variables for your players to study when considering the opponents:

- How far off the net is the set?
- In what zone is the ball set?
- What is the height of the set?
- What is the position of the spiker's body and arm in relation to the ball?
- What hand does the spiker hit with?
- What type of swing does the spiker use?
- What are the habits of the spiker?
- What is the design and intention of the play?
- What is the spiker's attack angle?

TRANSITION POSITIONS

There are important things you must teach about blocking that do not come under the heading of skills. These things mostly concern transition positions when there is a free ball or a down ball.

Free Ball

The front row drops straight back to the 3-meter line and the outside hitters stay in the court. The center hitter stays in the middle of the court, while the back-row defenders split the court and face the place from where the ball is coming.

If the free ball is coming from deep in the opponent's court, then the defenders must play deeper. If it is coming from inside the 3-meter line, the blockers must move up and encourage the remaining team members to work over the blockers' heads. The setter must release as soon as a free ball is called.

All free balls should be played with an overhead pass. No one should leave the court until the free ball is passed. And everyone should call "free ball" every time!

Down Block

In the down block situation, the two blockers at the net see the hit and cover the half-speed shots and tips. They stay close to the net. The four primary defenders form a semicircle facing the attack, playing deeper on the line and more shallow cross-court. The setter must think dig first and release to set, only after making sure the hit is not going to his or her area.

BLOCKING PRINCIPLES

Finally, following are five principles to remember for good blocking:

1. Block offensively. Under virtually every situation, the blocker's goal is to stuff every ball.
   —Force the hitter to hit a secondary shot.
   —Never give up a straight down kill.
   —Always penetrate the net.
   The goal should be to instill in your blockers a philosophy of intimidation.
2. Do not block or jump if you perceive that the hitter cannot score (hitter is out of position, ball is very deep, ball is outside antennae, hitter is standing, etc.). Knowing when to block is critical.
3. Seal the antennae. If the ball is set to the pin or beyond, the outside blocker ensures that the ball cannot be hit between the pin and the block. This is an important rule.
4. If the ball is set tight, surround the ball! Never allow the hitter to hit straight down in front of the back row.
5. Know the keys to blocking. See the hitter making contact with the ball; see yourself block the ball. Follow the ball with your eyes, then head, then body. The sequence follows:
   —See the pass.
   —Watch the setter set the ball.
   —Pick up the hitter's line of attack.
   —Follow the ball with your eyes to its apex.
   —Shift your primary focus to the hitter, centering on the shoulders.
   —Watch the attackers make contact.

—Follow the ball's direction.
—Verbalize the path of the ball.
—Keep your eyes open and see the block; make contact with your hands.
—On most normal sets (approximately 1.5 m (4 ft. 11 ins.) from the net, the timing is for the blocker to jump when the attacker's hitting arm clears his or her eyebrows on the ascent. This is a key point!
—Position your block in front of the extension of the spiker's arm.
—The outside blocker's primary responsibility is to establish the position described in No. 9, then stuff the ball.
—The middle blocker's responsibility on outside sets is to attempt to close on the outside blocker; the middle blocker's primary responsibility is to block the cross-court angle.

SUMMARY

Blocking is used to stop the ball from coming across the net and to deflect the ball into the blocking team's court. Players should go through a seven-step sequence and should master eight skills in performing a successful block. Skills include knowing when to block; proper footwork; body, hand and arm positioning; reading visual keys; timing; coordination; and studying opposing spikers. The keys to successful blocking are always the same: talk-work hard-analyze -penetrate. The responsibilities for the right, left and middle blockers differ somewhat and blockers should know the responsibilities for their positions. In addition, players should also know how to block the multiple attack and they should know about transition positions for a free ball and for a down ball. It is also important that players be aware of and remember the principles and keys of blocking.

Photo by Eric Seiffert

Chapter 13

SERVING

Bob Gambardella

The score in rally game is 15-14, your favor. The majority of the fifth game has been side-out volleyball and the opposition calls its last time-out. After the time-out, your server gets to the end line, the referee blows the whistle and your player serves the ball into the net for a side-out.

This situation has happened to all coaches at one time or another. It can break the momentum of the team and give your opponents a boost to get fired up. Now let's turn the tables and think about how the entire team feels when a member serves an ace. It always puts a spark of enthusiasm in your team's play.

Coaches look at serving in one of two ways: serving for points or serving to get the ball over the net and relying on the team's defense either to stop (block) the ball at the net or to play tough transition and score points. We should train our players to serve for points.

SERVING TOUGH = GETTING POINTS

It takes time to learn how to serve for points. First, you must work on the mechanics of serving with all of your players so that each player's serving efficiency is at the same level as the rest of the team's play. Along with that, tactics must be taught. Different serve reception formations warrant different serves and serving strategies. A good serving team will force its opponents to make critical errors throughout the entire match.

This chapter deals with serving techniques and tactics. The first step toward becoming a good serving team is for the coach to develop a philosophy of serving that best suits that particular team. With younger players, a coach might want to focus more on mechanics, whereas with older players or more experienced players, focus on teaching different types of serves that are tactically advantageous to the serving team.

SERVING TECHNIQUES

As a rule, better volleyball teams usually use a wider variety of serves, hitting different parts of the court with different trajectories, spins and speeds. This section presents the techniques for the overhand float serve, the round house floater serve, the top spin overhand serve, the underhand serve and the jump serve.

The Overhand Float Serve

The overhand float serve is the most widely used serve in volleyball. "Float" means that the ball has no spin and no predetermined flight path; air currents and other factors can affect its flight. Approximately 90 percent of collegiate and international volleyball players use this serve. It requires a sufficient amount of upper body strength, along with coordination of all body parts. This is a good serve because of its combination of placement and a floating action. Figures 13.1-13.5 show this skill in detail.

Lower Body. The server's feet are almost perpendicular to the net, shoulder-width apart. There

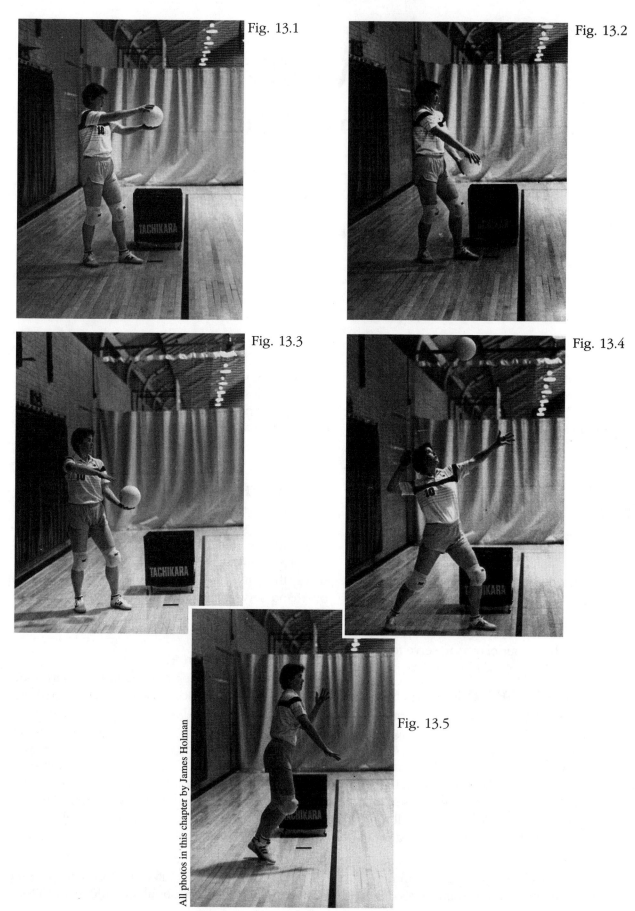

Fig. 13.1

Fig. 13.2

Fig. 13.3

Fig. 13.4

Fig. 13.5

All photos in this chapter by James Holman

is a slight flex in the knees. The weight is mostly on the back foot. If younger players find this stance difficult, they can adapt it to suit their more limited abilities.

Upper Body. The waist is open (almost perpendicular) to the net. The hitting arm is up just about shoulder height, bent at the elbow and slightly cocked away from the ball. The hand tossing the ball is 38 to 50 cm (approximately 15 to 20 ins.) away from the body, depending on the individual.

Serving Action. The toss is in front of the server, approximately 50 to 75 cm (approximately 20 to 30 ins.) above eye level. The hitting arm should be drawn back (with the thumb close to the ear, in a "bow and arrow" fashion, keeping the elbow up) as the ball is making its ascent and should start to move forward as soon as the ball starts its descent. The exact nature of the toss depends on the quickness of each player's armswing. The lower the toss, the quicker the armswing. Contact is made in the middle of the ball with the lower third portion of the hand (the heel of the hand). During the contact phase, the upper body moves into a position parallel to the net. There is a minimal amount of follow-through with the hitting arm. The lower body starts the transfer of weight as soon as the ball is tossed and the transfer ends immediately after the contact. The wrist remains stiff throughout the contact phase. Players should avoid putting a spin on the ball. Younger players especially will have a higher tendency to snap the wrist upon contact. Making quick contact with a stiff wrist will yield a higher percentage floater serve.

Problems associated with this serve are usually caused by a lack of upper body strength, improper weight transfer, an incorrect toss or incorrect hand contact. Following are some specific serving problems and their causes:

- If the ball is served into the net or out of bounds wide, improper footwork is usually to blame. Check to see whether the server is actually picking up the rear foot; doing so tends to tilt the upper body in a downward position. When the serve is wide, it usually means contact with the ball was off-center. Concentration in serving is the key.
- If the ball has a slight spin, the server is snapping the wrist upon contact. The wrist must remain rigid throughout the contact phase.
- If the ball is out of bounds past the opponent's end line, there is usually too much force on the

ball. The server should think about placement on the court rather than trying to contact the ball as hard as possible.

- If the ball drops before it reaches center court, either the player is not strong enough or the ball was hit incorrectly. Beginners and young players often do not have enough upper body strength to get the ball over. Such players may need to resort to another serve until they are able to master the floater. For example, the round house serve may show better results because there are more upper body muscle masses involved.

The Round House Floater Serve

Most coaches are not comfortable teaching this serve, so they never introduce it to their teams. Instead, they feel that a player who cannot serve an overhand float should use an underhand serve. Using the underhand serve guarantees getting the ball over the net; however, its action or float is nonexistent. As a result, the opponent gets an easy ball to pass.

The Japanese developed the round house serve (or Asian floater) for their women to compensate for a lack of upper body strength. The serve uses more muscle groups than the overhand float serve to give players a ball that will float. The serve has a very unpredictable flight (float) path, as does the overhand floater, but moves much more quickly than any floater type serve. In addition to its float, this serve, when correctly performed, has a flat trajectory and at any given moment will quickly drop toward the floor. Figures 13.6-13.13 show the round house serve in detail.

Lower Body. The feet are about waist-width apart, positioned almost perpendicular to the net. Legs are straight, but not locked at the knee. The weight is evenly distributed between the balls and toes of the feet.

Upper Body. The torso is slightly coiled. The hitting arm is extended out in front with the elbow locked when touching the ball. The tossing arm is about waist high and grasps the ball mostly with the fingertips. (Note that tossing the ball with the fingertips rather than the palm of the hand gives a more precise toss.)

Serving Action. The toss has to be precise. It must be made directly above the server's head, approximately 75 cm to 1 m (approximately 30 to 40 ins.) above eye level. If the ball is contacted in front of the server, it will have a downward trajectory

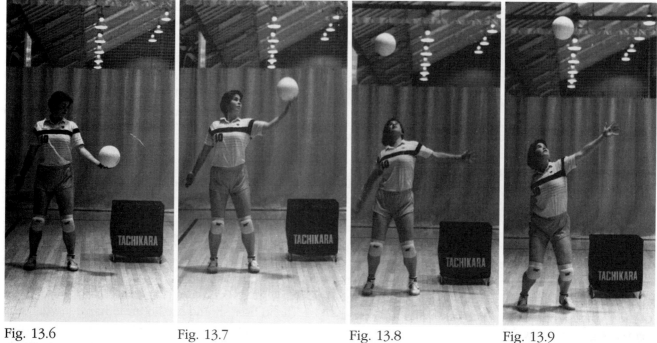

Fig. 13.6   Fig. 13.7   Fig. 13.8   Fig. 13.9

(winding up in the net). Contact behind the server will cause an upward trajectory (winding up out of bounds). Remaining straight and locked at the elbow, the hitting arm starts to draw back toward the buttocks. As the arm reaches its preparatory phase, it will then start to move up and over the server's head, where contact with the ball is made. Remember that the actions of the toss and striking arm have to be synchronized. If not, the serve is difficult to execute. The contact is made with the lower third part of the hand striking the middle of the ball while the upper body uncoils. There is a minimal amount of follow-through in order to ensure the correct action (float) on the ball. The weight transfer happens during and after the contact phase.

These problems are associated with the round house serve:

- Because of lack of knowledge in the coaching profession, coaches do not feel confident in teaching this serve.
- There is often a lack of repetition. Not enough time is spent on training players to serve.
- An imprecise or improperly timed toss hurts this serve even more than most serves.

Top Spin Overhand

The top spin serve is another serve that is not used enough in competition. In addition, this serve is not recommend for beginners. Instead, it is for the more experienced players who would like to add another dimension to their serving game.

This serve incorporates the same mechanics as the spike, except that the serve is done on the ground. It is a great serve to use as a changeup (as in baseball). If the opponent is not ready for the top spin, it usually yields a point or gives a more predictable play for the blockers to block.

The top spin serve has a trajectory that travels in a direct flight path, but at a faster velocity than the float serve. The server's timing and coordination are very important because the slightest deviation from proper execution can cause an errant serve. The top spin has a higher percentage of efficiency (aces) than the floater; however, it usually has a higher incidence of errors, as well. Figures 13.14-13.20 illustrate the key components of the top spin serve.

Lower Body. The feet are almost parallel to the net, approximately waist-width apart. There is a slight flex in the knees. The weight is distributed equally on both feet with a flat-footed stance.

Upper Body. The waist is open (coiled), approximately 30 to 40 degrees in relation to the net. The hitting arm is extended and relaxes when touching the ball. The tossing arm holds the ball at the level of the waist with the fingertips and fingers approximately 20 to 25 cm (approximately 8 to 10 ins.) from the body.

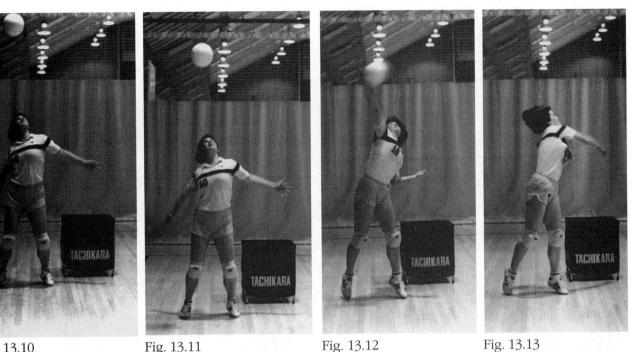

Fig. 13.10   Fig. 13.11   Fig. 13.12   Fig. 13.13

Serving Action. The toss varies from 90 cm to 1.5 m (approximately 36 to 60 ins.) above eye level. The toss is thrown up in a direct line with the hitter's arm off center (left or right) in relationship to the hitter's sagittal plane. When tossing for this serve, the server should put a forward spin on the ball. With a higher toss, this spin helps to keep the ball in a straight line in its pre-contact phase. The spin initiated by the toss also makes the contact phase easier to perform. Contact is made below the center of the ball: first, with the heel of the hand; and second, by snapping the wrist to initiate a whole-hand contact with the ball. The two-part contact phase starts the two actions of the ball. The heel contact dictates the speed of the ball and the snap of the wrist and follow-through will dictate the quickness of the spin. The faster the spin, the quicker the ball moves toward the ground. The follow-through is the same as in spiking, with a good range of motion throughout the serve.

Underhand Serve and Jump Serve

Two other serves worth mentioning are the underhand serve and the jump serve. The underhand serve has been with the sport since its beginning. It is an easy serve to execute and the level of success in getting the ball over the net is very good. However, using this serve in collegiate or other higher forms of organized volleyball is probably detrimental to the serving team. Because of the nature of the serving action, the serve causes the ball to travel in a parabolic flight path, which resembles a free ball situation for the opponent. Since it is easy to execute, the underhand serve is a good serve for very young players or beginners because the emphasis at their levels is on keeping the ball in play.

Although the jump serve has become an exciting, integral part of the game, its beginnings have been traced back to the 1960s. The jump serve is rather difficult to master because of all of the variables involved in it. Strength, coordination and proper movement are prerequisites to the mastery of the skill. The jump serve produces more points, but at the same time, it can cause a considerable number of errors. A team that is only an average passing team will make more errors when confronted with this type of serve. Presently, we see the jump serve has taken its place in the collegiate men's game with much success.

The start position for the jump serve varies from 3 to 4.6 m (10 to 15 ft.) from the end line, depending on the server's stride. The jump serve has a pre-contact approach, as in spiking, which leads into a vertical jump. Once a start position is established, the toss and approach should be learned. The toss is initiated with two hands. The toss has to be high enough and moving sufficiently in the direction of the server's end line to allow enough time for the server to make an approach and takeoff. After the coordination and timing of the toss are mastered, the height of the toss

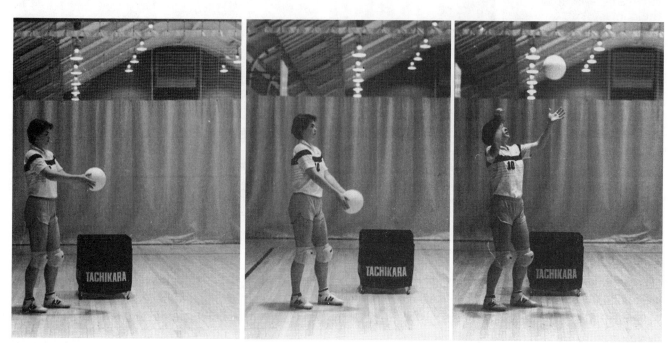

Fig. 13.14   Fig. 13.15   Fig. 13.16

Fig. 13.17   Fig. 13.18   Fig. 13.19   Fig. 13.20

is the biggest problem for proper execution of the jump serve (as it is for all serves). The mechanics of spiking also apply to jump serving with one exception: the contact with the ball. Contact should be the heel-snap contact, but it needs to occur below the midpoint of the ball, ensuring a curved trajectory that passes well above the net.

After serving technique has been developed, one other factor needs to enter into training: serving under pressure. You must use your imagination to set up situations that are game-like. For example, imagine that the score is 14-14, or the score is 14-2, or the teammate before you has just served into the net. The more your training can place the server in game-like situations, the more that training will pay off in actual games. Now that the rule change of serving anywhere behind the end line is in effect, you should experiment with your players' different strategies along the end line.

SERVING TACTICS

Before considering tactics in serving, the coach has to set guidelines for the team's performance. An example would be: first, get the ace; second, force the opponents to give you a free ball; and third, serve a ball that cuts down on the opponent's offensive options, thus making it a more predictable set to block. Depending on what those guidelines are for your team, you should teach your players to employ these tactics:

1. Always serve to the opponent's weakest player and do not ever let up.
2. Serve to a player who has just made a mistake.
3. Serve to a player who has just substituted into the game.
4. Serve to the weakest spot(s) in the receiving formation so as to force the opponents to make major adjustments to cover those weak areas.
5. Serve to areas in between players (hit the seams).
6. Use their setter as a key for placement of your serve. For example, when their setter is penetrating from the left back position, serve cross-court short.
7. Use the Pavlovian serve (developed by the USA men's team), a serve that is contacted immediately (without thought) after the referee's whistle.
8. If in doubt, serve to the deep corners, especially cross-court deep.

Directional Serving. It has been said that a coach has only a limited number of moves he or she can make (time-outs and substitutions) during a game. Directional serving gives the coach an additional, important way to stay directly involved in the game. Every time the team serves, the coach can decide where the serve should go. With the court divided up as shown in Figure 13.21, this decision can be signaled in from the bench. When the coach wants the player to serve area no. 1, the coach holds out one finger; area no. 2, two fingers; and so on. Area no. 6 is represented by a fist. Serving to different areas can be very effective in attacking weaknesses of an opponent's serve reception formation, thus reducing the opponent's quick attack potential.

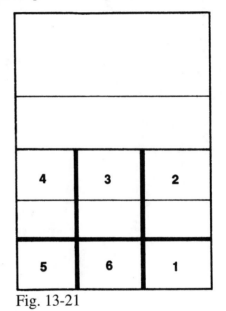

Fig. 13-21

SUMMARY

In order to serve for points, coaches must work on teaching players the mechanics of serving, serving tactics and techniques and the various types of serves. Types of serves include: the overhand float serve, the most widely used serve in volleyball; the round house floater serve, developed by the Japanese (a serve with an unpredictable path but the fastest floater type serve); the top spin overhand serve, a serve for experienced players that incorporates the same mechanics as the spike; the underhand serve, an easy serve to execute; and the jump serve, a serve that is difficult to master. Players must be able to serve under pressure and to learn to do so, must train in game-like situations. It is important for coaches to teach serving tactics, but they should do so only after setting guidelines for the team's performance. One way for coaches to stay directly involved in serving is by implementing directional serving during games.

Photo courtesy of the University of Minnesota

Chapter 14

RECEIVING THE SERVE

Rosie Wegrich

Receiving the serve is a critical volleyball skill, one that must be mastered before any team attains a high level of play. Without the pinpoint passing accuracy that results only from effective serve reception, there can be no multiple or quick attacks. Good serve reception requires a system of responsibilities achieved mostly through synchronized movement and communication among all six players on the court. The prerequisite to any such system, however, is the mastery of the necessary individual skills. These skills include early movement to the ball (anticipation) combined with proper technique (efficiency), both accomplished while tracking a moving object (the ball) that is subject to sudden direction and velocity changes. Adding to the difficulty of the skill, the pass that results from serve reception must be controlled and directed to a given area of the court at least 80 percent of the time. As the level of play in volleyball rises, the serves increase in difficulty and the target area shrinks in preciseness.

Effective service reception begins with each player assuming the proper ready position (made up of lower and upper body position); proper movement before and during contact; accurate side passing; good training; and teamwork. These components of effective service reception are the organizing points of this chapter.

LOWER BODY POSITION

The components of the lower body position are the feet and the knees. With those in proper position, players can reap the advantages of correct lower body positioning.

The Feet

I prefer to teach foot position by stressing the stance with the right foot forward and the feet slightly more than shoulder-width apart. This position assumes the offense is initiated from beyond the right of center court. In this way, the player can draw impetus from the left leg to push through the ball and direct it toward the right. The player's feet are rotated slightly inward to distribute the weight properly on the inside balls of the feet. This position readies the player to move in a split second. Coaches should remind players to avoid sitting back on their heels as the server strikes the ball.

Fig. 14.1

The Knees

The knees are slightly flexed in a medium position level (120 degrees flexion), thus, the passer is allowed to move efficiently to the oncoming served ball. The knees must be kept slightly ahead of the toes in order to aid the player's speed, especially the starting time. To develop a habitual pattern of proper positioning, a player should repeat this ready position in the learning stage. Full extension of the knees for service reception should be avoided. A full, deep squat position level (defensive posture) should also be avoided. Both of these body positioning levels will inhibit the kind of movement speed-effective serve reception requires.

UPPER BODY POSITION

The two key elements in proper upper body positioning are the trunk and the arms.

The Trunk

The trunk or spine should be flexed forward at the hip joint and waist and curved slightly down. You can describe this as "roll the shoulders down and forward." This position distributes the center of gravity over the balls of the feet, further preparing the player to move forward into and through the ball during contact.

The Arms

As the player prepares to pass the serve, the arms are apart and ahead of the body and slightly flexed at the elbow joint. The elbows should not be extended, because such extension promotes a tightened, restricted shoulder joint. As the player arrives at the pass position, or if the player is not able to stop and the ball must be contacted at this moment, the hands are grasped together simultaneously as the elbows extend. Players who have their hands grasped together may lose their balance, but there are times when a receiver has no choice but to prepare the arms to receive while still moving. A good training rule for readiness discipline is to have the arms ready and presented to the ball before it penetrates the vertical plane of the net.

In the correct upper body positioning, the trunk leans forward so the player's center of gravity is over the balls of the feet. The player's head must face the server during service. This time period is used to evaluate the server's unique cues (body language). Simple evaluative cues include the server's body positioning (line or cross-court), the server's location behind the end line (deep positioning or shallow), the type of toss and the server's direction of focus. A player's movement will be quicker if he or she can anticipate the serve first and then get to position before the ball arrives.

MOVEMENT PRIOR TO CONTACT

The important elements before contact with the ball are court position and anticipation.

Court Position

I prefer my players to start deep in the court, about one stride in from the end line for the two primary receivers (right and left back). This positioning gives the receivers added time to track the oncoming served ball and it promotes the idea that the player must have forward movement into the ball. In addition, it protects the receiver from having to back pedal to pass a deep served ball. It also eliminates the risky turning movement (side pass) to play the ball that the player has allowed to get too close to his or her body. Generally, then, players should start deep and always move forward to pass the ball. They should then stay deep until they have evaluated the depth of the serve so as not to let the ball get too close to their bodies.

Anticipation

Many receivers move forward before they have made a complete evaluation of the depth of the serve. The resulting reception often produces a shanked pass or one that requires an off-balance contact, thereby increasing the potential for reception error. Remind players that "you play the ball, do not let the ball play you." In more precise terms, fine adjustments of movement before contact with the ball in order to have a balanced posture at the time of contact with the ball will reduce the failure rate of service reception.

Gaining position prior to contact should be the goal of every player when learning how to pass a serve. To me, gaining position means to remain facing the ball as long as possible (maintain the ball/body relationship). Later, as they become more proficient in basic ball control, your players can learn the turning movement to receive serves off one side of the body (the side pass).

Fig. 14.2

Fig. 14.3

Fig. 14.4

Fig. 14.5

CONTACT WITH THE BALL

Critical points of ball contact include hand position, eye contact, proper contact for a slow serve and proper contact for a high velocity serve.

Hand Position

Early presentation of the arms to the ball enhances the passer's potential to execute the pass successfully. At this time, the receiver has tracked the predicted location of the serve and is now ready to grasp the hands together (Figure 14.2). The hands are interlocked just past the first joint of each finger. The thumbs are parallel and next to each other and the wrists are hyper extended down toward the floor (Figure 14.3). This wrist joint positioning keeps the ball from contacting the hands, which makes a poor passing surface. The ball should rebound off of both arms simultaneously, just above the wrist bone. The shoulders are flexed and curved forward to reduce the distance between them. From a biomechanical viewpoint, the scapulae move away from each other to a more lateral position.

Eye Contact

During contact with the ball, the receiver should complete the sequence of focusing on the ball not only as it travels through the air, but also as it contacts and leaves the arms (Figure 14.4). Many passing problems occur because players have not disciplined themselves to sustain that complete focus of attention. Often the passer will look at the passing target during contact and make an errant pass because the ball contacted one arm of the platform. A good motto to go by is to "get a picture of the ball as it leaves your arms." Keep the head down as the ball leaves the platform. During partner passing drills, each player should keep eye focus on the ball but should not move his or her head until the ball reaches the partner's arms. Then, as the ball rebounds back, the player brings the head up and focuses on the oncoming ball. This simple exercise will help to train the receiver's proper attentional focus.

Contact for a Slow Serve

As the receiver makes contact with the ball, the arms should be positioned well out in front of the body. The movement arc of the platform (arms) will vary with the speed of the served ball. For slow moving serves, the arc is increased. In this case, the receiver begins the arm action starting from a right angle relationship between arms and body. The arms move forward and up to slightly below shoulder level (Figure 14.5). If the style of pass trajectory for the team's offense is low and flat, then the contact with the ball is more on the back of the ball and the receiver stabilizes the torso in a more forward flexed position (Figure 14.6). If the desired pass trajectory is high and loopy, then the contact will be from under the ball and the receiver will straighten (extend) the torso and open the joint angle at the waist (Figure 14.7).

Contact for a High Velocity Serve

When attempting to receive a high velocity, flat trajectory serve, a passer must first be sure to present the arms early to the ball. Next, the passer should use one or two of the following techniques to improve control of the rebound. One option is to use the arm-drop motion after contact with the ball. This arm motion is toward the receiver's body, in the same direction as the oncoming ball. This causes a cushioning effect and will result in a slower, more controlled rebound. The passer should hold the torso in a fixed position with relation to the legs and lower body and remain in a forward trunk lean position (Figures 14.8 and 14.9). The second option to consider when passing a high velocity serve is to contact the underside of the ball and put underspin on the ball. The resultant pass trajectory will be slightly more vertical and higher. This will give the setter added time to arrive at the set position.

RECEIVING THE SERVE

The goal for all receivers when faced with passing a high velocity serve should be to: 1) keep the ball on your side of the net and not trap the setter against the net; and 2) control the rebound speed by slowing it with arm retraction or giving it underspin in its trajectory for added height. As Figures 14.8 and 14.9 show, by moving the arms through the ball smoothly, the player has a prolonged contact time with the ball, which results in more potential ball control.

SIDE PASSING

During those unpredictable game situations when a receiver has positioned too close to the ball, or is late arriving to the predicted passing position, he or

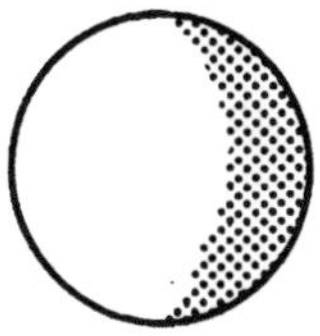

**ARM CONTACT
ON BALL
(FLAT TRAJECTORY)**

Fig. 14.6

**ARM CONTACT
ON BALL
(REVERSE SPIN)**

Fig. 14.7

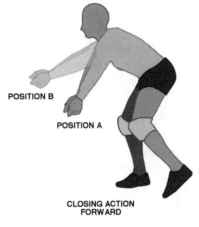

POSITION B

POSITION A

**CLOSING ACTION
FORWARD**

Fig. 14.8

POSITION A

POSITION B

**ARM RETRACTION
FOR HIGH VELOCITY
SERVE**

Fig. 14.9

she must pass the ball by turning to the side. The ball contact point is outside the player's center of gravity, the result of the body positioning after the player has pivoted toward the direction of movement. When turning toward the left, the player pivots on the left leg and draws the right leg forward directly ahead of the left (rear) leg (Figure 14.10). The lead shoulder (right) should be lowered by means of flexing the trunk down and forward. This angles the platform (arms) correctly toward the ball. This process will assure simultaneous contact of both arms with the ball. The movement is reversed when turning toward the right.

The initial action of the arms begins behind the center of gravity and then follows forward in an upward-sideward rotation of the trunk. The specific cues coaches should give when teaching this skill are first to remind players to drop the lead shoulder and raise the back shoulder and then to remind them to close through the ball (horizontal arm action and trunk rotation) in the direction of the target. The platform is the last body part that will give the rebound the desired direction. At the moment of contact, the ball should be played off of the lead leg. If the ball is contacted off of the rear leg, the rebound will most likely be out of bounds, making it extremely difficult for the setter to get to the ball to set it. Coaches should also insist that their players discipline themselves to complete eye contact with the ball during the entire execution of the pass. This is even more critical to the success of the side pass than it is when the ball is perfectly in front of the midline of the body. One last point concerning side passing: during the follow-through phase, the elbows and wrists may bend in order to give added direction to the pass.

TRAINING MOVEMENT PATTERNS

One of the most basic elements of successful serve reception is the speedy movement patterns you teach your players. The efficiency and the form of movement should be of prime concern to all coaches and players. These movement patterns need to be thoroughly learned until they become so habitual that the players do not have to think about how to move to pass any serve. Only thus can players become

Fig. 14.10

able to extend their focus on the ball while moving to gain the best passing position. The best passers are those who can anticipate the flight of the serve and can be at the passing position before the ball's arrival. Attention to these cues on a subconscious level will promote positive serve receptions.

The important elements of movement patterns include side movement (side shuffle) positioning, the step-crossover close motion, the forward run step, the sprawl pass, the turn and run and the back pedal.

Side Movement (Side Shuffle) Positioning

The most basic pattern is the movement to the side, known as the side shuffle. The movement is initiated by pushing off the leg opposite the direction you want to go. For example, if you wish to move right, then the left leg initiates the movement. The feet should remain rotated slightly inward and pointed straight ahead during the movement. The trunk is held in a stabilized, forward-flexed position, which keeps the center of gravity over the soles of the feet. Any movement up and down should be eliminated because of the time it takes to move the trunk due to the redistribution of the center of gravity that such up and down movement requires (back on the heels when the trunk is raised, onto the balls of the feet when the trunk is lowered). The knees are rotated slightly inward, which keeps the hips and shoulders facing straight ahead during movement.

Fig. 14.11

Fig. 14.12

A common error I see when teaching this skill is that many players open the lead leg (rotate the leg outward) in the direction of movement. This rotation forces the hips and shoulders to turn in the direction of movement and the player passes from an off-centered ball-to-body relationship, which increases the chance of an unsuccessful pass. During the side shuffle, the player keeps the head erect and looks up at the oncoming served ball.

The side shuffle has its limitations. First, it is one of the slowest movement patterns (along with the back pedal). Therefore, it should be used to cover only short distances of less than 1.8 m (6 ft.). High, flat serves can find the player caught too close to the ball when he or she has used the side shuffle pattern to gain passing position. A turning movement at times would be the more logical method of reception in order to get the body further behind the ball. In Figure 14.12, the player has had adequate time to play the ball in front of the body. If receivers can gain position around the ball, their chances of executing a perfect pass are improved.

Step-Crossover Close Motion

Another method of moving and getting around the ball is known as the step-crossover close. This is how it works: If moving to the right, the first step is taken with the right leg, which is pointed in the direction of movement. The trailing leg (the left) crosses over in front of the lead leg. As the left foot is planted, it is rotated to face straight ahead. In the third step, the right foot draws forward and swings around next to the left foot. This closing action closes the body (feet, hips and shoulders) to face the oncoming served ball. The player should face the passing target position at the moment of contact.

The advantage of this method of movement is that more distance can be covered in the same amount of time it takes to execute the side shuffle. The important emphasis in learning this is on the second step — the realignment step. Be sure the players understand that there is a simultaneous pivoting on the second step as they plant. Failure to complete this pivot will result in a poor body alignment and the players will find themselves facing away from the passing target.

Forward Run Step

The most often used method of movement is the forward run step. This step is used when the serve has lost its momentum and drops short at the deep receiver's feet. The ability to move forward in a flexed trunk position requires excellent quadricep and lower back strength. This is a situation in which players will have to grip their hands together during movement. It is the last chance to prevent the ball from hitting the floor. Also, the players' arms may bend at the elbow so that they may get their arms under the ball. A rushed pass will require the players to continue their movement forward past the point of contact in order to give underspin to the ball. This will prevent the ball from going tight to the net — or worse — across the net, allowing the opposing blockers to spike the ball straight down. During extreme cases, if the receiver is very late in getting to the served ball, a sprawl pass may be the only remaining choice of reception. The player strides (lunges) forward with the outside leg (the left back would stride with the left leg). This brings the body (trunk and platform) into a horizontal position. As the player contacts the ball, the arms move in an upward arc through the ball. I refer to this action as "closing through the ball." The arms slide along the floor during the follow-through phase of the contact.

Turn and Run

The turn and run method of movement is used either to go a long distance very rapidly or to go a short distance when the player needs to get somewhere as quickly as possible. Simply, the player turns or pivots in the direction he or she wishes to travel and sprints to the ball. During movement, the player should stabilize the trunk in a forward-flexed position. A low trunk position will give the receiver added time to get under the ball due to the lowered level of contact. It will also give a more vertical trajectory than would a high platform (which will drive the ball low and flat and therefore quickly toward the net). The main goal when passing on the run is to retain ball control in an off-balance posture. The setter at the net just needs a settable pass in this type of situation. Figure 14.13 illustrates the way the ball will spin toward the passing target from each side of the court.

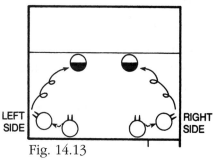

Fig. 14.13

Fig. 14.14

Figure 14.14 shows the correct body posture as the player completes contact. It shows the post-contact phase, as the player continues with arms up and through the ball. The assumes reception from the left side of the court, with the passing target located to the right of center.

Back Pedal

The final method of movement is the back pedal. This movement requires the player to keep the trunk forward over the base. This body posture is necessary because it keeps the player's center of gravity on the balls of the feet as they move backward. If the player draws the torso up, the center of gravity will shift to the heels, which will promote stumbling and awkward movement. The player must get well beyond where the ball will land in order to pass at a level between the knees and the waist. Getting caught halfway ready to pass — that is, too close to the ball — creates a body posture of trunk extension and an upward trajectory pass. In this situation, the player should turn and pass the ball off one side of the body. This will allow the ball to travel a longer distance before it has to be contacted, giving the passer more time to prepare for contact.

The back pedal should be used only for short distances of less than 1.5 m (5 ft.). It is a slow but necessary method of moving backwards. For longer distances, a side shuffle or turn and run is more adequate than the back pedal. These last two methods should not be needed if the reception pattern is such that most player movements will be to the side or forward.

Teaching Movement and Communication

Movement in volleyball is an essential building block in developing a team that can play with speed, safety and communication. Each player should make an aggressive move toward the ball to communicate his or her state of readiness to play. A player who turns a shoulder and "opens the lane" for the person behind him or her communicates that he or she in fact does not intend to play that ball. Late, tentative movement causes confusion, especially in the passing lane.

From a teaching perspective, a progression starting with the side shuffle, followed by the step-crossover close and finishing with the turn and run step, will prepare your players to move sideways. The back pedal step should be taught in conjunction with the forward run. Once the form is correct, add a ball and require the players to catch it, emphasizing proper body posture with the ball. Try to reduce any subconscious stress that may develop when players are unable to pass and move simultaneously for the serve. Once movement and balance are solidly established in their repertoire, then you may combine movement and skill. Remember never to skip the progressions of learning; always assume your players need review and repetition. This will make your practice time more satisfying, especially when you put the team together on the court for the first time and they all know how to make that sure, confident movement to the served ball.

SELECTED DRILLS FOR FOREARM PASSING

All receiving drills should begin at an easy level, with all serves coming from half court. A specific target (i.e., setter) should be present during all drills to provide direct feedback to the receivers of their forearm pass skill. I also believe that players will learn better if they are allowed to do just one facet of the skill (such as receiving the serve to the right of the passer) repeatedly and are allowed to stay in the drill for a consecutive number of repetitions, such as 10 attempts. When the skill shows improvement and consistency, the coach should then set a success goal for the receiver to achieve. If you have players who have consistent serves, then have them run the drill. Competition can be set up between the server and the receiver. For example, the server scores a point if the receiver is aced or passes the ball over the net. At the collegiate level, as the skill is more established, a point can be scored if the pass does not arrive in a designated area. All such game-like drills, however, have to be constructive, not destructive, or they become a waste of time in terms of learning. The coach's explanation of the objectives of the drill should be well thought-out.

Drill No. 1: Half Court Serve (Slow Speed) Directed at the Player. Practice receptions from the RF and RB. Emphasize squaring off (facing toward the inside of the court) to target. Progress to the CF, LF and LB. Note: When passing from the left side of the court, remind the player to lower the inside (right) shoulder and laterally flex the trunk, dropping the right half of the torso slightly. Impetus from the lower body should come from the outside (left) leg.

Drill No. 2: Movement Receptions. Helpful Hints: The coach should initially inform the receiver where the ball will be served. Short-range movement (side shuffle) will be used. Coaches should emphasize proper body alignment to the players. Next, emphasize as early an arrival to the passing position as possible. Figures 14.15, 14.16 and 14.17 show some of these drills.

Drill No. 3: Receptions From LF and LB. Helpful Hints: Side passing requires the player to lower the inside shoulder and the player should play the ball ahead of his or her body. Usually, if the player faces the sideline at about a 45-degree angle, the proper ball-body relationship will be achieved. Figures 14.18 and 14.19 show these drills. Note for Figure 14.19: Added player to practice opening lane. The left-front player should repeat the approach jumps if required to open the lane to let the left back pass. Remind LB receiver to maintain focus on the ball at all times. The player in front should not be a source of distraction.

Drill No. 4: Trash Can Run. Directions: The coach gives a signal to a player to start movement (such as side shuffle, turn and run, back pedal, forward run).

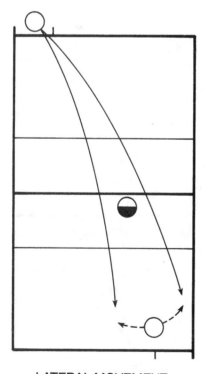

LATERAL MOVEMENT

Fig. 14.15

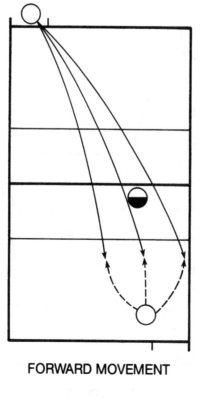

FORWARD MOVEMENT

Fig. 14.16

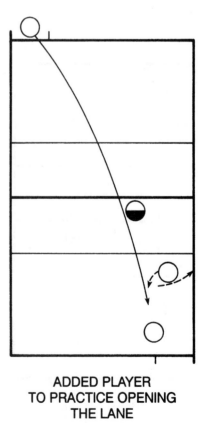

ADDED PLAYER
TO PRACTICE OPENING
THE LANE

Fig. 14.17

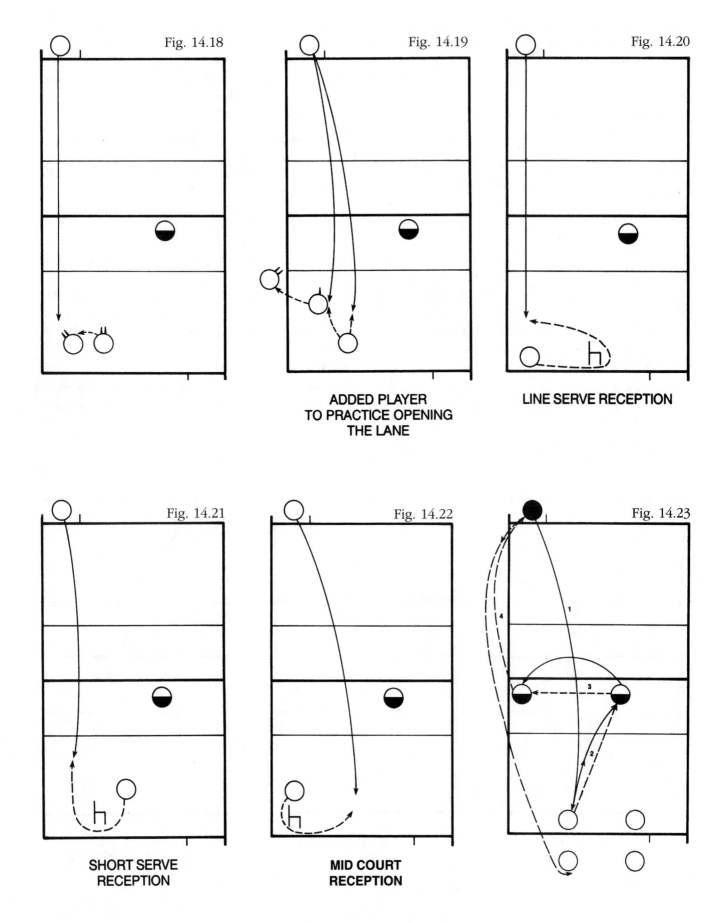

Fig. 14.18

Fig. 14.19

**ADDED PLAYER
TO PRACTICE OPENING
THE LANE**

Fig. 14.20

LINE SERVE RECEPTION

Fig. 14.21

**SHORT SERVE
RECEPTION**

Fig. 14.22

**MID COURT
RECEPTION**

Fig. 14.23

As the player makes the first turn, the coach serves the ball in the direction of the player's movement. Note: Tell players that they cannot leave their starting positions until they receive your signal. Emphasis: Receivers must practice patterns of movement at a maximum speed and must maintain body balance as they pass. Figures 14.20-14.23 illustrate this drill.

Errors/Corrections

Error: The player shanks the pass out of bounds.

Correction: Check to see if the player is sustaining complete eye focus when the ball leaves his or her arms. Check the receiver's head level — is it up, looking ahead at the passing target while the ball makes contact with the receiver's arms?

Error: The pass only goes to mid-court from a back-row reception.

Correction: The player's level of platform is too horizontal during contact. The player's torso may have extended (straightened) before contact, causing a redistribution of the center of gravity backward. Also, the hip joint angle may have opened too much as a result of the torso extension. Keep the angle closed and the body flexed forward. If the level of serve caught the player by surprise, the passer's body may be too close to the ball. Suggest to the player that he or she utilize the turning movement and pass the ball from the side. Remind the player to lower the inside (lead) shoulder and rotate the trunk through the ball. Also, side spin on the ball should be into the court.

Error: The pass goes across the net to the opposing blocker at the net.

Correction: Stabilize the arm action during contact; use a drop motion of the arms during contact; or try redirecting the arms under the ball and giving the ball underspin.

Error: The server serves a top spin serve which drops on the floor in front of the back-row receiver.

Correction: The player has failed to recognize the type of toss the server executed. Most top spin servers will hit under and then up the back side of the ball. Receivers should notice the ball spinning for the first 9.1 m (30ft.) of distance and move forward to meet the ball. This serve gains its momentum in a dropping action, much like the hitter's wrist action as the ball is spiked. If you are prepared for this serve, you should begin two or three steps behind the place where you predict the ball will land. Then, as you read the serve's trajectory, you move forward to meet the ball with a hop-to position.

Error: The front-row receiver passes the ball over the net.

Correction: The level of the platform should be slightly raised when receiving in the front court area. Players should attempt to give underspin to the ball and respond with more of a vertical trajectory pass. This will allow them to pass, then attack either a quick play or a semi-quick play. A good server who has the ability to stand 6.1 m (20ft.) behind the end line and serve the front row a dropper can cause severe reception problems. By putting underspin on the pass, the contact time is lengthened, allowing for more potential ball control.

SUMMARY

Proper service reception is achieved through synchronized movement and communication between players, but the prerequisite to this is the mastery of individual skills. Skills involved include: anticipation, proper technique and tracking the ball. Effective service reception begins with the proper ready position and proceeds to proper contact with the ball, including contact for a high velocity serve and side passing. In addition, movement and movement patterns must be well-learned. Important elements of movement patterns include side movement positioning, the step-crossover close motion, the forward run step, the sprawl pass, the turn and run and the back pedal.

Photo by Randy Nolen

Chapter 15

TACTICS AND STRATEGY IN VOLLEYBALL

Marilyn Nolen

Every sport has strategies so common that they are applied almost automatically. These expected forms of play are used in response to various recurring sport situations. Like other sports, volleyball has certain such strategies which, when properly executed, improve the soundness of a team's game and increase the chances for success. Volleyball's basic strategies can be seen clearly in terms of the sport's six basic skills — digging, setting, spiking, blocking, serving and receiving the serve.

DIGGING

Centered around digging, sound defensive play requires a considerable amount of coaching involvement and teamwork. As in each of the other five basic skills, there are certain strategies each individual player must have. First, each player must learn to form the prescribed defensive pattern(s) — that is, to get into the correct position before the ball is hit. A catch-and-throw method of teaching can help beginners, especially, learn the necessary defensive patterns.

For successful digging and defense, each player must get ready to play the ball before it is hit by the opponents. The only way to be prepared is if every player expects to be hit with the ball every time it is attacked. Thus, every player assumes a defensive ready posture in anticipation.

Another key point for successful digging and defense is that your players must try for every ball; they should never allow a ball to hit the floor without at least being touched. Secondly, they must commit themselves to trying for every ball with two hands.

Good defensive training begins with giving a team many repetitions in the basics described here. Although these patterns may seem simple, effective use of them will bring a team greater defensive success.

SETTING

Setting the ball for the attack is strategic at even the simplest level of play. Depending on the quality of the pass, a coach must be able to rely on a setter to make sound, consistent decisions. Following is a list of strategic demands on the setter, in ascending order of difficulty.

1. The ability to set the ball to the left front position is the most important skill for the setter to acquire. A coach can develop this ability by emphasizing that fact and by constant drills in practice.
2. With any set, the ball should be delivered well. Good delivery means that the ball is touched legally, set high enough and positioned properly relative to the attacker.
3. After becoming consistent in the skills outlined in Nos. 1 and 2, the setter's primary goal should be to set a good set to a good attacker. This goal requires the setter to know who the right attackers are, something that must be emphasized in practice. The setter should be especially aware of the primary attackers — those who score high statistically.

109

4. A poor set should never be made to a secondary hitter (a statistically lower attacker). What becomes a poor set when made to a secondary hitter may well have been a good set, or at least an acceptable one, if it had been made to a good hitter. In other words, often it is the hitter's ability that makes the difference in whether a particular set is poor, acceptable or good. Secondary spikers require good sets.

5. When setting a good set to a secondary hitter, the setter must have a specific shot planned for that spiker. Obviously, this requires a good deal of thinking by the setter (as should be expected in better intermediate and advanced play). Planning for a specific shot depends on observing the block positioning of the opposition and specifically setting for either a line or a cross-court attack. By paying attention to which attackers the opposing blockers are keying on, the setter can often get the secondary attackers in one-on-one situations. With one blocker versus one attacker, the attacker has a decided advantage. Simply notifying secondary spikers of open shots on the opponent's court before the set is made to that spiker will often result in a successful shot. This kind of communication should occur when the ball is dead before service. Because opponents often place the least effective blockers opposite the secondary attackers, the setter can look for these switches, being especially aware of size mismatches, and communicate the situation to the spiker prior to the next volley.

6. At a critical time, the setter should not set a cold hitter (one just coming into the game or one who has not been set often throughout the game) or an unsuccessful attacker.

7. Neither critical, high-risk sets nor trick sets and plays should be used at the end of the game — and especially not at game point.

8. When your team is making points, continue to use the sets that are working. Change strategies in the game only when opponents are successful at stopping the attack.

SPIKING

When plays and advanced attack systems are developed along with setting ability, the spikers have less pressure to incorporate individual spiking strategy because deception is planned into the system. Nonetheless, at every level of play, each attacker must develop some individual competence, especially to use in less-than-perfect situations. The strategies described here will give even beginning attackers statistical success. Once again, this list is in ascending degree of demand upon the spiker.

1. The ball must be hit into the opponent's court, even from a terrible set. The ball must be kept in play.

2. The hit should be to the opponent's disadvantage.

3. The ball should be killed (put down to gain a point or side-out). The kill is the most difficult shot to make consistently and often an error will result if the kill is the attacker's only focus. To become a good spiker with consistent statistics, Nos. 1 and 2 must be the primary focus, with kill attempts occurring only on the good sets. Success results from consistent play — without undue risk — taking on poor sets.

The attackers must develop skills to hit every type of set. Beginners or intermediate players may need to poke or dink sets that are too low or too close. Advanced players, on the other hand, must acquire the ability to attack these sets. Sets that are back from the net and deeper than the hitter's normal range require high contact and a considerable amount of top spin. In advanced play, these sets still should be skillfully attacked, rather than given as free plays to the opponents. This requires a lot of practice time.

In training attackers to become intermediate level players, a coach should have them develop two power shots, the line shot and the cross-court shot. However, it is equally important that they know when to use a power shot and when to dink or tip. The dink or tip is most effective on a good set, but the attacker must know what defense is being used by the other team before incorporating the tip. Obviously, just giving the ball directly to an opposing defensive player is not effective. The tip is best used in surprise, especially after the hitter has been spiking effectively and powerfully. In other words, it is best to dink after opponents have acquired respect for the attacker's power.

BLOCKING

Blocking is an advanced skill, one which becomes especially complicated and high-risk when more than one player is blocking. In low skill levels, and especially with beginners, the best strategy is not to block unless the set is close. The degree of success in the skill of blocking is very low at any skill level.

The distance of the opponent's set from the net is a key for blockers. The further away the ball is from the net, the less need there is to block. Unless the opposing spiker has two developed power shots, one properly positioned blocker is sufficient. A two-person block should only be used if the opponent's ability warrants it.

Advanced play presents a middle blocker with another strategic decision: when to commit to blocking center on a quick set (thereby giving the opposing setter an opportunity to set up a one-on-one situation — one blocker versus one spiker — in an outside position near the sideline). Coaching and statistical input are usually required for the middle blockers to be successful in making these decisions. However, the middle blocker should be aware of these two fundamental strategic considerations:

- Honor the middle when the opponent's primary spiker is attacking the middle.
- Overblock the line when the set is to an outside position and very close to the net.

Honoring the middle (guarding the middle closely) is necessary when the opponent's primary spiker is attacking the middle regularly with success. There are some further strategic considerations in this situation, however. A perceptive blocker can pick up certain cues and recognize when to honor the middle. Many setters only set the middle on the perfect pass. In addition, setters often develop observable habits, such as keeping their arms straight when setting the middle, or perhaps dropping their hands. The setter is sometimes out of range to set the middle attack, especially when the pass pulls the setter away from the net. With these cues in mind, the blocker will know much more reliably whether honoring the middle is required in each situation.

Overblocking the line should occur when the set is delivered by opponents to an outside position along and very close to the net. In this case, it is necessary to overblock the line to prevent the ball from being tipped, hit or wiped off of the outside blocker. Overblocking requires the outside blocker to position the inside hand on the ball.

SERVING

Service strategy depends on the ability of athletes to perform the skill. Each player must have a reliable serve that measures up to the skill level of the competition. In addition to a reliable serve, their repertoire should also include a higher risk but stronger service attack. Generally, either the coach or an advanced player determines the positions to serve into the opponent's court or lineup. Still, every player makes a decision as to how to serve aggressively upon rotating into the service corner. Ultimately, the player decides how much risk to take. Players should take the opportunity to be aggressive in the following circumstances:

- When seriously behind in score.
- When points are never made in a particular serving rotation.
- When the score is stuck in the middle of the game, especially in the middle game of the match.
- When the team's ability to side out is high.

Safe serving is more strategic in the following instances:

- When serving the first ball after winning the coin toss for service.
- After a time-out.
- After serving several points in a row.
- After a long rally.
- After the player in the preceding rotation has missed the serve.
- Any time after 12 points have been made in the game.
- When a strong front line rotation is at the net for the team.

RECEIVING THE SERVE

Receiving the serve is undoubtedly the most critical skill for establishing a team's success. Perfection in passing depends upon both the team's skill level and the effectiveness and power of the opponent's serve. These factors, listed in ascending order of difficulty, should be considered when receiving the serve:

1. Avoid being aced; try to at least touch the served ball.
2. Make the pass playable. Get it in the air somewhere.
3. Pass the ball between yourself and the setter.
4. Target the pass to the setter.

If the team cannot side out because of poor passing, change the receiving pattern. This alteration includes moving the pattern forward or back, flooding to one side or covering an ineffective passer.

Any time passing is unsuccessful in a 6-2 offense,

change immediately to a 4-2. The best passers should be in optimum position to receive the statistically highest percentage of serves (near the middle of the court). In tense situations, strong passers should extend their range and cover extra court area, in addition to assuming the responsibility for getting the ball passed. In extreme situations, the best passers can take every serve.

If failure to side out is the result of a poor attack, the serve reception pattern should be varied to position the best attacker to spike — left front. In beginning to intermediate play, the setter cannot be relied upon to perform a good set to any position but left front. This limitation requires patterns designed to allow the setter to set the best spiker in the left front position.

SUMMARY

Following is a summary of the points presented in this chapter:

Digging
- Learn to form defensive patterns.
- Get physically ready to play the ball before it is hit. Expect the hit.
- Try for every ball. Try for the ball with two arms.
- Defense must be trained. Catch and throw is a good method. If a player does not perform the trained duty, especially in forming defense (getting to court position after proper training), then substitute.

Setting
- Develop the ability to set to the left front; this is the most important target.
- Always deliver the ball well.
- Make a good set to a good hitter.
- Make a good set to a secondary hitter, but plan a shot for that hitter. That is, notice whom the opponents are keying on. Get the secondary attackers into one-on-one situations, then set them for a line or angle hit.
- Never give a poor set to a secondary hitter. A bad set for a poor hitter may be a good, or at least acceptable, set for a good hitter. Secondary hitters require very good sets.
- Do not set a cold hitter or a hitter who has been unsuccessful at a critical time.
- Do not use trick or critical sets at the end of a game, especially at game point.

- When making points, continue to use the sets that are working. Change strategies in the game only when opponents stop the system.

Spiking
- Hit the ball in the court, even on terrible sets.
- Hit to the opponent's disadvantage.
- Concerning kills: Skill must be developed to hit every type of set. That is, for close sets poke if necessary; for deep sets reach high and use top spin.
- Develop two power shots.
- If the dink is used, the hitter should know what defense the other team is in. The dink is most effective on a good set.

Blocking
- Practice each situational condition so that players acquire trained responses.
- In low skill levels, do not block unless the set is close. Depth of set is important.
- The further back the ball is from the net, the less need there is to block.
- Make sure an opponent deserves a two-person block.
- Concerning blocking the middle: When the setter sets it regularly with success.
- When the main hitter is in the middle.
- When the setter has range to set the middle or shows a tendency to set it. That is, does the setter set middle only on perfect passes? Does the setter drop the arms or keep the arms straight, providing the blocker with a cue?
- On close and wide sets, overblock to the outside to avoid being used (get the inside hand on the ball).

Serving
- Serving can be either aggressive or safe, depending, in part, on the ability of the player. Thus, the key to tough serving is increasing your players' skill levels.
- Use aggressive serving when: The team is seriously behind in score.
- The player never makes points in the serving rotation. (The other team plays the serve like a free ball).
- The ability of your team to side out is high.
- When the score is stuck in a middle game.
- Use safe serving when: The team has just won the serve.
- After a time-out.

- After serving several points in a row.
- After a long rally.
- When the person in the rotation ahead of you missed the serve.
- Any time after 12 points.
- When there is a strong front line (hitters or blockers).

Receiving the Serve

- The pass must be playable. Avoid being aced, especially when no one even touches the ball.
- Pass between self and the net.
- Target the pass to the setter.
- If the team cannot side out and poor passing is the problem, change the pattern:

- Move up or back.
- Flood to one side.
- Cover the person being served.
- Any time you cannot get the pass in a 6-2, immediately change to a 4-2.
- Put the best passers in position to pass. Let the best passers take everything.
- If failure to side out results from poor hitting, change the serve reception pattern to get the best hitter in position to hit. This position is usually the left front. At the lower skill levels, one cannot count on the setter getting the ball anywhere but left front.

Part 3

ADVANCED ELEMENTS
TEAM PLAY

Photo by Dan Houser

SYSTEMS OF PLAY

Ruth Nelson and Frances Compton

There are probably as many volleyball offensive systems in use today as there are coaches. Most coaches start out using one of the basic systems, but by the time it has been adapted to the specific abilities of their players, it has become a system unique to that program. Basically, a system is determined by how the setter penetrates — whether the setter(s) moves in to set from a front-court or a back-court position. This, in turn, is determined by the team's passing ability and the abilities of the setters.

While defensive systems are named with words and colors, offensive systems are named with numbers. Commonly used offensive systems include the 4-2, 5-1 and 6-2. The first number refers to the number of players who are designated hitters and the second the number of setters. Sometimes the numbers add up to more than six because the setters are also hitters.

In the 6-2 system, for example, the two setters each set while playing in the back court and hit after rotating to the front court.

The options and variations for each system are almost unlimited. Many factors will influence a coach's selection of an offense. It is best to start with a basic plan and get more sophisticated as coach and players gain experience and knowledge.

OFFENSIVE PROGRESSION

College coaches have the distinct advantage of being able to recruit players to complement their preferred offensive systems. Coaches of younger players usually find it necessary to fit the system to the players. A coach may want to begin by using an offensive progression while evaluating the setting and hitting potential of your players.

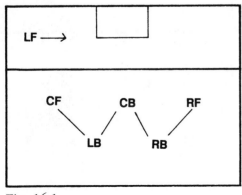

Fig. 16.1

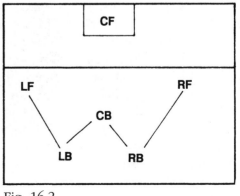

Fig. 16.2

Setting by Position

A simple way to begin is to designate a setter by rotational position. For example, have the center front set for a two-hitter attack, or have the right back player set for a three-hitter attack. Whoever rotates into the designated position (left, center, or right) becomes the setter. I call this a 4-0 when a front-court setter is used and a 6-0 when a back-court setter is used. (The zero means that there is no designated player who sets, only a designated setting position.) Designating a setter by rotational position has a great deal of merit in terms of developing players' understanding of offensive concepts, as well as aiding their total skill development.

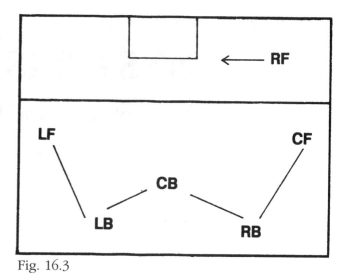

Fig. 16.3

Front-Court Setter Systems

Once a coach has identified the setters, he/she must consider whether or not to use a front-court setter or a back-court setter to run the offense. A front-court setter allows for easier passing formations and generally less confusion among hitters, since there are only two. The target area for passing in a standard 4-2 is larger, so the passes do not have to be as accurate (Figures 16.1-16.5). Players pass to a position on the court rather than to the setter. Another advantage is that the setter is already positioned in the front court and generally has a shorter and straighter movement path to the ball.

In a front-court setter system, hitting responsibilities are easy to define. All sets in front of the setter will be hit by the left front player, while all sets behind the setter will be hit by the right front player, unless combination plays are used. A front-court setter system can be made a great deal more sophisticated by using a "fake" hitter; this option will be discussed in a later section.

The front-court setter system may be less demanding on the passers and setters, but it places greater demands on the hitters. Strategically, the hitters must be smarter and more effective in a front-court system because they are usually hitting against a two-player block. In a basic front-court setter offense, there are fewer nick attacks or combinations, so the middle blocker has time to move to the outside to block. Thus, in addition to spiking the ball, the hitters must use tips, off-speed shots and blockers' hands (wipe-offs). They must also use position hitting to find the holes on the court. Learning to exploit the blockers' weaknesses is also important. For example, hitters

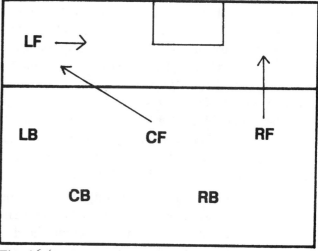

Fig. 16.4

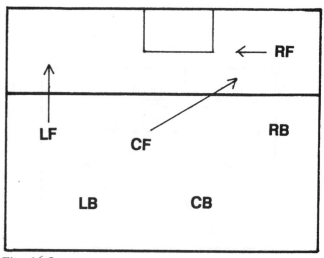

Fig. 16.5

Fig. 16.6   Fig. 16.7

should learn to hit cross-court when the middle blocker is slow or late moving into position. Thus, if there are several smart and capable hitters and the players are average in passing and setting, a front-court setter system may be just right.

Back-Court Setter Systems

In this system, a player moves in from the back court to set so that three hitters instead of two can be in the front court. A back-court setter system allows the coach to be more creative with the team's offense. This creativity tends to promote interest among the players as they become involved in the challenge of learning the system. As players become more experienced, the excitement of making the offense more complex keeps them from becoming complacent. A coach really does not know the potential of his/her players until a challenging situation arises. Running a three-hitter attack with a back-court setter sets the stage for future development — including plays, combinations, fakes and back-court attacks.

Passing determines the level at which a team can play. If a team has a very good setter, he/she can work with average passing. If it has an excellent passing team, an average setter can run a three-hitter attack. If the opponents are comparable in skill, then set selection (choosing the hitter and the hitter position) will make the difference.

Remember, the efficiency of the pass is determined by the strength of the team's own servers. If teammates serve tough to each other in practice, it will be a much better passing team. Also, remember that winning is not necessarily an indicator of offensive effectiveness. Winning shows that one team scored points on serving and blocking, as well. A team cannot win on offense alone.

A coach may want to use a progression to move into a back-court setter offense. Begin by using a setter from the back court on free balls only. The team should be able to pass free balls to the setter with accuracy. With good positioning of the setter, the hitter should be able to make proper approaches and the setter can execute the set as planned. On serve receive, try staying with a front-court setter if the passing tends to be off-target. By following this progression, the players will become familiar with the concepts of the 4-2 and 6-2 offenses. When passing breaks down, there are then more options.

Eventually, a coach and a team will progress to the point where they can run plays to capitalize on the hitting strengths of the individual players and to confuse the opponent's defense. Having the option of moving a hitter to another position to enable him or her to hit the best shot is naturally advantageous. In order to have this option, the setter must learn to make good sets and good decisions. Set deception will come with experience.

The trend in passing is to pass the ball lower and faster. Using lower, faster passes facilitates better timing between the setter and hitter and allows the defense less time to position. However, the pass should always be high enough that the setter has the option of jump setting. Jump setting gets the ball to the hitter faster, makes the blocker commit and reduces the chance of the setter setting the ball below the top of the net.

A fast attack is not limited to one set to the middle attacker. In using a fast attack, the hitter is trying to hit the ball before the defense has time to position. The setter can fast set anywhere at the net. In order to use a fast attack, however, the setter must make precise sets.

In the back-court setter system, passing and setting must be more exact. The hitter's job, aside from learning the patterns, is not as demanding as it is in a front-court setter offense. In fact, the system is designed to create better situations for the hitters. Instead of going against a double block every time, the hitters should be one-on-one with their respective blockers. This offense can be very simple or create your own options. Coaches may be surprised at what the players can do. Offer them the challenge!

BASIC OFFENSIVE SYSTEMS
The 4-2

The 4-2 is a front-court setter offense with four hitters and two designated setters. There are two different ways to run the 4-2 offense. The standard 4-2 uses a center front setter with a left and right side attack. The right side 4-2 allows for greater use of the middle attack. These systems are explained below.

Standard 4-2. In the standard 4-2, the setter moves to the middle of the front court as soon as the ball is contacted on the serve. The setter has basically two options: set the left side attacker, or back set to the right side player (Figures 16.1-16.5). Play sets are not usually seen in the standard 4-2.

The advantages of this system are its simplicity, a larger passing target, easier setter movement and less confusion among hitters. However, if a setter is small and there is a short block in the middle, the opponents may try to exploit this weakness. Also, as mentioned before, the hitters are usually hitting against a double block.

Right Side 4-2. In the right side 4-2, the front-court setter moves to the right side of the court as soon as the ball is contacted on the serve. The setter can set the left side attacker or the middle attacker. The setter can position at the net (Figures 16.8, 16.9 and 16.10) or pretend to be a back-court setter and line up behind

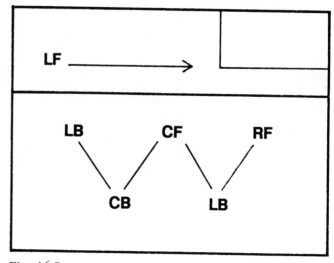

Fig. 16.8

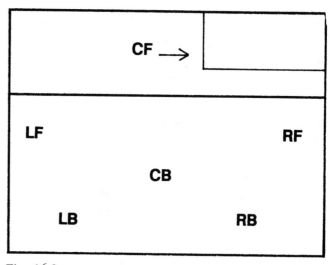

Fig. 16.9

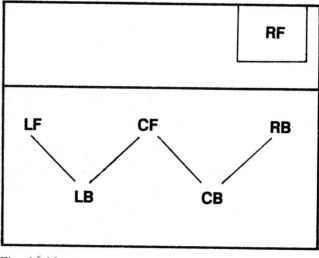

Fig. 16.10

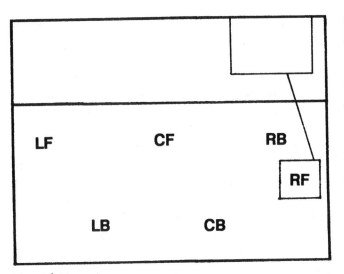

Fig. 16.11

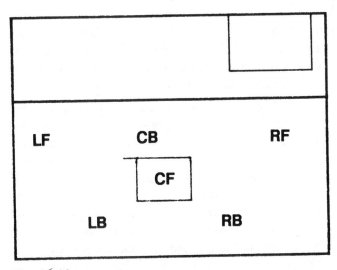

Fig. 16.12

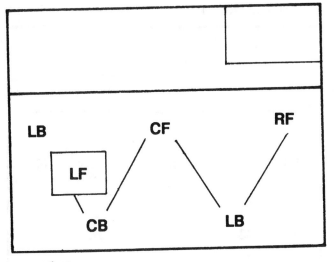

Fig. 16.13

the respective back-court player (Figures 16.11, 16.12 and 16.13). For example, when playing the right front position, the setter lines up behind the right back player as the fake hitter. The setter must move into legal position before the ball is contacted on the serve. The setter usually steps in front of the back-court player as the ball is tossed for the serve. Overlapping will be called if the setter fails to move into the correct position before service contact. It is important for the setter to jump set as many balls as possible so that the opposing blockers do not know if the setter is going to tip, hit or jump set to the hitters.

The advantage of the right side 4-2 over the standard 4-2 is that there can be a middle attack while still maintaining the benefit of simple setter movement. It is easier for the setter to set the middle attack area because it is not confined by the antennae; in addition, this lack of confinement makes the middle area more difficult to defend. The left side hitter can now hit against one blocker, or at least a late middle blocker, because the middle hitter has held the middle blocker. If the setter is small, have a taller player in the middle for blocking purposes against a team that runs a three-hitter attack. If the back-court player is used successfully as a fake hitter, the center hitter should also find a one-on-one hitting situation.

There are a few disadvantages to this system. The passes must now be made to the right side, requiring a little more accuracy than passing to the middle of the court. If a coach chooses to disguise the two-hitter attack as a three-hitter attack, have the setter line up in the back court. This technique makes the setter's movement path longer, requiring more quickness. There is also more opportunity to overlap. Thus, with the right side 4-2, one can overcome some of the disadvantages of the standard 4-2, but will still have only two eligible hitters.

Player Positioning for the 4-2. Start out with the two setters opposite each other in the lineup. If there is a significant difference in the abilities of the two setters, put the best setter in the center front and the second best setter as the center back. The best hitter starts at the left front, with the second best hitter at the right back. If the second best hitter is not the No. 1 or 2 server, then start a tough server at the right back. Place the third best hitter at the left back and the fourth best hitter at the right front. If the No. 4 hitter is not a tough server, then use a substitute to serve after the first rotation (Figures 16.14, 16.15).

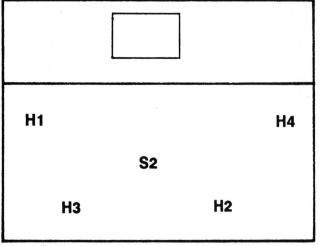

Fig. 16.14

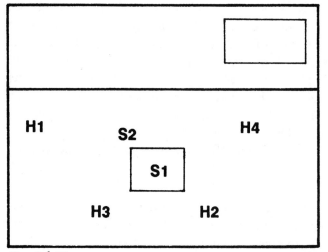

Fig. 16.15

The 6-2 is a back-court setter offense with a three-hitter attack. All six players are hitters and two of these players are also designated to set when they are in the back court. Having a back-court setter gives the team a left, middle and right side attack. In the 6-2 offense, the setter moves into setting position after the ball is contacted on the serve. The passes must be made to the setter just right of the center front position.

The biggest advantage of this system is the potential for hitting options. It allows the coach and setter to create plays. Hitter specialization can make a tremendous difference in offensive effectiveness and the coach can capitalize on the unique hitting abilities of each player. Better communication is required because of the more intricate movement of hitters and this tends to improve team cohesiveness. The blockers must look at three hitters instead of two, so there should be favorable hitting situations.

When running the 6-2 attack, four players are in the front court and this can create confusion, especially on off-plays and transitions. Passers must be able to pass the ball to the setter with accuracy. A three-hitter attack requires more decision making by the setter and with fast sets, there is a greater chance of setter error. Therefore, a coach must devote more time to training the setters. The setter can no longer jump and hit or tip the ball over the net because this would be a back-court hitter violation. The setter must learn to set good sets from bad passes. Also, spiker coverage is generally weaker with a fast attack because players do not have time to get to their ideal coverage positions.

Player Positioning for the 6-2. Setters are usually placed opposite each other in the lineup. If they are not opposite, then one setter will set more rotations than the other setter. This situation could be used to an advantage. For example, have the better setter set at right front, right back, center back and left back. As a result, the second setter will not have to set from the more difficult left back position.

Assuming that the setters are opposite each other in the lineup, their starting positions will still depend on their hitting abilities. It is vital to place comparable hitters opposite one another. Thus, a coach must first rank the skill levels of the hitters and setters. Usually, the best setter starts in the right back if the second best setter is a strong hitter. If the second setter is not the No. 1 or 2 hitter, as is often the case, then start the better setter at the center back, the second setter at the center front and the best hitter at the left front. Place the No. 2 hitter at the right back, the No. 3 hitter at the left back and the No. 4 hitter at the right front (Figure 16.16).

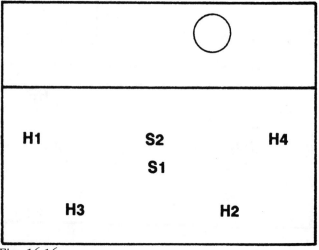

Fig. 16.16

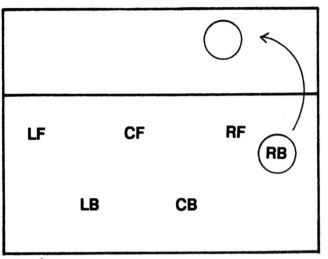

Fig. 16.17

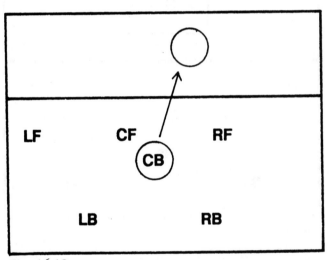

Fig. 16.18

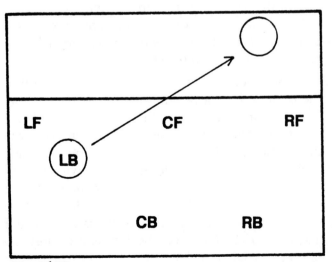

Fig. 16.19

The 5-1

The 5-1 is basically a combination of the 4-2 and 6-2 offenses. In this offense, there are five hitters and only one setter. When the setter is in the back court, a three-hitter attack is run (Figures 16.17, 16.18 and 16.19). When the setter is in the front court, the attack is run with two hitters (Figures 16.1, 16.2, 16.3; 16.8, 16.9, 16.10). College teams usually use a middle attack (right side 4-2) when the setter is in the front court, but a standard 4-2 offense with the setter setting from the middle may also be used.

Many of the advantages and disadvantages of this offense have been pointed out in the discussion of the 4-2 and 6-2, but there are some pros and cons that are unique to the 5-1 system. Relying on one setter will give that setter a far greater opportunity to develop setting skills in practice, as well as in actual competition. The hitters adjust to the one setter and there is less confusion as to who should set the ball on transition. Because of this greater experience, fewer setter errors should take place.

The problems occur when the setter is not mentally or physically prepared to play. Substituting for a 5-1 setter could mean a very difficult adjustment for a team. Also, most 5-1 setters are smaller than the majority of the hitters on the team. If the setter is not a strong hitter and blocker, the opponents will certainly use this weakness to their advantage.

At the international level, the 5-1 system is used by most of the top women's teams. These teams use the 5-1; training two setters to run such a highly sophisticated offense is far too difficult for them. Even with very talented setters of equal ability, it is very unlikely that two setters who must share setting duties on a 50-50 basis could develop the same capabilities as one setter who sets the whole system. Thus, if a team has one setter whose ability is far greater than the others and who has the temperament and endurance to do the job, this system has the potential to be extremely effective.

Player Positioning For The 5-1. There are many trade-offs to consider when deciding on the most suitable lineup for the players. Following is one suggestion for positioning players for the 5-1 starting lineup: The setter usually begins at the right back if the team is serving (or the right front if the team is receiving), establishing a three-hitter attack for the first three rotations. If the setter starts at the right back, the hitters could be positioned as follows: the

No. 1 hitter at the left front, the No. 2 hitter at the center back, the No. 3 hitter at the center front, the No. 4 hitter at the left back and the No. 5 hitter at the right front (Fig. 16.20)

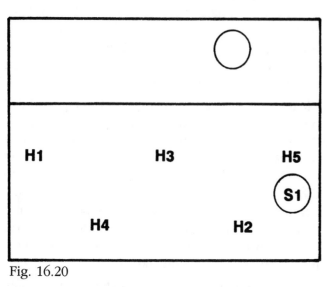

Fig. 16.20

OFFENSIVE VARIATIONS

There can be any combination of back-court and front-court setters and hitters. The challenge is to utilize the abilities of each player to the team's greatest advantage. Experiment and try different combinations in order to arrive at the system that is best for a particular team in any given year.

The 6-3

One variation that I have found particularly effective is the 6-3. In this system, all six players are hitters and three players share back-court setting duties. This system enables a coach to work the younger setters into the lineup to train along with the more experienced setters. Another big bonus is that the setters, who are usually the best all-around players, can now be used for passing and defense in the vulnerable left back position. As a result, there is more versatility in pass/receive formations. When passing breaks down with a back-court setter, there is always a setter in the front court. There are also more options on transition when the setter cannot move in to set. The lineup is more flexible because the two best setters do not have to be opposite one another (Figure 16.21).

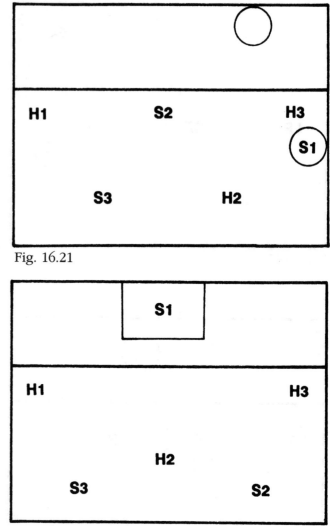

Fig. 16.21

Fig. 16.22

The 3-3

The 3-3 system is essentially the same as the 6-3, except the setters set from the center front and the right front positions instead of the right back and the center back. The benefits of this system are the same as the benefits of the 6-3 (Figure 16.22).

Left Side Attack. In a left side attack, the setter runs the offense from a position left of the center front instead of from the right side of the court. The setter has the middle and right side attackers in front with the left side attack behind. This variation is designed to help the setter get in faster when playing the left back or the left front positions. It also allows a front court setter who is right-handed to attack easily. The main reason for running the left side attack is that it allows a faster attack on the left side against the opponent's right front blocker. The attack can be even

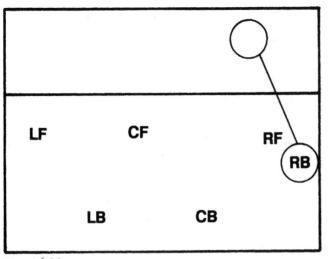

Fig. 16.23

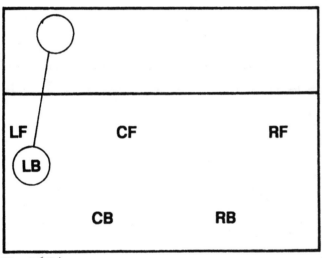

Fig. 16.24

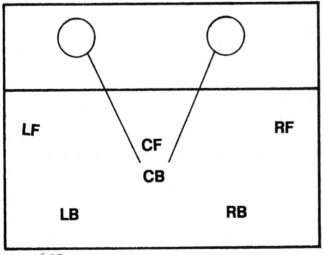

Fig. 16.25

faster if the center hitter is left-handed. The right front blocker is usually the setter or a weaker blocker because most teams attack fast on the right side of the court.

The following figures show a number of attack options: a right side attack when the setter is at the right back (Figure 16.23); and a left side attack when the setter is at the left back (Figure 16.24). When the setter is at the center back, she moves to the right side if the ball is served cross-court and to the left side if it is served down the line (Figure 16.25). This movement is done because it is easier to pass the ball straight ahead than cross-court.

In order to run the left side attack, coaches must train their passers to pass left. There is nothing difficult about passing left, except that players are programmed to pass right from an early age. If a team is running a number of plays, the setter has the difficult task of reversing the set positions.

SPIKER COVERAGE

Spiker coverage is not essential unless a team is getting blocked. In spiker coverage, players move into a position to back up the hitter in case the hit is blocked by the defense. If the ball is blocked, the covering players can get the ball up and prepare to attack again. The key to knowing where to cover is to watch the blockers' hands and the placement of the set.

If the set is off the net, the coverage should be tight because the ball could come down in front of the hitter. Close coverage is also necessary when the blockers are tall and are penetrating over the net. In this case the ball will probably be blocked down. If the blockers are blocking straight up but not over the net, then coverage should be deeper in the court.

As a general rule, the three players closest to the hitter take a low position near the 3-meter line and the other two players balance the entire back court. The setter usually follows the set. The three closest players should not reach back to play balls. Instead, those balls should be played by the back court players. Spiker coverage for the standard 4-2 offense is shown in Figures 16.26 and 16.27.

This spiker coverage pattern is described as a 2-1-2. There are two players in fairly close, one slightly deeper and two in the back court. On a left or right side block, the no. 1 slot is filled by the middle hitter

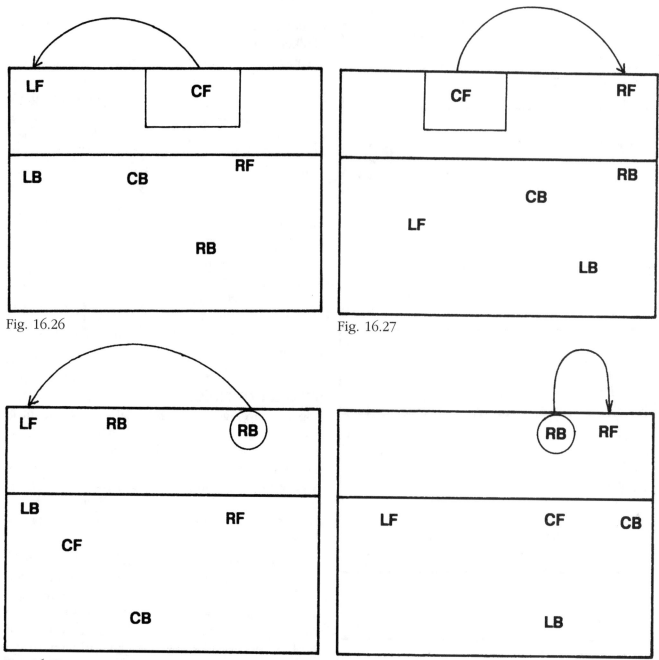

Fig. 16.26

Fig. 16.27

Fig. 16.28

Fig. 16.29

(Figures 16.28 and 16.29) unless the hitter drives for a fast set. In this case, the setter fills the number 1 position (Figures 16.30 and 16.31). When covering the center hitter, the coach may designate which player fills the number 1 slot. I usually designate the left back player (Figures 16.32 and 16.33). When a front-court setter sets from the right front to the left front, have the setter pull off of the net instead of following the set (Figure 16.34). If the setter follows the set and the ball is bumped up, then all of the front court players are bunched up on the side where the team was just blocked (Figure 8.35).

For a basic offense, spiker coverage should be complete. When fast plays are used, coverage becomes less defined because the players simply do not have time to position properly before the ball is hit. Many times the coverage will be the two players closest in and two in the back court. If the pass is poor, the setter will not have time to get into position. Players must learn to balance the coverage when the setter cannot move in.

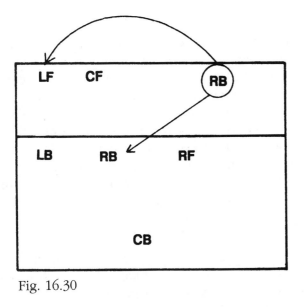

Fig. 16.30

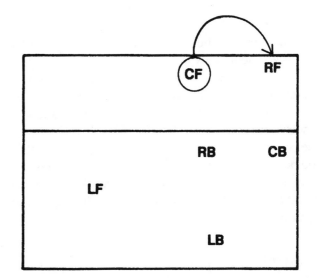

Fig. 16.31

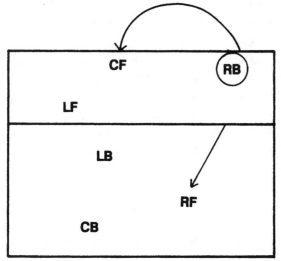

Fig. 16.32

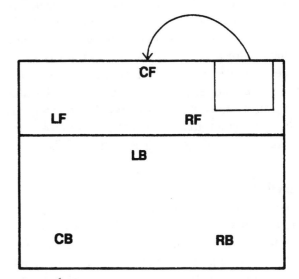

Fig. 16.33

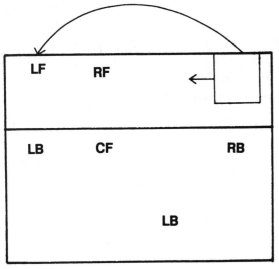

Fig. 16.34

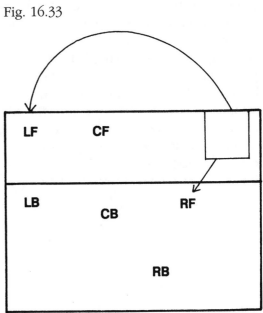

Fig. 16.35

MATCHING UP

Even after coaches have established an effective offensive lineup, they may find that in certain rotations, the opponents are outscoring the team by a wide margin. Consequently, adjustments must be made. First, try switching blocking assignments or substituting for a weak blocker. Next, alter the set selection. If these measures do not work, try to match up differently in the next game. Possibly rotate the lineup so as to match your best player against the opponent's best player. Another option is to match your best hitter against the opponent's weakest player or a short setter.

Total Team Preparation

The importance of developing every player in order to achieve the concept of total team development cannot be stressed enough. All players must master all of the basic fundamentals. Very often tall players concentrate on hitting almost to the exclusion of passing and setting, while shorter players do exactly the opposite. Hitting effectiveness depends to a large degree on the quality of a team's ball control. Before you begin categorizing hitters and setters, make sure that all of your players are working hard at developing all of their skills.

Flexibility

Every system has its strengths and weaknesses. There is no set system that will work perfectly for your team without adaptations. Analyze the individual abilities of your players and design your system. Allow enough time for the system to succeed, but do not be afraid to make changes if it is not functioning properly. Players are generally more flexible and adaptable than one might first think. Remember, also, that with change, expect some initial failures. Do not be discouraged. The team will gain a better understanding of how to achieve offense effectiveness as it works through the problems. The enthusiasm players show as they experience success with a system will be worth the efforts.

SUMMARY

A coach should determine which system of play to use by taking into account a number of factors, including the team's passing ability, the setter's ability and the way the setter penetrates. Each system has many options and variations available, and to select a system, it may help to designate a setter by rotational position. There are both front-court setter systems and back-court setter systems, and either a front-court setter or a back-court setter can be chosen to run the offense. A front-court setter system is less demanding on the passers and setters, but it places greater demands on the hitters.

A team may utilize any combination of back-court and front-court setters and hitters. The coach should design the system by analyzing the abilities of the individual players and then employing the combination that is best for the team.

Offensive systems are named with two numbers. The first number denotes the number of players who are designated hitters and the second number denotes the number of setters. Basic offensive systems include the 4-2 and the 6-2. The 4-2 is a standard front-court setter offensive system that includes the standard 4-2 and the right side 4-2. The 6-2 is a back-court setter offensive system. The 5-1 system is a combination of the 4-2 and the 6-2 systems.

The 6-3 system is an offensive variation that can be particularly effective. In this system, all six players are hitters and three players share the back court setting duties. The 3-3 system is another variation similar to the 6-3 system, except the setters set from the center front and right front positions.

The coach must make adjustments in the rotation if his or her team is being outscored. If the team is getting blocked, spiker coverage is necessary. A coach may also choose to switch blocking assignments, substitute for a weak blocker, alter the set selection or match up players differently in the following game.

Photo by Dan Houser

Chapter 17

OFFENSIVE COMBINATIONS

Doug Beal

In 1965, most U.S. volleyball teams ran the 4-2 attack (four spikers, two setters). One setter and two spikers were at the net at all times and most sets were high and wide. The most frequent variation was a quick set to the side or the middle. An attempt in 1966 to standardize the names of various sets yielded the following terminology (Figure 17.1):

- The four (or shoot) — a low set to the sideline;
- The three — a medium set about halfway between the spiker and the setter;
- The two — a set about two feet above net height right next to the setter;
- The one (or quick, popularized by the Japanese) — a ball set right next to the setter so that the spiker can attack it on the way up rather than on the way down; and
- The zero (or regular) — the usual high, wide set.

Still in use today, this system has been further complicated in two ways:

1. Some teams have redefined one or two signals — a three might be a quick 10 feet away from the setter or a five could be a soft lob back to the weak side.
2. Many more types of sets have been defined.

This chapter traces the evolution of the terminology associated with offensive systems as a way of introducing the offensive systems themselves. Then it explains in detail the general concepts, fundamental approaches and offensive series used by the USA national teams in order to show in detail one fully-developed approach to offensive combinations.

Today, a three-spiker attack is popular — anyone at the net may attack the ball and the setters are the people in the back court. This may be called a three-spiker attack, a multiple offense or a 6-2. With so

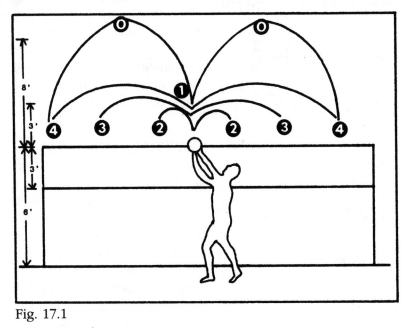

Fig. 17.1

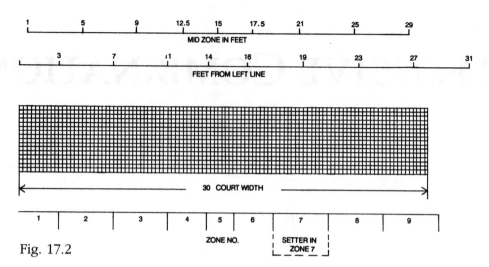

Fig. 17.2

many combinations of setters, sets and attackers, a more sophisticated system of naming sets became necessary. The attack positions along the net and the height of the set needed to be included. Several systems were tried and in 1972, the Kenneth Allen team from Chicago (coached by Jim Coleman) worked out a variation of an earlier system of Val Keller's that worked in the following way (Figure 17.2):

• The first of the two digits that name the set designates the attack position along the net and the second the height of the set above the net.
• There are nine attack zones symmetrically distributed across the net, with zones one and nine extending outside the court.
• Sets are made to attack zones of designated width and if the set is within the zone, it's acceptable.
• Regular sets are assumed to be higher than 2.4 m (8 ft.) above the net and are designated by a zero as the second digit.

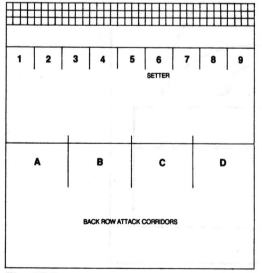

Fig. 17.3

• Special sets vary up to 2.4 m (8 ft.) above the net and super-high sets are 4.6 to 6.1 m (15 to 20 ft.) above the net.

Thus, a 52 is 61 cm (2 ft.) above the net and hittable in the center of the court (the 5 zone). A 30 is a regular height set (2.4 to 3 m or 8 to 10 ft.) hittable between 2.1 and 3.4 m (7 and 11 ft.) from the left sideline (the 3 zone). An 89 is a super-high set about 1.5 m from the right sideline (the 8 zone). The 9 designates super-high (4.6 to 6.1 m or 15 to 20 ft.). Thus, with the exception of zero, the lower the second digit, the lower and faster the set is.

As 1984 U.S. Olympic men's gold medal coach, I modified the nine-zone system (Figure 17.3) by naming nine symmetrical positions with numbers 1 and 9 not outside the antennae (thus 6 becomes the most common position for the setter/target). Each slot is 1 meter wide. For the first time, attack corridors were designated (A, B, C and D) for back-row attackers. This is now the generally accepted method of terminology for U.S. offensive systems. It will be used throughout this chapter to explain offensive combinations.

GENERAL CONCEPTS

The idea behind the offense of the U.S. national teams is to force the blockers to pinch in because of the attackers' inside moves. Then the attacker can get the ball to the outside of the outside blockers, forcing them to reach away from the court to block the ball. We want to give our attack a cumulative effect by always initiating our offensive patterns the same way. Each attack approach requires very specific footwork and attack angle, but individual differences are allowable if the desired effect is obtained. All attackers run their patterns all of the time; continuous movement in the play set roles is essential to developing the cumulative effect we want.

The setter jump sets whenever possible; the offense and the passing are designed for jump sets. The setter's responsibility is to establish the same correct position every time. It is the attacker's responsibility to establish the correct position and timing relationship with the setter.

If possible, we threaten with all five attackers. Players must understand and be able to execute both individual and team offensive tactics effectively. We concentrate our attack on the deep corners off the quick sets and off many play set combinations.

We use a specific one- or two-word communication system. If this system is insufficient, we verbally call the play or set and rely on beating the defense with execution. The setter can audibly call off any play that is not developing properly; attackers then go to the next highest option. This strategy generally keeps the player in the same slot but raises the set or slows the play down. Some situations will signal automatic pattern adjustments. For example, when any pass crosses the midline to the left, the play set hitter options to a 94 (called by the setter or the hitter).

FUNDAMENTAL APPROACHES

This discussion assumes right-handed players; for a left-handed player, reverse left and right side attack positions. (A left-handed middle attacker requires further modifications in the system.) All approaches off of service reception are basic four-step approaches (RL, RL) except that of the middle hitter, which will most often be three-step (LRL) and sometimes two step (RL). The approach angles are straight lines as detailed in Figure 17.4

The Left Side (Number 4 Attacker) Approach

Hitting high outside, the left front player in position 4 moves to about a 45-degree angle to the net and takes a full accelerating four-step approach (Figure 17.5). Hitting the 13 or 14, the left front moves more up to the line with a quicker, more abbreviated approach. The player must start more closely to the 3-meter line. The timing on the 13 has the setter touching the ball as the number 4 attacker is going into the last two (RL) steps of the approach.

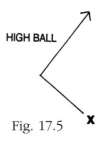

HIGH BALL

Fig. 17.5

HIGH
The Middle Attacker Approach

The middle attacker may line up in a variety of receive positions. But the approach and the result will always be the same. The keys to a successful middle attack are:

- The hitter's ability to establish a consistent position and timing relationship with the setter;
- The hitter's ability to see the setter, blockers and opponents' court;
- The hitter's ability to be in an attack-available position every time; and
- The hitter's developing range out of the middle.

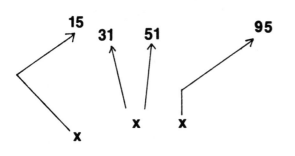

Fig. 17.4

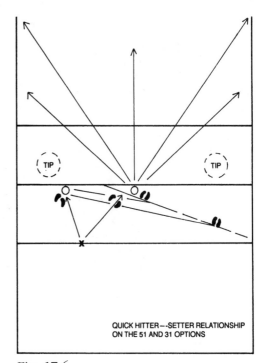

QUICK HITTER–-SETTER RELATIONSHIP
ON THE 51 AND 31 OPTIONS

Fig. 17.6

The attacker never goes past the imaginary line created by the setter's feet and the net (Figure 17-6). The takeoff point is actually 50 cm (1 ft. 8 ins.) behind the line and the ball is contacted at the line. The line for the 31 runs from the setter's left foot to the 3 slot.

Three steps (LRL) or two (RL) may be used. The two-step approach is usually used in fast transition. The second and third steps are often not as long and as low as the basic approach, simply because there is not as much time, especially in transition. There is little opportunity for a strong heel-toe action, especially with the left foot (a third step). The feet hit almost flat-footed. The armswings (back and front) are also abbreviated. A very upright swing, with little backswing, is preferred. Quickness of attack and range of attack are most critical.

The quick hitter must get the hitting arm up as quickly as possible to provide a target for the setter.

The shoulders are at a 45-degree angle to the net, parallel with the imaginary line developed by the setter's feet. The ball is hit with a quick, short, upright armswing, since the big wind-up is not possible or particularly desirable. Also, the attack is mostly based on wrist action, with little time for shoulder rotation. The setter, in certain situations, may lead back to the hitter's left shoulder to force a rotation to get by an over-playing block.

The approach begins essentially from the same spot on the left edge of slot 4 at the 3-meter line. If the serve goes over the hitter's left shoulder, the hitter pivots facing the ball, uses the left foot to plant back toward the receiver, uses a rocker step and quickly goes left-right-left. If the ball goes over the hitter's right shoulder, the hitter pivots facing the ball, rocker steps off the right foot and goes left-right-left. The middle attacker is able to go to the 31 or 51 from the same spot (Figures 17.7, 17.8, and 17.9).

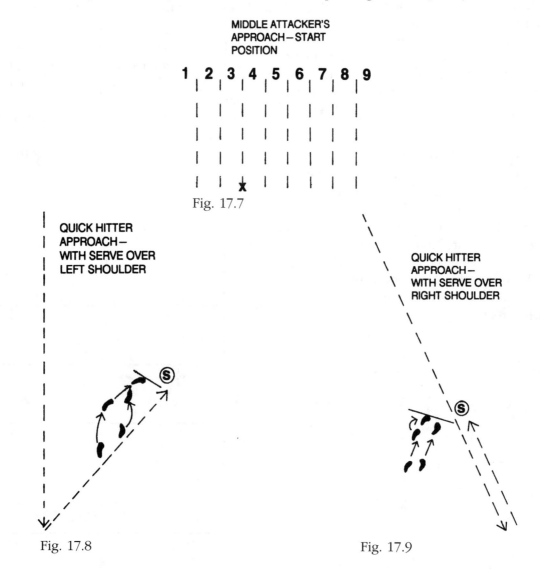

MIDDLE ATTACKER'S
APPROACH – START
POSITION

1   2   3   4   5   6   7   8   9

Fig. 17.7

QUICK HITTER
APPROACH –
WITH SERVE OVER
LEFT SHOULDER

QUICK HITTER
APPROACH –
WITH SERVE OVER
RIGHT SHOULDER

Fig. 17.8   Fig. 17.9

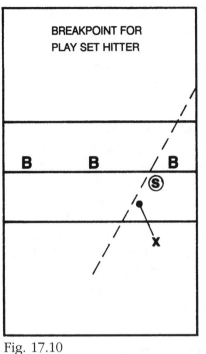

Fig. 17.10

The Play Set Hitter (Position No. 2)

The play set hitter (no. 2 position) initiates the break approximately 2.4 m (8 ft.) from a point on the net where the setter is in a direct line between the hitter and the opposing left side blocker (Figure 17.10). The play set hitter approaches each set on a straight line after either an appropriate fake or the break.

In terms of timing, the play set hitter makes a break just as the middle hitter is lifting off and the setter is contacting the ball. The left (or second) step of the four-step approach is planted approximately 2.4 m (8 ft.) deep, directly behind the setter, as the setter is contacting the ball.

For a wide X (33), the hitter (after the break) takes a long third (right) step, then plants the left foot in a position that puts the shoulders at a 45-degree angle to the net and allows the hitter to long jump to ball contact. For the regular X (43) the move is the same except slightly abbreviated. The tandem is hit in a position behind and between the setter and the middle hitter. The approach is right-left after the break, but shorter than the X plays. The fake X (73) is a pivot off the left foot break, then a right-left short drift to contact behind the setter. The flair-out (93) is the same pivot as the fake X (73) but uses a long right-left move with maximal long jump. The hitter floats to contact, catching up to the outside set. The ball is contacted outside the body line.

The X plays fade off the net so the ball is contacted 50 cm (1 ft. 8 ins.) behind the quick hitter. The flair-out is set parallel to the net or slightly toward the pin.

Deep Hitter Approaches

The back-row attacker hits release sets or play sets that are 1.8 to 2.4 m (6 to 8 ft.) high. There is no need for faking in the approach because the front-row play action is designed to screen back-row movements. The approach is the basic four-step approach. The lift-off should be just behind the attack line, with the left foot the closest. The hitter long jumps to the set. Timing is based on the design of the play and height and depth of the set. The position of this set is approximately 2 m (6 ft. 6 ins.) back from the net.

OFFENSIVE SIGNALS

Offensive signals can be given three ways:

1. Each spiker audibly or visibly calls each specific set.
2. The coach predetermines a specific play to match each defense the opponent shows.
3. The setter calls the team patterns.

Generally, I believe the setter should determine the team patterns (much as a carefully trained quarterback calls his own plays). While it is probably a good idea to allow communication between the spiker and the setter (a modification of No. 1), ultimately the setter should be able to determine specific weaknesses in the opposition, react to the situation and call for an offensive pattern that takes advantage of the current offensive strengths and defensive weaknesses.

Just as a baseball, basketball or football team has certain set patterns called by predetermined signals, so the volleyball team needs a series of patterns with specific signals. While the specific terminology of the nine-zone system described earlier in this chapter is useful during technical discussions (practices, time-outs), during competition you need a system that is more conducive to visible and audible communication. With one simple signal, the setter needs to be able to tell each of the three spikers his or her specific job on the current play. Thus, for example, Option 1 (signaled by using only the index finger) tells the left spiker to be ready for a regular (10), the center front spiker to hit a quick (71), and the right front to hit a back lob (93). By seeing that signal and recognizing that play, each spiker also knows his or her role in the overall team pattern.

Thus, there are three elements to the way an offensive combination is signalled:

1. A quick signal (hand or verbal) for quick communication during competition.
2. A two-digit number (or even number and letter) designation for accurate description and discussion.
3. The name of the team pattern or play.

Thus, on the team level, one play may be known as insides (or left inside, right inside); its sets may be designated as LF-52, MF-31 and RF-90 (92); and its signals may be thumbs up (left) or thumbs down (right). This may perhaps seem unwieldy, but in practice it works quite well. Tables 1 and 2 at the end of this chapter list the signals and sets used by the USA national team. Each coach and team will, of course, have their own different signals and sets.

OFFENSIVE SERIES AND RATIONALES

A play series consists of a group of plays designed to create specific effects on an element of the opponent's defense. The following discussion includes descriptions of six offensive play series, with illustrations and the rationale for each. (The parts of each series are listed in Table 3 at the end of this chapter.) Until they pass a test on the pattern presently being worked on, your team should not attempt another progression. Beginning with a pass, the team should successfully execute the pattern in 80 out of 100 attempts.

The 51 and 31 Series

The goal of the 51 and 31 series is to freeze the middle blocker and force the opponent's left side or No. 4 blocker to reach outside the court. The timing is designed to create seams in the block and a piston effect on the opponent's block. Used effectively, with good serve-receive and continual quick-hitter pressure, the combinations within these series can create uncontrolled movement on the block and shake the block timing. Table 3 and Figures 17.11 and 17.12 give more details on this series.

The Reverse Series

The reverse series forces the opponents' block to their left, opening up our left side. This series can be thrown in between the 51 or 31 series after the opponent has made adjustments to the 51 or 31. Also, this series permits the team to change assignments for the hitters, allowing the flexibility either to change tempo or to put a particular hitter on a specific blocker (Figure 17.13).

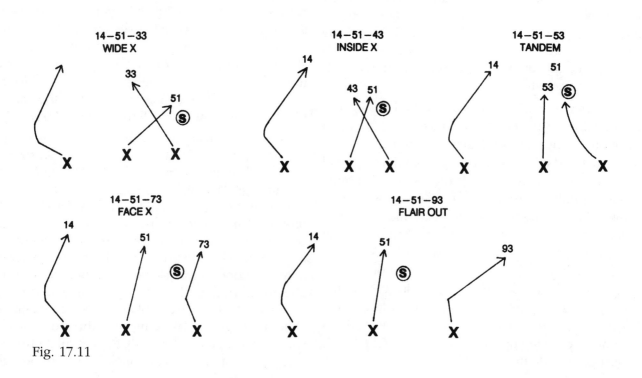

Fig. 17.11

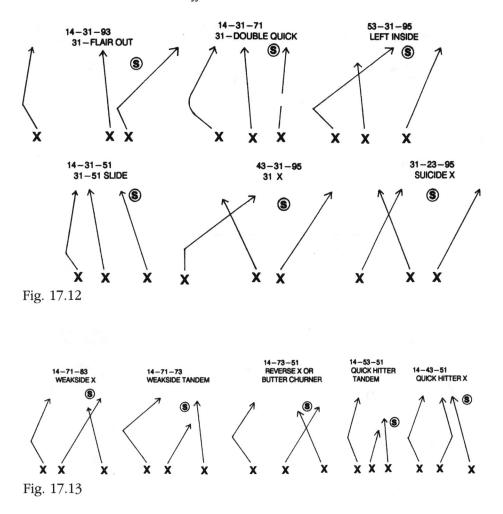

Fig. 17.12

Fig. 17.13

The Isolation Series

The isolation series is used only occasionally and with discretion. It has three purposes: to change tempo, to isolate and nail one blocker, and in critical point-making situations after the opponent has made a long, methodical comeback and/or after there have been many sideouts (Figure 17.14).

The deep hitting series is used to maximize all of the team's fire power, to change the angle and timing in the opponent's defense and to add an option if the team is in a front-row setter system (Figure 17.15).

The Spread Series

Once the other series have pinched the blockers inside, then the offense must get the ball to the outside of the blockers with low trajectory sets out to the pins. Blocking is most difficult when the blockers are forced to reach outside the court to block (Figure 17.16).

Innovations and Specific Sets

Four variations on the series described above are:

• Controlled deep corner hitting off quick sets and play sets: Most defenses are geared to play defense close in against the quick and play set attack. The corners are usually wide open.

• The fading X set (1 to 1.5 m or 3 ft. 3 ins. to 4 ft. 11 ins. off the net): The offense must add as many problems or variables to the opponents' blockers as possible. Timing a deeper set after gearing up for a tight set is difficult.

• Deep attack play sets: The use of the back-row attackers has traditionally been with high release sets. The intention is to put maximum pressure on planning and timing the block by using long back-row sets.

• The wide series: The offense gets the ball to the outside very rapidly, and then, slightly slower, to the middle as a safety valve.

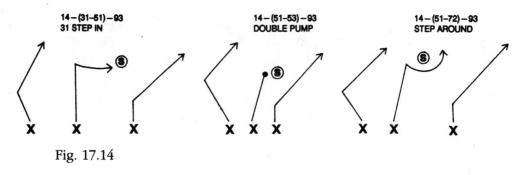

Fig. 17.14

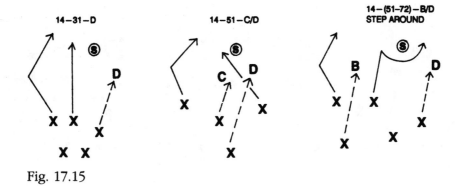

Fig. 17.15

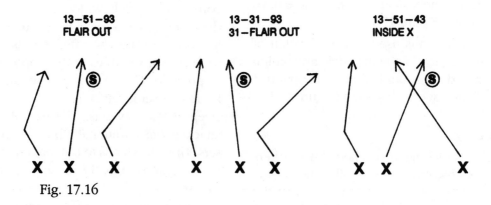

Fig. 17.16

SUMMARY

The names of various sets were standardized in 1966, but since then some of the sets have been redefined and new sets have been added. In 1972, a variation of the earlier standardization was composed. Each set is named with a two-digit number; the first number designates the attack position and the second number designates the height of the set.

All approaches off of service reception are basic four-step approaches and the middle hitter's approach is three-step or two-step. The various approaches include the left side approach, the middle attacker approach, the play set hitter approach and the deep hitter approach.

Offensive signals can be given three ways: the spiker can call each set; the coach can predetermine the play; or the setter can call the team patterns. The best way may be for the setter to determine the team patterns, because he or she may be best able to choose the offensive pattern that takes advantage of the current offensive and defensive situation.

The team should have a series of patterns with specific signals and the setter must be able to signal these visibly or audibly. There are three ways an offensive combination can be signalled: a hand or verbal signal during competition; a two-digit number; or the name of the team pattern or play.

A play series is a group of plays designed to create specific effects on an element of the opponent's defense. The team should be able to execute the pattern successfully 80 percent of the time. Six offensive play series are: the 51 and 31 series, the reverse series, the isolation series, the deep hitting series and the spread series. Four variations on the series are: controlled deep corner hitting off quick sets and play sets, the fading X set, deep attack play sets and the wide series.

Note: The first three paragraphs of this chapter are an adaptation of material first presented in "Recent Changes in the designation of Offensive Systems in Men's Volleyball" by Jim Coleman, in *International Volleyball Review*, Vol. XXIX (Jan.-Feb. 1973).

SET TERMINOLOGY		
HAND SIGNAL	**SET**	**DESCRIPTION/ZONE WHERE HIT**
Index finger	one set	Hitter is at peak of jump when the setter contacts the ball — the zone in relation to setter, 5–8.
	one and 1/2	Hitter takes off when the setter contacts the ball — the zone in relation to the setter, 5–8.
Index & middle fingers	two	Hitter is on the first step of a three-step approach when the setter contacts the ball — zone 5 & 6 — center of the net.
Wave of back of hand away from body.	31	Hitter takes off when the setter contacts the ball — zone 3.
Wave of back of hand with flash of two fingers.	32	Hitter on first step of three-step approach when the setter contacts the ball — zone 3.
Four fingers pointing down	Four (fast) 12	Hitter on first step of three-step approach when the setter contacts the ball — zone 1 (12).
Five fingers pointing down.	Five (fast) 92	Hitter on first step of three-step approach when the setter contacts the ball — zone 9 (92).
OTHER SETS		
Fist	regular	zone 1, 5–6, 9
Four fingers — pointing up	regular — four	zone 1 (14)
Four fingers — pointing down	regular — five	zone 9 (94)
Index & middle finger on fist of other hand.	high two	zone 5–6

On the above four sets, begin approach when the ball is halfway in its flight, at the peak of its arc.
"Once you start your approach, do not stop until you hit the ball." (ARM SWING: FORWARD – BACK – FORWARD)

Circle formed index finger & thumb (OK signal)	pump – one	Fake one set then hit a two (low).

Table 1: Quick Communication Signals

PLAYS	**PLAY**	**SETS**	**SIGNAL**
1. Insides	a. Left inside b. Right inside	LF–52 MF–31 RF–90 (92)	Thumbs up Thumbs down
2. X or Fake X	a. X b. Fake X	LF–10 (14 or 12) MF–61 RF–52 LF–10 (14 or 12) MF–61 RF–82	Cross fingers Index & middle Wave of cards Index & middle fingers
3. Outsides	a. b.	LF–14 (10) MF–31 RF–82 (71–back) LF–14 (10) MF–31 RF–95 (92)	Pinky out Index finger & pinky out
4. Combine out- sides & insides	a. b.	LF–52 MF–31 RF–82 (81) LF–52 MF–31 RF–95 (92)	Thumb up & pinky out Thumb up, pinky & index out
5. Green/yellow back court switch (back court fakes)	Yellow Green	MF–90 LF–14 (12) RB–Fake 61 RF–82 (81) MF–10 LF–32 LB–Fake 61 RF–92	
6. Trick plays— back court fakes, pump ones			
7. Blocking serve plays			
8. Setter tipping (as back court player)			
9. 5–1 disguised as 6–2; setter tips or hits front court.			

Table 2: Team Pattern Signals

SERIES	NUMBERED SETS	PLAY NUMBER	NICKNAME	COACH'S SIGNAL
51 SERIES Quick hitter has option of hitting 51 or 71 based on position of MB, except on play #4	14–51–33 14–51–43 14–51–53 14–51–73 14–51–93	1 2 3 4 5	Wide X Inside X Tandem Fake X Flair Out	
31 SERIES	14–31–93 14–31–71 52–31–95 14–31–51 43–31–95 31–23–95	1 2 3 4 5 6	31–Flair Out Double Quick Left Inside 31–51 Slide 31 X Suicide X	Hook 'em Horns
REVERSE SERIES	14–83–71 14–73–71 14–73–51 14–53–51 14–43–51	1 2 3 4 5	Weakside X WeaksideTandem Reverse X: Butterchurner Quick Hitter Tandem Quick Hitter X	
ISOLATION SERIES	14–[31 51]–93 14–[51 53]–93 14–[51 72]–93	1 2 3	31 Step In Double Pump Step Around	
BACK ROW SERIES (Plays referred to here indicate the setter at the net). These can be run with 3 front row attackers.	14–31–D 14–51 Slide C/D 14–51 Step Around B/D 51–33X A/C/D 51–93 A/B/D 31–93 A/C/D	1 2 3 4 5 6		
SPREAD SERIES	13–51–93 13–31–93 13–51–93	1 2 3	Flair Out 31 Flair Out Inside X	

Table 3: Offensive Series

Photo Courtesy of Fresno State

Chapter 18

SERVICE RECEPTION

Dave Shoji

Volleyball coaches change their serve reception formations for many different reasons. Hiding a weak passer and running a quick attack are two of the reasons for variations of the standard W formation. The most important consideration in deciding what pattern to use for serve reception is a team's ability to cover the court efficiently. The next most important consideration is that the setters be able to get to the desired area quickly enough. If either of these considerations is not met by the current service reception, the coach's offensive system cannot be implemented at all. Thus, the serve reception system being used must satisfy these two requirements.

This chapter describes the basic service reception formation (the W) and its use with the 4-2 system, the 6-2 system (including the cup formation) and a number of special formations based on the 5-1 system.

THE W FORMATION

The W formation is the most versatile, reliable service reception formation for most beginning teams. The W formation uses five passers to cover the court, regardless of front- and back-row considerations. The players are positioned as shown in Figure 18.1. Thus, the term W formation is used.

The formation should be placed on the court according to where the server stands. A general rule is that players 1 and 3 should stand on a direct line from the server to the corner of the court (Figure 18.2). Serves that fall in the shaded area are considered low percentage to attempt, so passers are concentrated between the two shaded areas. The rest of the formation requires even spacing between all players.

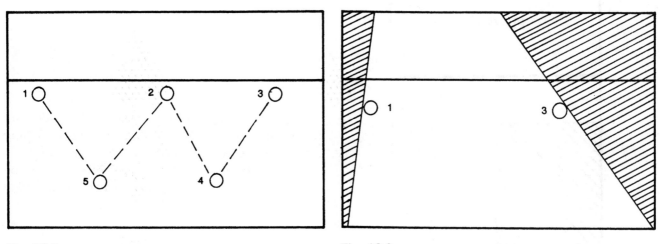

Fig. 18.1   Fig. 18.2

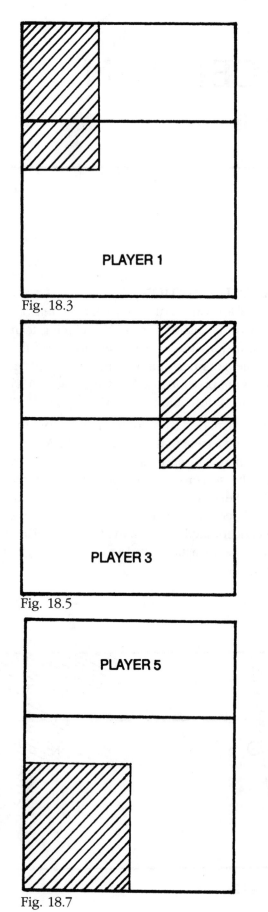

Fig. 18.3

Fig. 18.5

Fig. 18.7

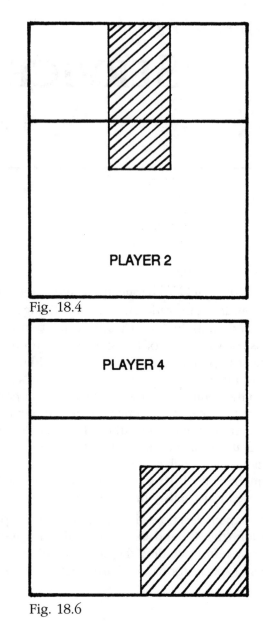

Fig. 18.4

Fig. 18.6

The passing responsibilities in the W formation are shown in Figures 18.3, 18.4, 18.5, 18.6 and 18.7. Note that players 4 and 5 have much more area to cover than do players 1, 2 or 3. These players must be aware of this fact and be ready to cover this wide area.

The 4-2 System

The W formation can be utilized with a 4-2, 5-1 or 6-2 offensive system. In the 4-2 system, the setter may be placed at the net and the two remaining front-court players lined up in positions 1, 2 or 3 (Figure 18.1). More specifically, when the setter is in the left front position, the hitters may be placed in the spread formation (Figure 18.8).

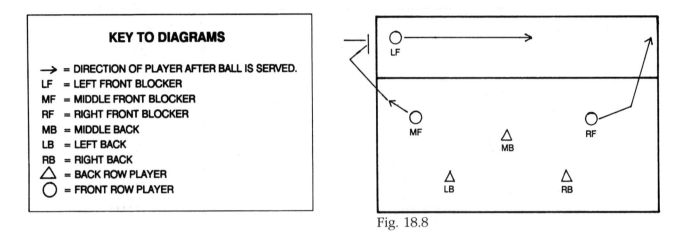

Fig. 18.8

The hitters may also be lined up in a shift formation, with attackers hitting the left front and the middle front as shown in Figure 18.9.

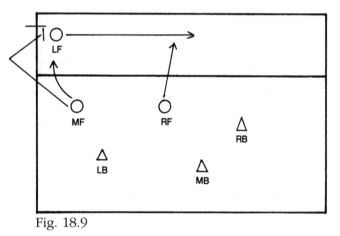

Fig. 18.9

A third option would be for the spikers to be shifted on the right side of the court, hitting from the middle front and the right front positions (Figure 18.10).

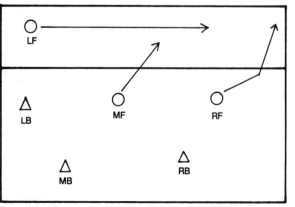

Fig. 18.10

When the setter is in the middle front, the same three options are available. The spikers are at the left and right front positions. (Figures 18.11, 18.12, and 18.13).

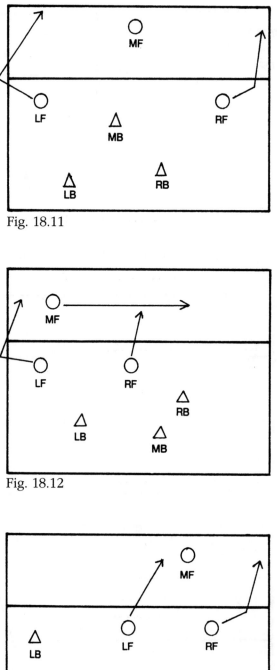

Fig. 18.11

Fig. 18.12

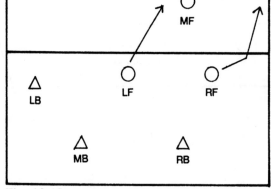

Fig. 18.13

When the setter is in the right front, the same three options are available. The spikers then are at the left front and the middle front positions (Figures 18.14, 18.15, and 18. 16).

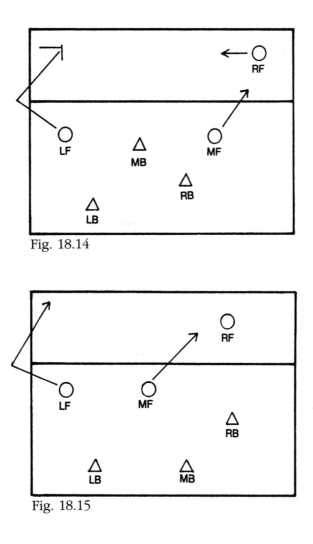

Fig. 18.14

Fig. 18.15

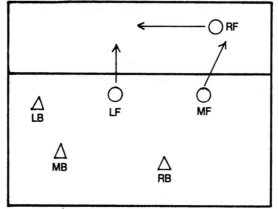

Fig. 18.16

The position of the setter before the ball is served may be varied to try to deceive the opposing team. The setter may appear to be a back-row player so that your team seems to have three attackers. Figures 18.17, 18.18, and 18.19 provide three examples of this.

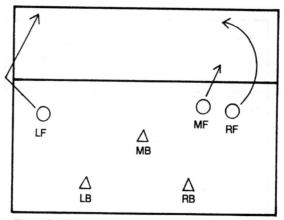

Fig. 18.17

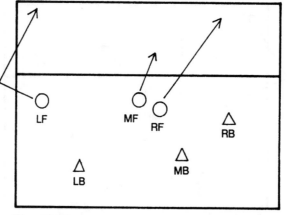

Fig. 18.18

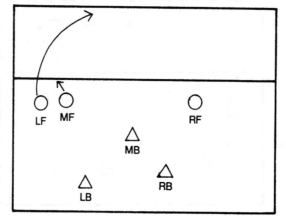

Fig. 18.19

The 6-2 System

In the 6-2 offensive system, a back-row setter with three attackers is utilized and the alignment is basically the same. The setter starts behind a front-row player and moves to the net after the ball is served. The ideal position for the setter is between 2.4 and 3.7 m (8 and 12 ft.) from the right sideline. This position allows the setter to face the left and middle attackers (Figure 18.20).

When the setter is in the right back, he or she stands to the right and behind the right front player. When the ball is served, the setter runs to the designated (shaded) area (Figure 18.21).

When the setter is in the middle back, he or she lines up on the right behind the middle front player (Figure 18.22).

A setter who is in the left back may line up two different ways. In Figure 18.23, the setter lines up to the left and behind the left front player. In Figure 18.24, the setter lines up to the right and behind the left front player. The setter cuts diagonally across the court to the desired area. In either case, this is the most difficult position from which the setter must reach the right front area.

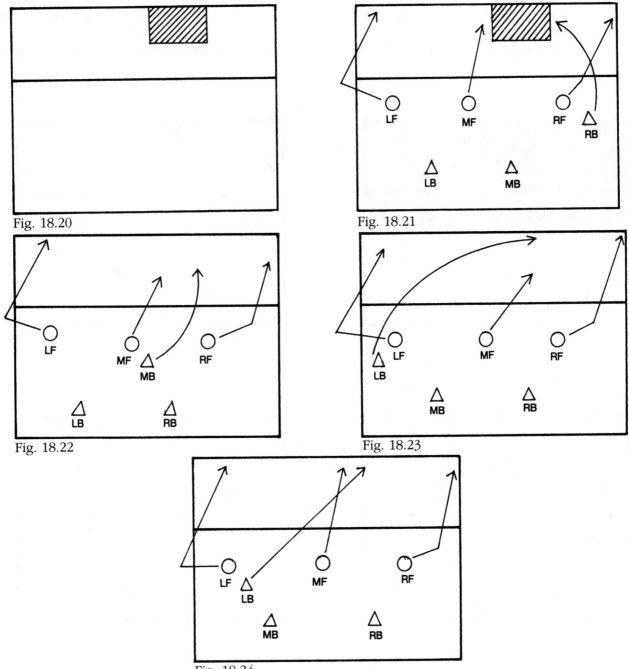

Fig. 18.20

Fig. 18.21

Fig. 18.22

Fig. 18.23

Fig. 18.24

The Cup Formation

The four-player or cup formation is also used with the 6-2 offensive system. The main reason for using the cup formation is that the middle (quick) hitter does not pass, which enables the hitter to hit a quick set easier. The middle front area is covered by the left and right front players. The back-row players have the same responsibilities as they do in the W formation (Figure 18.25).

Left Front Responsibility/Right Front Responsibility

When the setter is in the right back, the quick hitter is at the net. After the ball is served, the quick hitter comes back off the net to approach for the quick hit as the setter runs to the right front area (Figure 18.26).

If your quick hitter is in the right front in this rotation, bring the right front player to the net with the setter and place the middle front player to the right side of the court. This allows the quick hitter to get to the middle of the court faster (Figure 18.27).

When the setter is in the middle back, both the setter and the middle front player come to the net. After the ball is served, the setter backs into position and the quick hitter gets off the net for the approach (Figure 18.28).

Two other options may be used when the setter is in the middle back. Both options force the setter to stand in the middle of the court as if passing. Once the ball is in play, however, the setter must quickly run to the

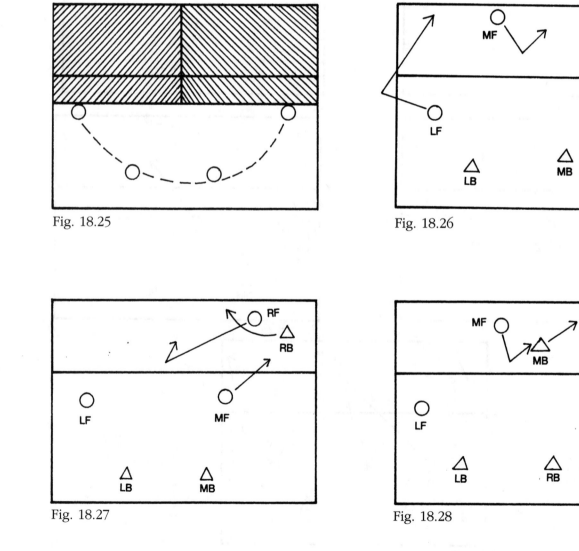

Fig. 18.25

Fig. 18.26

Fig. 18.27

Fig. 18.28

setting position. In Figure 18.29, the quick hitter is in the left front and the middle front hits outside on the left. In Figure 18.30, the quick hitter is in the right front and the middle front hits outside on the right.

When the setter is in the left back, he or she comes to the net with the left front player, but stands behind that player. The setter may move to the right so as to line up just to the left of the middle back. This allows the setter to be closer to the right front area. There are two options from this formation. Either the left front or the middle front player may hit the quick set, with the other hitting outside on the left. Figure 18.31 illustrates Option 1 and Figure 18.32 illustrates Option 2.

The 5-1 System

Some teams on the international level have designed special formations to take advantage of great passers and/or hide weak passers. These patterns vary widely and coaches should be very careful when utilizing these methods. Other factors are often involved in formulating these service reception patterns, such as the role of back-row attackers in a particular offense. Figures 18.33, 18.34, 18.35, 18.36, 18.37 and 18.38 show six formations that utilize a 5-1 offensive system with the same two players doing all of the passing. Needless to say, these two players must be exceptionally quick and must also have great passing skills.

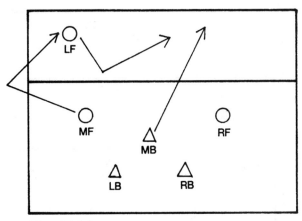

Fig. 18.29

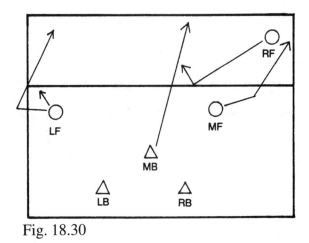

Fig. 18.30

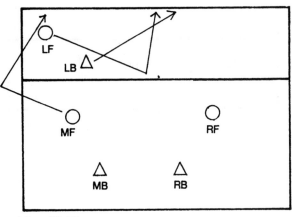

Fig. 18.31

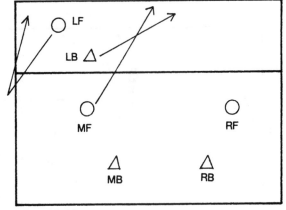

Fig. 18.32

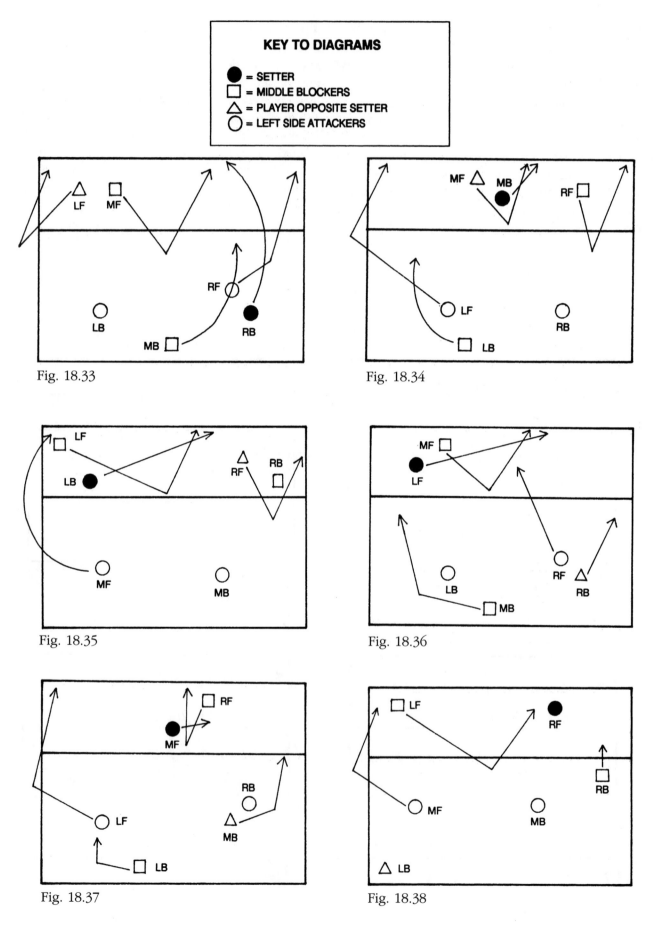

Fig. 18.33

Fig. 18.34

Fig. 18.35

Fig. 18.36

Fig. 18.37

Fig. 18.38

In the formation shown in Figure 18.33, LB and RF pass the entire court. MB moves to the right to hit a back-row set. In the formation shown in Figure 18.34, LF and RB again pass the entire court.

In the next rotation, the same two passers are now in middle front and back as seen in Figure 18.35. Then RB moves to the right to hit the back-row set, which is the third option, and RF may hit the play set or swing to the left (Figure 18.36).

In Figure 18.37, LB does not pass. MB swings to the right to hit the back-row set. In Figure 18.38, RB may hit the back-row set.

A team that wants to utilize three passers may line up in the manner shown in Figures 18.39, 18.40, 18.41, 18.42, 18.43 and 18.44. In this three-pass system, the middle blockers do not pass at all. The player opposite the setter and the outside attackers pass the entire court. The three passers' responsibilities change from the previous systems. They now must cover less court from side to side, but must cover more court from the end line to the net. This may be an advantage in one way, but a disadvantage in another.

In the previous two systems (two-player and three-player receive formations), there is always a front-court player involved in the passing. When this front-court player moves deep to pass a serve, this player may not be able to be involved in the offense. Therefore, the team must have other hitting options. Usually teams will involve a back-row attack, with the back-court middle blocker hitting this set. The middle blocker must maneuver into position when the serve is in the air.

SUMMARY

When trying to decide what pattern to use for serve reception, the most important consideration must be the ability of the team to cover the court efficiently. The second consideration should be whether or not the setter or setters can get to the desired area quickly enough.

A coach can implement his or her offensive system when these two considerations have been met.

The basic serve reception formation is the W formation and it can be used with the 4-2, the 6-2 and the 5-1 offensive systems. Coaches and players should know the positioning options available to them with each system.

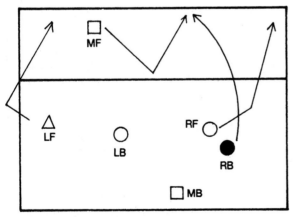

Fig. 18.39

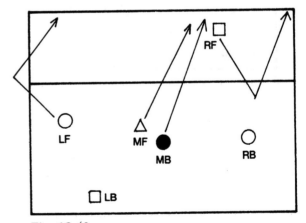

Fig. 18.40

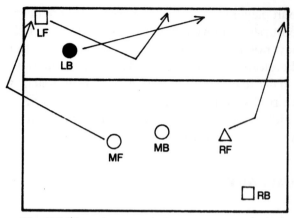

Fig. 18.41

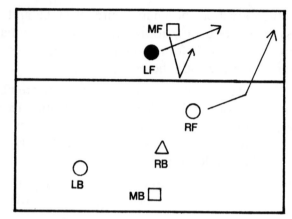

Fig. 18.42

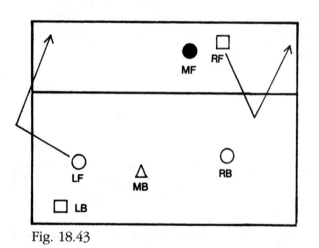

Fig. 18.43

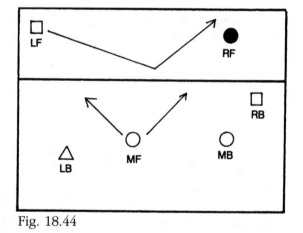

Fig. 18.44

Photo by Dan Houser

NET DEFENSE
OPTION BLOCKING
Jim Coleman

For the team desiring a fixed system for every blocking situation, this article has little to say but "good luck." For the team wishing to optimize the capabilities of its athletes, there is much to be gained for virtually any team at any level.

One of the reasons that the 1984 USA men's Olympic team was among the best in the world was that its members very successfully employed a rather complex system of option blocking, yet they were talented enough that standard blocking systems may have worked almost as well. Teams with less-talented athletes have more to gain by choosing the correct blocking options.

THE BASIC PREMISE OF BLOCKING

At the 1974 World Championships for men, I found that blocking was the best predictor of tournament rank. I also found that as a predictor of point spread, blocking was second only to attacking. Because of these statistical findings, it seems apparent that the teams with the best blocking will win the most games, matches and tournaments.

There is an abundance of literature on blocking techniques. Coaches will launch into long discourses on the various techniques of blocking, but few pay attention to the tactical strategy of blocking. Blocking technique is generally considered to be the most difficult skill to learn and as a result, many coaches believe that an outstanding blocker will play almost irrespective of other skills.

In recent years, there have been tremendous improvements in offensive strategy, while defensive improvement appears to be either in techniques or in the execution of predetermined patterns. Defensive patterns are routine and have altered little in the past few years. In fact, defensive strategy may even have fallen backward during this era. Today, defensive positions are often dictated by offensive considerations, whereas 20 years ago defensive patterns were based upon defensive considerations. It is false economy to preempt good defense in the guise of offensive potential. Without defense, offensive considerations are a moot point. Thus, it is not wise to make defensive decisions based upon offensive considerations.

The Role of Probability

All volleyball strategies should be established on a probability basis. That is, all strategies should be designed so as to give the highest probability for total success of the team. Thus, great offensive potential is of little value if there is no defense. Likewise, great defensive potential is of little value if there is no potential for transition to an effective offense.

Interestingly enough, very little is known about the probabilities of success in volleyball. The majority of decisions are made on gut-level feelings rather than on hard data. As a matter of fact, almost no coaches — or even researchers — approach volleyball on a probability basis. Yet players and coaches alike copy each other with some intuitive feelings that what is being copied is high probability volleyball.

Parallel Sports

For initial considerations, the basic tactical ideas in similar sports must be studied. Basketball and football are similar enough to volleyball that much can be learned from their strategies.

Zone vs. Man-to-Man. In both basketball and football, defense takes one of two general forms: either zone or man-to-man. The same is true in volleyball. There are two implications to the zone/man-to-man idea. The original idea was that if the blocker did not stuff the ball (essentially man-to-man), the block should screen out an area of the court (zone). With predictable zones of the court screened out from hard attacks, the digging zones on the court are diminished in size and the probability of the ball being dug when hit into a digging zone is increased.

Today, there is another possibility for the man-to-man defense: a blocker is designated to follow a specific spiker no matter where the attacker may move, making for perhaps a more pure form of man-to-man defense. This parallel between sports can continue, for in the man-to-man concept, if my attacker does not get the ball, I then have the opportunity to become an assist blocker to help my teammates.

Mismatching Abilities. Basketball and football strategies call for producing mismatches of ability on offense and for matching abilities on defense. Thus, in basketball, the offensive team continues to run, pass and screen until a player is entirely free to shoot or until a strong shooter is matched (mismatched) against a weak defender. On defense, strengths are matched against an opponent's offensive strengths and defensive weaknesses are hidden by matching them against an opponent's offensive weaknesses. These same considerations should be made in volleyball. However, volleyball is different from basketball and football in that players must play both net and back-court and the decision time to run a play is limited by the number of hits (three) per side.

In basketball defense, a weak defender is better than no defender; hence, even a tiny guard attempts to harass the giant center who is shooting. However, in volleyball this is not a wise option because a weak blocker tends to be worse than no blocker. A weak blocker often turns the mediocre spiker into an offensive superstar. The weak blocker is not only "used" by the spiker, but also disrupts the digger's ability to play effective defense. A good defensive option, which few coaches choose, is not to block.

Another consideration from football which we may apply is to stack the defense on each play against the most probable offensive option on that play. For instance, if a football team has to defend against third down and 15 yards to go, the defense will drop off linemen and replace them with pass defenders. If there is a fourth down and 6 inches, the defense will load with defensive linemen and linebackers.

In volleyball, there are not these substitution options, but there are options on the deployment of the defensive players. Each time a team serves, the serving team, now on defense, has the option of blocker deployment. Probability dictates that the best blockers should be deployed against the receiving team's most probable offensive option. If the serving team scores because the attacker is not successful, the probability that the same attacker will get the next set is diminished and blocking may need to be changed. With wise calculation of probabilities and a little luck, weak blockers often will never have to block on an entire trip across the net. At the same time, the defensive team will score points.

Defensive Deployment

Two other strategies can improve the probabilities of strong blockers blocking and weak blockers not blocking. The first is to make a good choice of serving targets. Effective serves to sidelines or to selected front-court receivers can limit the receiver's offensive options. This strategy may increase the probability of strong blockers blocking and weak blockers avoiding the block. Second, blockers can fake movements to a given position and in this way confuse the opposing setters. Often setters are so engaged in keeping track of weak blockers that they become ineffective setters.

Not only do defensive teams have the option of blocker deployment, but they also may choose various defenses. In a given game or match, a specific defense or defensive modification may be chosen. Sophisticated teams have many options. For instance, a team may choose to vary defenses on each serve and may keep the defense hidden until it is too late for the offense to know what is happening. The USA men's team won the 1967 Pan Am Games and defeated the Soviets in the 1968 Olympic Games using a hidden defense system. The center back player kept an intermediate position until the ball was approaching the opponent's setter. At that moment, he moved into the predetermined red (6-up) or white (6-back) defensive position.

Today it is common for a team to run different defenses based upon specific hitters or on specific sides of the court. A team may run a standard defense against a power hitter hitting from the left side of the court, and, at the same time, may run a rotation defense against a different hitter who is hitting from the right side of the court. There are teams which always run standard against left side attacks and a rotation against right side attacks.

A wise coach frequently bases the starting team's rotational position on various offensive and/or defensive match-ups. Often high-jumping, slow blockers do not do well against combination plays, but will stop high regular sets quite well. On the other hand, shorter, quicker blockers do well against combinations, but are helpless against the high regular sets. Creating the appropriate match-ups may increase a team's probability for success.

The Assist Block

Not all blockers have equal blocking abilities, yet weak blockers are repeatedly given assignments which would challenge power blockers. This practice can be avoided. Many times weak blockers are assigned to block next to more skillful blockers. When this situation occurs, the good blocker should be given the freedom to position the block and to block in a one-on-one manner, with the weaker blocker assuming the role of the assist blocker.

The assist blocker performs two functions. First, the assist blocker fills the hole next to the principle blocker. This prevents the low, off-the-arm shots which sometimes plague good blockers. Second, the assist blocker soft blocks, which has two effects: 1) it forces the spiker to hit higher, and 2) it makes the ball easier to dig. By concentrating on soft blocking rather than on blocking kills, a player who is a weak principal blocker can avoid blocking errors and become a contributing assist blocker.

THE BOLD STRATEGY OF OPTION BLOCKING

The idea behind option blocking is that in order to gain defensive probabilities, the blockers will commit to, or overload on, a play, a player or a position. There are four separate but not completely independent components of option blocking. These are: 1) read versus committed blocking; 2) positional commitment; 3) positional overload; and 4) stack blocking.

Read Versus Committed Blocking

The quick middle sets (sets 51, 61 and 71) were conceived with several goals in mind. The first, obviously, was that they could score points. The second was that, since the spiker jumped before the ball was set, the blocker would also have to jump early (committed block) in order to stop the attack. If the blocker committed before the ball was set, the blocker, with feet in air, would have a difficult time moving to block balls set quickly to the outside. The immobilization of the center blocker is quite an effective technique against most teams. The third goal was to give the center blocker as many choices as possible, because the more choices the center blocker has to process, the slower is his or her reaction to the specific set being made.

Today, bigger and smarter center blockers are taking another option to stop the middle and to be effective on other sets. They are not jumping with the quick attacker. Instead, they are waiting for the ball to be set and attempting to read the setter-hitter combination. They are often conceding the high, quick, middle attacks and are tiptoe blocking the more common lower, slower or mis-timed plays. They are then free to move to combination plays or outside sets. Center blockers who are tall and have good perception of the entire offensive system of their opponents are doing very well with the read blocking maneuver.

Positional Commitment

In this form of option blocking, the blocking team commits a player to a specific potential quick set. The option blocking tactics used by the USA men's team in 1979 and 1980 were as follows: option four blocking, option three blocking and option two blocking.

Option Four Blocking. The defensive left front blocker, position 4, is committed to jump with — to block — the opponent's quick middle attack (71 set). The reason for using this tactic is to defend against a probable X or crossing pattern. With the middle hitter stopped by the outside blocker, the middle blocker can concentrate on stopping the opponent's second attacker coming into the middle on the crossing pattern. If the play is run into offensive zones 8 or 9 (to the left of the committed blocker), the offense has won the tactical battle. At this point, the defense has two weak hopes. The committed blocker may be able to recover enough to make a blocking attempt. The best chance for the defense is for the zone 5 digger (down the line) to be prepared to dig the unblocked shot. For this reason, it is important that the diggers be knowledgeable about the blocking options being employed. If the zone 5 digger knows that unblocked digging is the first responsibility, the digger will have a chance to be successful. If there is no knowledge of the probability of this unblocked attack, the probability of digging success is quite low. In the commonly used defenses today, too often the outside blocker gets caught guessing on the inside block and the zone 5 digger is caught unaware of this extra responsibility. Thus, while processing other less likely possible shots, the zone 5 digger misses the major, unblocked one.

Option Three Blocking. The center blocker, position 3, is committed to jump with — to block — the offensive quick hit (sets 31 to 71). For many years, this has been the standard defense to stop middle attacks. The primary blocking will be one-on-one and the defense will be vulnerable to crossing patterns. In order to defend against the crossing patterns, the outside blockers may pinch toward the center blocker. With this strategy, the threat of the crossing play has virtually assured offensive success to relatively quick outside sets (14s and 94s). This success has been made even more probable by the choice of outside blockers. Usually the bigger, better blockers are in the middle, committed to the "one" sets which take little mobility to stop and the smaller and/or less mobile blockers on the outside are responsible for the quick, mobile actions which they are incapable of stopping.

Option Two Blocking. In option two blocking, the front right blocker (position 2) is committed to jump with — to block — the offense 31 set (many teams call the 31 a 3 set — a quick set about 3 m or 10 ft. from the left offensive sideline). The reason for using this defense is to stop a probable 31 set, to defend a left side X-play or to defend the left inside plays. This option leaves the defensive right side (position 2) vulnerable to quick outside attacks (14 sets). Considerations here are similar to those discussed in the section on option four blocking.

Positional Overload. Positional overload deserves the greatest amount of consideration, for it is the boldest of the option blocking tactics and it holds the most practical application for a team that is mismatched on defense. It is also the most easily applied by a less-experienced team. Two concepts are important in positional overload:

1. Overload the blockers on the best or most probable hitter.
2. Invite the opponent's weak hitter to be set.

To approach this concept, consider the case in which one very weak blocker is at the net, along with two relatively strong blockers, and they are facing an opponent who has three respectable hitters. Some coaches would choose to have all three blockers in blocking roles, but there is another alternative, and that is to use only the two good blockers and allow the other player to dig. If this third player cannot block, it is hoped that he or she is a good digger. Assign one blocker, commonly the blocker second in ability, to go man-on-man with the opposition's best outside hitter on the net. Have the other blocker assigned to block both other hitters, but cheating toward the better one (Figure 19.1).

With this blocking alignment, the weak blocker is now a digger, which is that player's preferred position. Now there is one certain blocker on the best hitter and occasionally there will be two blockers on that hitter's high sets. There will always be a blocker on the no. 2 hitter and there will usually be a blocker on the no. 3 hitter. Of course, the defense invites the setter to set the number 3 hitter, hence, a defensive victory. It is often found that the no. 1 blocker is perceptive enough to pick up crossing patterns of the no. 2 and 3 hitters. Many times the best blocker will have a greater probability of stopping the crossing patterns alone than two blockers would if one of those blockers is very weak.

The essence of positional overload is to continue this manner of thinking to cover the situations in which blocking assignments different from the routine ones should be considered. In the most common of

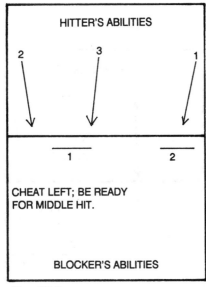

Fig. 19.1

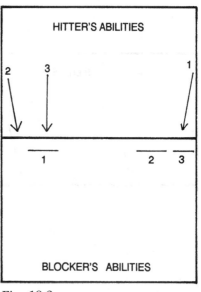

Fig. 19.2

these, two blockers are used to stop the more routine, but more devastating, power hitters, while one blocker defends against two less powerful hitters. The defensive alignment might be the one shown in Figure 19.2.

Defensive position 2 has been overloaded to stop the most probable hit. The weaker hitters are invited to attack the ball, while the most perceptive blocker is allowed to do what he or she does best and that is to move to block the ball unhampered by surrounding blockers. It is strongly recommended that this option be considered any time the offensive team passes poorly. It is also probable that there are times when the blockers wish to disguise this overload until the offensive setter sets the ball.

The deployment of blockers will depend upon the individual blocking skills and the relative skill levels of the offensive players. If the no. 1 hitter is so dominant as to get "all" of the sets, then the defensive no. 1 blocker should probably go with that hitter. When the no. 3 blocker is not a strong principal blocker, the no. 2 and 3 blockers should shift positions. In this situation, the no. 2 blocker should be allowed to go one-on-one against the strong hitter, with the weaker blocker blocking in the middle, using an assist block to stop lower, cross-court shots (Figure 19.3). Similar strategies may be worked out with the best offensive hitters in other attacking positions.

Overload blocking should be considered if the offense is using a front-court setter. Too many teams

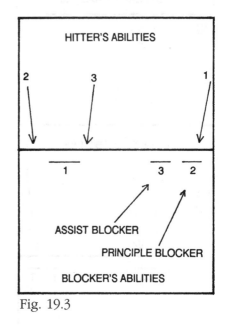

Fig. 19.3

deploy weak blocking tactics only for the resulting offensive simplicity (Figure 19.4). Offensive transitions do not occur if the ball cannot be dug — this system invites defensive disasters.

In this common defensive strategy, the best two blockers are enamored with the offensive no. 2 hitter faking in the middle. Meanwhile, the offensive power hitter is having a field day against the setter, who is a weak blocker. The defensive considerations should be as shown in Figures 19.5, 19.6 or 19.7.

With the appropriate choice of these alignments, the offensive "outside cannon" will not have a free

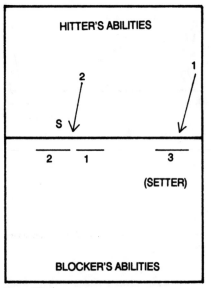

Fig. 19.4

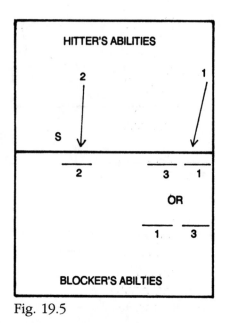

Fig. 19.5

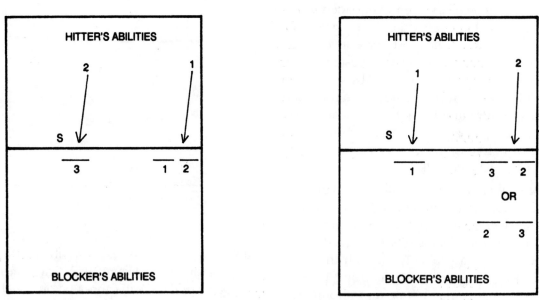

Fig. 19.6

Fig. 19.7

KEY TO DIAGRAMS

N = NORMAL OUTSIDE BLOCKER
C = COMMITTED BLOCKER
S = STACKED BLOCKER
Ⓢ = OFFENSIVE SETTER
S = STACKED BLOCKER FOLLOWS TO
     COMBINATION (POSITION 2) B.

shot at killing the ball. But there will be some defensive challenge to this powerful hitting. With the deployment of the no. 3 blocker (setter) either on the outside or in the middle, there are two advantages:

1. The offensive transition, which has a higher probability of happening now can still take place.
2. If no. 3 should be an assist blocker, the assist blocker may be better in the middle (Figures 19.5 and 19.7) because balls hit over no. 3 will be more easily dug. If no. 3 is on the outside, the probability of the weak blocker being "used" or "tooled" is great.

Stack Blocking

The stack blocking system is commonly used against teams that use crossing patterns effectively. A blocking stack consists of one blocker positioned near the net in normal blocking position and a second blocker positioned slightly behind and to the side of the first blocker. The first close blocker is normally committed to the fast attacker sets (sets 51, 71, and 81). The second stacked blocker then follows the attacker hitting the combination set.

For instance, if an offensive team runs an X or a fake X play, the committed blocker will jump with the quick middle attack (set 71). The stacked blocker will follow the offensive position 2 (right side) hitter (Figure 19.8). If the fake X is run, the stacked blocker blocks on the outside. If the X is run, the stacked blocker becomes the middle blocker.

There are a great number of options with blocking stacks. If, in Figure 19.8, the fake X or normal outside sets are most common, the stacked blocker is stacked on the outside of the committed blocker. If the X is most common, the stacked blocker should then stack on the inside of the committed blocker (Figure 19.9).

Stacks can be used on the right side of the court if there is a high probability for an offensive left side combination and a 31 set. These are less common than the right side combinations. In addition, other options are available to stacked blocking teams. Often the stacked blocker will be perceptive enough to read the setter on the quick sets and will be able to assist the committed blockers.

It is not always the normal middle blocker who is the committed blocker in the stack. The choice of blocking positions should be decided by probabilities of attack and blocking success. So the usual middle

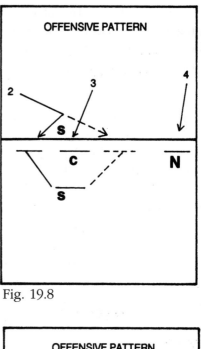

Fig. 19.8

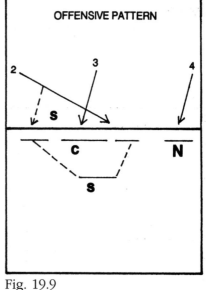

Fig. 19.9

blocker often will be the stacked blocker. If the best attacker is in position 4, the normal middle blocker may be moved to the outside to go one-on-one with the best hitter, while the other blockers participate in the stack.

SUMMARY

Offensive tactics have occupied the minds of many coaches during the past decade. Because of this emphasis on offensive strategies, defensive tactics have remained stagnant. It is time for blocking strategies, and thus total defensive strategies, to be reevaluated. Tactics, not techniques, should be emphasized. Rapid improvement in blocking effectiveness can be achieved by enhancing blocking tactics. For higher probability defense, coaches should consider the possibilities of option blocking. Coaches should choose strategies based on the greatest probability of success. To improve the probability of strong blockers blocking and weak blockers not blocking, choose a serving target or blockers can confuse opposing setters by faking movements. Various defenses may be chosen by defensive teams and a team may choose a defense based upon specific hitters or on specific sides of the court. It may be a good idea to base the starting team's rotational position on various offensive or defensive match-ups.

Option blocking allows players to gain defensive probabilities. There are four components of option blocking: read versus committed blocking; positional commitment; positional overload; and stack blocking.

REFERENCES

Beal, Douglas. (1984 USA men's Olympic coach). Personal communication.

Coleman, James E. *The Relationships Between Serving, Passing, Setting, Attacking and Winning in Men's Volleyball*. Unpublished thesis, George Williams College, 1975.

Coleman, James E. *A Statistical Evaluation of Selected Volleyball Techniques at the 1974 World Volleyball Championships*. Unpublished dissertation, Brigham Young University, 1975.

Coleman, James E. and Terry Ford. Option blocking. *Journal of the National Volleyball Coaches Association* IV, no. 2 (May, 1983): 3-12.

Coleman, James E., William Neville and Bea Gorton. A statistical system for volleyball and its use in the Chicago women's volleyball association. *International Volleyball Review*, 27 (1969): 72-73.

Coleman, James E., William Neville and Greg Miller. The four-point statistical system used for backcourt defense. *International Volleyball Review*, 28 (1971): 38-39.

Miller, Greg. Statistical artifacts and suggestions. *International Volleyball Review*, 29 (1972): 37-38.

Photo by Dan Houser

FLOOR DEFENSE:
BACK COURT DEFENSE
Terry Liskevych and Bill Neville

Offense captures an audience's immediate attention; defense wins matches and eventually wins championships. The best defense combines two factors: sound techniques (in blocking and individual defense) and teamwork (to take as much of the floor as possible away from the opposition). The best team defense reacts quickly and spontaneously to the requirements of any situation. This chapter presents the functional philosophy, technical principles and formations of floor defense.

FUNCTIONAL PHILOSOPHY

There are three components to the philosophy of defense: the right attitude, an appreciation of tactical considerations (the role of the block and the placement of diggers) and effective communication.

Attitude

A coach must instill in players the attitude that no ball will hit the floor at any time; that no ball is impossible to retrieve; and that every ball will be played with maximum effort every time. No value judgment on whether or not a ball is playable is ever made during play. The athletes simply play as hard as they can and make every effort on each sequence until it is terminated. This behavioral attitude is referred to as relentless pursuit. Relentless pursuit means that each player believes "every ball comes to me" and "I will play every ball." This conditioning will heighten players' levels of concentration and physically prepare them to respond.

Before a coach will be able to condition players to believe they will play every ball, he/she will first have to convince each player that, "While I am in my defensive area, I will position myself so that every ball will come to me." For example, if the opposing attacker were set to spike a ball from outside the antenna in the left front position, the left back player would position himself or herself in an advantageous area to dig the cross-court spike.

Controlled aggression is also required to get into position on the court and to be prepared to dig physically. A volleyball player cannot play defense with reckless abandon. Such recklessness would be disruptive and would make the team's defense ineffective. Promote an attitude of highly aggressive behavior that is controlled enough to work in a coordinated team effort.

The key points concerning defensive attitudes are as follows:

• Think "relentless pursuit."
• Believe "every ball comes to me."
• Get into position!
• Play with controlled aggression.

In summary, defense is an attitude — a total commitment to the fact that every ball is playable until proven otherwise (until after a sincere, maximum effort fails).

All players respect other players who give their maximum effort all of the time. Relentless pursuit on defense is undoubtedly the clearest evidence of this level of intensity. A team can win many points, games and matches through continued defensive prowess.

Tactical Considerations

Tactical considerations include two components of team defense. The first component is the block, the first line of defense. The second component is placement of the diggers (to be discussed later).

Role of the Block. The first tactical decision is to determine the block's role. Will the block be deployed primarily to take away an area of the court or will the purpose always be attack blocking? At a higher level of play, athletes can combine those two kinds of blocking based on specific situations. For example, a ball that is set tight should be attack blocked on the opponent's side of the net, even in a game or match when the primary tactic is to block cross-court areas.

Area blocking dictates where the opponents can hit: they can hit anywhere except where your players are blocking them. The back-court defense fills in around the block. Attack blocking dictates that the opponents cannot hit the ball anywhere — the block is everywhere. This tactic is effective for good blocking teams that are reasonably sure they can stop the ball at the net, but deployment of the back-court defense is more difficult. In either system, the floor defense must build around the block and what it is doing. But the blockers must recognize that they also have some back-row responsibilities. The diggers should not feel required to dig the whole court.

Placement of Diggers. An important tactical consideration for floor defense is placing the best diggers in the areas that are most likely to be attacked in each specific situation. As in blocking or attacking, it should always be a goal to put your team's strengths in the most advantageous positions. In floor defense as well as in blocking, deploying your best diggers or blockers and making necessary adjustments will require switching. Switching as it relates to blocking is termed "option blocking." This concept also applies to digging and team defense.

Switches can be called:

- During time-outs (initiated by the coach).
- Prior to the serve (by an experienced, responsible player).
- On a bad pass situation (such as a simple switch when a high ball to the opponent's no. 4 hitter is the only logical option and the middle back

switches to the left back).

Switching the best diggers into the areas most likely to be attacked is very logical. As you look at each rotation, you must identify your best diggers and determine where they best perform their skills. You should adjust your defensive personnel based on the opponent's arsenal and how your opponents deploy in any given situation.

For advanced or experienced teams, a designated back-row player can be given the responsibility of setting the defense. This individual must consider each player's ability to get into position. For example, the server who needs to get over to the left back may be limited in serving effectiveness or may simply be ineffective against the fast attack, or because of transition responsibility, the setter may need to play right back.

Switching adds to the complexity of playing the game and it is not necessary when there is no significant difference among the skill levels of your athletes (or in the skill levels of the opposing players). The return for making the switch must be justified.

Another individual tactical consideration requiring switching is if an off-side blocker cannot establish strong defensive position. Automatically that player should cover the tip. To establish court position, the back-row defenders must key on the blocker's moves and adjust accordingly, balancing the court.

The previous paragraphs focused a good deal on individual tactics, highlighting individuals switching positions for various reasons. This is also true of tactical adjustments in the team's defense. It is actually more common to see a complete team switch from a player — back to a rotational or player-up defense. These tactical adjustments are usually made because of the opponent's tendencies. The situations in which to make the switch are the same as previously mentioned. A common defensive tactical adjustment is to combine two different floor defenses to accomplish a desired coverage. A floor defense can be played with different blocking assignments or philosophies — whatever it takes to be effective in stopping the opposing team.

COMMUNICATION

There must be ongoing, clear communication during all defensive situations. Coupled with the communication must be the consistent adherence to the rules of defense. Furthermore, the same trigger word must be used.

There are three types of communication:

1. The communication of direction.
2. The communication of execution.
3. The communication of confirmation.

It is not always necessary to use the three types in every situation, but the players must be trained and prepared to use the communication necessary to complete a smooth play. Each type of communication uses different trigger words.

Communication of Direction

Trigger words include:

- Switch — the middle back on a high ball would change with either wing to present optimal digging.
- Rotate — a defensive captain calls movement.
- Tip — alerts an adjustment.
- Deep — stay on perimeter.
- White or Back — which type of defense to use.

Communication of Execution

Trigger words include, "Mine," "Me," or "Ball" — an execution trigger word such as "Mine!" should be uttered every time by the player about to make contact.

Communication of Confirmation

Trigger words include, "Yours," "Okay," "(Name)" — all confirm that the ball belongs to the other player.

Communication should be monosyllabic, concise and clear. One of the most devastating blows to a team's tempo is losing a point or serving opportunity because of a failure to communicate.

TECHNICAL PRINCIPLES

Before exploring the technical principles involved in playing defense, one should realize that the largest part of defense is played before the ball is attacked. If we look at the defensive sequence, it will become clearer:

1. Assume the base or starting position.
2. Read the developing play.
3. Adjust position.
4. Move to the final court position.
5. Take final body position.
6. The ball is attacked.
7. Reaction position is retrieved or pursued.

As you can see, five steps in the defensive sequence occur before the ball is attacked.

When teaching defense, one might break it down into the following steps:

1. **Starting or base position.** Any time a player hits the ball over the net to the opponent he or she should immediately get into a starting/base position. In all cases, the player should strive to be in a starting position before an opponent touches the ball.

2. **Read position.** This position is decided by the pass to the setter, the set direction and the spiker's approach. The ideal is to be in the read position by the time of the hitter's foot plant at take-off. Sixty to 70 percent of the athlete's success in defense is related to this step in the sequence. This step determines the athlete's area of responsibility. The defensive posture the player assumes should allow both forward and lateral movement. This is achieved by positioning on the inside balls of the feet with a rounded back and arms bent in front of the body. This type of stance allows the player to lean into the attack. Caution must be taken not to rush in or move while the ball is being contacted.

3. **Adjust position.** This position is the spot from which the player initiates actual defensive play. The player focuses in on the spiker and fine tunes the area of responsibility to a primary zone of effectiveness. Like a computer, the athlete analyzes the last bits of information to set the exact stationary position. The digger computes the spiker's relationship to the ball and net and the relationship of all of these factors to the block. This information is analyzed at breakneck speed and the result is the adjusted position for the digger. This position must be assumed as the attacker begins to swing at the ball.

4. **Reaction position.** An athlete actually plays the ball from the reaction position. The digger reacts from the adjusted position into the primary zone of effectiveness to play the ball. This movement is made immediately after the attacker hits the ball. During the reaction to the ball, the body should not contact the floor until after the digger has made a play on the ball. The arms should be between the ball and floor, coming up to meet the ball. The

ball should be played in front and within the midline of the body whenever possible and the feet should be more than shoulder width apart at contact. There should be minimal armswing except for directional control. The best control can be achieved by simply angling the platform to the target. If the athlete is completely off-balance after contact, an emergency technique (i.e., collapse, dive or roll) may be employed as a landing that will prevent injury.

5. Emergency position. The emergency position covers the secondary zone of effectiveness. It would be used, for example, when a ball touches off the block or is hit to an open area. The player's focus is primarily on the ball and he or she moves as quickly as possible to make some kind of play on the ball to keep it off the floor. The more experienced players will also concern themselves with positioning during the play so the ball will rebound near a prescribed target or area. After the play on the ball, the athlete will be required to execute some method of landing (i.e., dive, roll or slide).

The On Help Principle. The on help principle is an important but neglected principle in defense. "On help" means to play a position so that teammates are on the court side of you. For example, your cross-court defenders should play with their backs to the sideline or facing the opposite sideline. As you visualize this when the dig is made, the player is playing the ball toward the rest of the team, which will thus be in a position to better help play the ball. Another example would be a line digger playing with the foot on the line and in front of the inside foot so the rebound angle is "on help," or back toward the team and court.

The Pursuit and Relay Principle. The pursuit and relay responsibility principle is another important but neglected principle in defense. The block should be touching most attacked balls. Some will be terminal ricochets, but most will be deflected to the back row, where defensive pursuit is possible. The usual deflection that is pursuable goes deep out of the back of the court. Most often the middle back defender, by virtue of court position, will have first contact pursuit responsibility. The wing digger closest to the trajectory follows, prepared to make second contact. The rest of the team should automatically move toward the pursuit in preparation for the third contact. If the ball is deflected off of the block and out of

bounds, the wing digger nearest the ball pursues, followed by the middle back. The absolute necessity is pursuit by everyone.

Additional Principles. Other principles of a technical nature that deserve to be mentioned are the following:

1. Always play the ball in front of you.
2. Lean into the attack but do not rush it.
3. Never move after the armswing has started.
4. Play every ball with two hands.
5. All defenders must know their second contact responsibility.

Defensive Positioning

Defensive positioning occurs prior to the attacker's contact with the ball. The most important aspect of defense is reading the play correctly. Positioning on the court is a series of adjustments that are always mental and sometimes physical. Taken in stages, a player must anticipate:

1. Overpass.
2. Setter tip or spike on second hit.
3. Set direction.
4. Set position — zone, deep, on, quick.
5. Attacker approach — under (early), late.
6. Attacker tendencies — line, cross-court, deep, sharp, seam, off hands, straight down, offspeed, roll, top.

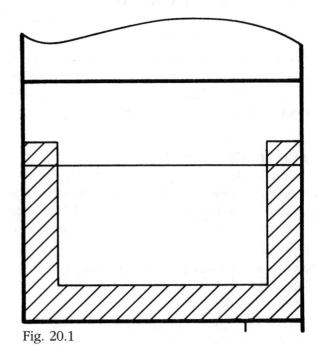

Fig. 20.1

Philosophy and Principles of Defense Checklist

Objectives of Defense

- To position yourself between the flight of the ball and the court.
- To dig the ball to zone 7 (settle for nothing less than perfection) so that the setter has all options available.
- Nothing will hit the floor at any time — relentless pursuit.
- Always follow the ball with your eyes during every instance that it is in play.
- Put yourself in a position so that you can play every ball coming over the net — "every ball is coming to me."
- Do not hit the floor if you do not have to. Never be on the floor before your arms contact the ball. The floor and the ball can be contacted simultaneously.
- Recognize that you are responsible for a defensive area, not just one precise spot.
- Always attempt to play the ball with two arms.
- Be aggressive, but under control — controlled aggression.

7. Over block — weak blocker, hole, position (block line, block cross-court, block both, give seam).
8. Use of antennae and court to your advantage.
9. Need for perimeter defense — It is easier and much more efficient to move toward the center of the court than away from the center of the court. This is opposed to the theory of centrality which dictates that everyone always congregates in the center of the court. Thus, wing players (positions 1 and 5, RB and LB) should use the sideline as their guide. In middle back defense (position 6, MB) the middle back should use the endline as the guide. Be sure to remember the area where most balls are hit in an international match (Figure 20.1).

10. The importance of parallel movement. There should be parallel movement between players who are digging in the back court (Figure 20.2). For example, the six players on defense must respond as a unit, even though there is separate coordination within the first line of defense (blockers) and the second line of defense (back-

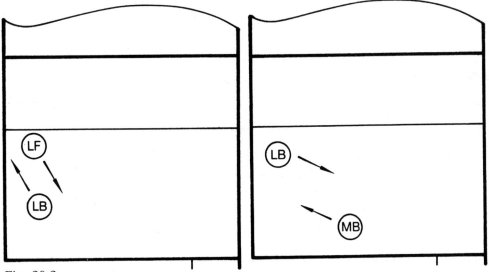

Fig. 20.2

row diggers).

Blocking. The block is the foundation of the defensive alignment. A back-row adjustment will be made if:

1. You are blocking with one, two and/or three players.
2. You attack block or area block.
3. You are blocking line or blocking cross-court.

Design your defense according to:

1. The strengths of your players.
2. The areas where your opponents are most apt to hit.
3. The weaknesses of your players.

Attitude. The most important aspect of defense at the international level is attitude. It is most difficult to teach, because it involves:

- Hard work
- Discipline
- Concentration
- Perseverance
- Desire

Physical position. Before and at the time of the attacker's contact with the ball, the defender should:

1. Stand on the inside balls of the feet.
2. Be ready to move forward and laterally.
3. Lean into the attack, but not rush it.
4. Stand with a bent back and bent knees.
5. Place the arms in front of the body.

6. Take a step before moving the arms.

At the time of the defensive player's contact with the ball (your contact):

1. Keep the arms between the ball and the floor and parallel to the floor.
2. The arms should come up to meet the ball, not go down with the ball.
3. Always play the ball in front of you.
4. If at all possible, keep the body's midline behind the ball.
5. Use minimal armswing except for directional control. The forearms should be angled toward the target.
6. The feet should form a stable base at contact.
7. If the ball is not directly to you, lunge first. Dive and/or roll as a last resort.
8. If the ball is hit above your waist (knuckler), you must play it with a fist (overhand) or turn and take a step to play it.

DEFENSIVE FORMATIONS
Base or Starting Position

All defensive activity begins from the base or starting position, which is determined by the opponent's offensive abilities. The most common base position in collegiate play is the one seen in Figure 20.3. The distance from the net is very arbitrary and depends on the opponents' offense. If a team attacks quickly from the middle, the starting position for the back-row diggers moves closer to the net.

The theory of centrality is an important factor in establishing a base position (Figure 20.4). The tendency is for everyone to congregate at the center of the court because everyone moves forward and never backs up. If forward movement, then, is the easiest movement to make, it should be the last

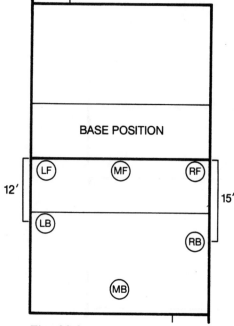

Fig. 20.3

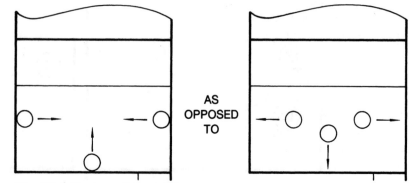

Fig. 20.4 Center of Centrality

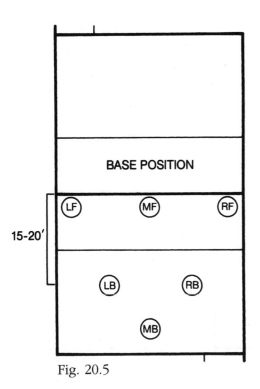

Fig. 20.5

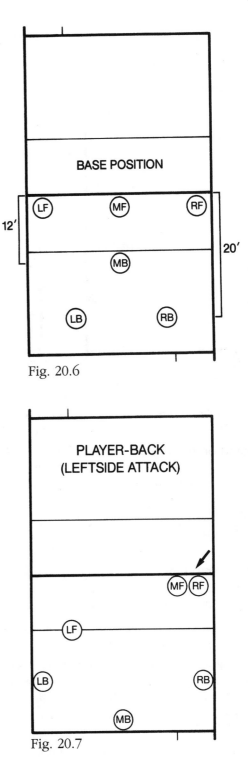

Fig. 20.6

Fig. 20.7

movement that has to be made. In applying this concept to defend against the short, quick attack, the defense would start close in order to be in position ready to play the quick attack. The movement of the defensive players would have to be backward with a reaction forward, as opposed to starting back, moving forward and then reacting backward.

In Figure 20.5, another variation to the base position is offered. This is usually used against a lower-level opponent, one which has a tendency to play the second ball over the net.

Another consideration for establishing the base position would be the type of defense you are going to play. Figure 20.6 shows an example of a base position that might be used for a team that plays opponents who may pass the first ball in error over the net or attack with the second ball. It also is an easy base position to use if you intend to use a player-up defense. Therefore, a secondary consideration is the ease of transition from your starting position into your read position.

Player-Back Defense (White or Standard)

The player-back defense is a perimeter defense that primarily covers the outer areas of the court, while the block covers the center of the court. All defenses are variations of this basic defense. In Figure 20.7,

you will observe the zones of responsibility when an opponent is attacking from the left front or their number 4 position. The non-involved blocker retreats and straddles the 3-meter line, always facing the attack. The blocker should open to the court first and then slide away from the net. The middle back is always on the endline. The middle back makes primarily

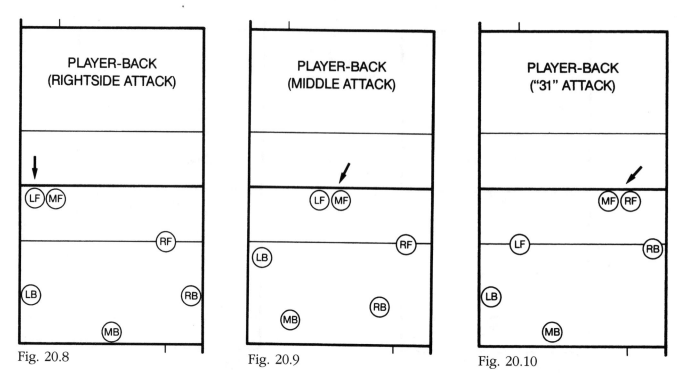

Fig. 20.8   Fig. 20.9   Fig. 20.10

lateral movements in order to cover from corner to corner. A common error occurs when the middle back begins to creep too close, because then a lateral and backward move must be made. A teaching technique that may help in training a middle back player is to put a piece of tape 2 feet from the endline, from sideline to sideline. This will emphasize the primary area of responsibility. The middle back player (no. 6) positions in the seam of the block and reads and adjusts from there. Compare Figure 20.7 to Figures 20.8 and 20.9; observe the difference in positioning based on the seam of the block.

In the player-back defense, the right and left backs cover the balls in the middle of the court. The cross-court diggers should play with their backs to the sideline. In Figure 20.7, the left back should position just off the inside hand of the block. When the middle blocker is involved, the player positions off this blocker's inside hand, back to the sideline, deep in this zone of responsibility. This player is the main cross-court digger. The right back player in Figure 20.7 covers against a line shot spike or tip. In Figure 20.8, with the attack from the opponent's right front, the right back player becomes the main cross-court digger.

If you are defending against a quick attack, like a 31 set, always try to have two blockers up. In Figure 20.10, the movement of the back-court defense is shown in respect to this situation. The right back

moves up to cover the tip, while the middle back moves into the strong shot of the hitter, which is usually in line with the direction of the hitter's approach. This may change once you determine the particular tendencies of that hitter. Figures 20.11 and 20.12 show the defense formation for a quick set in the middle or behind the setter.

For a high set in the middle, the left front and right front blockers should move in and set up on the middle blocker, forming a three-player block as shown in Figure 20.13. This situation may also occur against a high set to the left or right sides. As shown in Figures 20.14 and 20.15, if the block is well-formed, good and solid, the left and right back players will adjust to cover the tip. The middle back would position to be in line with the approach angle of the spiker.

The next group of diagrams (Figures 20.16, 20.17, and 20.18) shows the probable backcourt alignment when only one blocker is able to jump to defend at the net.

The group of diagrams beginning with Figure 20.19 deals with the areas of responsibility, movement patterns and tip responsibility. Figure 20.19 shows the areas of responsibility during a left side attack. The areas are outlined with dotted lines, showing the general area each player is to cover. Figure 20.20 shows movement patterns so that all movement is coordinated to avoid collisions. If a ball is hit to a

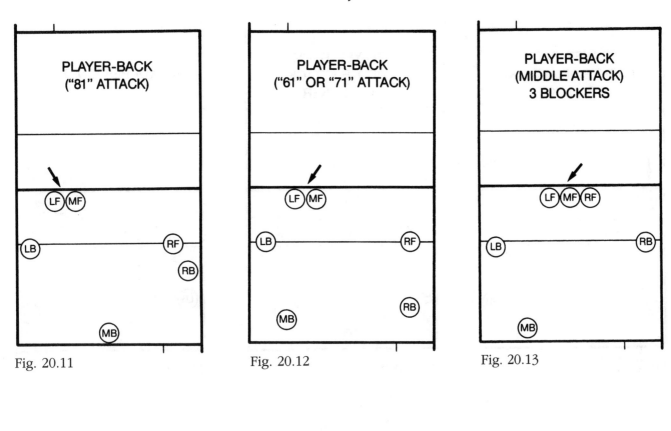

Fig. 20.11

Fig. 20.12

Fig. 20.13

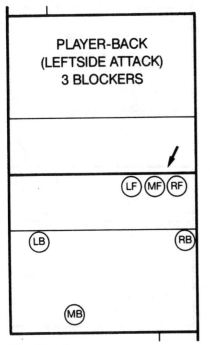

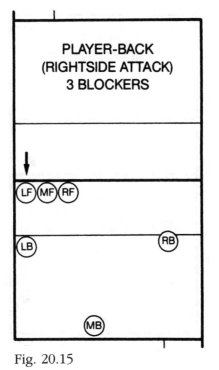

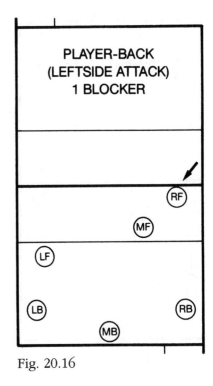

Fig. 20.14

Fig. 20.15

Fig. 20.16

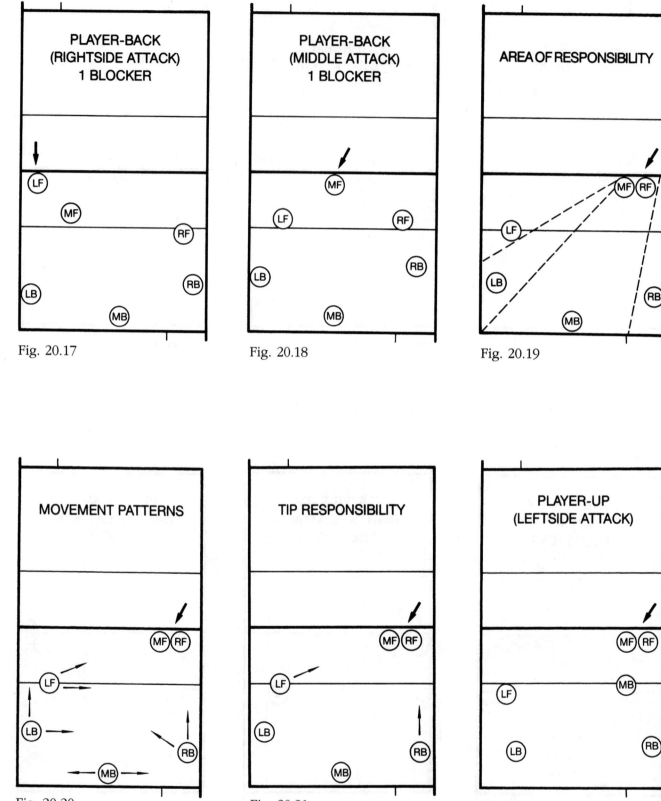

Fig. 20.17

Fig. 20.18

Fig. 20.19

Fig. 20.20

Fig. 20.21

Fig. 20.22

seam, then both players go for the ball. One goes short or in front and the other goes long or behind. This is the concept of parallel movement. The last of these diagrams, Figure 20.21, shows tip responsibility in this defense. If the set is inside or the block takes the angle away, the left front player releases to cover the tip. If the block seals line or the set is on or beyond the antenna, the right back player releases for the tip.

Player-up Defense (Red or Six-up)

The player-up defense primarily involves covering the center of the court and limiting the perimeter coverage to three players instead of four. This variation of the player-back defense positions a defender near the middle of the court behind the block. In Figure 20.22, observe positions when an opponent is attacking from the left front or the no. 4 position. The non-involved blocker retreats just beyond the 3-meter line, back to the sideline. The blocker should open to the court first and then slide away from the net, staying closer to the sideline than in the player-back defense. The left back now plays near the endline. This player should be playing the season in the block and be concerned mainly with balls over or off the block deep into the court. Compare Figure 20.22 to Figure 20.23, observing the differences in the positioning of the left back and right back players based on the side of the court being attacked.

In this defense, the player-up covers balls in the middle of the court. The player-up should play behind the seam in the block at approximately 3.7 m (12 ft.) deep, as shown in Figure 20.22. This player is primarily responsible for covering tips, roll shots and touches of the block that fall short. In Figure 20.23, with the attack from the opponent's right front, this player assumes a position similar to that described above, except closer to the other sideline.

In Figure 20.22, the right back player is the primary line digger. This player positions approximately 6.1 to 7.6 m (20 to 25 ft.) deep, depending on the ability of the opposing attacker to hit the ball down. The line digger must also consider the formation of the team's block in establishing the correct position.

If defending against a strong middle attack, always try to have two blockers up. In Figure 20.24, the movement of the back-court defense is shown in respect to this situation. The right back moves toward the baseline and covers the cut-back shot over the

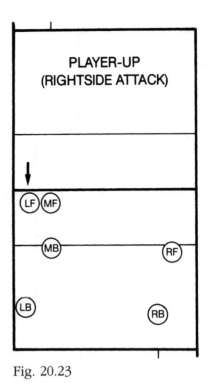

Fig. 20.23

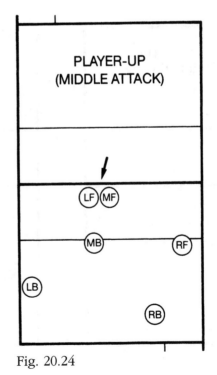

Fig. 20.24

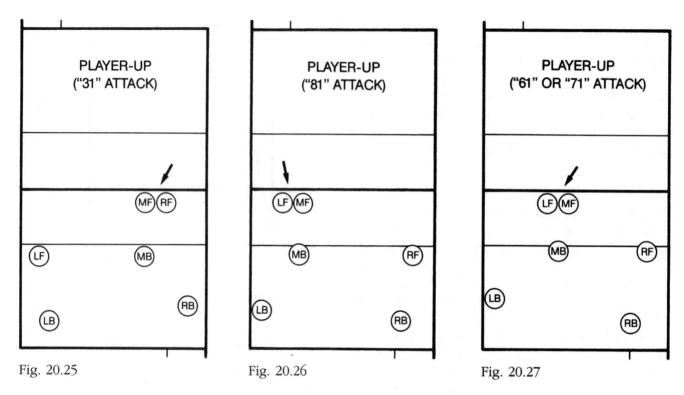

Fig. 20.25   Fig. 20.26   Fig. 20.27

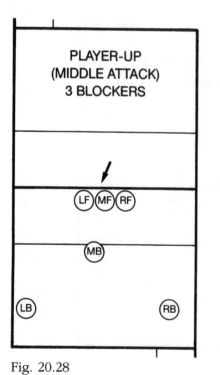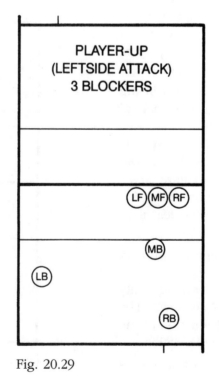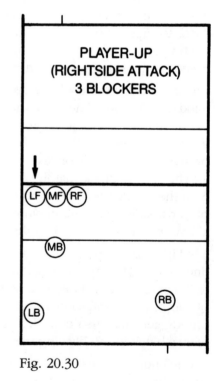

Fig. 20.28   Fig. 20.29   Fig. 20.30

block. The left back player covers over the block cross-court or inside the left front blocker if the block leaves a lot of court. The left front assists the middle blocker while the right front moves in to cover the cut-back shot of the hitter. This may change once you determine particular tendencies of the hitter. Figures 20.25, 20.26 and 20.27 show the defense formation for quick attacks from the middle or behind the setter.

For a high set in the middle, the left front and right front blockers should move in and set up on the middle blocker, forming a three-player block as shown in Figure 20.28. This situation may also occur against a high set to the left or right side. As shown in Figures 20.29 and 20.30, if the block is well-formed, good and solid, the left middle back will adjust to cover the tip. The right back and left back will play the perimeter of the court.

The next group of diagrams (Figures 20.31, 20.32 and 20.33) shows the probable back-court assignments when only one blocker is able to jump to defend at the net.

The group of diagrams that begins with Figure 20.34 deals with the areas of responsibility, movement patterns and tip responsibility. Figure 20.34 shows the area of responsibility during a left side attack. The areas are outlined with dashed lines showing the general area each player is to cover. Figure 20.35 shows movement patterns so all players' movements are coordinated to avoid collisions. If a ball is hit to a seam, then both players go for the ball: one goes short or in front and one goes long or behind. This is the concept of parallel movement. The last of these diagrams is Figure 20.36, showing tip responsibility in this defense. In the player-up defense, one person is always given this responsibility. These diagrams have illustrated the middle back player.

Rotational Defense

Strong Rotate. This defense is a movement defense primarily covering the corners of the court and the area immediately behind the block. This defense is a variation of the player-back defense.

In Figures 20.37 and 20.38, observe that the rotation is in the direction the ball was set. This is sometimes called the strong rotate since the defense is rotating toward the ball. The non-involved blocker retreats deep, positioning below the attack line facing the

attack. The opposite wing player rotates deep to cover the cross-court corner. In Figure 20.37 it happens to be the left back player. The middle back player also rotates toward the ball to cover the deep line corner. Simultaneously, the wing player on the line rotates up behind the block to cover a tip. In Figure 20.37 this would be the right back player. This rotation defense limits you to only three players covering the perimeter of the court but leaves one player available for tip coverage responsibility.

Figures 20.39 and 20.40 show attacks out of the middle; the rotation is based on which blocker assists the middle blocker. In Figure 20.39, the left front helps the middle blocker, forcing the rotation to the left. In Figure 20.40, the rotation is to the right since the right front assists on the block. In this situation the right back releases for tip coverage, forcing a rotation to the right.

In Figure 20.41, using a three-player block against a middle attack complicates this defense since either of the wing players can release to cover the tip, leaving two remaining deep players. These players can play the corners or most frequently attacked areas.

If you are defending against a quick attack, like a 31 set, the philosophy of trying to get two blockers up should still prevail. In Figure 20.42, the movement of the back-court defense shows the rotation to the right, releasing the right back for tip coverage. The rotation will be limited since the play is so quick, making it more difficult to cover the corners. Figures 20.40 and 20.43 show the defense formation for a quick set in the middle or behind the setter.

In the case of high sets, it may be possible to have three blockers up. Figures 20.41, 20.44 and 20.45 show the formation following strong rotational principles. The rotation is always to the side from which the ball will be attacked. If the corners are a major coverage priority, you may be all right. As the diagrams illustrate, you are now short one back-court defender; therefore, your priority is to block the ball.

The next group of diagrams (Figures 20.46, 20.47 and 20.48) shows the probable back-court alignment when only one blocker is able to jump to defend at the net.

Figures 20.49, 20.50 and 20.51 illustrate the areas of responsibility, movement patterns and tip responsibility for the strong rotate defense.

Counter Rotate (Blue or Slice). The counter rotate

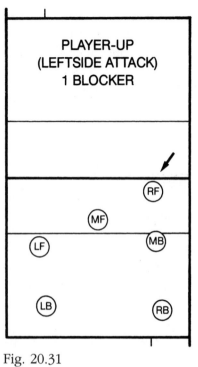

Fig. 20.31

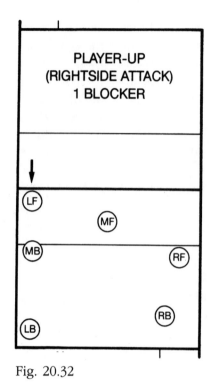

Fig. 20.32

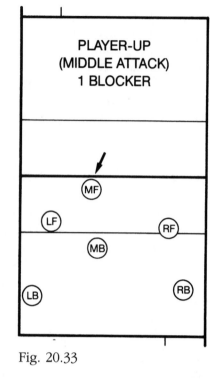

Fig. 20.33

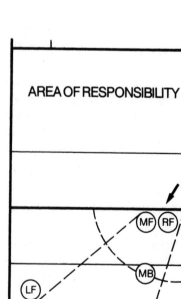

Fig. 20.34

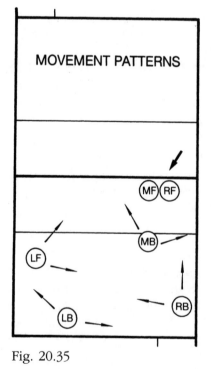

Fig. 20.35

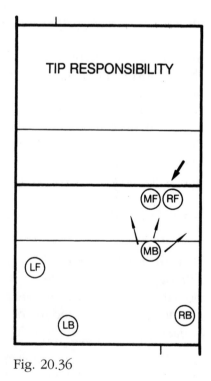

Fig. 20.36

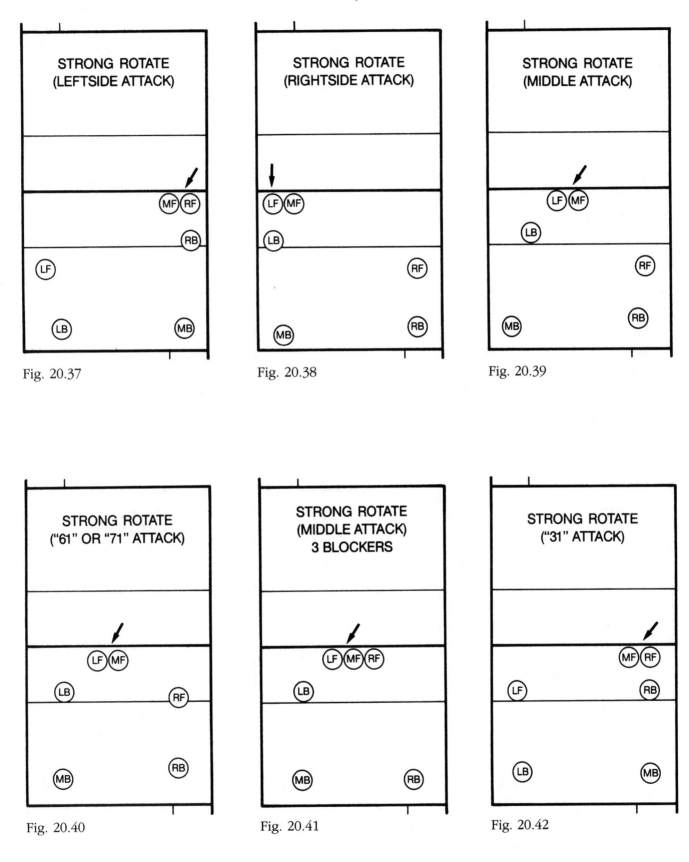

Fig. 20.37

Fig. 20.38

Fig. 20.39

Fig. 20.40

Fig. 20.41

Fig. 20.42

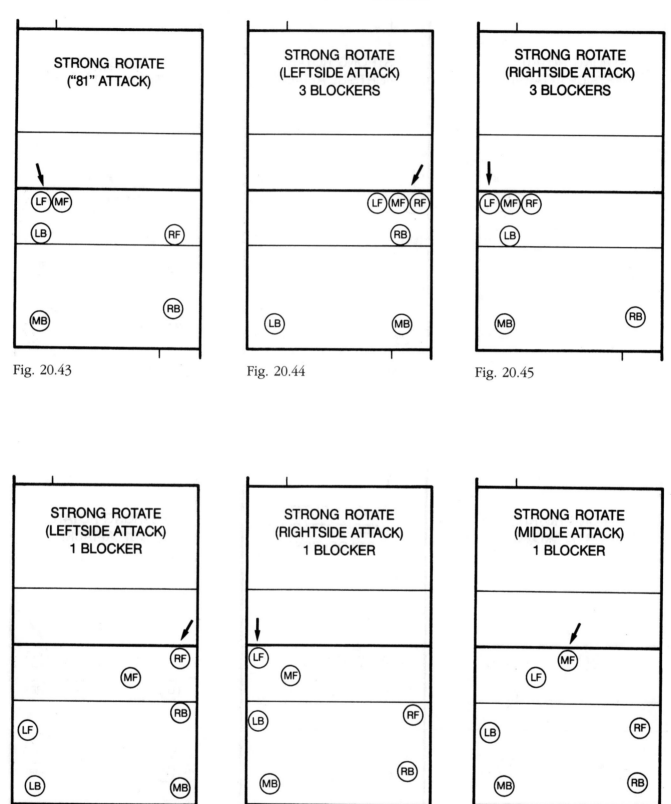

Fig. 20.43

Fig. 20.44

Fig. 20.45

Fig. 20.46

Fig. 20.47

Fig. 20.48

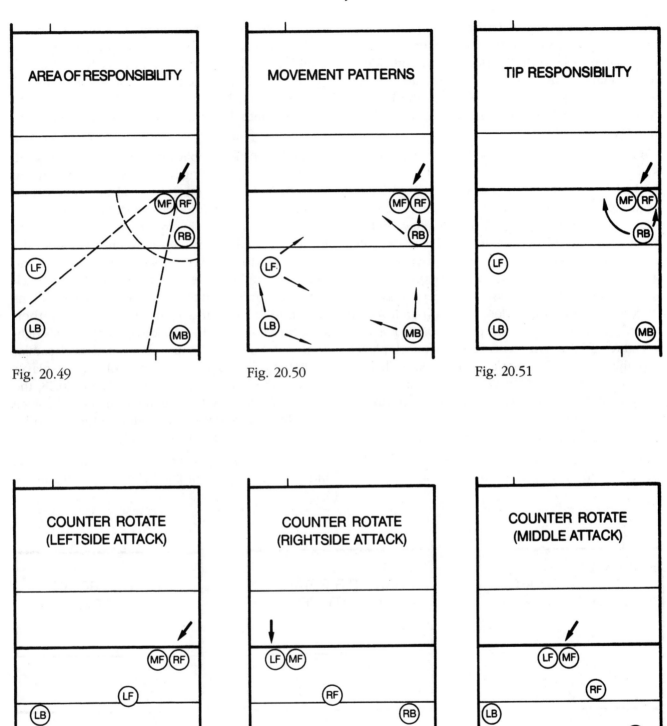

Fig. 20.49

Fig. 20.50

Fig. 20.51

Fig. 20.52

Fig. 20.53

Fig. 20.54

defense is also a movement defense that primarily covers the corners of the court and the area immediately behind the block using the off-side or non-blocking front-court player. The rotation in this defense is away from the side where the ball has been set. This defense is again another variation of the player-back defense.

In Figures 20.52 and 20.53, observe that the rotation is in the opposite direction the ball is set. Therefore, if the ball is set to the opponent's left front, the team rotates to the left. This is sometimes called a counter rotate since you rotate in the opposite direction from which the ball is set. The non-involved blocker rotates in behind the block, pushing the other players to rotate so the line digger will back up, covering the deep line. The middle back will cover the deep, cross-court corner. The wing player closest to the non-involved blocker rotates up to cover the power cross-court shot. In Figure 20.52 it happens to be the left back player. With the non-involved blocker (sometimes called the off-blocker) rotating to cover the tip, this counter rotation defense also limits you to only three players covering the perimeter of the court.

In Figures 20.54 and 20.55 showing an attack out of the middle, the rotation is based on which blocker assists the middle blocker. In these two diagrams,

we illustrated the left front helping the middle blocker forcing the rotation to the right. Of course, the rotation would be to the left if the right front helped out in the block, which the left front, non-involved or off-blocker released to cover the tip. Figures 20.56 and 20.57 illustrate the 31 attack and the 81 attack.

In Figure 20.58, using a three-player block against a middle attack complicates this defense since all blockers are participating in the block. A rule of thumb to go by is the wing on the side of the usually non-involved blocker would then create the rotation by moving to cover the tip. In Figure 20.59, when the attack is coming from the opponent's left side, the last blocker to be involved would be the left front. Once the left front decides to block, the left back continues to rotate in to cover the tip. This positions the middle back and right back to cover their respective corners. The attack to the opponent's right front, as shown in Figure 20.60, causes a similar rotation to the right. In the case of a three-player block in the middle, as shown in Figure 20.58, the rotation would most likely come from the right since the right front traditionally would be the last to be involved in helping out the middle.

The next group of diagrams (Figures 20.61, 20.62 and 20.63) shows the probable back-court alignment

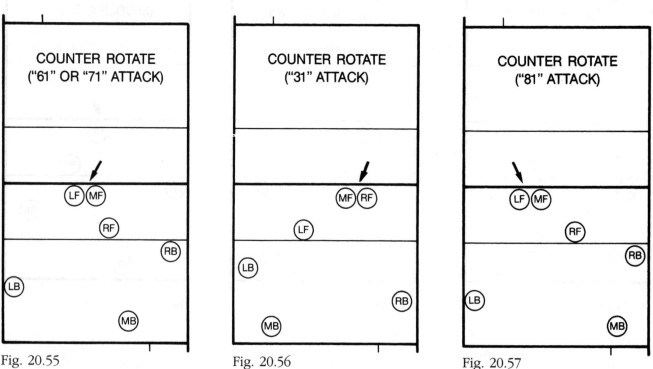

Fig. 20.55   Fig. 20.56   Fig. 20.57

when only one blocker is able to jump to defend at the net.

Figures 20.64, 20.65 and 20.66 again illustrate the areas of responsibility, movement patterns and tip responsibility for the counter rotate defense.

SUMMARY

Defense is a significant part of volleyball that accomplishes two things. First, defense scores points. The average team should score three to five points per game off of floor defense. Second, defense can change or solidify the momentum in the team's favor. A great dig or save can inspire a team, whereas lack of effort or missing easy defensive plays has the opposite effect.

The three components to defense are the right attitude, an understanding of tactics and effective communication. Most defense is played before the ball is attacked, and in teaching defense, it is helpful to teach a seven-step defensive sequence. In addition, players should be familiar with the principles of defense, including the on help principle and the pursuit and relay principle. Players must also know and practice the various defensive formations, especially the player-back defense, the player-up defense and the rotational defense. It is important for players to remember the old adage, "Offense scores points, but defense wins games."

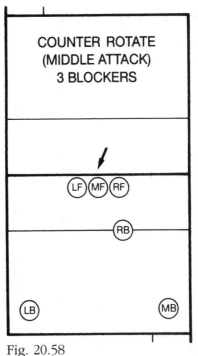

Fig. 20.58

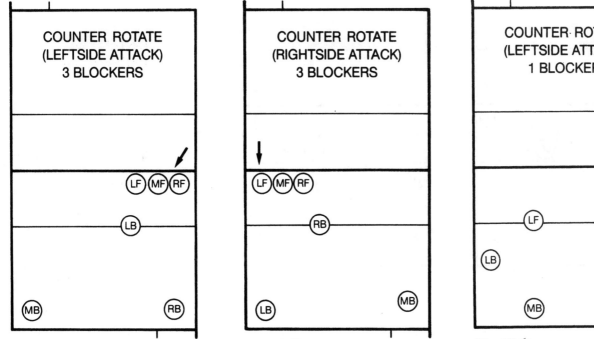

Fig. 20.59   Fig. 20.60   Fig. 20.61

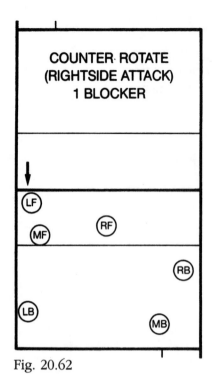

Fig. 20.62

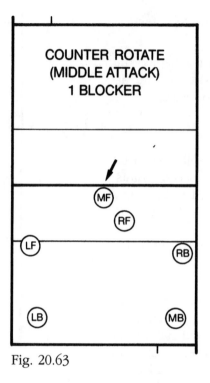

Fig. 20.63

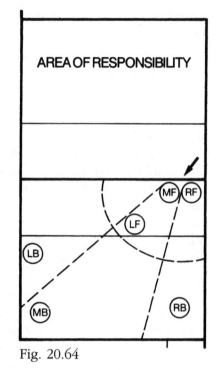

Fig. 20.64

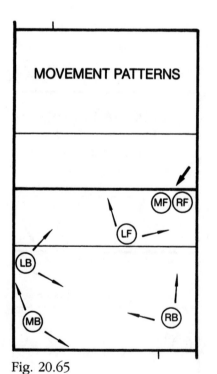

Fig. 20.65

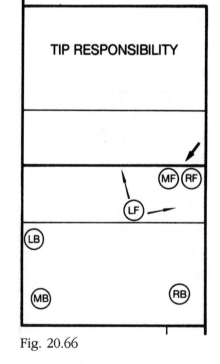

Fig. 20.66

Chapter 21

ELEMENTS OF TRANSITION

Andy Banachowski

Explaining the elements of transition on paper seems every bit as difficult as perfecting and performing them on the court. The difficulty begins with defining "transition" as it occurs on the volleyball court. The dictionary defines "transition" as a period of passing from one condition, activity or place to another. It sounds simple. In basketball, transition is easily observed as the players move from one end of the court to the other. In volleyball, transition seems to be most frequently explained as going from defense (digging) to offense (spiking). But there are many other transitional aspects of volleyball that also need to be discussed. Every time the ball crosses the net, many transitions occur. For example, switching from offense to defense can be just as important a transition as the generally accepted notion of going from defense to offense. Additionally, because of the rotational alignment of the game, many minor transitions can occur that will enhance a team's positioning and performance.

Before discussing these aspects of transition, the following comments on the relative importance of the transition game must be made. During the 1970s, volleyball was a pass-set-hit game that resulted in points mainly when the passing broke down. It still is, because passing is still crucial to a team's success, but it was even more so then. Until the rules were changed in 1977 so that the blocker's contact no longer counts as one of the three allowable contacts, a team would have only two hits to return the opponent's attack, assuming that the block touched the ball. This restriction usually resulted in a free-ball

pass over the net that gave the receiving team the opportunity to pass-set-hit again. Under these rules, transition was an even more vague concept. It was little understood, little practiced and little perfected. With the rule change that eliminated the blocker's contact as the first hit, transition became easier to execute and its importance became more apparent in determining the outcome of the game. Today, an effective transition game has become critical.

Many coaches still believe that serving and passing are the two most important factors in deciding the winner of a match, but if these two elements are equal, the next big determining factor is who can play the better transition game. This concept is especially true for the women's game, because men's volleyball is such a power-oriented game. (The next important element for the men is the block since their game consists primarily of pass-set-hit-block, resulting in a quick point or side-out, depending on which side of the net the ball hits the floor.) The women's game, although it has become increasingly more powerful over the years, still consists of rallies that excite the fans with outstanding defensive plays and continual action. There is much more transition played on the women's court, thus it is more important in determining the winner.

The most important element of transition is ball control. Quickness, agility and anticipation are additional skills that must be constantly employed. Finally, an understanding of the transition game and the formations used to run it are crucial to its success. There are two main types of transition: rotational transition and defense-to-offense transition.

ROTATIONAL TRANSITION

Rotational transitions are minor changes that can greatly enhance individual and team performances if executed quickly and properly. These transitions allow a coach to position a team for its best attack or defense. But if performed slowly or poorly, these transitions will usually negate the advantage.

The serving team should make its switches immediately upon contact of the ball by the server. In the front court, the middle blocker should quickly move to the middle, maintaining a position closest to the net. The outside blockers should quickly run to their assigned blocking areas, crossing behind the middle blocker when necessary. In their rotational position, the players should establish a minimal distance (without forming a screen for the server) from one another to allow for an even quicker switch. In the back court, players should also make switches to their assigned defensive areas as designated by personal coaching philosophy (specialization versus generalization) and defensive system. Caution should be exercised to avoid screening and overlap violations.

For the receiving team, usually only the designated setter will be making a rotational transition as the serve is contacted. The setter must move to the passing target area, while the other players concentrate on passing the served ball. After the ball is passed, rotational transition may begin to occur. Some teams like to make their back-court switches while the ball is being set so that they have completed their switching before they position themselves for hitter coverage. Then they can quickly move to their assigned defensive position after the attack is completed. For instance, a left back player who normally plays middle back can move into the hitter coverage positioning of the middle back position and thus establish the switching before moving back to defense. This makes the transition from offense to defense smooth since the players are already in their normal, more practiced defensive positions.

Other teams prefer to wait until after hitter coverage to make back-court switches, thereby emphasizing hitter coverage before transition to defense. This is a more sequential approach to the game and requires that each player be familiar with each coverage assignment.

In the front court, the attackers frequently cannot make any rotational switches until the attack has been completed. An exception would be to run a designated play with the hitters attacking from their defensive positions. For instance, a middle blocker who is in the right front area can be called upon to hit the X. This requires this player to move to the middle of the court to spike and it also positions the player for defense.

Once the attack has been completed (the ball crosses the net), front-court players can make rotational or positional changes following the same guidelines as on defense. Depending on the caliber and tempo of play, however, these switches are the most dangerous to make because this is the time that the opponents are trying to "out-transition" you. That is, they are trying to dig-set-attack your attack while you are switching positions. For you to switch slowly or at inappropriate times increases their chances of success in transition.

This type of offense-to-defense transition in the front court should be utilized with certain guidelines in mind. The middle blocker must always get to the middle. Outside hitters should only switch if the dig is not controlled within the court boundaries. If the dig is not controlled, then the player will have enough time to get to the desired position. If the dig is controlled, you will still have more success stopping their transition with the players in position, rather than with players getting caught in switches and/or being late for the play.

These elements of transitional play should be practiced any time scoring or side-out work is called for.

DEFENSE-TO-OFFENSE TRANSITION

To run a transition game successfully, in the sense of going from defense to offense, the key element is ball control. Whether a ball is dug from a spike or from a deflection off the block, the dig must be executed skillfully enough — with enough height and accuracy — to allow the players time to make the transition.

In a normal defensive alignment with the blockers "up" (blocking the spike) and the diggers positioned properly, your defense must come up with a dig that allows you to execute your transition offense. This dig must be high enough to allow the other players to position themselves for offense and accurate enough (to the normal target area) to allow you to run an offensive attack. As the digger prepares to play the ball, the other players must anticipate the next action and ready themselves.

If using a back-court setter, the setter must release from the back-court defensive position and get into the front court to set the ball. When the setter sees that the ball is hit away from the back-court position, he or she can release to a setting position. If the dig is not accurate, the setter can call for help from a teammate.

The front-court players must ready themselves for an attack: as the blockers are landing, they must locate the ball and move off the net to get ready to make their normal approach for an attack. Their path off the net should take them to their usual starting position for an attack. In doing so, they should follow a pattern that will avoid a collision with the back-court setter coming forward. The remaining front-court player, who is already back off the net in a digging position, needs only to move into the normal starting attack position.

All of these actions must be taken quickly because there is usually very little time for them, depending on the height of the dig. All the players must know their responsibilities — who is to dig, who is to set and who is to attack — and be skilled enough to perform them. They must be able to anticipate the action which will take place and have the agility and strength to perform these physical skills quickly.

If you have a front-court setter, as soon as the ball goes by the blockers, the setter must move to the target area for the dig, while the other front-court players get off the net and prepare to attack. This is the pattern that to practice repeatedly from a normal defensive position to make the transition swift and smooth.

Another situation that also must be practiced is called a free-ball situation, which occurs when the opponents cannot generate an attack and must forearm pass the ball over the net. The forearm pass is the key that can be used to trigger this formation for a team. Whenever you see the opponents begin to underhand pass the ball over the net, all of your players should call out "free ball" and respond quickly by assuming their free-ball formation. This formation should be the same as the service-reception formation. The ball comes over the net relatively slowly. If the team recognizes the free ball quickly, there is plenty of time for each player to get into position. The front-court players should back off of the net to their normal receive positions, which will also allow them to attack. The setter, whether front-court or back-court, moves to the normal target area for the pass.

Since this free ball is usually an easy ball to pass — and each player should be in the attacking position — this is the best time to run an offensive play to confuse the opponents. However, this is also a "must" time to score a point or side-out; the team should not do something so intricate that it will hinder the chances of scoring.

Another situation that may also occur is a down-ball situation. This is defined as a situation in which the coach feels the team's chances of digging the ball are better than the prospects of blocking the attack. It usually occurs when the opponent's set is not on target and the hitter can still swing at the ball, but not well enough to generate a potent attack. It can happen if the set is too deep in the court or too wide; the hitter is too late approaching and does not jump; or the attack is so weak as not to warrant blocking. When this situation occurs, someone designated to recognize it calls out "down ball." Often the middle blocker is responsible for calling down balls since that player should be most skilled at recognizing when to block and when not to block. Or, assign that responsibility to the team's most experienced player. All of the players, however, should be practiced enough to anticipate when the down ball situation is going to be called.

When a down ball is called, all players must respond quickly because the ball must still be attacked. Often the "down" call is late or inaudible to the back-court players. Quickness is even more important in this transition, since the players must move to a new digging position in such a short time.

Some teams like to use the same formation as a free ball for a down ball since it means the players only have to learn one formation. If the team employs a simple 4-2 offense, these formations can be easily accomplished, especially if the opponent's attack level is not too high. If the team is using a 6-2 or a 5-1 offense and the setter is in the back court, a coach may have difficulties trying to use the same free-ball formation for a down-ball situation.

One accepted theory is that if a down ball is called, the hitter must be in some kind of trouble and will probably try to hit a safe shot and keep the ball in play. To counter this situation, a coach might put his/her best digger in the middle of the court to dig. This player is the primary digger and has the green light to dig whatever can be reached. The wing diggers (line diggers) should position themselves in their respective area of the court at least 1.5 m (5 ft.) in from the sideline and slightly behind the primary digger. From this position, they should read the hitter and adjust accordingly. This positioning allows for the best coverage of the court where the hitter is most likely to hit the ball. If the opposing hitter has known tendencies, the formation can be adjusted accordingly.

The front-court players must also become active in the down ball formation. There are different ways to accomplish this. The left front player should move off the net to a digging position. The other two front-court players must also be active. One must get off the net to a digging position while the other should stay at the net, ready to get any ball just trickling over the net and to assume the role of setter once the ball is dug.

One strategy involves keeping the middle front player at the net and pulling the right front player back, which makes it very easy to get a balanced digging formation. This strategy works well if the middle front player is the setter, such as in a basic 4-2. However, if the middle front player is an attacker, it is much better to keep the right front player at the net (often the normal position for the setter) while bringing the middle front player to the right side of the court to dig. This strategy enables the team to have the same digging formation as previously described and gives the most benefits for a quick transition. The middle of the court is open for the primary digger to dig as many balls as possible, the middle attacker is off the net ready to attack and a setter (or designated setter) is at the net ready to set.

If the primary setter is in the back court and the hit is away from that position, the setter can release to the front court to assume the setting role. Coming into the front court, the setter yells, "I'm in" and the right front player will relinquish position to back off of the net and become an attacker.

If the back-court setter digs the ball or cannot release quickly enough, the right front player becomes the setter. This player must be a capable setter to run the offense or set a high set to an attacker. If the pass (dig) is close to the net, this player can attack the ball. This is an ideal position for a left-handed setter-attacker. If the pass is off the net, the right front player can call for help and a teammate can step in and set the ball.

DRILLS FOR TRANSITION

Perfecting the transition game requires a thorough understanding of each player's responsibilities and good communication among the players. It also requires a lot of practice regarding the skills and formations employed to be successful. Since ball control is essential, the most basic skill necessary is digging. The following pages describe digging drills:

Drill No. 1: Dig to Target

From a position above the net on the opposite side of the court, the coach can repetitively hit balls at a player who must dig the ball to a specific target area. The player should repeat a specified number of digs successfully to the target area and then alternate with another player who plays the same defensive position. Other players shag stray balls. A setter, who must run down each dig and set it to a specified target, can be added to this drill (Figure 21.1).

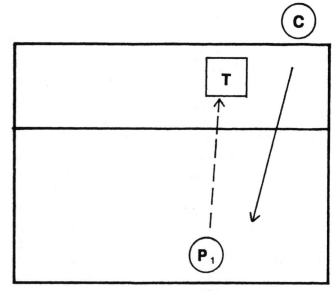

Fig. 21.1

Drill No. 2: Pass to Target

From the opposite court, the coach tosses balls across the net to two lines of waiting players. The player passes the ball (overhand or forearm passes) to a specified target. The player then shags the ball and returns it to the coach, returning to the opposite line to await another turn (Figure 21.2).

Drill No. 3: Dig Three Spots to Target

From a position above the net on the opposite side of the court, the coach hits a ball at a player (Pl) who must dig the ball to a specific target area. The player (Pl) then moves to another defensive position on the court and the coach hits a second ball. Then the player (Pl) moves to a third defensive position on the court to dig the third ball hit by the coach. The next player (P2) in line follows the same pattern. When all players have moved to the other side of the court, the drill continues with the direction of movement reversed. This allows players to work on moving to their right and left. The drill can be varied to require a successful dig to the target area before the player is allowed to move to the next digging position (Figure 21.3).

Drill No. 4: Half-Court Digging

This is a continuous action drill with the coach located on the same half court as the three diggers. The object is to keep the ball in play as long as possible. The coach spikes the ball at a player who will dig it, then one of the other two players must step in and set the ball to the coach. The digger and the non-setting player should balance the court until the setting player returns to a digging position. The coach will continue to hit the ball. All diggers must be ready to set the ball and communication among the players should be stressed to ease balancing and covering the court at all times (Figure 21.4).

Drill No. 5: Dig-set

The coach hits balls at two lines of players. The non-digging players must then set the ball to a specified target area. Two new diggers step onto the court to continue the action (Figure 21.5).

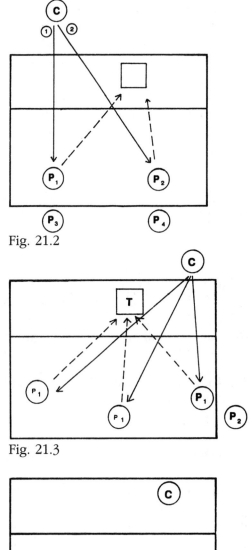

Fig. 21.2

Fig. 21.3

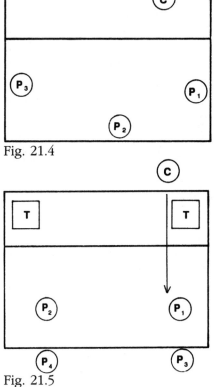

Fig. 21.4

Fig. 21.5

Drill No. 6: Back-Court Diggers

Back-court players are positioned in the down ball formation of the coach's choosing and then the coach continuously hits balls at the diggers until they dig a specified number of balls to the target area, or until a set period of time (i.e., two minutes) has elapsed. This will sharpen their digging skills and their teamwork (Figure 21.6).

Drill No. 7: Dig-Hit

A front-court digger (e.g., LF) must dig a ball hit by the coach from above the net on the opposite side. The player (Pl) must dig the ball to a setter who will then set the ball. The digger must then become an attacker and get into position to hit the ball being set. This drill works best when a second (P2) or third (P3) digger is included and the players alternate. One or two blockers can be added to make the hitting more difficult and the drill more realistic (Figure 21.7).

Drill No. 8: Back Court-Front Court Dig

This drill is the same as drill No. 7, but with an additional player on the court. This additional player is the back-court digger (e.g., LB) behind the front court digger (e.g., LF). Two balls are hit before the players change position. The first ball is hit to the left back digger and the setter sets to the left front player. Immediately after the attack, the coach hits a second ball at the left front player, who must get into defensive position after the first attack. The ball must be dug and set back to the player who will attack for the second time. Players then rotate positions, with a new player moving to the left back and the left back player moving to the left front. One or two blockers can be added and players should be encouraged to cover the hitter at all times (Figure 21.8).

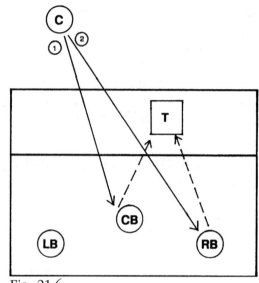

Fig. 21.6

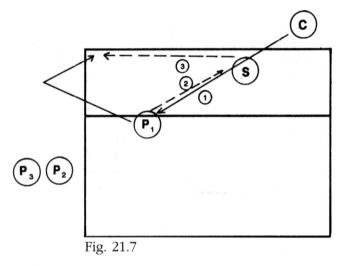

Fig. 21.7

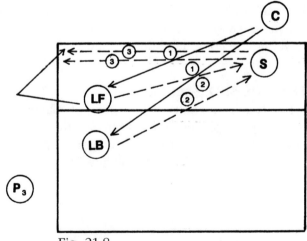

Fig. 21.8

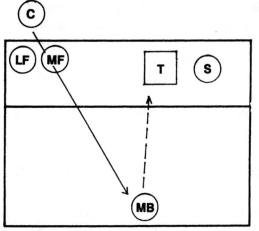

Fig. 21.9

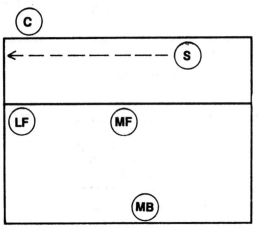

Fig. 21.10

Drill No. 9: Block to Hit

Two players take a blocking position versus a coach on the opposite side of the net. The coach will hit the ball over, around or off the blockers to a back-court digger. As the digger digs to the target area, a setter will come into the front court to set the ball to one of the blockers who has quickly moved off the net into an attacking position. The same blockers should stay in the drill until they have successfully completed a specified number of transition attacks (Figures 21.9 and 21.10).

Drill No. 10: Three Versus Three

Three players are positioned on each side of the net and their objective is to dig-set-hit the ball back and forth across the net successfully and successively. With beginning players, ball control should be stressed, with the goal being to keep the ball in play as long as possible. Whenever an error is made, a new ball is introduced at that point to correct the error and play continues. Multiple variations can be introduced to alter the drill. These include making all attacks from behind the 3-meter line or adding another set of three players on each side who exchange positions with the set of three on the court whenever the ball crosses the net (Figure 21.11).

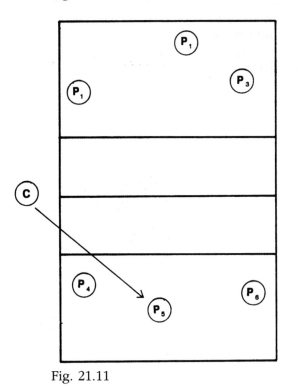

Fig. 21.11

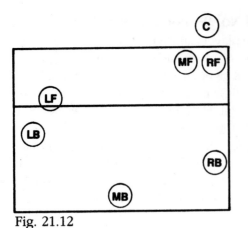

Fig. 21.12

Drill No. 11: Team Defense Versus Coach

The coach attacks balls against a team of players. This allows proper positioning on each play and gives the coach the opportunity to repeat exact situations. The players must play good defense and convert the transition to attack successfully. This is a very controlled drill and allows for excellent teaching. Players should be rotated frequently (Figure 21.12).

Drill No. 12: Six Versus Six, Free Ball

Two complete teams are on the court. One team is allowed only one hit to get the ball across the net the first time. The coach tossing the ball should make the toss so that the team will have to pass the ball across the net, thus assuring a free-ball situation. This allows the other team to practice free-ball situations continuously. They should run the free-ball plays you have designed and the ball should be played out with each team having three hits (Figure 21.13).

Fig. 21.13

Drill No. 13: Six Versus Six, Down Ball

Two complete teams are on the court. One team is allowed only one hit to get the ball across the net the first time. The coach should toss the ball so that an attack can be made, but deep enough off the net so that the blockers can call a down-ball situation. This allows the other team to practice down-ball situations continuously. The ball should be played out with each team having three hits. The team practicing down balls should have to perform a specified number of successful transitions before they are allowed to rotate (Figure 21.14).

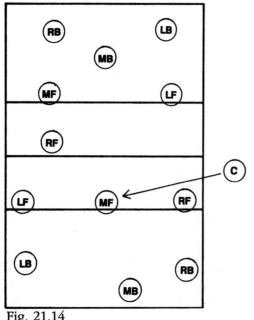

Fig. 21.14

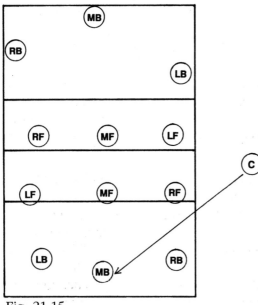

Fig. 21.15

Drill No. 14. Six Versus Six, Free Ball/ Down Ball

Two complete teams are on the court. One team is allowed only two hits to get the ball across the net the first time. The coach should toss the ball in a variety of positions so the different situations will be set up. This will force the defending team to distinguish regular defense, down-ball or free-ball situations and react accordingly. The ball should be played out with each team having three hits (Figure 21.15).

SUMMARY

Transition is a very important element of volleyball; it is probably the most important element after serving and passing. There are two main types of transition: rotational transition, which includes minor changes, and defense-to-offense transition. The main transition in volleyball would be going from defense to offense, but many minor transitions occur in every game.

Important components of transition are ball control and transitional formations. Transition plays must be made quickly and players must be familiar with various possible situations that may occur, such as free-ball or down-ball situations.

Each player must have a thorough understanding of his or her responsibilities and must be able to communicate effectively with the other players on the team. Players must practice drills emphasizing skills, formations and ball control.

Part 4

RELATED ELEMENTS
PROGRAM DEVELOPMENT

Photo by Gerry Vuchetich

Chapter 22

ADMINISTRATION OF A VOLLEYBALL PROGRAM

Stephanie Schleuder

Anyone who has coached knows that the time spent in the gymnasium is only a small part of a coach's job. At the collegiate level, a head coach's job description reads like a job description for the chairman of the board of a major corporation. The head coach's job involves a myriad of responsibilities, including staff supervision, public relations, budget management, program planning, recruiting and coaching. Ultimately, the success of any collegiate sport program can be directly related to efficient management.

This chapter presents an organized, practical approach to the administration of a collegiate volleyball program. Organizing a program in the configuration of a corporate structure can prove to be a valuable method of maximizing one's efforts as head coach.

PHILOSOPHY AND GOALS

Before beginning to plan the development of a volleyball program, a coach must have a clear understanding of where and how the athletic program fits into the hierarchical structure of the institution. Lines of authority and communication should be well-established (see Chart 1).

The philosophies of the university, formed by the board of trustees and the chief executive officer, are reflected in written statements depicting the institution's missions and policies. These philosophies shape all programs within the institution. Responsibility for developing an athletic program

which embodies the philosophies of the institution lies with the athletic director. The athletic director sets goals for specific sport programs and selects coaches who are responsible for meeting those goals. By consulting with the athletic director, the head coach, in turn, designs and implements strategies for operating the program within the parameters set by the athletic director and the institution.

Since the athletic director is the coach's direct link with the administration of the institution, and the director will make all decisions about the sport programs, it is essential that good communication exists between the athletic director and the coach. Probably the most vital component in creating a successful sport program is the compatibility of the coach's philosophies and goals with those of the athletic director. If disharmony exists here, the coach can do one of two things: The coach can modify philosophies and goals so that they are compatible with the athletic director's or the coach can develop a comprehensive plan to "sell" the athletic director a new package. Regardless of the approach, it is important that the two individuals come to an understanding. There should be a detailed outline of the program goals and needs and there should be a clear understanding of the strategies which will be used to accomplish the goals.

Any coach who presents an organized plan for the development of his or her program will increase the chances for gaining the support of the athletic director. Below is a sample of a presentation that is designed to outline a coach's goals and needs for developing

Chart 1

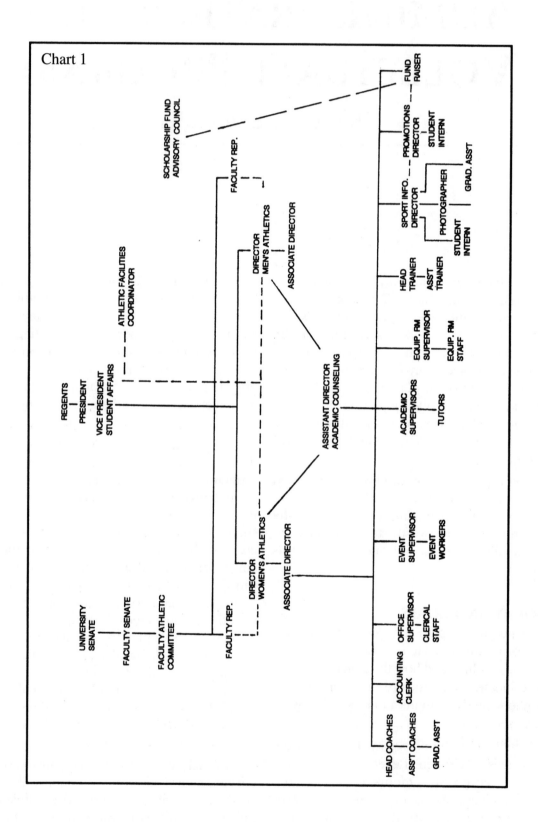

a volleyball program. Obviously, this outline should be written to reflect the individual goals and needs of a specific program and the coach who prepares it should also be prepared to defend each request. Comparisons with other successful programs can be most helpful in defending requests. In any areas where problems exist, it is essential for the coach to gather supporting data which will illustrate the necessity of the requests being made.

Outline for Volleyball Program Development

I. Performance Goals
   A. Year one: Qualify for the conference championship — have a winning record.
   B. Year two: Qualify for the conference championship while improving on the previous season's record.
   C. Year three: Qualify for NCAA championship play-offs by finishing first or second in the conference — be nationally ranked.
   D. Long-range: Be consistently competitive nationally; make an appearance in the Final Four.
II. Program Goals
   A. Gain national recognition — developed through consistent performance at highly competitive levels; evidenced by national rankings.
   B. Generate revenue — substantially increase attendance at home events.
   C. Develop support groups — start a booster club and identify local target groups for promotions.
   D. Improve public relations — through clinics, demonstrations and public speaking engagements — make the public more aware of the program.
   E. Develop respect — the volleyball program should be synonymous with quality; stress proper conduct of coaches and players, performance in matches and efficient organization of the entire program.
   F. Establish professional recognition — the coaching staff must be active in professional organizations and must serve in positions of leadership.
III. Program Needs
   A. Coaching staff
      1. Full-time assistant
      2. Second assistant/graduate assistant
   B. Improvement in services of the support staff
      1. Academic advising — tutors, study halls
      2. Athletic trainer — travels with team
      3. Secretarial — additional staff necessary
      4. Sports information — travels with team
   C. Full allotment of scholarships
   D. Increased travel budget — specific outline — type of travel
   E. Increased recruiting budget — specific outline
   F. Promotions and publicity
      1. Expanded media guide and brochure
      2. Event promotions
         a. Recruit a band, cheerleaders and mascot
         b. Target high school groups
         c. Target university students
         d. Target specific community groups
         e. Create gimmicks to draw spectators.
      3. Media coverage
         a. Print media
            i. Need pre-game coverage.
            ii. Need game reports and coverage.
            iii. Need human interest stories.
         b. Electronic media
            i. Secure radio broadcast contract.
            ii. Secure live or tape-delayed television coverage.
            iii. Provide radio and television with public service announcements for their own use.
   G. Facilities — availability at prime-time
      1. For practice during season
      2. For competitive events
      3. For off-season practice
   H. Equipment needs

Once the philosophy and goals of the program have been established and an evaluation of the program needs has been made, the coach should begin organizing the program with the resources available. Much can be accomplished with little money, a lot of delegation and a good master plan.

STAFF ORGANIZATION

Selecting a staff of well-qualified individuals who can work together toward common goals is clearly one of the most important tasks for the head coach. The head coach must determine the individual qualities which will complement and contrast with the coach's own. Regardless of the situation, the following would represent desirable qualities for any coaching staff member:

- Loyalty
- Creativity
- Integrity
- Honesty
- Enthusiasm
- Good communication skills
- Ability to motivate individuals
- Good knowledge of sport
- Self-motivation and the ability to work hard
- Goal orientation

All members of the coaching staff should have job descriptions outlining their duties and responsibilities. The head coach is responsible for supervising and evaluating the work of each staff member. Following are sample job descriptions for an assistant coach, a graduate assistant and a team manager. These are written in general terms. As a head coach develops a program, the job descriptions should become very specific in nature. Usually, the more clearly responsibilities are outlined, the more productive the staff will become.

Assistant Coach Job Description

Pre-season

1. Coordinate distribution of practice clothes, equipment, shoes and uniforms with the equipment room staff.
2. Organize physical testing materials for the first days of practice.
3. Coordinate the weight lifting program with trainers or the weight coach.
4. Organize travel plans:
   - Confirm motel reservations.
   - Secure game contracts.
   - Arrange for plane tickets and vans/buses.
   - Obtain maps and directions, when necessary.
   - Confirm practice facilities for road trips.
   - Prepare rooming lists for motels.
5. Coordinate the completion of all paperwork needed by the department for each player (i.e., sports information profiles, NCAA eligibility forms, medical releases).
6. Review the graduate assistant's and manager's job descriptions with each of them.

Practice

1. Assist in all phases of practice planning.
2. Conduct warm-up, conditioning and cool-down phases of practice.
3. Talk with trainers before each practice to check on the status of injured players.
4. Supervise the graduate assistant and the manager to make sure they are fulfilling their responsibilities.
5. Schedule individual practice sessions for players with specific weaknesses.
6. Schedule videotape review sessions with players as needed.

Matches

1. Gather players for the pre-game meeting.
2. Conduct and/or supervise the warm-up.
3. Perform designated pre-game duties assigned by the head coach (i.e., scout opposing hitters, turn in lineup).
4. Perform designated duties during the match as assigned by the head coach (i.e., suggest offensive strategy to fit the opponents' defensive changes).
5. Supervise the cool-down and gather the team for the post-game meeting.
6. Call in the match scores when necessary.
7. Meet with the head coach for match analysis and evaluation.
8. Supervise the graduate assistant and the manager in their responsibilities.

Recruiting

1. Prepare a recruiting budget and a master list of recruits.
2. Organize the recruiting files.
3. Organize contact sheets for each recruit and keep them up-to-date.
4. Organize a master schedule for:
   - Talent assessment — watching recruits in games and practices.
   - Home visits.
   - Campus visits.
5. Maintain contact with recruits throughout the year by:
   - Phone contacts.
   - Correspondence.
   - Weekly mailings.
6. Request videotapes and solicit recommendations from high school coaches.

7. Schedule, organize and conduct all campus visits.
8. Keep the head coach constantly apprised of all recruiting developments.
9. Assist in making final decisions regarding scholarship offers.

Scouting

1. Prepare a master schedule of opponents' matches.
2. Prepare a list of videotape requests for scouting purposes.
3. In consultation with the head coach, delegate scouting duties to staff members.
4. In consultation with the head coach, prepare scouting reports on all opponents.
5. In consultation with the head coach, evaluate and update all scouting reports after competition.
6. Receive and process opponents' requests for game videos.

Post-season

1. Organize an off-season conditioning and weight-training program in consultation with the trainers and weight coaches.
2. Gather off-season tournament information and schedule allowed competition.
3. Seek funding or sponsorship for the off-season if necessary.
4. Make travel arrangements for off-season competition.
5. Work with the head coach in setting up a competitive schedule for the following year.
6. Assist in preparing the budget for the following year.

Booster Club

1. Coordinate all club meetings with the head coach and the club president.
2. Coordinate the distribution of club membership materials.
3. Supervise the ordering and sale of club merchandise.
4. Meet with the departmental director of promotions to coordinate club promotional ideas with departmental promotion.

Facilities and Equipment

1. Meet with the facilities manager to coordinate schedules for all practices and matches.
2. Meet with the maintenance staff to arrange needs for practices and games (i.e., net setup, locker rooms, microphones).
3. Schedule facilities when opponents desire practice time.
4. Schedule practices at opponents' facilities.
5. Coordinate arrangements with the equipment room staff for home and away matches (i.e., laundering of uniforms).
6. Each spring, conduct a complete inventory of equipment and uniforms.

General

1. Assist in all phases of program planning.
2. Communicate and post office hours.
3. Be present at all staff meetings.
4. Be present at all player and coach conferences.
5. Attend all departmental social functions.
6. Assist in everyday office work, such as telephone calls and correspondence.
7. Attend as many athletic events as possible — support the entire athletic department.
8. Act and dress in a professional manner when representing the university.
9. When in public, support the head coach at all times.

Second Assistant/Graduate Assistant Job Description

Pre-season

1. Record and compile all physical testing materials and results (i.e., vertical jump, weight).
2. Help plan all scouting and recruiting schedules.
3. Review the managers' job descriptions so that their responsibilities are clear.

Practice

1. Assist in conducting drills and other assigned duties.
2. Help the manager set up the gym for practice.
3. Assist during individual practice sessions when needed.
4. Help put equipment away after practice.

Matches

1. Help with warm-up.
2. Set up videotape equipment when necessary.
3. Instruct the ball shaggers in the three-ball rotational system.
4. Assist with statistics as necessary.

5. Perform other game duties as instructed by the head coach.
6. Meet with the coaching staff following a competition to evaluate the match.

Recruiting and Scouting

1. Assist in evaluating high school prospects.
2. Complete a written evaluation after watching each prospect.
3. Help scout opponents when necessary.
4. Help with on-campus recruiting visits when necessary.

Booster Club

1. Write and distribute a monthly newsletter to members.
2. Organize post-game receptions for all home matches.
3. Attend and take minutes at all club meetings.
4. Act as the liaison between the club officers and the athletic department.
5. Assist in all areas of club operation.

General

1. Schedule weekly office hours with the head coach.
2. Help plan practices.
3. Conduct individual workout sessions when necessary.
4. Act and dress in a professional manner when representing the university.
5. Perform other duties as directed by the head coach.
6. When in public, support the head coach at all times.

Manager Job Description

Preseason

1. Prepare the gym for practice by checking with the head coach to find out what is needed.
2. Check all equipment and balls for proper maintenance.
3. Assist with practice as directed by the coaches.
4. Store all equipment at the end of practice.

Home Games

1. Check with the coach for any special preparations.
2. Make a checklist of all the equipment required for the match, and make sure everything on the list is available.
3. Set up the videotaping equipment.

Away Matches

1. Make a checklist for the equipment needed on the road. Be responsible for this equipment while traveling.
2. Prepare and bring a bag with extra uniforms, socks and knee pads.
3. Laundry and uniforms: Collect uniforms after each match for laundering.
4. Help pack and unpack the vehicle(s) used for travel.

Pre-match Duties

1. Set up the videotaping equipment.
2. Verify players' uniform numbers for the lineup sheets.
3. Greet the opposing team and see if they have any special needs.
4. Assist with team warm-up drills when necessary.
5. Secure and store all balls after the warm-up.

Duties During Matches

1. Keep statistics as designated.
2. Keep running totals of the substitutions and time-outs used.
3. Between games, compute designated statistical game totals for the coach's use.

Post-match Duties

1. Secure and store all balls and equipment, including video equipment.
2. Give the visiting coach a copy of the official score sheet.
3. Check the locker rooms to make sure that nothing was left and that the towels and uniforms are put away.

Statistics

1. Compile all statistics after matches and give them to the head coach.
2. Obtain a copy of the official box score from the sports information staff following all matches. If the team is on the road, also ask for a copy of the official score sheet.
3. Compile season total statistics and give them to the coach and the sports information director every Monday during the season.
4. Replenish the supply of stat forms when necessary.

SUPPORT STAFF

The support staff members are critical to the efficient

everyday operation of the athletic department. In most cases, members of the support staff operate in cooperation with the head coach — they are not people who report to the head coach. Because of this, the coach must learn to function with these peers in a professional atmosphere. Understanding the primary duties of each member of the support staff is an essential prerequisite to working with each one.

The Sports Information Director

The sports information director is responsible for the direction, development and implementation of all sports information released from the athletic department. This person serves as the spokesperson for the department by releasing pertinent information about the programs. Typical duties of the sports information director include:

- Writing, editing and distributing news releases to newspapers, magazines, radio and television stations and press services.
- Preparing information brochures.
- Keeping statistics, records and other news material valuable to the media.
- Gathering personal information on team members and distributing it to the media.
- Arranging press box services, including lineups and statistics, for home and visiting teams.
- Maintaining pictorial and information files.
- Supervising the taking of athletic pictures to be used for publicity purposes.
- Supervising the writing and editing of all programs sold at home.
- Supervising statistical crews at all home events and preparing box score forms for distribution at the end of each event.
- Communicating with the coach via weekly meetings during the season, post-game interviews and other meetings as necessary.

The Director of Promotions

The director of promotions is responsible for the direction, development and implementation of all special events and promotional activities for the department. The purpose of this position is to direct events (other than sports events) which will bring attention and/or funds to the department and to promote athletic events so that attendance will increase. Some typical duties would include:

Fig. 22.1 *A program will grow and become successful if everyone involved works as a team.*

- Cooperating with the fund-raiser and sports information director in all event promotions.
- Negotiating radio and television contracts for athletic events.
- Representing the department in speaking appearances before civic clubs, alumni groups, booster clubs and other organizations.
- Arranging such engagements for coaches.
- Organizing a promotional program for each sport season. Begin with identifying target groups and determining methods for reaching these groups.
- Developing a comprehensive marketing plan for season ticket sales.
- Securing outside funding for promotional programs and sponsorship of sporting events.
- Organizing special events that will raise money for the scholarship fund.
- Communicating with the coach via monthly preseason meetings for planning season activities and specially arranged meetings as necessary.

The Facilities Coordinator

The facilities coordinator is responsible for scheduling and maintaining all athletic facilities. All practices, special events and home events are cleared through this person, who is then responsible for coordinating individual sports schedules so that conflicts do not exist. The coordinator also schedules necessary maintenance such as floor cleaning, painting, refurbishing, locker room cleaning and all other related tasks. Communication between the coach and the facilities coordinator includes quarterly meetings to coordinate facility needs, memorandums for notification of upcoming situations and emergency meetings as needed.

The Event Supervisor

The event supervisor is responsible for hiring and training all staff to work at events and maintaining security at all events. The event supervisor works in conjunction with the facilities coordinator in preparing the competitive site for competition (i.e., setting up nets, taping the floor and assigning locker rooms). Some specific duties include:

- Hiring and training ticket takers.
- Hiring and training scorekeepers, clock operators and a public address announcer.
- Ordering and supervising setup of the public address system and the scoreboard.
- Contracting all officials and linesmen for home events.
- Securing and training ball shaggers.
- Opening the building prior to the game and securing the facilities following the event.
- Hiring or retaining security people to work during the event.
- Communicating with the coach in a pre-season meeting to coordinate needs for home events and in other scheduled meetings as necessary.
- Coordinating media needs with the sports information director.

The Accounting Clerk

The accounting clerk is responsible for preparing payroll and personnel forms, maintaining accounting records and handling cash. The accounting clerk is also in charge of advance checks for travel and purchase orders. In general, the person in this position deals with all budget items in the department.

Communication with the coach is through budget requests, travel vouchers, requisitions and monthly written budget status reports.

The Office Supervisor

The office supervisor is responsible for organizing and supervising all office workers, including the secretaries, receptionist and student workers. It is the supervisor's duty to make sure that the office runs efficiently and professionally. General office work performed by a coach's secretary would include these duties:

- Answering the telephone, taking messages and making appointments. Performing routine typing, copying and collating.
- Picking up and distributing mail.
- Maintaining files with correspondence and master lists for labels.
- Operating office machines.
- Ordering new supplies and keeping the office supply inventory.
- Running campus errands when necessary.
- Maintaining an accurate list of recruits and preparing weekly mailings.
- Assisting in making travel arrangements, including motel and plane reservations. Communicating with the coach via written work request slips and daily conversations and discussion of needs.

PROGRAM PLANNING

Once the coach has a thorough understanding of the workings of the athletic department, the process of planning the volleyball program becomes a more feasible task. Obviously, the interrelationships and intradependencies of the athletic department staff make careful planning an absolute necessity. Chart 2 maps out a yearly scheme for planning a collegiate volleyball program. It details the tasks that need attention and the time of year when each should be handled. Clearly, the head coach cannot attend to every item listed on this chart, but he or she must serve as the administrator of the volleyball program. The head coach must delegate responsibilities to the staff, work cooperatively with the support staff, and supervise the daily operations of the program.

Seasonal Conditioning

In order to elicit the best possible performance from athletes, it is essential that they be provided with a

TASK	SUMMER (June-July)	PRE-SEASON (August)	COMPETITIVE SEASON (September-December)	OFF-SEASON (January-May)
1. SEASONAL CONDITIONING	- general cardiovascular conditioning - weight training (strength) - speed, flexibility, agility, and endurance work	- specialized conditioning: agility, muscular endurance, flexibility - weight training	- general - strength maintenance - technical training - tactical training	- heavy weight training (strength) - jump training (plyometrics)
2. PRACTICE	- no organized team practice	- physical exams - physical testing - two-a-day practices until first week of competition - 2–4 hours per session	- Mon.-Fri. except on match days - 2–4 hours - videotape review session	- individual sessions - team practice, 1–5 days per week as allowed by NCAA rules
3. SCHEDULING	- print schedule for distribution in fall	- distribute schedules	- get verbal agreements for next 2-3 years in advance	- confirm schedule for following year - send contracts - schedule off-season competition
4. COMPETITION	- summer beach tourneys	- intrasquads and/or alumni matches	- competitive schedule - evaluate scouting and game plans	- off-season competition (player development)
5. RECRUITING	- initial contacts (phone, mail, and personal) - talent assessment at summer competition	- home visits - correspondence and phone contacts - plan schedule for campus visits	- home visits - campus visits - talent assessment—watch matches - correspondence and phone	- correspondence and phone - initial contacts for juniors (mail) as allowed by NCAA rules - signing of prospects
6. BUDGET	- redo budget based on finalized allocation	- submit team travel advance requests - submit recruiting travel advance request	- turn in expense vouchers from trips - update budget status	- submit budget proposal for coming year
7. ELIGIBILITY	- compute team and individual grade point averages - verify eligibility	- verify individual eligibility - submit team roster for conference and national governing body - athletes register for classes	- arrange tutors and study halls as necessary - update roster for championship competition	- compute grade point averages for athletes - verify eligibility of incoming freshmen (NCAA clearing house)

Chart 2

TASK	SUMMER (June-July)	PRE-SEASON (August)	COMPETITIVE SEASON (September-December)	OFF-SEASON (January-May)
8. TEAM TRAVEL	- make motel reservations - reserve vehicles for travel - make plane reservations	- confirm all reservations - send rooming list to motels - submit season itinerary to athletic director	- carry game contracts to events - confirm practice times and facilities - gather receipts and submit upon return to campus	- confirm off-season travel plans
9. VOLLEYBALL STAFF MEETINGS	- meet as necessary - train new staff members - motivate staff for coming year	- daily meetings to plan and evaluate practices	- daily meetings to plan and evaluate practices - pre- and post-game meetings - weekly recruiting update meetings	- regular practice planning meeting - weekly recruiting updates - hire new staff as necessary
10. SCOUTING	- Prepare list of video requests for opponents	- send video requests to opponents and process their requests	- prepare scouting reports for team use - review videotapes	- file scouting reports for future reference
11. EVENT MANAGEMENT	- contract officials, linesmen, scorers, timers, PA announcer, court manager - coordinate schedules and facility needs for year	- train scorers, linesmen timers - organize event workers - retain security personnel - secure ball shaggers	- conduct and supervise events	- evaluate event management
12. INVENTORY/ EQUIPMENT ORDERS		- distribute practice clothes, shoes, and uniforms to players - assign lockers	- handle emergency needs	- take inventory - order shoes, uniforms, etc. - collect uniforms, non-perishables
13. PUBLICITY/ SPORTS INFORMATION	- gather information for media guide - plan design and layout of media guide - preliminary plans for video highlight tape	- prepare promotional plan for individual players - distribute media guide - organize and conduct pre-season press conferences - take action and head shots	- prepare and distribute weekly updates of statistics and results - produce promotional tape - nominate players for honors	- mail season summary - publicize signing of recruits - update All-Time records
14. PROGRAM PROMOTIONS	- identify target groups for promotion plans - arrange public speaking engagements to talk about team - conduct demo and exhibitions	- arrange for bands, cheerleaders, etc. - arrange public service announcements for local media	- implement promotional plan - continually work with media - implement marketing plan for ticket sales	- evaluate past season's marketing and promotional plan - develop comprehensive marketing and promotional plan for coming year - arrange demos and exhibitions for public relations

Chart 2 (continued)

TASK	SUMMER (June–July)	PRE-SEASON (August)	COMPETITIVE SEASON (September–December)	OFF-SEASON (January–May)
15. AWARDS BANQUET			- set date and site for awards banquet - plan program needs coordinate with Booster Club	- select player honors and awards from past season - conduct banquet
16. BOOSTER CLUB	- appoint or elect officers - order perks to be given or sold to membesr	- conduct membership drive - plan events surrounding games - work with promotions director for special events	- conduct receptions and special events - mail monthly newsletter (throughout the year)	- plan and conduct post-season fund raising - host team awards banquet
17. CLINICS AND CAMPS	- conduct camps or clinics - evaluate success of event	- secure site, date, and facilities for next summer camp	- write and print camp brochure	- distribute brochure - hire staff - register campers - plan program and order equipment
18. EVALUATIONS	- complete year-end report - evaluate success of program for past year	- evaluate players—individual performance skills	- evaluate team performance - conduct player conferences	- evaluate staff performance - evaluate recruiting - evaluate support staff
19. PROFESSIONAL INVOLVEMENT	- attend clinics and workshops	- keep up-to-date on rule changes, trends, innovative ideas - join professional organizations - be active in conference activities	- attend national championships and national coaches' conventions - run for offices in national association	- volunteer services for professional groups - attend workshops and clinics

Chart 2 (continued)

well-planned program for conditioning. The purpose of this program is to bring the athlete to a level of peak physical performance at the appropriate time of the year. Volleyball demands high levels of muscular endurance, cardiovascular endurance, strength, flexibility, speed and agility. Conditioning programs, then, must be designed to develop these qualities.

The most logical time to stress strength development at the collegiate level seems to be during the off-season conditioning program. Weight-lifting programs should be designed to develop power and strength. Plyometric training (jump training) may also be incorporated into the off-season program.

The summer conditioning program should be designed to continue with strength-related conditioning. The summer period should also include programs designed to develop speed, flexibility, agility and general cardiovascular endurance. Circuit training and sprint training are commonly used to develop these qualities. In addition, acrobatic training is necessary for developing agility, flexibility and speed. Since the athlete usually works alone during the summer, these programs must be designed for individual work.

Pre-season conditioning should incorporate as many volleyball-related activities as possible. These specialized conditioning activities should stress further development of strength, flexibility, agility and muscular endurance. Most often, the coach designs intense, demanding practices that lend themselves to the development of these qualities.

During the competitive season, athletes are primarily involved in technical and tactical training. Conditioning during this portion of the season is aimed at maintaining existing levels of fitness. As post-season tournament competition approaches, there is a gradual tapering off of physical work. The goal of this tapering is to enhance the body's ability to reach peak physical performance.

Practice

Much like seasonal conditioning, the practice schedule varies with the time of year. Pre-season practices should be longer and should stress individual skill repetition and heavy physical work. During pre-season practices, team play is limited and emphasis is placed upon individual performances.

Fig. 22.2 *Well-conditioned athletes are able to perform difficult skills with little fear of injury.*

Moving into the competitive season phase of practice, the emphasis switches from individual performance to team-oriented drills that are designed to bring the team together as a unit. In the competitive season, repetitive drills are still used, but game situations become the central focus. The off-season provides opportunities for players to change techniques and improve fundamental skills. Although team play is limited during the off-season, it is important to provide some opportunities for play. Competition can serve as the athletes' reward for hard work.

Scheduling

At the collegiate level, scheduling is being done earlier and earlier each year. In most cases, conference offices put together master schedules several years in advance. When the conference schedule is complete, the coach may add non-conference matches or tournaments to the schedule. Some considerations in scheduling non-conference matches should be:

• Working within the budget.

- Adhering to institutional academic policies for days of class to be missed.
- Adhering to national governing body rules for the total number of allowable matches.
- Scheduling competition that challenges athletes (i.e., top 20 schools).
- Scheduling matches that allow travel to different parts of the country.

(The last two points are important when a team is being considered for berths in postseason tournaments.)

When the schedule is completed, contracts should be sent to each school. Form 1 shows the information found in a typical contract. (Note: Forms 1-10 appear at the end of this chapter.)

Competition

Playing the competitive schedule is the culmination of a year-long process of preparation. Once this period arrives, the coach should be organized well enough in all other aspects of the program that the principal focus of attention can be preparing the team for each match. Competition outside the primary season (off-season tournaments, intrasquads, etc.) should be subordinate to the regular season schedule. It should be clear to the athletes that the primary season is the most important competition during the year.

Recruiting

In all likelihood, the ability of a coach to identify and recruit talented athletes to the program has a high correlation with the success of the program. Although many factors have significant influence on the coach's success, rarely can a coach take average athletes and transform them into a team capable of competing with the best in the country. Briefly outlined below is the recruiting process:

I. Identifying prospective recruits no later than by their junior year. Identifying prospects often begins as early as their freshman year in high school.
   A. Subscribing to scouting services.
   B. Attending age-level tournaments.
   C. Contacting state high school coaches for recommendations.
II. Initiating contacts during the summer before senior year and into early fall (NCAA rules regulate when and how recruits may be contacted).

A. Initiating correspondence.
B. Initiating telephone contacts.
C. Making initial home visits.

III. Making final assessments of talent during the summer and fall of the senior year.
   A. Attending junior tournaments.
   B. Watching prospective recruits in high school matches — more than once if possible.

IV. Executing the final stages of recruitment in the fall and winter of the senior year.
   A. Continuing correspondence.
   B. Continuing telephone contacts.
   C. Scheduling a visit to the athlete's school.
   D. Making additional home visits.
   E. Scheduling a campus visit for each athlete.
   F. Continuing to watch athletes compete whenever possible.
   G. Offering scholarships and signing athletes.

Assessing the talent and potential of an athlete is obviously an important task for the coach. Form 2, designed by Doug Beal, USA national men's team coach, may be used for recording the potential of possible athletes.

Home Visits

Home visits are important in the recruiting process because they give the coach an opportunity to bring the program to the athlete and the athlete's family. Home visit appointments should be made at least two weeks in advance and should be scheduled at the convenience of the athlete and the athlete's family. In most cases, the visits should occur after the dinner hour and should be no more than two hours in duration. The primary objective of the initial home visit is to inform the athlete and his or her family about your program and to answer specific questions about the program. A typical home visit covers the following topics:

- Academics — bring specific academic information about the athlete's academic interests. Include academic advising, tutors, etc.
- University community — describe the university setting.
- Coach's philosophy — be ready to articulate your philosophy of coaching, both to the recruit and to his/her parents.
- University's commitment to the program — describe the type of support.
- Volleyball program specifics, including:

- Budget
- Scholarships
- Items provided to athletes, such as shoes, clothing, etc.
- Schedule and conference organization
- Type and mode of travel
- Facilities — practice and competitive
- Staff — number and quality of coaches
- Booster club
- Team and player promotions
- Dormitory facilities
- Program goals
- Description of returning players as it will relate to the prospect's status/position on the team
- Coach's expectations for athletes in the program
- Question and answer session
- Highlight video (if available)

Campus visit

The campus visit is a significant factor in the athlete's final decision. Whether the athlete selects your institution may well be determined by the perceptions of the program during one 48-hour period. It is therefore advisable for the coach to plan the athlete's visit carefully. Form 3 outlines the type of information the athlete should receive prior to the visit. The student host should also receive a copy so that arrangements can be made for the recruit to be in the right place at the right time. Forms 4 and 5 illustrate other types of information gathering tools that are helpful to the coach during the recruiting process.

Budget

Budget proposals are an annual ritual. Each spring, word comes down from the athletic director to prepare a proposal for the following year. The strategies for preparing these proposals vary depending on the financial environment at each institution. One strategy is to prepare a budget with built-in surpluses so that when it is cut, there will still be sufficient funds. Another strategy is to prepare a request which contains the bare minimum necessary for conducting the program. Whatever plan is used, be prepared to justify your requests. Once the actual budget is allocated, it is usually necessary to reassess the projected expenditures to ensure that you operate within the budget. Primary budget items should include:

- Salaries
- Supplies
- Equipment
- Team travel
- Coaches' travel — scouting, clinics, meetings
- Recruiting
- Officials
- Telephone
- Game filming, videotape
- Player promotions, team promotions
- Memberships, subscriptions
- Scholarships
- Publications, media guide

Forms 6, 7, 8, 9 and 10 are examples of forms which can be used in making travel arrangements, requesting funds for travel and returning unused travel funds.

Scouting

Currently, most scouting is done from videotape rather than by a coach traveling to watch a match. This method usually allows the coach to gather even more information than can be recorded at a "live" match. Having access to the opponents' game videos also allows the coach to share specific parts of the video with the team, emphasizing certain points.

Scouting your opponents can provide your team members with valuable information for an upcoming match. However, the scouting report is most valuable to the coach. A good scouting report helps in structuring practices that allow a team to be more prepared to face the competition. With information from the scouting report, the coach may wish to make lineup changes, defensive adjustments, offensive changes, changes in serving strategy or any number of other alterations. The key to providing team members with scouting reports is to know how much information to share. Sometimes the athletes can be so concerned with the opponents' tendencies that they fail to concentrate on their own play.

Scouting can become a very complex process of gathering data on opposing teams. A coach must decide what the relative value of detailed information will be to the team. Coaches who are unable to scout opponents may find it helpful to make notes about the opponents after the match. By attaching the box score to the following list of notes, the coach can at least be more prepared to meet the same team in the future. These items may be important notes to keep on your opponents:

- Offense employed
- Offensive tendencies and most successful play sets
- Defense, defensive adjustments
- Starting rotation
- Substitution patterns
- Serve receive formations
- Poor passers
- Best servers and type of serve
- Best blockers and blocking strategy
- Outstanding hitters and tendencies
- Ability of setter(s)
- General evaluation of match
- Mental toughness — do they fall apart — who is the key player

Event Management

The coach should delegate all the responsibilities of the event management to other members of the coaching staff or to the support staff. The coach will want to supervise this process carefully, since the image of the entire program is reflected by the manner in which the competitive events are run.

Inventory/Equipment Orders

The support staff in the equipment room should be charged with the responsibility of taking inventory and advising the coach about the condition of equipment and supplies. With this information, the coach should place necessary orders each spring. In most cases, institutions require that supply equipment orders be placed out on bid. To ensure that you receive exactly what is desired, be sure to list all specifications and brand names.

Publicity/Sports Information

The sports information director has primary responsibility for publicity and sports information. The coach should serve as a consultant in preparing highlight tapes, media guides and other informational materials regarding the team. The sports information staff should also assist with preparing paperwork for nominating players for post-season awards.

Program Promotions

The coach again serves as a consultant in promoting the volleyball program. In order to promote the program, it will be necessary for the coach to conduct demonstrations and exhibitions, work with the media and be actively involved in public speaking. Advice from marketing experts is useful in developing a comprehensive promotional plan and a marketing plan for selling season and individual game tickets.

Awards Banquet

Most athletic departments sponsor an annual banquet for all sports. However, these affairs rarely provide adequate time for a coach to recognize individual team members as he or she would like. For this reason, a separate volleyball banquet is a desirable event and it can be as informal as a picnic or as formal as a banquet. The coach should determine the types of awards that will be presented to the players. The booster club can be helpful in planning and sponsoring the year-end volleyball awards banquet.

Booster Club

A booster club can do a great deal to enhance the image of a program. Such a club provides a base of support for your team. Set some goals for the booster club, such as increasing attendance at games, increasing public awareness of the program and providing supplemental funds for special volleyball projects. Enthusiastic leadership for the booster club is essential. Provide booster club members with special seating at home games and arrange some post-game receptions so that the club members can interact with the team and coaches.

Clinics and Camps

The coach should become involved in conducting clinics and camps. Clinics are usually directed at educating other coaches, whereas camps usually teach skills to athletes. Both camps and clinics offer the coach an opportunity to showcase the program. Summer camps can also provide opportunities to develop young athletes who may help your program in the future. Summer camps can also provide an additional revenue source.

Evaluations

All areas of a program must be constantly evaluated if improvements are to be made. Evaluations conducted orally with staff and players are valuable for the participants, but these conversations should be accompanied by written evaluations. A year-end report should include an evaluation of every phase of the program.

Professional Involvement

If the sport of volleyball is to grow, it is imperative for coaches to join and become actively involved in their national associations. Professional associations such as the American Volleyball Coaches Association (AVCA) were founded for the express purpose of promoting volleyball. The coach should also attend as many clinics as possible to keep abreast of current trends.

Enhancing Your Program

Once a coach has established a well-organized program, it may be time to begin soliciting the expertise of individuals outside the department or university to complement and enhance the existing training program for athletes. Many professionals are willing and even anxious to have an opportunity to volunteer time working with elite athletes. Professionals in these areas may give a competitive edge to your team.

- Sport psychologist (team and individual athletes)
- Vision training expert (individual)
- Media training expert for athletes
- Mentor program with community support to assist athletes in academic interests

SUMMARY

A volleyball program should have well-defined goals and philosophy, which should be compatible with those of the university. The responsibilities involved in the administration of a collegiate volleyball program are great, but the magnitude of the job can be lessened if a systematic approach is taken. A well-organized volleyball program should accomplish three things: First, it should provide the athletes with every possible opportunity to succeed; second, it should be a positive reflection of the university's philosophy; and it should reflect the pride and professionalism of the coach.

CONTRACT

This agreement, made and entered into on the _____ day of _____,
19 ____, by and between the Athletic Associaiton of [college/university] _____
_____ and the athletic authorities of _____,
_____ their duly authorized agents, is in accordance with the following conditions:

- Sport:_____
- Place:_____
- Date of Event:_____
- Time of Event:_____
- Practice/Warm-up Time:_____
- Agreement on Officials:_____
- Special Agreements Concerning the Scheduled Event:
   - Locker Room:_____
   - Uniforms:_____
   - Equipment (training room, supplies, etc.):_____
   - Competitive Rules:_____
   - Financial (entry fees, guarantees, etc.):_____
   - Other:_____

Official Representative of Visiting Team	Official Representative of [COLLEGE/UNIVERSITY]
Coach_____ Telephone (____)_____ Address_____ _____	Coach_____ Telephone (____)_____ Address_____ _____
Director of [Men's/Women's] Athletics	Director of [Men's/Women's] Athletics
_____ Signature	_____ Signature
Univ. Phone (____)_____ Home Phone (____)_____	Telephone (____)_____ Please sign and return white & yellow copies to:

Distribution:
White copy: Home Athletic Director
Yellow copy: Home Coach
Pink copy: Visiting Athletic Director
Gold copy: Visiting Coach

[College/University]
[Men's/Women's] Athletic Department

_____
_____

Form 1: Sample contract uses for regular season matches.

PLAYER EVALUATION REPORT

PLAYER_____ RH_____ LH_____ HT_____ WT_____
Position_____Vertical Jumping Ability_____(standing jump/two-step approach)
Year in school_____ ACT_____ SAT_____ _____ Class rank_____ GPA_____
Honors (League, State, National)_____
_____

USVBA Experience: Years_____ Club Name_____ Club Coach_____
_____

RATING CODE: 5 – Superior,   4 – Excellent,   3 – Good,   2 – Fair
[Circle one in each category]

__SPIKING__   5   4   3   2
What angle does player usually hit?_____
Can player hit the line?_____
Is he/she bothered by a 2–3 man block?_____
Does he/she spike deep sets as well as close?_____
Can he/she hit fast playsets?_____

__SERVING__   5   4   3   2
Type of serve player uses: Overhead Floater____ Overhead Spin Serve_____ Japanese Floater_____
Does he/she usually serve to the same spot and same depth?_____
Can player serve to the six positions on the court?_____
Is he/she an aggressive server?_____

__SETTING__   5   4   3   2   (Only for setters)
Is player able to set combination plays?_____
Can he/she effectively set fast to the sides?_____
Can player short set the middle?_____
Can he/she set the ball effectively with an underhand pass?_____
Can he/she set very high sets accurately?_____
Are sets close to sideline or in toward middle?_____
Does player always set direction he/she faces?_____
Does he/she tip-off overhead set?_____ How?_____
Can player jump set?_____

__BLOCKING__   5   4   3   2
Is player a good outside or center blocker?_____
Does player have good quickness?_____
Does he/she penetrate over the net?_____
Can player jump with: elbows_____hands above top of net_____?
Is he/she an aggressive blocker?_____

__PASSING__   5   4   3   2
Does player always have good lateral range in receiving zone?_____
Is he/she equally proficient in hard, soft, spin, and float serve receptions?_____
Can player pass consistently to target area?_____

Form 2: Player evaluation report for prospective athletes.

−2−

__SPIKE DEFENSE__ 5 4 3 2

Does player handle hard spikes well?_____

How fast does player react to dinks?_____

Does he/she dive and roll with ease?_____

How efficiently does player get a ball hit away from him/her?_____

__ATTITUDE__ 5 4 3 2

Is player a competitor?_____

Is he/she a pressure player?_____

Is player coachable?_____

Is he/she motivated?_____

OVERALL EVALUATION

(Circle one number in rating code that best describes him/her as a total volleyball player.)

5 – SUPERIOR

This player can execute offensive and defensive skills with a high degree of consistency. Player is able to analyze or anticipate opponents. Excels under pressure.

4 – EXCELLENT

Player may not excel in all areas of the game, but is outstanding in one facet of the sport. For example, outstanding on offense but is back-courted.

3 – GOOD

Average skills, not outstanding. Steady player, but does not excel in one particular phase of the game.

4 – FAIR

He/she may lack playing experience, but has potential to become a good player.

This player is capable of playing:

DIVISION I_____   DIVISION II_____   DIVISION III_____   J. C._____

University or College preference_____

Area of study_____

Remarks_____

_____

_____

_____

_____

Date_____

Player evaluation report (Form 2, continued).

CAMPUS VISIT ITINERARY

NAME _____

HOST/HOSTESS _____

<u>ARRIVAL</u> – DATE/TIME _____

  – Airline _____
  – Flight Number _____

HOUSING ACCOMMODATIONS _____

<u>MEETINGS/ENTERTAINMENT</u>

ACADEMIC ADVISOR _____

HEAD COACH _____

CAMPUS TOUR _____

PHOTO SESSION _____

TRAINERS _____

ENTERTAINMENT _____

OTHER ACTIVITIES _____

_____

_____

<u>DEPARTURE</u> – DATE/TIME _____

  – Airline _____
  – Flight Number _____

Form 3: Campus visit itinerary. Should be mailed to the prospective athlete before his or her visit.

VOLLEYBALL ATHLETIC GRANT APPLICATION

Date_____

Name_____ Date of birth_____
 Age_____ Height_____ Weight_____ High school graduation yr_____

Home address_____
City_____ State_____ Zip code_____
Home phone_____ Social security number_____

High school_____ School phone_____
School address_____
Coach's name_____

High school class rank_____ Total number of students in class_____
Grade point average_____ ACT test score_____
                            SAT test scores_____ _____
What college, if any, have you attended?_____
JC graduated_____

Father's name_____ Father's occupation_____
Mother's name_____ Mother's occupation_____

What extracurricular activities, other than sports, have you participated in during high school? List
any special honors or awards. _____
_____
_____

What career or profession might you like to pursue? What will be your college major?_____
_____
_____

VOLLEYBALL INFORMATION

Years of participation_____ Favorite or best position_____
Standing vertical jump_____ Running approach jump_____ Reach_____

List any summer camps you have attended_____
_____
Individual honors_____
Team record and accomplishments_____
_____

[Please attach any individual or team statistics that are available.]

Form 4: Athletic grant application, which should be completed by the prospective athlete and
returned to the head coach.

—— VOLLEYBALL RECRUITING CONTACTS ——

NAME _____

HIGH SCHOOL _____

HOMETOWN _____

HEIGHT _____   POSITION _____

PROFILE _____
_____
_____

PERSONAL CONTACTS

	Date	Made by	Where	Comments
1.				
2.				
3.				
4.				
5.				
6.				

PHONE CONTACTS OR CAMPUS VISITS

Date	Made by	Comments

Form 5: Recruiting contact sheet. Most institutions are required to keep accurate records of the number of personal contacts made with recruits. This form is also helpful in keeping a recruiting history for each athlete.

TRAVEL ARRANGEMENTS

COACH_____ SPORT_____

DATE OF TRIP_____ DESTINATION_____

....

HOTEL/MOTEL

Hotel accommodations needed?_____ In what city?_____

Dates needed_____ Number of Singles_____ Doubles_____ Quads_____ Other_____

....

CARS/VANS/WAGONS

# Needed:	Destination	Pickup date/time	Return date/time
Cars ____	_____	_____	_____
Vans _____	_____	_____	_____
Wagons ____	_____	_____	_____

....

BUS

Destination_____

Departure date & time_____

Shuttle needed?_____ Approximate departure time, return trip_____

....

FLIGHT INFORMATION

Destination_____ # of reservations_____

When you must be at destination_____

Earliest possible time of return_____

[List names in traveling party]

....

MEALS

of persons_____ # of days_____ $ per day per person_____

Total_____

....

RENTAL CARS

Type and # needed_____

....

ENTRY FEE

Entry fee required?_____ Amount_____ Payable to_____

[Please note any special requirements on back of form.]

Form 6: Team travel arrangement form. Should be completed and turned in well in advance of actual travel.

STAFF/RECRUITING TRAVEL INFORMATION

Coach_____ **Team**_____

Date of trip_____ Destination_____
Hotel/motel_____
Address_____
Telephone_____

Reservation confirmation number_____

ROOMS

<u>Type</u>   <u>Price</u>   <u>Dates reserved</u>

Single_____   _____   _____
Double_____   _____   _____

TRANSPORTATION

Rent-a-car information_____
                                 _____
Instructions_____
Gasoline expense_____

MEALS, etc.

Meals for_____days

Tickets for events (program, parking, etc.)_____

Recruiting of_____
Other purpose_____

TOTAL ADVANCE:_____

Form 7: Staff travel information. Should be completed at least two weeks prior to departure.

TEAM TRAVEL ROSTER

TEAM_____

TRIP TO/FROM_____

DATE_____

ROSTER

1. _____   14. _____

2. _____   15. _____

3. _____   16. _____

4. _____   17. _____

5. _____   18. _____

6. _____   19. _____

7. _____   20. _____

8. _____   21. _____

9. _____   22. _____

10. _____

11. _____

12. _____

13. _____

Manager _____   Trainer _____

Coaches _____

_____

_____

Form 8: Team travel roster, which lists all members of traveling party. Submit prior to departure.

TRAVEL EXPENSE VOUCHER

Name_____   Requisition No._____

Sport_____   Check No._____

Destination_____   Amount of Advance_____

Purpose of Trip_____   Budget No._____

Dates_____

This form should be turned in as soon as possible.. Please list "to" and "from" when turning in receipts from taxi expenses. Upon return, please remit the amount you did not spend, if any, in the form of a personal check payable to_____.

| | | | | | | Meals | | |
Date	Description of Misc.	Car Rental	Hotel	Misc.	B	L	D	TOTALS
Totals								

NOTES:

Amount of advance   _____

Total amount spent   _____

Amount due University _____

Amount due you   _____

Form 9: Travel expense voucher, to be completed after return to campus. It is a detailed listing of expenditures, with receipts attached.

TEAM ITINERARY

DATE	DEPART (CITY)	ARRIVE (CITY)	MATCH/DATE/TIME	MOTEL	MODE OF TRANSPORTATION

Form 10: Team itinerary.

Photo courtesy of ASUCLA

Chapter 23

PHYSICAL TRAINING FACTORS

Greg Brislin, M.S., C.S.C.S.

It is commonplace now for most coaches to incorporate some sort of strength training and/or conditioning program into their overall volleyball plan. In fact, coaches want information on how to incorporate these programs rather than reasons why to incorporate them, as in times past. Developing an efficient, practical and effective program is a challenging task for a qualified, experienced strength and conditioning coach, let alone for a coach with many other responsibilities and little or no experience in the field.

Due to demands on time, lack of knowledge or inexperience, body building, basketball or other sport programs are often used as guides in developing programs for volleyball teams. Although these programs may help develop some areas of the athlete physically, they are inappropriate for the needs of the sport of volleyball or for improving sport-specific athletic performance.

Programs developed for collegiate or national volleyball, while suitable for sport performance improvements, are often not appropriate for the age and development of younger, less-experienced players. Implementing programs too difficult or inappropriate for a team may increase the frequency of injury, decrease performance and create frustration from lack of improvement.

Deciding what is important and appropriate when designing a program for your athletes depends on a number of issues that range from time and equipment considerations to changes in exercise intensity. Practical, effective training programs lead to improved sport performance and the prevention of injury — the ultimate goals of any program. The "anything is better than nothing" approach is simply a waste of time, expense and effort.

The ability to blend the physical components of athletic skills and to integrate them with the technical skills of volleyball so that optimal volleyball performance is achieved is the task of the Volleyball Conditioning Specialist (VCS). This chapter will help you understand the role of the VCS, improve your knowledge as one and evaluate and develop a program that is effective for your team.

THE VOLLEYBALL CONDITIONING SPECIALIST

Deciding how to develop a training program, how much to emphasize it and what to include in it is determined by the Volleyball Conditioning Specialist (VCS). This individual is not necessarily a "strength" coach, but may serve a number of roles on the team from the head coach to the equipment manager. Regardless of the other responsibilities this person may have, he/she is the individual ultimately responsible for designing and implementing a program with two specific goals in mind.

An appropriately designed program will eliminate or reduce the severity of injuries suffered by the athlete and improve the player's athletic skills through the development of the physical components of the sport. Blending these components with the technical skills of volleyball will develop optimal sport performance.

A VCS should be competent in a number of areas, but recognizing that no one is proficient in everything, he/she should recognize individual weaknesses and know who or where to turn to as a resource when dealing with those issues. Obviously, a VCS should be familiar with all aspects of the technical and tactical skills of the game of volleyball. He/she should also be familiar with all of the tools available to achieve athletic skill development and injury prevention.

Through field tests and subjective observation, the VCS should be able to identify the individual technical and athletic needs of the player and measure the effectiveness of an athletic skills development program in relation to volleyball performance. The VCS should be familiar enough with the components of athletic skills (agility, mobility, footwork, recovery and on-court conditioning, stability/balance and explosive power) that he/she can relate them to volleyball skill development.

He/she should be able to design a year-round program that effectively integrates athlete and volleyball skill development on an individual basis. A VCS needs a basic understanding of the concepts of progression/overload, rest/recovery, the classification of exercises and the physiology and biomechanics of volleyball. He/she should be able to identify correct exercise technique and correct errors in execution of an exercise.

Since injury prevention should be key in program design, a VCS should be able to be familiar with common volleyball injuries; how to help reduce the severity and/or occurrence of injury through proper program design; and communicate effectively with medical personnel during the functional rehabilitation process of an injured athlete. A VCS should be able to offer counsel or identify resources on nutritional questions and issues and effectively motivate players to adhere to training programs.

PROGRAM DESIGN CONSIDERATIONS
The Athlete

Individualizing a training program is crucial to achieving maximum effectiveness. To individualize a program best, one must create a profile of the player or players who will be using the program. Characteristics such as the age of the athlete and the developmental age of the athlete, which is sometimes not the same as the chronological age, are obvious first concerns. An athlete who is chronologically 14 years old may be more physically mature like an 18-year-old. Training her/him by chronological age

would undervalue the program and not meet the needs of the athlete. Conversely, training an athlete who may be 16, both by physical maturation and chronologically, like a 21-year-old may predispose her/him to injury.

Consider the volleyball experience level of the athlete. This will help in determining how much an athlete can be challenged physically. How long has the athlete been competing in volleyball? Is it one year or five years? At what level does the athlete currently compete? High school, club, college? Different levels deserve different training emphasis. A veteran player will have different physical abilities and will probably be able to handle higher training intensities.

Has he/she participated in other sports? What previous experience with strength training, conditioning and/or equipment does he/she have? Will the athlete need more instruction time with exercises or equipment? Progression of exercise and intensities will revolve around these issues.

Review the medical history of the athlete. Has the athlete had past injuries and have they been treated? Is the injury chronic or acute? Has the athlete been through rehab and is he/she continuing therapy? Are certain athletes under any restrictions or limitations? Preventing future injuries benefits the athlete and the team and is central to the periodization model.

Measuring the athlete's physical condition through a number of physical tests provides input of the player's athletic strengths and weaknesses. The information from the tests can give you a basis to start from when considering individual needs from the plan.

Equipment

A second important factor to consider when outlining your plans is the equipment that is available to you for training. Are you fortunate enough to have a fully equipped facility for your use? Is there nothing available? Do you have any funds to purchase equipment? Take an inventory of everything. Even the simplest and least expensive equipment can be used effectively. A variety of inexpensive training tools like jump ropes, dumbbells, resistance bands, medicine balls and elastic tubing can be utilized properly to improve athletic performance.

If equipment is available, how accessible is it? Will other teams be utilizing the facility at the same time? These questions will become important when deciding what equipment would be most effective in the time allotted.

Understand the limitations and possibilities of the equipment. It will make future decisions regarding what exercises to incorporate and how to work the training into your available time much easier.

Time

Consider how important training is to you and your team goals. What other non-training considerations affect this decision? How much time do you have to devote to running an effective training program? Do you have capable assistants to help handle the load? Do you have an experienced or inexperienced team? An inexperienced, unskilled high school team with a four-week pre-season and only two hours in the gym to practice on a daily basis would be hard-pressed to commit an hour a day to training. The time needed to instruct a new exercise regimen to this team may not be available. Priorities of the game, such as individual skill training and team defense skills, would certainly take precedent. This is not to say that the training is unimportant, but incorporating the physical training into skill drills would take advantage of time and facility problems for a situation such as this.

Devote what you can to physical training but maximize your time. An effective performance enhancing and injury reduction program can be accomplished in as little as 20 minutes a day!

Sport Specificity

Sport-specific training refers to the utilization of resistance, conditioning and plyometric exercises that improve the on-court performance of the skill demands of the volleyball player. These exercises may place demands on one or a combination of one or more of the athletic competencies of agility, mobility, footwork, recovery and on-court conditioning, stability/balance and explosive power. They are functional in nature in that they mimic one or a combination of one or more movements of a skill like a standing block or a jump serve. The more specific the exercise to a skill demand, the more effective it will be in enhancing performance in that skill.

Safety

Emphasizing safety to all athletes should be a prime directive and through evaluation of the aforementioned elements, you should be able to design protocols safely for each of your players. Sound warm-ups, stretching and cool down exercises should be included in every workout.

Form should never be sacrificed for weight. Proper lifting techniques should always be emphasized. Learn the proper techniques for exercises that you plan to use in your program, even if you cannot do them yourself. Give good instruction on lifting techniques or have someone qualified in teaching exercise techniques provide instruction. Re-evaluate your athlete's technique at each workout and correct improper form immediately.

Use spotters when using free weights and for highly technical and difficult lifts. Weight belts, grips and weight gloves should be used when appropriate.

Teach athletes to be aware of their surroundings at all times. Have them use common sense and allow no horseplay. Learn their limitations with different exercises and weights and get them to understand their own limits.

Physiology

Understanding the metabolic requirements of the sport is necessary to develop conditioning programs appropriate for each athlete's needs. Despite belief by many, the most recent research of the energy demands of volleyball determine that it is primarily an anaerobic sport.

Physiologically, there are two basic metabolic systems that provide energy for muscular work, the aerobic and the anaerobic systems. Both systems unleash energy for the muscle to use by the breakdown of adenosine triphosphate (ATP), although each goes about it in a different way.

Aerobic activities require the use of oxygen to break down glycogen to produce energy in the form of ATP. The aerobic metabolic system begins to be activated after 60 seconds of continual activity and is the primary energy source for events lasting greater than 90 seconds. Long distance running, cycling and swimming are examples of sports that receive the majority of their energy from this system. This process generates tremendous amounts of ATP for long-term events and utilizes fats as a primary fuel for activities lasting longer than 20 minutes.

The anaerobic system is composed of the ATP-CP system (alactic) and the anaerobic glycolysis (lactic acid) systems. Both provide high levels of energy in short time frames. The ATP-CP system supplies energy for activities of short duration and high intensity. The release of energy from the breakdown of creatine phosphate (CP) produces ATP for muscular contraction in a rapid fashion. Since the muscle is unable to store large amounts of CP or ATP, this system is depleted in a short time (<20 seconds) before needing replenishment. If an athlete rests immediately following the movement or event, up to 75 percent of the original stores of CP are replenished after 30 seconds and can be fully restored in two minutes. A standing or approach jump is an example of the type of powerful, short-lived event that primarily relies on this type of energy production.

Events like the 400 m sprint that last between 20 to 90 seconds derive their energy from anaerobic glycolysis. This system breaks down glycogen into ATP in a similar method to that used by the aerobic system, but without the use of oxygen. Lactic acid, a by-product of this process, builds up in the muscle during exercise because oxygen is not present. This build-up causes muscular fatigue and limits activity after approximately a minute and a half. Recovery can take up to two hours to regenerate 40 percent of original levels of this energy system.

The ability to recover rapidly for a second bout of an event is critical in volleyball. During a typical rally, a middle blocker may attempt a block, come off the net, make an approach, spike the ball and make a second block attempt all in the space of a few seconds. The athlete's metabolism needs to rebound quickly to provide energy from one explosive move to the next.

Training protocols should be adapted to the energy requirements of the sport. Research places the average rally lasting four to eight seconds, depending on the level of play and how equally matched the teams may be, and the average longest rallies last from 15 to 18 seconds. The length of time of both activities easily falls within the demands of the ATP-CP energy system. To maximize the athlete's sport-specific conditioning demands, the length of time it takes to complete a conditioning exercise should mimic the activity on the court. In other words, the majority of conditioning exercises should take no longer than 20 seconds to complete.

To enhance a player's recovery time between bouts, we consider the rest intervals between activities. The time between energy demanding explosive movements (averaged across a match) has been reported to be approximately 22 seconds for front-court players and 40 seconds for back-row players. The work-to-rest ratio is approximately 1:3, the ideal work-to-rest ratio to apply to improve anaerobic endurance.

The importance of understanding this metabolic information is in its application. Since volleyball is primarily an anaerobic sport, conditioning should be primarily anaerobic in nature. As mentioned above, most conditioning exercises should be between four to 20 seconds in length, with a rest interval lasting three times that of the work interval.

Volleyball does have an aerobic component, but research shows that frequent on-court practice and match play is sufficient to develop and maintain aerobic conditioning levels. This is not to say that it does not have a place in a training plan, especially in the off-season. Aerobic conditioning improves the cardiovascular system and enhances removal of lactic acid build-up accrued through anaerobic conditioning. Thus, it has an additional effect of improving anaerobic endurance. It is not recommended to make it a primary exercise or to make it the cornerstone of the conditioning program, but to make it a supplementary exercise best suited in limited use for off-season periods or in the rehabilitation of an injured athlete.

Biomechanics

Understanding the mechanics of the sport allows a coach to recognize whether an activity is sport-specific and if it is beneficial to her/his players. Mechanics are important for proper execution of a drill or activity. Correcting a player's approach mechanics, like one who makes a goofy-footed approach, will eventually lead to better hitting mechanics and a better volleyball player. Understanding the mechanics of strength training or plyometric exercise and comparing them to sport movements can help a coach decide whether to include them in the athlete's training regimen.

Better understanding of the forces and dynamics associated with the game can lead to better recognition of potential injury situations, also. A coach who observes poor armswing mechanics in a player that may predispose her/him to injury can design a more appropriate and individualized injury prevention training routine for the athlete.

A VCS should review the movements of each of her/his volleyball player's practice, play and film from a biomechanical perspective. He/she should observe the athletes' movement patterns, how hard an athlete lands (ground reaction forces), joint stresses brought about by poor posture and poor mechanics and take that information into account when individualizing the player's training program.

Components of the Program
Injury Prevention

Essential to the development of a high-performance athlete is keeping the athlete healthy and injury-free. The effect of commonly occurring injuries like ankle sprains, shin splints, shoulder or rotator cuff injuries, low back and knee strains can be reduced through integration of sound injury prevention exercises into the overall periodization scheme.

Practicing injury prevention activities should be a lifelong endeavor. Every athlete at every level should regularly train with these types of exercises year after year throughout every phase of their program. A good strength base develops strong muscles, bones, tendons, ligaments, improves the overall structure and stability of the joint and improves the athlete's body control. When injured, an athlete with this kind of training base will often suffer a less severe injury and will recover from it more quickly than an athlete who may be more unstable, unbalanced and less structurally sound.

Injury prevention exercises include rotator cuff exercises for shoulder injury prevention; anterior tibialis exercises for prevention of shin splints; back exercises for low back injury prevention; and ankle exercises to help reduce ankle injury. There are a vast number of other exercises and their variations that can easily be employed in the periodization program.

It is important to communicate with medical personnel when it comes to adding these exercises into your program. A coach should have a good working knowledge of the mechanisms of these injuries, how they occur and who on the team may be predisposed toward which injuries. The expertise provided by athletic trainers, physical therapists and physicians can help a coach successfully add the right exercises to her/his program and to recognize situations that could lead to injury and how to correct them.

Communication with these individuals is essential when dealing with an injured athlete. Understanding how the injury was managed and functionally integrated with the rest of the body during the rehabilitation process will help avoid a recurrence of the injury and help the coach set realistic goals for the athlete's return to training.

Exercise Technique and Progression

There are a number of excellent books available for the purpose of describing strength training exercises and their techniques and although it is beyond the scope of this chapter to describe all exercises available for a coach with all equipment, learning to teach perfect technique and understanding exercise progression is an important concept to avoid future injury. As with learning to pass, practice makes perfect — but only perfect practice leads to perfect technique.

As a VCS, you should make it a priority to learn the techniques that you demand from your athletes. If you are unfamiliar with any exercise or technique, have an experienced strength coach teach the techniques. Learn about the exercises and how to watch for incorrect technique. Teaching improper technique can lead to chronic and/or potentially disastrous injuries. Be honest with yourself for your athletes' sake. If you do not understand an activity, get someone qualified to instruct it or do not use it until you do. This is especially important when wanting to use highly complex, technical exercises like the squat, clean or snatch.

Inexperienced athletes need to be taught simple exercises first and have them repeatedly perform these exercises correctly before moving on to more complex activities. Generally speaking, weight machines are safer to use and easier to teach to inexperienced athletes than complex free weight exercises. For example, a simple exercise like the leg/knee extension should be taught and the technique perfected by the athlete before teaching and incorporating a more complex activity like a squat or power clean.

Correct errors immediately and reinforce good technique. Poor technique practiced over and over may result in injury. Daily review through observation is required to stop incorrect technique before it becomes a habit.

Develop core musculature first. Abdominal, back and hip muscles are crucial to volleyball performance, as they are involved in every movement on the court. Core mass lifts like parallel or lateral squats and incline press and lat pulldowns are recommended for development of these areas. Center development by focusing on these areas first, then work toward the extremities or assist areas for optimal results. Underdevelopment in the core musculature may lead to poor exercise technique and body position during lifts or exercises.

A note on Olympic lifts needs to be raised here. Although these exercises have been touted as the ultimate exercise for developing sport-specific power and strength, they are highly technical lifts that require expert instruction to be done correctly. Many facilities lack the equipment to be able to perform them properly. More functional exercises like a medicine ball granny toss can develop the same gross motor movement and recruitment with less instruction, equipment and safety concerns.

Teach an exercise that is more technical, like an Olympic lift, through a progression. The more complex the exercise, the more components there are to performing it correctly. Break the exercise down into these components and teach them individually. Have the athlete perfect the first component before moving on to the second. Explosive lifts like the power clean and snatch should be taught through progression.

Start with no load and add resistance gradually. As in teaching a bench press, use a broom stick to teach form before moving to a weighted bar then on to weights or dumbbells. Too much weight may lead to cheating, which can compromise body position; in turn, the compromise may create stress in susceptible areas like the low back.

Be aware that fatigue may cause poor exercise technique. During a long, hard practice, an athlete's skill techniques likely will break down. When an athlete is fresh, her/his passing technique may look great, but as the practice continues, fatigue causes posture to degrade and he/she begins to get flat-footed. The same can occur during training. Continuing to train under these circumstances can lead to injury, poor recovery and overtraining.

Table 1 — Exercises of Various Muscle Groups

Muscle Group	Type of Group*	Exercise
Abdominals	C	Crunches
		Twist Crunches
Low Back	C/IP	Press Ups
		Back Extensions
Legs/Hips	C	Step Ups
		Lunges
		Squats
Chest	C	Push Ups
		Incline Press
Back	C	Bent Over Rows
		Lat Pull Downs
Shoulders	A	Military Press
	IP	Rotator Cuff Exercises
Arms (Triceps and Biceps)	A	Biceps Curls
		Triceps Extensions
Calves	A	Heel Raises
Combination Exercises		
Legs, Back, Shoulders, Abs, Arms, Calves	C, E	Power Cleans
Shoulders, Arms, Chest, Back	C	Dips

C = Core; A = Assist; IP = Injury Prevention; E = Explosive

Table 1 provides a brief example of exercises for various muscle groups. Remember to make workouts fun and invigorating and use a variety of exercises to train the same muscle groups or power or strength needs throughout the season. Not only will musculature recuperate better, but it has a positive psychological effect, as well.

Every workout should begin with a period of warm-up lasting at least 10 minutes. During this period of time, the athlete performs light to moderate activities that will work the muscle groups and joints that will be emphasized during the training session. Warm-up is not the same as static stretching, which will be discussed later. Stretching activities, if incorporated, should be performed after this warm-up period. Warm-up activities increase blood flow to the muscles, tendons and other tissue. The increased flow prepares muscles, tendons, ligaments, the central nervous system and other tissue for maximum effort by performing these exercises with submaximal effort.

Flexibility/Stability

Flexibility plays an important role for athletes, but true flexibility in reference to performance is an often misunderstood concept. Flexibility is often viewed as a static concept — the ability to touch one's toes or do the splits — and is often used as a warm-up unto itself. In reality, flexibility in regard to athletic performance is not a static quality, but is quite dynamic. It is the combination of strength and flexibility that allows a joint to go through a large range of motion under control. It is dynamic or functional because it allows an athlete to extend and reach that extra six inches to play up a ball that is out of her/his defensive range.

Although assessments like the sit and reach or shoulder elevation provide reference points for future measurements, especially post injury, since they are static measures they do not translate well into the functional ability of an athlete. Dynamic flexibility is different for everyone. The shape of one's joints and bone structure and the ability to perform movements through a wide range of motion are the determining factors for flexibility. In other words, a statically flexible athlete may not have good range of motion in a volleyball skill which may limit performance. On the other hand, a statically inflexible athlete may have tremendous dynamic range of motion and can perform exceptionally well at the same skill.

Work dynamic flexibility exercises into the warm-up or conditioning programs that work the range of motion of skills of volleyball. A well-designed resistance and plyometric training program will also improve dynamic flexibility because of increased control and stability of the joints exercised. Never use static stretching or ballistic (bouncing) stretches for warm-ups. Stretching prior to warming up a muscle may decrease coordination and may increase risks of muscle injury. As mentioned above, they should be incorporated after the warm-up in as dynamic a way as possible.

Static stretching or propriorceptor nerve facilitation (PNF) stretching exercises are beneficial as a cool down exercise. PNF stretching is a more active stretch where a partner will provide resistance against the limb being stretched. Only athletes well-coached in these stretches should be allowed to perform them. Since the musculature is well-supplied with blood and the nervous system is fully activated, the muscles are more conducive to being stretched passively. These exercises help relax stretch receptors in the muscle, allowing a greater dynamic stretch for the next day's exercise bout.

Strength

The textbook definition of strength is force exerted against a resistance. Strength expresses itself as a component of power in the dynamic setting of volleyball. Power is the ability to exert maximal strength (force) through time. Just as athletes need to be brought along a progression from simple to complex exercises, so, too, do athletes need to be brought through a progression of strength development from general to special to specific strength.

General strength refers to traditional resistance training that is not necessarily sport-specific. It consists of general exercises that develop muscular strength and size, depending on set/rep protocols, that improve flexibility, muscle recruitment and coordination through limited range of motions. These exercises are more linear, single plane exercises and are less functional in terms of sport specificity. Weight resistance or selectorized machines represent a group of exercises that fall into this category. Younger, less physically developed and less-experienced athletes should spend the majority of their training in this area.

Special strength is resistance training that incorporates joint movements similar to those in the sport. They are more specialized like plyometric exercises or exercises using dumbbells, resistance bands, tubing, boxes, etc., that mimic a particular sport's skill. These exercises should be introduced along with a general strength program for athletes who are older and more physically developed.

Specific strength is similar to special strength, although much more specialized toward sport specific movements. The speed component is higher and

Table 2 — Examples of Strength

Activity	General Exercise	Special Exercise	Specific Exercise
Spike	Dumbbell Pullover	One Arm Pullover	One Arm Medicine Ball Throw
Block (Jump)	Squat	Jump Ups	Jump Squat w/ Weight Release
Block (Upper Body)	Military Press	Push Press	Two Handed Medicine Ball Put

increases in intensity are greater with relation to training age, level of physical ability and time in the periodization cycle. High-level athletes should perform these exercises, along with appropriate amounts of general and special strength exercises, for maximal performance gains.

Table 2 illustrates different exercises for a volleyball specific movement for each strength category. Every volleyball activity can be developed through general, special and specific strength exercises.

Progression/Overload

Overload is the principle of training describing the need to increase the load/intensity of exercise to further adaptation. It is central to the periodization plan and is the reason that the number of sets, repetitions and intensity changes through every phase of the macrocycle. After a system gets exposed to a certain training intensity, in this case a muscle-connective tissue-neural system, it adapts until the load becomes easier to handle. This can be accomplished through improved recruitment of muscle groups or increased muscle size or strength. When the load becomes tolerable, the system needs to be challenged with a different intensity to again adapt and improve.

Conditioning and Recovery

Noting that volleyball is primarily an anaerobic sport, training this metabolic system needs to be addressed. Conditioning drills should be introduced in progression as mentioned for strength exercises. Beginners or poorly conditioned athletes need to start with simple exercises with fewer repetitions between sets and progressing to more sets and repetitions as athletes mature. They also need some basic aerobic conditioning, although this should not be the core of their program.

Conditioning exercises, as discussed in the physiology section of this chapter, should be designed to mimic the anaerobic demands of volleyball. Since most activities on the court last less than 20 seconds, most conditioning exercises need to reflect that same time frame. The only equipment necessary for the exercises are a flat, open space (preferably a gym floor) and a timer. Exercise examples include volleyball court suicides, 20-meter sprints, six- to 20-second full court jumps or hops and any obstacle course that will take six to 20 seconds.

Plyometrics

Often considered just jump training, these exercises blend the properties of speed and strength to form a training method to develop explosive, functional movements in multiple directions and planes. Plyometric exercises utilize the stretch-shortening cycle found in sports that is characterized by a rapid deceleration of the body followed by a quick acceleration in an opposite direction. The stretch-shortening cycle uses the ability of the series elastic element (S.E.E.) in the muscle-tendon structure to store energy when stretched to produce explosive concentric or positive actions. These exercises include hops, bounds, leaps, skips and medicine ball throws.

Stretch receptors in the muscle and tendons normally limit the range of stretch of a muscle to prevent injury. When this structure is forcefully overstretched, energy is absorbed in the S.E.E. and released during contraction of the muscle. The greater the force of the prestretch, the more energy is available for positive work during the contraction. The faster the contraction following the prestretch the greater the acceleration.

These exercises are performed at maximal or near maximal rates of force development or high acceleration and are considered in the categories of special or specific strength exercises. The most effective of these exercises simulate movement patterns, velocity and/or acceleration of the movements of volleyball. They should be taught in a progression as any exercise and are training level specific; a certain base level of strength and coordination need to be developed before they can be introduced for use by the athlete. Younger athletes or those with little plyometric training, poor balance, low leg, abdominal, back and/or hip strength or are predisposed to lower leg injuries should perform low level plyometric activities for longer periods of time, even months, before progressing to moderate level movements. As the athlete shows proficiency in drills of lower stress and their strength base develops, they can be challenged with higher level drills.

These exercises should be performed after adequate warm-up. They should not be performed when the athlete is fatigued. Doing so exposes the athlete to potential injury because the nervous system and musculature are fatigued. Maximal force production and acceleration cannot be exerted when muscles are fatigued, defeating the purpose of the exercises. These exercises should emphasize quality over quantity. An athlete should fully recover between sets

Table 3 — Minimum Physical Requirements per Level

Beginner	Intermediate	Advanced
Standing Long Jump Own Height	Proficiency in Low Level Drills	Proficiency in Medium Level Drills
5 Push Ups	1 to 2 Months Basic	Free Squat 1.5 to 2.0 x
5 Squat Thrusts	Strength Training	Own Body Weight
Jump Rope - 30 seconds	Free Squat 1.0 to 1.5 x	Leg Press 2.0 to 2.5 x
Proficiency at jumping	Own Body Weight	Own Body Weight
Stand with balance 5 seconds	Leg Press 1.5 to 2.0 x	Mature Athletes
on one leg bent at the knee.	Own Body Weight	25 Push Ups

Table 4 — Plyometric Stress Continuum and Exercises

Intensity	Low	Medium	High	Shock
Athletic Level	Beginner	Intermediate	Advanced	Very Advanced
In Place	Jump Rope	Cycle Jumps	One Leg Hops	In-Depth Jumps
	Net Touches	Jump Ups	Frog Kicks	x
Short Response < 10 reps	Standing Long Jump	3 Cont. Long Jumps Standing Triple Jump	5 Cont. Long Jumps Double Leg Box Jump	Cont. Hurdle Hops Box Bounds
Long Response > 10 reps	Skipping Leaps	Bounds Power Skipping	Hops Speed Bounds	x x
Vertical Displacement	Squat Jumps Ice Skater	Lateral Hop Low Box Depth Jump	High Box Drop Jump x	x x
Horizontal Displacement	1 or 2 Foot Take Offs and Landings	Single Hurdle Jumps Skis	5-10 Hurdle Rebound Jumps 5+ Hops	Box Hurdles Short Approach Bounds
Upper Body	Light Medicine Ball Tosses	Upper Body Box Drops	Heavy Med Ball Throws Clap Push Ups	Drop and Rebound Push Ups

Modified from N.S.C.A. Recommendations

in order to maximize gains in explosiveness. In other words, to develop maximal explosiveness and acceleration, you have to train when fully rested.

In order to develop maximal force and acceleration, plyometric training needs to be done in conjunction with a strength training program. Studies show that the combination of the two maximizes results. In effect, strength gains through resistance training increase force production, thereby increasing potential acceleration through plyometric training.

Exercise technique and progression of training are extremely important to avoid injury. A coach should seek qualified instructors to teach and/or monitor the plyometric exercises of choice.

Table 3 represents suggested minimum physical requirements for beginners, intermediate and advanced athletes. Table 4 represents the plyometric stress continuum and suggested exercises.

Testing

Testing should be used to measure an athlete's current physical and physiological status characteristic to the sport and to measure the effectiveness of an implemented conditioning program. By utilizing the information, which will outline an athlete's strength and weaknesses, a coach can be more effective in individualizing an athlete's training program.

Testing on a regular basis throughout the training year, say every six to eight weeks, will provide information on an athlete's progress in the current program. Improvement on the test battery raises the confidence level of the athlete and the coach in the current program. The coach will then be able to set realistic goals for the next training cycle and the athlete will be motivated to achieve similar results during the next series of tests.

A lack of progress or negative results can alert the coach of potential problems like overtraining. If these results are indicative of the entire team, then a coach may need to re-evaluate the overall conditioning program and alter it accordingly. If the results are representative of one or two individuals, the coach may re-evaluate the individuals' programs or look at other factors such as on-court performance. If there is a drop in overall performance, then the coach may take a closer look at the athlete's physical and psychological status.

Testing an athlete regularly will also provide important data for an injured athlete's rehabilitation progress. When an injured athlete scores at or higher on tests taken nearest to her/his injury date, then a coach can have full confidence that the athlete is completely ready to return to play.

Information gathered over a number of years on an athlete can allow a coach to distinguish between natural physical maturation and training effects. A coach can readily determine if a player continued conditioning over the off-season or he/she did little to keep the edge maintained at the end of the last peak of training.

Testing may not determine an athlete's volleyball performance. Some controversy exists in the application of tests to performance in the sport. This means that there is a question of validity of these tests — the ability of a test to measure what it says it measures. Volleyball abilities are subjective and may not be measured quantitatively. Obviously, the player who can jump the highest is not necessarily the best volleyball player; as a result, he/she may not make the team. The important issue to remember is that an athlete should not be discouraged from participating on a team if physical tests are the only measure of performance. Understanding this difference can avoid potential problems with athletes, parents, administrators and coaches.

There are a wide variety of tests available to measure a wide variety of sport-specific movements. Table 5 lists a small sample of tests for different athletic demands for volleyball. These suggested field tests are just a sampling of those available. More sophisticated tests are available but require more expertise and equipment to administer.

Rest

The most undervalued component of any program is rest. Rest periods are essential to athletic development. As will be addressed later, rest breaks need to be worked into every phase of training. From a physical perspective, this may be anything from

Table 5 — Examples of Possible Skill Tests

Athletic Skill	Test
Power Lower Body	Vertical Jump Approach Jump
Strength Upper Body	Bench Press
Strength Lower Body	Parallel Squat
Speed	20 Meter Dash
Agility	T-test 5-10-5 Drill
Anaerobic Endurance	30 Second Cone Hops

allowing at least 48 hours before the next strength training bout or taking a few days off after a particularly difficult power training series. The body requires some time off on a regular basis to replenish completely energy reserves, hormone levels and to allow minor injuries like muscle strain or soreness to heal and get away from repetitive training.

Program Design — Periodization

Periodization of training is nothing more than setting down a year-long conditioning plan with the goal of physically peaking the athlete at the competitive portions of the year. To make the program most effective, the coach must evaluate the program considerations previously mentioned, especially those concerning the athlete, and the competition schedule. In designing the plan the coach must determine the off-season, pre-season, in-season (including post-season play) and just as importantly, periods of active rest.

The periodization plan is laid down in a series of cycles. Macro-cycles refer to large blocks of training time, usually in months, and micro-cycles refer to smaller blocks of time, such as weeks. Reaching an absolute training peak at the onset of the competitive season is achieved through the creation of a number of relative peaks throughout a number of macro- and micro-cycles. Within each cycle, training time, training intensities, strength training, plyometric exercises,

Table 6 — Suggested Time Commitment to Strength Development by Level

Level	Age* (years)	Training Experience	General Strength	Special Strength	Specific Strength
Beginning	<14	0 - 2 years	50 - 60%	30 - 40%	10%
Intermediate	15>20	2 - 4 years	40 - 50%	25 - 30%	15 - 20%
Advanced	20>	> 4 years	30%	30%	40%

* = Adjustments into a higher or lower category should be made based on physical abilities.

conditioning, volleyball practice workloads and competition schedule are all considered to maximize the program while avoiding overtraining and associated injuries.

Level of Experience

When determining workloads and exercise selection, we again revisit the training level of the athlete. Generally speaking, athletes below the age of 14 with less than two years of training experience should be considered beginners. Athletes between 15 and 20 years of age with two to four years of training experience should be considered intermediate athletes and those older than 20 years of age with more than four years of experience are advanced athletes. Again, categorize an athlete on her/his own merits. A 14-year-old who plays three team sports with six years of training experience may be considered an intermediate athlete, while a 21-year-old with eight months experience may need to be trained as a beginner. Table 6 suggests the relative amount of time a coach should commit to selection of exercises for each developmental level.

When reviewing experience level for a periodization plan for an athlete, consider where he/she is in the continuum of development. Selection of exercises should be dictated by where the athlete falls in this continuum. A coach will look at the volleyball skills of a freshman in college, envision what the athlete can potentially do as a senior and plan how to improve and teach those skills over the next four years. The same type of overall planning needs to be kept in mind when planning a training program. Where will the athlete be in four years? The younger, inexperienced athletes need more base strength development whereas the older, more experienced athletes need more specific training to achieve their highest potential. Pushing an athlete into a level that he/she is not physically ready for may help the team in the short term, but may have potential ramifications

for the athlete in the future. It is not uncommon for athletes to be sidelined during their senior season due to overtraining injuries and fail to be selected for the college program that they had hoped.

The Phases

It is through the manipulation of six phases of programming over the course of the training cycle that peak physical condition is attained at the beginning of the competitive season. They are the hypertrophy, strength, power, peak, maintenance and active rest phases. Each phase has its own specific goals and requirements for training.

The hypertrophy phase is generally associated with the off-season. It is the period of time that training focuses on making anatomical adaptations to exercise in the muscle and nervous system and associated tissues. This period develops the foundation of the athlete upon which higher levels of training are built. Volume of exercise is high, while intensities are relatively low. Rest between sets and exercises is relatively low. This phase is ideal for introducing complex power lifts and exercises since an athlete can focus on the technique of the exercise with little or no weight. Younger or beginning athletes should spend a greater portion of their off-season training in this mode. As an athlete advances in age and physical maturity, he/she spends less off-season time working in this area and more in the other phases. The majority of exercises during this phase should be of the general strength training or those thought of as traditional weight training type.

Volume of exercise is reduced and intensity or load increases during the strength phase of training. Rest breaks increase as well, since load is higher and a less fatigued muscle is required to maximize strength gains. Complex exercises should be practiced with more speed and slightly higher weights. Increasing force production in the musculature gained in the hypertrophy phase is the goal of this training phase.

Intermediate and advanced athletes devote more time to this phase since they have more years of general strength training experience. More special strength exercises are introduced during this phase.

Conversion of strength to power and more sport-specific movements is the goal of the power phase. Speed of movement and load/intensity increase since exercise technique should be perfected by the time this phase is reached. Volume of exercise is lower and rest intervals get even longer. Specific strength exercises are the mode of training, while fewer general or special strength exercises are utilized.

The peak phase is just as it describes. It occurs during the pre-season at a time when the athlete's physical abilities should peak. Training now focuses on maximizing all of the power, strength and metabolic gains achieved in the past several phases for performance improvements. Volume of exercise and frequency are low, while intensity and speed of movement are at their highest. Specific strength exercises are the primary mode of training.

The maintenance phase lasts throughout the season. In fact, recent research indicates that training should continue even into the post-season. Many coaches discontinue training during the post season to focus on team priorities, but studies indicate that continuing this phase into post-season play gives a physical advantage to teams. This phase seeks to preserve the power and strength developed during the preceding year. A blend of exercises is ideal with intensities approximating those found in the off-season and strength phases.

Active rest is the period of time immediately following the in-season. Athletes should be encouraged to continue some type of training or other sports play, but to avoid volleyball specific work. This should be a physical and psychological break from volleyball specific activities, although not from all physical work. Table 7 gives a suggested overview of the time frame for these phases for a high school athlete and Table 8 lists the phases and relative information on exercises, intensities, etc., for the periodization chart in Table 7. Compare the training time frames for a collegiate athlete in Table 9 versus those of the high school athlete in Table 7. Note the changes in length for each phase between the two tables. Athletes who play year-round in club and school ball pose particular problems when trying to manipulate these training phases. Careful consideration of the athlete's physical demands is required when planning their training cycles.

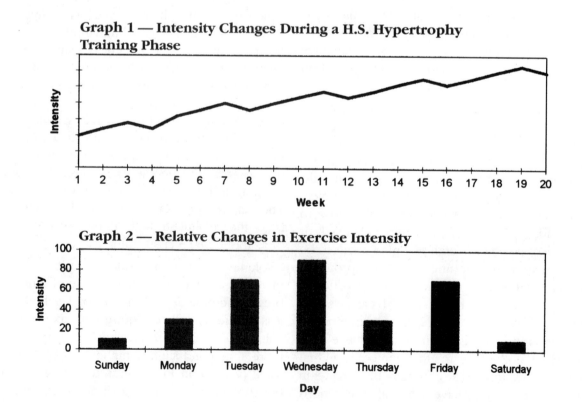

Graph 1 — Intensity Changes During a H.S. Hypertrophy Training Phase

Intensity vs *Week* (1–20)

Graph 2 — Relative Changes in Exercise Intensity

Intensity vs *Day* (Sunday, Monday, Tuesday, Wednesday, Thursday, Friday, Saturday)

Table 7 — Sample High School Periodization Chart

Dec	Jan	Feb	Mar	Apr	May	Jun	Jul	Aug	Sep	Oct	Nov
Off-Season							Pre-Season		In-Season		
Hypertrophy					Strength	Power		Peak	Maintenance		AR

Table 8 — Sample High School Strength Periodization Phase Chart

Phase	Weeks	Days/ Week	Exercises / Day	Sets/ Exercise	Reps/ Set	Rest (min)	Intensity
Hypertrophy	18 to 20	3 to 5	9 to 15	3 - 5	10 to 12	1 to 2	30 - 60 %
Strength	4 to 6	3 to 5	9 to 12	3 - 5	6 to 8	2 to 3	70 - 85 %
Power	8	2 to 3	3 to 5	2 to 3	3 to 6	3 to 6	85 - 100%
Peak	2 to 4	1 to 3	3 to 5	1 to 2	3 to 6	3 to 6	100 - 120 %
Maintenance	8	1 to 2	6 to 9	2 to 3	6 to 8	2 to 3	60 to 80 %
Active Rest	4	NA	NA	NA	NA	NA	NA

Table 9 — Sample Collegiate Periodization Chart

Jan	Feb	Mar	Apr	May	Jun	Jul	Aug	Sep	Oct	Nov	Dec
Off-Season		Spring In-Season			Off-Season		Pre-Season		In-Season		
Hypertrophy		Strength	Power	Strength		Power	Peak		Maintenance		

Table 10 — Sample High School Anaerobic Conditioning Periodization Chart

Phase	Weeks	Days/ Week	Exercises / Day	Sets/ Exercise	Reps/ Set	Rest (min)	Intensity
Hypertrophy	18 to 20	2 to 3	4 to 8	4 to 10	10 to 12	1 to 2	L
Strength	4 to 6	2	2 to 6	3 to 8	6 to 8	2 to 5	L to M
Power	8	2	2 to 6	2 to 6	3 to 6	3 to 5	M
Peak	2 to 4	1 to 2	2 to 6	1 to 6	3 to 6	Full Recovery	H
Maintenance	8	1 to 2	2 to 4	3 to 6	6 to 8	2 to 3	L to M
Active Rest	4	NA	NA	NA	NA	NA	NA

L= Low, M = Moderate, H = High, NA = Not Applicable

Table 11 — Sample High School Plyometric Periodization Chart

Phase	Weeks	Days/ Week	Exercises / Day	Sets/ Exercise	Reps/ Set	Rest (min)	Intensity
Hypertrophy	18 to 20	2 to 3	2 to 3	2 to 4	10 to 30	2 to 3	L
Strength	4 to 6	2	3 to 5	2 to 4	10 to 20	2 to 5	L to M
Power	8	2	3 to 5	3 to 5	5 to 15	3 to 5	M
Peak	2 to 4	1 to 2	3 to 5	3 to 5	3 to 8	5 to 7	H
Maintenance	8	1 to 2	2 to 3	2 to 4	10 to 20	2 to 5	L to M
Active Rest	4	NA	NA	NA	NA	NA	NA

L= Low, M = Moderate, H = High, NA = Not Applicable

Table 12 — Exercise Order by Day for Two Different Seasons

Off-Season Mode	Sun	Mon	Tue	Wed	Thu	Fri	Sat	In-Season Mode	Sun	Mon	Tue	Wed	Thu	Fri	Sat
Strength Training		X		X		X		Strength Training		X			X		
Anaerobic Conditioning			X		X			Anaerobic Conditioning				X			
Plyometrics		X			X			Plyometrics				X			
Injury Prevention		X	X	X	X	X		Injury Prevention		X	X	X	X	X	
Practice		X	X	X	X	X		Practice		X		X	X	X	
Match Play								Match Play			X				X
Rest/Recovery	X						X	Rest/Recovery	X						

Progression/Overload and the Phases

The principle of progression or overload needs to be implemented throughout every phase of the macrocycle. As seen in Tables 7 and 9, the manipulation of exercises, sets, reps and intensities change from phase to phase. However, the level of intensity should change within every phase, as well.

The intensity/load should change from week to week and can change from workout to workout. Weeks of reduced intensity, sometimes called a back-down week, should be introduced every so often, i.e., every third to fourth week, to allow the athlete some recovery before being challenged again. For example, during a 20-week high school hypertrophy phase, a coach might work in a back-down week every fourth week to allow the athlete some recovery. Graphically, this manifests itself as a gradually increasing progression with a number of relative peaks during the phase (see Graph 1). The advantage to this peaking allows a back-down week before starting the next phase of development.

The variation of intensity continues down to the microcycle, the smallest cycle of planning. Changes in intensity and load, as well as exercise order, are all important in order to prevent overtraining or overuse injuries. Graph 2 illustrates how exercise intensity can vary during a week and Table 12 depicts how workout sessions and modes are varied during the week during two different seasons for maximum benefit.

Nutrition

Achieving optimal performance requires commitment of the athlete to a well-balanced nutritional plan. Research reports strong evidence that an athlete's diet directly affects her/his performance. Combined with a solid, well-designed and implemented conditioning program, a good diet can improve endurance, decrease fatigue and improve recovery time.

Carbohydrates

As mentioned previously, glycogen, which is stored in muscle and in the liver, is the fuel of muscular contraction. Its breakdown in the muscle fuels the anaerobic energy system. The more glycogen stored in the muscle, the greater the capacity for work by the muscle. If an athlete does not have an adequate supply of glycogen, he/she tires easily.

Glycogen is a type of sugar and is the stored form of carbohydrates, which are generally distinguished as simple and complex. Complex carbohydrates should form the cornerstone of the athlete's diet, composing at least 60 percent of the total number of calories consumed daily. Complex carbohydrates are found in foods like pastas, breads, cereals and vegetables. Simple carbohydrates are found in fruits, candy and soft drinks and are generally burned quickly for energy after ingestion. Complex carbohydrates can be stored as glycogen for future work by the muscles. Although most foods containing simple sugars should be avoided, fruits are highly recommended since they supply important vitamins and minerals.

Proteins

Proteins should compose approximately 15 percent of the daily caloric intake and fats should equal no more than 25 percent of the daily calories. Despite popular belief, excessive protein intake has not been shown to increase lean muscle mass but is more important for growth and development and reparation and maintenance of injured tissue. Diets too high in protein can cause excess urination and may cause dehydration. According to statistics, most Americans consume more than adequate amounts of protein in their daily diet. Even the most competitive bodybuilders who insist on taking in excessive amounts of protein get plenty from standard fare. Volleyball players are not bodybuilders and most get sufficient levels of protein from a regular diet. Protein can be found in beef, poultry, dairy, seafood, beans and nuts. Low-fat protein sources are lean cuts of beef, grilled or broiled seafood and chicken, skim milks and low-fat cheeses are selection of choice.

Fats

Fats pose a number of problems for athletes. They are digested slowly so a meal high in fat eaten prior to a match will decrease performance as blood is shunted away from muscle to aid in digestion. Also, excess fat in the diet is more easily stored as body fat than proteins or carbohydrates. As in the case of a high-protein diet, a high-fat diet usually translates into a low-carbohydrate diet, thereby reducing the potential for glycogen repletion and availability for muscle.

Vitamins and Minerals

Vitamins and minerals are essential for overall health and performance. Some vitamins, like potassium and calcium, are important in muscular contraction. Some minerals, like chromium and magnesium, are involved in the metabolic energy systems and deficiencies in these vitamins and minerals could limit performance and recovery time of these systems. Fat soluble vitamins like A, D, E and K can be stored by the body because they are fat soluble, but most must be ingested regularly to maintain adequate levels in the body. A well-balanced diet can supply most of the vitamin and mineral needs of most athletes. Since athletes, especially younger ones, often do not eat well on a regular basis, vitamin supplements are recommended.

Water

Water's role in optimum performance is probably the most overlooked by athletes and coaches. Water is important in the storage of muscle glycogen, the transportation of important metabolic nutrients, including oxygen, and the removal of byproducts like lactic acid from working muscle. Few individuals get their daily recommended water and most athletes tend to perform in a dehydrated state. Recommended levels of water for each age group are listed in Table 13.

Athletes should be encouraged to drink as much water as possible. A glass of water is recommended every 15 to 20 minutes of a practice, match or training session. Water should be taken in even more frequently during hot and/or humid conditions. Never let thirst be your guide. Your body often lets you know you are thirsty when you have become too dehydrated. Have athletes drink frequently even if they are not thirsty.

Table 13 — General Nutritional Recommendations by Group

	Recommended Number of Servings						
	Cal/Day	Dairy	Meat*	Fruit	Vegetable	Grains #	Fluids
Cal/Serving	-	90-250	200	60	60	80	-
Youth	2000	3	2	8	5	8	10
Teen (JR)	3500	4	2	10	5	20	10+
Adult	3000	2	2	10	5	17	10+
Professional	4000	4	4	10	5	25	12+

* = also includes Fish, Poultry, Nuts, Cheeses, Beans

\# = also includes Breads, Pasta, Cereals

Modified from High Performance Demands A High Performance Diet

By maintaining adequate water levels, the athlete stays hydrated, allowing for greater storage of carbohydrates by the muscles. This enhanced energy storage can improve muscular contraction and endurance. Excess water also promotes more efficient chemical processes within the cells, thereby reducing fatigue.

Supplements

Athletes are inundated with the call in magazines, on television, in newspapers, etc., to take dietary supplements to enhance performance. This supplement promises energy boosting and that supplement promotes fat burning. Most of the claims made by the advertisements for these supplements are unsubstantiated by scientific research and the products are of questionable value.

Any supplement should be carefully researched before being recommended for athletic consumption. This includes asking the manufacturer for referenced, peer-reviewed, published literature supporting the supplement's claims. If you still have questions about the product's value, consult a qualified nutritionist or dietitian. Athletes should be counseled that a balanced diet will provide all of the essential vitamins, minerals, carbohydrates and proteins necessary for optimal performance without the addition of supplements.

Points to Ponder

Coaches should exercise caution when advising an athlete or a team on nutrition. Information in Table 13 describes general recommendations for athletes at different age levels, but ideally each athlete should have his/her caloric needs determined by a registered dietitian or nutritionist. This is especially true if an athlete has a weight management problem or concerns about body image.

Nutritional demands also need some degree of periodization. Different times of the year require different amounts of caloric demands. Information in Table 13 is appropriate for pre- and in- season time frames, but during off-season or transitional periods, caloric requirements should be adjusted to reflect the lower training demand.

Resources

There are many valuable resources that a coach can turn to when questions come up about training or nutrition. The National Strength and Conditioning Association (NSCA) and the American College of Sports Medicine (ACSM) are two federally recognized leaders in the exercise science and application fields. Nutritional resources include the American Dietetic Association and the Nutrition Council of America. Organizations like the Sports Medicine and Performance Commission of USA Volleyball, the American Volleyball Coaches Association, Gatorade Sport Science Review and the United States Olympic Committee (USOC) are also highly accessible resources that can help or direct you to individuals who can assist you.

Books and magazines distributed by these organizations or by their members are reputable sources of information. Theses and other resources can be obtained at your nearest university or college science libraries. Many of the above-mentioned resources have their own Internet site, but be wary of all the information that you see on the Internet. It is a blessing and a curse. It allows you to interact freely and access information by the boatload, but read what you see with care and verify the source of the information and the information itself before you use it.

Do not be afraid to ask questions and to seek answers. It will make you a better coach and your athletes will benefit in the long run.

Summary

Reaching an athlete's optimal performance level involves developing the athlete physically. By understanding the sport more thoroughly and the methods available to train an athlete appropriately according to the needs of the sport, the coach can plan an effective training program that improves the strengths and athletic skills of the athlete while preventing or reducing injury and improving her/his weaknesses.

A VCS should have a working knowledge of all of the aspects of training and the resources available to her/him. By improving her/his knowledge about the numerous aspects that lead to improved performance, the team will develop better players and have a better coach.

Definitions

Duration-The length of time an athlete trains for a given exercise or session.

Frequency-How often the athlete trains in a given time frame.

Intensity/Load-Stress or tension placed on muscle. It is usually represented by weight lifted but is also affected by the number of sets, reps, rest intervals and duration of workout.

Mode-The type of exercise or resistance being used.

Reps/Repetitions-One complete movement of an exercise.

Rest/Recovery-Time between sets, exercises or workouts.

Sets-A group of repetitions of an exercise.

Volume-Total work done determined by the number of exercises, sets, reps and frequency of the workout.

References

Alejo, Bob. Individual and team training and the role of the volleyball conditioning specialist. *Performance Conditioning for Volleyball*, 3(7): 7.

Armitage-Johnson, Stephanie and Daye Halling, (ed.). (1990) National Strength and Conditioning Association, *Strength Training and Conditioning for Volleyball*. Champaign, IL: Human Kinetics.

Baechle, T. (ed.) (1994). National Strength and Conditioning Association, *Essentials of Strength Training and Conditioning*, Champaign,IL: Human Kinetics.

Bompa, Tudor. (1993). *Periodization of Strength: The New Wave in Strength Training*. Ontario, Canada: Veritas Publishing, Inc.

Bompa, Tudor. (1995). *Power Training for Sport*. Ontario, Canada: Veritas Publishing, Inc.

Brislin, Greg. Cost effective exercises for volleyball. *Performance Conditioning for Volleyball* 1(7): 6.

Brooks, G. and T. Fahay, T. (1985). *Exercise Physiology: HumanBioenergetics and its Applications*. New York, NY: MacMillan Press.

Chapman, Neil and Eric Lawson, Eric. (1996). Strength Training for Volleyball Players, manual for Youth National Team Volleyball Camp.

Chu, D. (1992). *Jumping Into Plyometrics*. Champaign, IL: Leisure Press.

Day, Barbara. (1991). *High Performance Demands A HighPerformance Diet*, Louisville, KY: Barbara Day.

Gambetta, Vern. (1997). Stretching the truth. *Training and Conditioning*, Vol. 7, No. 2.

Gambetta, Vern. (1996). Strength in Motion. *Training and Conditioning*, Vol. 6, No. 4.

Hakkinen, K., M. Alen and P.V. Komi. (1985). Changes in isometric force and relaxation time, electromyographic and muscle fiber characteristics of human skeletal muscle during strength training and detraining. *Acta Physiol Scand.*, 125:573-85.

Komi, P.V., (ed.). (1992). *Strength and Power in Sport*. London: Blackwell Scientific Publications.

Kontor, Ken. (1996). Lifting on your own. *Performance Conditioning for Volleyball*, AVCA Pre-Conference Seminar Manual.

Kunstlinger, U., et al. (1987). Metabolic changes during volleyball matches. *Int. J. Sports Med.*, 8(5):315-22.

Viitasalo, J.T., et. al. (1987). Endurance requirements of volleyball. *Can. J. Spt. Sci.*, 12(4): 194-201.

Photo courtesy of Purdue University

Chapter 24

PSYCHOLOGICAL FACTORS IN VOLLEYBALL PERFORMANCE

Nathaniel Zinsser, Ph.D., Craig Wrisberg and Vanessa Draper

Introduction

Athletes, coaches and scientists have been searching for the keys to superior athletic performance since the beginnings of organized sport. With each passing decade, and with each new wave of technology, new answers have been found to the questions, "How should athletes train in order to develop their talents?" and "How can athletes ensure that they perform at their maximum levels in the pressure-filled competitive arena?" These answers have led to a series of breakthroughs in human performance. At the turn of the 20th century, athletes learned from medical science the basics of exercise physiology and biomechanics. In the decade of the 1930s, the science of strength training added a new dimension to athletic training — one which rapidly evolved over the next 20 years as new technologies produced new equipment and facilities. In the 1960s and '70s, biochemical research led to the discoveries of nutritional supplements and synthetic drugs which could enhance performance. Having largely exhausted the possibilities offered by advances in physical and biomedical training, elite athletes in the 1980s started turning to psychology, to the power of the mind in sport as a way of finding a further competitive edge. Now in the 1990s, the science of applied sport psychology has advanced to the point where it is a valuable and indispensable element in the training of the modern athlete.

Despite this interest, many coaches have not had the opportunity to develop their intuitive understanding of the mental skills affecting performance to the point where it can be effectively communicated to their athletes. This chapter will introduce the specific mental skills which are crucial to volleyball performance and will suggest ways to include such mental training in a competitive volleyball program. Among the key skills are the ability to concentrate and control attention during any situation; the ability to control how athletes talk to themselves and interpret events so they can become more confident each day; the ability to stay physically relaxed while under stress; and the ability to prepare fully for any competition through visualization. Also, the ability to set and prioritize personal and team goals and specific actions to follow in pursuit of these goals is important for sustaining motivation and using time wisely.

The importance of these skills to sport success cannot be overestimated. The ability to throw away any and all fear during competition, to handle distractions and to remain positive in the face of setbacks is characteristic of all truly great athletes. These are the qualities which will determine the outcome of a competition between two equally talented and well-trained athletes or between two evenly-matched teams. Honestly ask yourself how much of success in volleyball is due to physical factors such as strength, speed and skill and how much of that success is due to mental factors such as confidence and concentration at the moment of truth. While athletes have historically reported that mental factors account from 25 percent to 75 percent of success in sport, very few of them devote any time to developing these mental skills systematically. Consider how little sense it makes to leave factors as important as these up to chance.

Applied sport psychology is a relatively new science and the notion of mental training to enhance athletic performance is still greatly misunderstood. Most of this misunderstanding stems from the popular tendency to associate the words "psychology" or "mental" with either sickness or an inability to cope with the problems of living. This association is logical, in that modern psychology evolved from medicine, and like medicine, it is focused primarily on helping unhealthy or dysfunctional people to function normally. However, it is critical to understand that applied sport psychology is focused on helping individuals who are already healthy and well-adjusted to go far beyond "normal" and achieve the "supernormal" levels of performance that are occasionally attained by world-class athletes. The terms "performance enhancement" or "effectiveness" can be used to express this crucial difference between the needs of the motivated, talented athlete and the needs of the individual who requires counseling or therapy to function adequately.

Cognitive Training for Confidence

The most consistent finding in peak performance literature is the direct correlation between self-confidence and success. Every coach and player knows and remembers confident players with whom they have been associated. They are the people you want to have in the rotation when the match is on the line, the people whom you do not give up on even when they have lost the first game. This high level of confidence is not an accident, nor is it the result of physical talent, opportunity or previous success. Confidence in competitive sport is the result of particular thinking habits, which, when consistently practiced, enable athletes both to retain and benefit from the experiences in which they have been successful and release or restructure the memories and feelings from the less successful experiences. The result of this "selective perception" is the priceless trait called confidence.

Developing confidence entails two prerequisite steps. First, players must understand that their thoughts about their ability, the demands they face and of the environment they are in determine to a large extent the way they feel inside. These immediate

feelings, in turn, directly affect performance because they produce objectively verifiable changes in muscle tension, blood flow, hormone production and attentional focus. Confident players, then, deliberately direct their thoughts onto those aspects of the environment and onto those aspects of self which produce powerful, confident feelings. Second, players must be willing to pursue honestly the question, "Am I really thinking in a way that will give me the best chance of success?" For anyone playing volleyball, the real opponent is within themselves in the form of self-criticism, self-doubt and hesitation — all of which are caused by ineffective cognitive habits. This means the athletes with great confidence have simply learned to win the battle with themselves. While this is indeed a difficult battle, it is also the challenge which makes sport such a great experience with so much potential for self-satisfaction.

Confidence develops when players take the responsibility to control their own thinking and perceptual processes. That means deliberately focusing the mind — the thoughts and memories which create energy, optimism and enthusiasm. Every human being develops during childhood the ability to focus his or her mind selectively on a particular thought, feeling or memory and in the process, screen out or de-emphasize other thoughts. The consistent, daily and hourly use of this natural "mental filtering" is the process that allows a player to retain and benefit from the experiences in which he or she has been successful and release or restructure the less successful experiences.

Explaining events according to these guidelines and deliberately perceiving them selectively does not mean that one ignores mistakes entirely or adopts a totally unrealistic view of one's ability and circumstances. It means that one views mistakes and failures rationally, using them as aids to improvement, rather than dwelling on them unproductively. Taking notice of one's errors or shortcomings is a great way to grow, as long as it is done with an eye to the bigger question, "How do I use this to help me improve right now?" Watching a game film and noting technical errors is a good idea, as long as one a) simultaneously makes note of the good points revealed on the film; b) decides right then and there what to do about those errors; and c) while correcting those errors remains focused on one's good points and bright future. Athletes with great attitudes do criticize themselves occasionally, but this criticism is always kept in its proper perspective. The athlete with an effective explanatory style thinks, "It is just these few mistakes; they do not affect the rest of my game and they are balanced out by all of these other things I did well." Compare this with the less-effective statement, "I made tons of errors; they spoiled every part of my game, and they are going to keep on happening." To summarize, an optimistic explanatory style is one in which errors are treated as temporary, specific to that one practice or game, and atypical of one's potential, while one looks at successes as more permanent, more general and certainly more indicative of one's true abilities.

Once a player has made the decision to think effectively, there are limitless opportunities to act on it and thus develop confidence. Every practice session presents the opportunity to focus on and retain a few key moments of success or improvements. Every competition against an opponent who is highly ranked or has been successful against you presents an opportunity to think, "I am better then he/she until they prove otherwise" as opposed to "They beat us before so they will be really tough." Every time one's efforts at improvement are frustrated by events beyond their control (coaches, officiating, weather, travel), there is the choice to become caught up in anger and blame or to take the time to find something useful — something helpful that happened in that situation and keep the mind focused on this one positive experience.

In each of these situations, one course of thinking leaves the athlete feeling optimistic and energized while the other course leaves him or her demoralized and psychologically disadvantaged. Which style of thinking would give the best chance of success in this competitive world? The bottom line is that if players are to make it they have to decide that they are going to focus on the qualities and abilities in themselves and on the aspects of the environment which allow them to get to where they want to be. They will either focus their mind on the positives in their volleyball experience, and thus build themselves up, or they will focus on the negatives and thus drag themselves down; there is no middle ground. This predisposition to keep one's mind on the positive aspects of one's life and sport performance, even in the face of setbacks and disappointments, is a hallmark of the successful athlete, a trait Seligman

(1991) refers to as learned optimism. Top performers realize they have a choice to make and they deliberately choose to be positive.

Relaxation Training

Athletes perform best when they are optimally aroused, both physically and mentally. Physical arousal is defined by the amount of muscle tension that an individual experiences. Too much or too little muscle tension can hinder skill performance, while an optimal amount facilitates coordinated movement. The same is true for mental arousal. Each athlete has a certain level of mental arousal at which he or she performs best. Some athletes need to "psych-up" in order to perform successfully, while others need to "psych-down."

In addition to pre-competition adjustments, performers often need to monitor and alter their arousal levels during competition. This is where the "effective thinking" skills mentioned previously become tremendously important, because what one player perceives as a stressful game situation, another may see as exciting and challenging. For example, an experienced, risk-taking individual might regard a match-point serving situation as an opportunity to shine and win the game single-handedly. However, an inexperienced, less-confident player might consider this same situation as a threatening, sure-to-fail proposition. For both of these players, there is a feeling of increased mental arousal and physical tension. If either becomes aroused beyond his or her optimal point, that player can "choke." Therefore, players need to monitor their levels of arousal consciously in order to make the adjustments that will bring their mental and physical tension within an optimal range. If peak arousal can be maintained, peak performance will usually result.

When we realize that a player is over-aroused, we have a tendency to scream, "Relax! Concentrate!" More than likely, the player is not comfortable with this tension any more than we are and our anxious cries do little to remedy the situation. A better strategy would be to address the root of the problem before the problem occurs. The athlete who is trained in muscular relaxation and attentional control techniques can begin to take control of his or her mental state and level of arousal. He or she will then be in a better position to handle competitive anxiety successfully when it occurs.

Muscular relaxation methods are based on two assumptions: that muscular tension can be due to emotional stress and that learning to reduce one's muscular tension can help in reducing such stress. Relaxation techniques teach the athlete to focus on various muscle groups and help develop control over the amount of tension within the muscle. A typical relaxation session begins with the athlete (or athletes, if in a group session) in a comfortable, reclining position, preferably in a quiet room where there will be no distractions.

Initially, the athlete should be talked through the relaxation procedure by another trained individual. However, with practice, individuals can perform the technique on their own. Most muscular relaxation procedures follow the same general format and use similar terminology. The instructor usually begins the session by having the athletes close their eyes, inhale deeply and exhale slowly, relaxing completely. The instructor may choose to prepare a monologue which directs the athlete's attention to the various muscle groups, isolating and relaxing each group, and moving systematically through the body from head to toe. Again, the objective is to have the athlete become aware of any isolated muscular tension and become adept at consciously relaxing those muscles.

Being able to achieve a relaxed state spontaneously has two advantages in athletic competition. Not only is it useful prior to competition as a means of relaxing and adjusting arousal levels, but it can also be employed during competition to relieve tension in muscle groups essential to performance. For example, as a player prepares to serve a match point, the last thing needed is tight shoulder and neck muscles because the coordinated effort of these muscles is needed for successful serve execution. Therefore, it would be most beneficial for the player to pause before serving, mentally check those muscle groups to see if excessive tension exists and consciously relax those muscles before attempting the serve. Muscular relaxation training can enhance a player's ability both to recognize the tension and to do something to relieve it.

Attention Control Training

Relaxation procedures and mental rehearsal of skills can be done prior to a competition to help optimize skill and arousal levels. But pre-game preparation and mental readiness will not make a difference unless the athlete can also maintain this readiness throughout the match. To do so, your players must also be able to alter or adjust their attentional focus. It is not much of an advantage to have a player who is physically able to kill the ball every time he or she goes up to attack if the player is consistently so distracted by the blocker or by negative thoughts that he or she mis-hits or hits into the block. This type of player can be greatly helped by attentional control training.

Clinical sport psychologist Robert Nideffer categorizes attention according to the dimensions of direction (internal or external) and width (broad or narrow). An internal focus is one in which the individual attends to his or her own thoughts or analysis of a situation. An external focus is one in which the individual concentrates on the activity going on around him or her. For example, in volleyball, the serving player should have an external focus while observing the opposing team's serve receive positioning. The focus then becomes internal as the player decides which type of serve would be most effective in this situation. Finally, a switch to an external focus occurs as the eyes are fixed on the ball that is to be hit.

Attention can also be described as broad or narrow, depending on how specific the focus is. If a blocker is watching the play unfold on the opposing court, looking for general clues as to the direction the set is headed, then the blocker has a broad focus. However, when it has been determined that the ball is going to the middle hitter, the blocker would then narrow focus to the hitter and concentrate entirely on the ball and the hitter's arm and hand. Thus, both direction and width of focus are important during attentional control.

There are two keys to attentional control: knowing the most appropriate focus for different game situations and being able to shift from one focus to the other. For example, the server mentioned earlier must shift focus several times before ever hitting the ball. Similarly, if an attacker is aware of when and where the focus should be, potential blockers become another source of information rather than a distraction. As the spiker watches the play develop on his or her court, the attentional focus is broad and external. It should become broad and internal as the spiker realizes that the ball is coming to him or her and begins to determine alternatives for action (e.g., tip, hit cross-court, hit down the line). In order to decide which alternatives to execute, the attacker must again shift to a broad, external focus and assess the opposing blockers' defensive positions. Once a strategy is determined, the attacker must shift to a narrow, internal focus while preparing to approach and hit the ball, concentrating on his or her movement toward the ball. While actually executing the hit, the hitter should have a narrow and external focus, concentrating on the ball and the blocker.

These shifts are neither as complicated nor as difficult to achieve as they may sound. Under non-stressful conditions, these shifts are made rather easily and naturally. But when an athlete becomes tense or anxious, the attentional "flow" can be interrupted. Attentional control training helps the athlete recognize when he or she is losing the "flow" and offers a way to regain control. The first step to regaining control is what Nideffer refers to as "centering."

Centering is a momentary internal check of one's mental and physical state. The athlete checks and adjusts breathing and muscle tension. Being centered can be thought of as feeling balanced and steady. With practice, an athlete can begin to center in the time it takes to inhale and exhale. Nideffer suggests the following technique:

Take a standing position, feet shoulder-width apart, knees slightly bent. Inhale deeply from the abdomen. Feel the tension in the chest and shoulders and consciously relax these muscles. As you exhale, relax the muscles of the thighs and calves and feel your body rest more heavily on the ground. You are balanced and steady and ready to direct your attention to the upcoming task or competition.

Centering is a "time-out" that allows the athlete to clear the mind of distracting or negative thoughts and regain a feeling of balance and control. This sensation of control must be followed by a sequence of thoughts and feelings that channel the attention appropriately and put the player in the optimal state of mental and physical arousal. This sequence or routine will vary for each individual player, but it must include: 1) a deliberate decision to focus the mind on a successful outcome of the upcoming play — the ace, the dig, the set, the spike, the block — whatever may be called for from his or her position; and 2) another deliberate decision to focus the eyes on the one key focal point for beginning of the point, the ball or the position of the receivers, etc. Once these steps are completed, the player is in the best possible attentional state to react automatically and instinctively to the movement of the ball and to communications on the court.

This "between point routine" (Rotella, 1995) may be employed by a server who may use it while preparing to serve or any player may center while waiting for the server to serve and play to begin. In order for the procedure to be effective in the heat and excitement of a match, it must first be practiced and routinized so thoroughly that the player cannot fail to do it between each point. Having this between-point routine will help the player clear the mind and balance the body, thus allowing him or her to attend to the external cues essential to successful performance (e.g., the ball coming off of the server's hands, the opponents' block, the opponents' attack).

Mental Rehearsal

Relaxation methods are sometimes coupled with another psychological technique called mental rehearsal. Mental rehearsal in sport involves mentally practicing specific motor skills, attending to every detail of the skill and visually imaging successful performance of the skill. Because it requires an internal focus of attention, mental rehearsal is not effective in combination with relaxation sessions. Creating a mental image of a skill is much easier if the athlete has achieved a moderately relaxed state, with a mind relatively clear and free of distractions. For example, a defensive specialist who has achieved a moderate level of relaxation might be instructed to rehearse the following situation mentally:

Imagine that your team is serving and you are playing left back. You hear your teammate serve the ball and watch it fall deep in the other team's court. The opposing left back plays the ball and their setter sets the ball to their left front hitter. You watch the hitter closely and notice the body position as the approach is made. As the hitter goes up, he or she is angled toward you and is looking at the inside of the block. The hitter's arm and hand come through and cut the ball around the inside of the block. You position yourself low, with your weight a little forward and your arms outstretched. The ball is coming at you but is falling short. You dive and feel the ball snap off of your hand as you pop the ball to your setter, who sets back to the right front for a down-the-line kill.

Such mental practice of skills has been found to be

a very useful addition to physical practice. It will not, however, take the place of physical practice. In order to make mental practice most effective, the following points should be considered:

- Mental practice should be used in conjunction with physical practice, not in place of it.
- Mental practice periods should only last from two to five minutes.
- Mental practice sessions should be as realistic as possible and should always involve a successful performance by the player rehearsing.
- Mental practice is useful both for beginning players and for the rehearsal of intricate skills (e.g., a one-on-one blocking situation).
- Mental practice is most effective when the athlete learns to rehearse in "real time," that is, the time it actually takes to go through the skill physically.

Another important consideration when using mental practice is the basic ability of the athlete to create the mental image of a skill. Not all players are able to create vivid, enduring images of a performance. Some will report quick flashes of figures that are only outlines. But, like any skill, the more mental rehearsal is practiced, the better the performer will get at creating proper images. What is important is that all athletes be encouraged to take the same perspective one would take if actually performing rather than if observing a performance. A player who takes that internalized perspective can create and rehearse the physical feelings that accompany the skill. These feelings are extremely important for successful motor skill learning and performance. Learning to "feel" the skill physically improves the athlete's ability to rehearse in "real time." Being able to associate physical feelings with mental images makes imagery easier, more lifelike and more effective as a practice method.

Following are some guidelines to follow when incorporating mental rehearsal into the total practice routine:

- Use relaxation procedures first to create the optimal mental state for mental imagery.
- Make sure that each athlete knows precisely what skill or phase of a skill to image (i.e., attacking against an outside block or blocking a middle hitter).
- Encourage all athletes when they are imaging to take the perspective they would have if they were actually performing the skill, rather than if they were observing as a spectator.

- Emphasize the importance of learning to rehearse mentally in "real time." Have the athletes mentally rehearse an activity as they time it on a stopwatch. Then have them physically rehearse the same activity, also to a stopwatch. Compare the times. If they are not accurate, the athlete does not have a grasp of real time imaging and should practice this exercise until real time rehearsal is achieved.

Goal Setting

Athletes and coaches alike have aspirations of being "number one." Early in the season there is often talk of "winning it all come tournament time." Too often, this ultimate goal is the only goal. Sometimes, we as coaches do not place enough importance on short-term, specific goals that will get a team to the point it wants to be at the end of the season. We also sometimes fail to recognize that each player should be working toward personal goals, as well as team goals, for the two go hand-in-hand. Thus, proper goal setting is an important factor in improving team and individual performances and in enhancing training results. Proper goal setting can also be a source of motivation if handled correctly.

An effective way to ensure that goal setting is a positive experience for both individuals and the team is to conduct private coach-athlete sessions in which, together, the coach and player discuss the player's role on the team and the related skill areas and training tasks that that player needs to emphasize. When both player and coach understand and agree on the nature of the player's contribution to the team and the important tasks that player performs, then specific goals and procedures for evaluation can be established. The following sections offer general guidelines for goal setting in a volleyball program.

Goals Must be Realistic: Challenging, But Within Reach

Players must honestly assess their abilities and limitations when considering a goal for performance. For a novice hitter with a 50 cm (20 in.) vertical jump to set a goal of putting every middle hit within the 3-meter line is probably unrealistic given that player's experience and jumping ability. That this goal is unrealistic should be pointed out to the player and the suggestion should be made to revise the goal so that it will be more realistic. For example, this player's goal might instead be to hit progressively closer to the 3-meter line a higher percentage of the time on predesignated evaluation dates throughout the season.

Goals Should be Specific and Have a Time Frame

Evaluation is an important part of goal setting. In order for a goal to be evaluated, it must be specific and include predetermined target dates for evaluation. The player and coach should estimate the level of performance that is desired and attempt to project the amount of time it will take to reach that level. For example, a player who is putting only 50 percent of his or her serves in the court at the beginning of the season might set up the following sequence of serving goals:

> 60 percent by (date)
>
> 70 percent by (date)
>
> 80 percent by (date)
>
> 90 percent by conference tournament (date)

The specificity and the time frame make it easier for players to chart their progress and to see it on paper. Moreover, deadlines tend to be motivating (again, if the goals are realistic).

Leave Room for Revisions

Providing for the revision of goals is not meant to imply that goals should be lowered at the first sign of failure. However, if it becomes obvious that the original goal was not appropriate or realistic, a player needs to feel that it is acceptable to revise the goal and bring it within reach. If a player determines that one training goal is to lose 15 pounds of body weight and after several weeks of healthy dieting and workouts is only able to lose eight but is playing the best volleyball ever and feeling good, perhaps the goal weight should be reconsidered. Players need to be given this flexibility because pressure to achieve may become a burden if goals are inflexible and unrealistic.

Put the Goals in Writing

Having something in writing usually adds a seriousness to the player's commitment to goal achievement. Written agreements may take several forms. For example, players may write up contracts that outline their goals; include methods or procedures of evaluation; and establish target dates for evaluation.

Coaches might post charts of player and team progress (e.g., graphs charting team serve percentages or individual vertical jump improvements). Making goals visible encourages accountability in each of the individual players, motivating all to do their part to enhance team performance.

Individual Goals Must be Compatible with Player Roles and Team Goals

Volleyball has become extremely specialized at most levels. Players have specific roles on a team and it is important that they are aware of these roles before setting goals. If a coach intends for a player to play in only a defensive capacity, it is useless to have that player spend time constructing goals for hitting and blocking skills. Put simply, training goals and performance goals should be related to each player's role and responsibility.

A final point to consider when setting goals is the importance of short-term goals. Long-term goals are important, but players need to realize that it takes the achievement of a series of progressive, short-term goals to reach the final goals successfully. Goal setting and evaluation of progress should be ongoing before, during, after and in-between competitive seasons.

Summary

A number of psychological techniques have been developed to help players reduce stress and gain the mental skills needed for athletic competition. These techniques include: cognitive control for confidence, relaxation training, mental rehearsal, attentional control training, and goal setting.

Confidence is developed through following procedures of selective perception, which allow an athlete to retain and benefit from successes while releasing and restructuring setbacks and disappointments. Each athlete has a level of mental and physical arousal at which he or she performs best and players should monitor and adjust their arousal level accordingly, both before and during play. Relaxation is used for players who are overly aroused. To perform this training, players recline, close their eyes and go through a relaxation procedure. Mental rehearsal involves mentally going through specific motor skills and visually imaging a successful performance of the skills. Attentional control training consists of having players adjust their attentional focus, internal or external, broad or narrow. The two keys to attentional control are knowing the most appropriate focus for different game situations; being able to shift from one focus to another; and having a well-rehearsed between-point routine. Goal setting involves setting realistic personal and team goals and working toward reaching them.

References

Cratty, Bryant J. (1983). *Psychology in Contemporary Sports*. Englewood Cliffs, N.J.: Prentice-Hall.

------------------. (1984). *Psychological Preparation and Athletic Excellence*. Ithaca, N.Y.: Movement Publications.

Klavora, P. and Juri V. Daniel. (1979). *Coach, Athlete and the Sport Psychologist*. Champaign, IL: Human Kinetics Publishers.

Nideffer, Robert M. (1981). *The Ethics and Practice of Applied Sport Psychology*. Ithaca, N.Y.: Movement Publications.

------------------. (1985). *Athlete's Guide to Mental Training*. Champaign, IL: Human Kinetics Publishers.

Rotella, Robert. (1995). *Golf is not a Game of Perfect*. New York: Simon and Schuster.

Seligman, Martin. (1991). *Learned Optimism*. New York: Alfred A Knopf.

Photo by Randy Nolen

Part 5

STATISTICS

Photo courtesty of Springfield College

Chapter 25

GRAPHING STATISTICAL PERFORMANCE

Linda Delk

The benefits that can be derived from statistical information are numerous and varied and the importance of statistical data cannot be denied. Data can be used in determining starting line-ups, in developing strategies against opponents, in determining effective player positioning, in goal setting and more. Using statistics to monitor player and team performance is also an effective tool in providing a variety of information to the coaching staff and players.

It is important when discussing statistics with players that they understand that the data are most effectively used in monitoring their own personal performance.

Unfortunately, players often use statistics to compare their performance with other players rather than being focused on their own. When players focus on their personal performances, statistics can show declines in individual player performance (as well as the team's performance) that otherwise may not be noticed when simply comparing one player with another. For example, the best hitter on a team could enter a hitting slump, with performance declining over the last three matches. If the player and the coach simply compare the performance to other team members, the player may still be performing statistically above other teammates, even though the player's own performance has begun to decline. As a result, the decline could go unnoticed and neither the player nor the coach might be aware that a problem has begun to develop.

At the team performance level, a team could be winning games regularly but the total team performance could be slipping. Graphing player and team performance will provide visual feedback and will show downward trends that may be halted more quickly.

In order to graph a player and/or team performance, a statistical system for recording information based on numerical values must be selected. The use of percentage-based data is probably the easiest statistical method available. The statistical system I recommend is contained in the *National Volleyball Statistics Manual* (1992), published by the American Volleyball Coaches Association.

A coach should be thoroughly familiar with the manual in order to interpret the information effectively to players. Secondly, the coach must determine which performance areas are to be graphed. The areas of serving, passing and attack lend themselves readily to graphing and can provide valuable information. Finally, although it is not necessary, it is helpful for the coach and players to have established individual player and team goals. These goals provide the standard for minimum expectations of performance and will help to determine if each person, as well as the entire team, is meeting expected levels of performance.

The following information is provided in order to demonstrate performance graphing. The definitions and statistical information are paraphrased from the *National Statistics Manual* of the AVCA.

Section I - Attacks
Article 1

- Attack attempts: Any time a player attempts to hit the ball over the net, including the spike, set, tip or hit as an overhead contact. An attempt should not be charged to a player who is attempting to put a poorly set ball over the net just to keep it in play.
- Kill: Any time an attack is unreturnable and directly causes the opponent not to return the ball or any time the attack leads directly to a blocking error by the opposition. A kill results in a point or side out.
- Error:
   a. Ball is hit out of bounds.
   b. Ball is hit into the net, resulting in four hits.
   c. Ball is blocked down by opponent to attacker's side and cannot be kept in play.
   d. Attacker net fouls.
   e. Attacker is called for a centerline violation.
   f. Attacker is called for an illegal contact.
   g. Attacker hits the ball into the antenna.

The formula for Attack Percentage (Kill Efficiency) can be found in article 2 of the statistics manual.

$$Pct = \frac{\text{Total Kills - Total Errors}}{\text{Total Attempts}}$$

$$\text{e.g.,} \frac{8-4}{20} \times 100 = 20\%$$

Section 3 - Serving
Article 1

- Attempts: When a player attempts to serve the ball over the net.
- Ace:
   a. The ball hits the opponent's court untouched.
   b. The ball is passed but cannot be kept in play.
   c. Official calls a violation on the receiver (e.g., lift).
   d. Receiving team is out of rotation (overlap).
- Error:
   a. The serve hits the net or fails to clear the net.
   b. The serve is out of bounds or hits the antenna.
   c. The server foot faults or takes too much time.
   d. The server serves out of rotation.

The formula for Serve Percentage can be found in article 2.

$$Pct = \frac{\text{Total Attempts - Errors}}{\text{Total No. of Serve Attempts}}$$

$$\text{e.g.,} \frac{20-2}{20} \times 100 = 90\%$$

Article 5 - Serve Reception

- Attempt:
   a. When a player attempts to or should have attempted to pass the served ball.
- Error (a reception error):
   a. Ball strikes the floor in the area of the player.
   b. Player passes the ball but it cannot be kept in play by teammates.
   c. Player is called for reception violation by the official (i.e., lift).

The formula for Serve Reception Percentage is:

$$Pct = \frac{\text{Total Attempts - Errors}}{\text{Total No. of Serve Reception Attempts}}$$

$$\text{e.g.,} \frac{15-3}{15} \times 100 = 80\%$$

For coaches at beginning levels of play, the serve reception percentage may be a sufficient statistic to utilize. The information basically tells us how many balls the team is passing that are up and playable. Frequently, however, coaches are concerned with the quality of the pass to the setter's position and a more detailed system of evaluation is required.

A suggested system for recording the quality of a pass is by the numerical designation of the values 3, 2, 1 and 0. The numerical values are expressed as follows:

- 3: The perfect pass. The ball is directed to the setter's zone perfectly. All attack options are available. The middle 1 can be set, as well as all designated play options.
- 2: The pass has eliminated the middle 1 set or other play options. The pass is of sufficient enough quality to allow the setter to set the offense to the front and back side hitters or a simple high middle set. The quick middle attack is no longer a reasonable option.
- 1: The pass is of poor quality which results in only one setting option. The setter is scrambling to make a set and may be forced into passing the ball (as

opposed to setting the ball) to the attacker. Another characteristic of a "1" pass is that the setter may not be able to get to the ball at all and another player must step in and set the ball to the attacker.

- 0: The receiver is aced. An error in reception has occurred. The pass results directly in a point for the opponent. The ball may or may not be touched by a receiver.

Recording data in this fashion still allows you to determine the serve reception percentage discussed earlier. In this case, each number recorded represents a reception attempt and each zero recorded represents a reception error. You would simply count all of the reception attempts (total attempts) then count the number of zeros (errors) made by the passer and apply the serve reception percentage formula to the data.

However, the data will allow the coach also to determine a pass average for each player, as well as determine a perfect pass percentage. The pass average will tell the coach (and player) what the quality of the pass to the setter's target area is on the average.

To illustrate the formulas and data collection, imagine that a player's 15 passes were recorded as follows:

3-2-1-3-0-3-3-2-3-2-0-3-3-2-0

The Sum of the Quality Points equals 30. Just add the 15 numbers together. The number of attempted passes equals 15 (count each number). Therefore, 30 divided by 15 equals a Pass Average of 2.0.

The formula for Pass Average is:

$$Avg = \frac{\text{Sum of Quality Points}}{\text{No. of Attempts}}$$

$$e.g., \frac{30}{15} = 2.0$$

The Perfect Pass Percentage reflects how frequently the passer enables the setter to run all three attack options. (It does not mean that the setter must run the middle, only that the middle is an option and has not been eliminated because of a poor quality pass.) Using the same figures from the above example, of the 15 passes made, nine passes were designated as "3"s.

As a result, the formula for the Perfect Pass Percentage is:

$$PP\% = \frac{\text{No. of "3" Balls Passed}}{\text{No. Attempted Passes}}$$

$$e.g., \frac{7}{15} \times 100 = 46\%$$

Once data are collected from your first match of the season, players and coaches can begin to graph their personal and/or team performance. This information in itself can be used to analyze consistency of performance by the team and players. However, I believe the data is best utilized when players establish individual performance goals for themselves. A coach needs to assist players in recognizing and establishing acceptable levels of performance for the team, as well as for each individual.

In establishing player and team performance goals, you should consider acceptable standards for your particular level of play. For example, it is generally acceptable that nine out of 10 serves should be over the net and in the opponent's court. In attacking, players need to be hitting at a minimum of 20 percent efficiency in order to be minimally competitive. And to compete most effectively at a national level, we need to hit as a team at 24 percent efficiency (and preferably better). In passing, a passer should be able to pass nine out of 10 balls that are up and playable (Pass Efficiency). We would like players to pass at a 2.2 minimum pass average and pass 50 percent of the opponent's serves perfectly (PP percent), allowing us to run the middle option 50 percent of the time. These figures would be considered minimum standards of performance for the team and if we can perform at this level we can be competitive.

The coaches utilize this information in establishing a baseline of performance for the team graph. This is indicated by drawing a red line on the horizontal plane along the appropriate numerical designation for that statistical category. We then challenge the players to exceed these minimal goals by establishing higher criteria for performance and these become our team goals. For example, I would like the team to serve at 95 percent efficiency, pass closer to a 2.4, have a perfect pass percentage of 60 percent and attack at 26 percent efficiency.

This line is represented on the graph in blue ink along the horizontal plane at the appropriate numerical designation. When our team statistics are graphed and we fall within the range created by the two lines (minimum acceptable team performance and team goals), we are (probably) playing at a sufficient enough level to win. Whenever the team's performance surpasses the team goal, we feel we have had a superior night of play. From the graphs, coaches may also notice a middle-of-the-season decline (a slump) in total team performance, indicating a need for a break from practice or a change-of-pace practice to refresh and revitalize team members. The coaching staff charts the team's performance and the graphs are posted on the team bulletin board and statistical information is entered on the graph after each competition to allow players to see how the team performed.

All players draw a red ink line on their graph indicating the minimum accepted standards for performance for the team. Typically, first-year players utilize minimum acceptable performance levels for their personal goals while three- and four-year players are establishing personal goals based on previous years' performances. For example, a returning senior may have served at 93 percent efficiency during the junior year; as a result, the player sets a new goal of serving at 95 percent efficiency, thereby creating a challenge to improved performance. A primary passer who passes at a 2.2 pass average may wish to set a new goal of 2.4. In this fashion, new standards are based on what has already been accomplished and each player is challenged based on personal performance levels.

Once players have established their personal goals for their categories, they return to the graph and draw another line (we use blue ink) to represent the standard they wish to attain in each of their performances. As each match's information is entered on the graph, the players readily see if they have met their established goal and/or the minimum team goal. What we hope to see over the course of a season is a gradual but steady improvement and a consistency of performance in attaining the personal goal. As the season progresses, we should see the players performing at or above their target goal and the team's overall performance should be a gradual climb toward their highest performance level near the end of the season.

Plotting the Data

Graph paper is used to plot the data. The horizontal axis is used to record the season schedule and the vertical axis is used to record the numerical data for each category to be graphed. Always begin with a "0" at the intersection of the horizontal and vertical axis. (Refer to Figures 25-1 to 25-4 that demonstrate specific graph development.)

Attacking

The majority of athletes will have an attack percentage

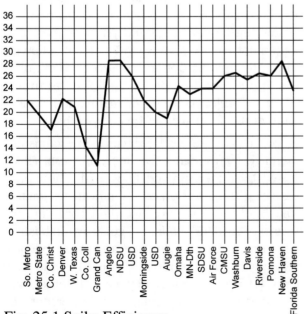

Fig. 25.1 Spike Efficiency

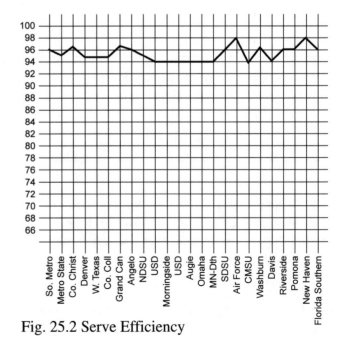

Fig. 25.2 Serve Efficiency

between 0 percent and 40 percent. In Figure 25.1, the numerical data for the vertical axis is entered in increments of two up to 20 percent, then in increments of 10 up to 100 percent. Our team goal is to hit at 26 percent, with a minimal acceptable performance of 20 percent (indicated by a red line). In the event a negative attack percentage is attained by a player, the data would be marked at 0 percent efficiency with a notation of the actual negative hitting percent.

Serving

It may be convenient to number the vertical axis in large increments up to 70 percent or 80 percent. Most players will serve above this percentage regularly. Most athletes should be able to perform in a range between 80 percent and 100 percent efficiency. Therefore, it will be more important to have smaller increments (consider two increments between numbers) at the higher performance levels. Athletes should attempt to serve at a 90 percent efficiency and this is our minimal acceptable team performance. We establish 95 percent efficiency as our team goal (see Figure 25-2).

Serve Reception Percentage

Theoretically, players should be passing at a 90 percent efficiency (nine out of 10 are up and playable). The statistical range most often attained is 70-100 percent. The numerical increments along the vertical axis should be smaller at the higher level percentages to record the data most effectively. (No graph is shown for this category.)

Pass Average

The increments can easily be marked in 10ths of points beginning at 0 and continuing through 3.0, the highest pass option value assigned. We establish a minimal acceptable performance of 2.0 with a team goal of passing a 2.4 pass average (see Figure 25-3).

Perfect Pass Percentage

We would like players to be passing at least 50 percent of the balls directly to the setter position to allow us to run the middle attack option off of serve receive. Our minimal accepted standard then is 50 percent and we establish a team goal of 60 percent (see Figure 25-4).

Conclusion

Other data that can be graphed include Kill Average, Block Average, Dig Average and Setter Assist Average. By developing graphs in these areas, all major statistical categories will be visually available for analysis and players will be able to analyze their own performance data more readily. Over the course of a four-year career, players will actually "see" their year-to-year progress within a program, their improved performance over the course of the years and an increased consistency performance.

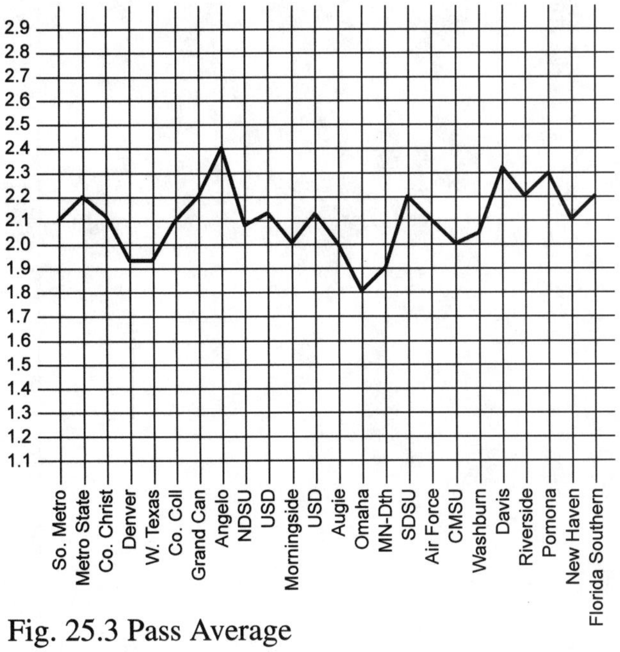

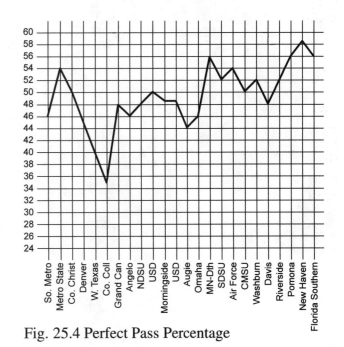

Fig. 25.3 Pass Average

Fig. 25.4 Perfect Pass Percentage

Photo courtesy of the University of Wisconsin

Chapter 26

KEEPING VOLLEYBALL STATISTICS WHILE DIRECTING A MATCH

M. Eileen Mathews

Statistics are valuable to programs at all levels. Determining exactly which statistics are useful, gathering that data and appropriately interpreting it are difficulties a coach faces.

Necessity dictated the development of a statistical charting system that gives coaches the ability to collect data while directing a match. The following system accomplishes this with minimal effort and maximum results and serves as a complement to the data gathered from the scorebook.

All of the standard statistical data (passing, setting, attacking, blocking and serving efficiencies) are gathered by this system. Additionally, one critical piece of information, namely the series of (ball) contacts for each player (overlooked by other systems) is charted with this method. The series of contacts identifies a single contact as it relates to a previous contact or group of contacts. Thus, the contribution of the pass and the set to the successful attack or to the attack error can be identified. The same is true for detecting defensive problems. Information of this type is valuable in determining the specific source of the ball handling error(s) and better equips the coach to make appropriate adjustments.

Basic System

The basic system is described first and the more detailed "beyond the basic system" is discussed last. Both methods use player numbers to indicate ball contact. Consider the first contact to be a pass, the second a set and the third an attack.

Pass

When the pass is directed to the target, record the passer's number. For a pass that is off the target but playable (set your parameters) and within the attack area, circle the passer's number. If the pass is off the target and unplayable, slash the passer's number.

6	⑥	6̸
good pass	playable	error

Set

The second contact is the set. Rate the set in the same manner as the pass. When the setter executes the appropriate set to the target, record the contact by marking the setter's number. For a set off the target but playable, record by circling the setter's number. If the set is unplayable, or a setting error occurs, slash the setter's number.

7	⑦	7̸
good set	playable	setting error

Attack

Evaluate the attack with some qualification. The hitter's number is recorded for a successful attack that is played by the opposition. A kill is recorded by adding a "K" after the player's number. If an attack error occurs, a slash is drawn through the player's number. In addition, specific errors are noted in the following manner: An "N" is placed behind the player's number for an attack that is hit into the net; an "O" is used for an attack that is hit out of bounds; and a "b" is used for an attack that is blocked. These are the five possibilities:

9	9K	9N̸	9Ó	9Ɓ
attacked	kill	hit into net	hit out	blocked

Blocking

Blocking is designated with an uppercase "B" after the player's number to indicate a block that controlled the hitter or a touch on the block. Use an "S" after the player's number to indicate a stuff block and a slash through the number and the "B" to indicate a blocking error. Be sure to distinguish between an offensive player with an attack error due to being blocked "b" and a defensive block using a "B".

9B	9S	9Ɓ
control block	stuff block	block error

Serving data can most easily be collected using just three events: A successful serve that is played by the opponent is denoted by a check; an ace is noted by an "A"; and a serving error is marked using a slash. Record the player's number in the right-hand column of the data sheet. Next to the player's number record the result of the serve.

6	✓	A	/
good	serve	ace	error

Contact Series

Examples of a series of three contacts — pass, set, attack — can be found in Table 1.

Table 1

6-7-8	6 passed to the target 7 set to the target 8 attacked into the opponent's court
⑥-7-8̸N	6 playable pass not to target 7 set to target 8 attack error — into the net
6-7̸	6 passed to the target 7 setting error — unplayable
-7-8K	7 setter makes first contact, set to target 8 kill

Beyond the Basic System

Passes can be graded, sets rated and attacks evaluated. In order to detail the quality and the result of the contact, add a rating for each contact. Adapt the data to your own system and needs.

Pass

The rating system of 0, 1, 2, 3 records the result as a superscript next to the passer's number. The superscripts in this case represent scores to calculate passing efficiency.

6^3 controlled pass to the target
6^2 playable pass, but not to the target
6^1 poor pass, tight, shanked but on the court
6^0 passed off the court, low trajectory pass, not playable

Set

Record playsets and specific information about the set the same way. A two-number system is used to describe the set executed. The following examples use offensive zones numbered 1-5 beginning on the outside. The set height is also recorded using 1-5 (1 being a quickset and 5 being a high set). The first number indicates the net zone and the set height. Thus, a high outside set would be noted with a superscript of 15 while a middle quick attack would be a 31 (see Figure 26-1).

Fig. 26.1

zone 1	zone 2	zone 3	zone 4	zone 5
5' outside	5	5' middle	5	5' weakside

Attack

The remaining data to be recorded for the hitter are the target areas of the attack. Using the opponent's defensive alignment, record the court area to which the attack is directed. In the example on the next page (see Figure 26.2), a basic center back defense is used to illustrate court assignments.

Fig. 26.2

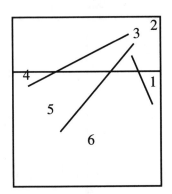

9K^5 a kill by No. 9 to area 5 of the opponent's court

9^4 an attack by No. 9 to area 4 of the opponent's court, where the ball was played

Blocking

Additional blocking data is recorded by noting the result of the attempted block. After the basic notation of the player's number followed by "B" for an attempted block, indicate the set that was delivered to the hitter.

9SB^{13} player 9 stuffed the hitter on a high outside set that terminated play

9B^{31} player 9 committed a blocking error on the attempt to block a 31

Examples of the contact series: pass, set, attack while detailing the quality and result of the contact can be found in Table 2.

Serving

Serving data is kept in the upper right-hand section of the data sheet. Player numbers are recorded at the time of service and a superscript is added to indicate the service area. Errors are recorded by indicating the type: "N" for net serve and "O" for serve out of bounds and an "F" for foot fault. Thus, serving data looks like the following examples:

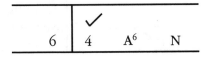

Player No. 6 served a ball to zone 4
The second serve was to zone 6 and resulted in an ace
The third serve was hit into the net.

Table 2

8^3-7^{55}-9^5

Player No. 8 passed to the target
Player No. 7 directed a high set to the weakside
Player No. 9 attacked to area 5 of the opponent's court. The ball was played by the opponent.

8^2-7^{31}-$9K^4$

Player No. 8 passed the ball but not to the target
Player No. 7 executed a quickset to the middle
Player No. 9 killed the ball to area 4 of the opponent's court

8^0-7^{51}-$9N$

Player No. 8 shanked the ball
Player No. 7 made a great play to set a 51
Player No. 9 made an attack error, ball in the net

8^3-7^3-

Player No. 8 sent a pass to the target
Player No. 7 failed to execute a 53, resulting in a setter error

8^2-7^{31}-96

Player No. 8 passes off the target, but the ball was playable
Player No. 7 set a 31
Player No. 9 is blocked for an attack error

$9S^{51}$

Player No. 9 stuffed the opponent on a 51 set

The systems described allow collection of simple or complex information that can be tailored to program needs. Determine the kind of information needed to evaluate with statistical data then choose those skills or events as the basis for data collection. Be creative. Design a notation that is logical and one that meets your needs.

Game # _____3_____   v.___Ki-Be 9/29___   Score ___14-16___

8SB	1 - 7 - 10K	~~10~~	
⑩- 7 - 9K	9 -~~7~~	10 - 7 - 11K	
10 - 7 - 9	1 - 7 - 10K	⑩- 7 - 11	
~~10~~	⑪- 7 - 8	2 -~~7~~	
10 - 8K	8T - 11 - 7 - ~~9~~N	2 - 7 -11	Serving
9SB	~~11~~ - 7 - 9	~~2~~	
9/5 SB	~~10~~	1 - 7 - 11	10 / A / N O / /
~~2~~	~~11~~ - 7 - 9	⑫-~~7~~- 1	
~~10~~	8SB	⑪- 7 - 11	5 /
10 - 7 - 9K	11 - 7 - 9	110	
10 - 7 - 10	~~10~~ - 9S - ~~90~~	~~12~~	9 A / / / /
⑨- 7 - 10	9SB	⑨- 7 - 11K	
9 -⑦- 11	11T - ~~10~~	11B	12
~~7~~	11SB	9 - 7 - 10K	
~~8~~	11B	~~10~~	7 / / / / /
9 - 7 - ~~5~~N	7 - 1C - 11		
9 - 7 - 11K	10 - 7 - 9K		11 / /
9 - 7 - 11K	11 -⑦- 8		
⑩- 7 - 10	~~10~~		2 / / A / / / / N
1 - 7 - 10	1 - 7 - 9K		
			1 N / / /

Player	Kills	Attempts	Errors	Serving %	Aces/ Errors	Assists	Errors	Blocks	Blocking Errors	Notes
10	3	8		4/7 .57	1-2	1-7	7/14			
5		1	1	1/1 .100				5		
9	5	8		5/5 .100	1-	-4	1/9	2.5		
12							1/2			
7				5/5 .100		11-	1/2 -3			
11	4	10		2/2 .100			2/8	4		
2				7/8 .875	1-1	-3	2/4			
1	1	1		3/4 .75	0-1	-1	1/6			
6/8	2	5	2					3		
Totals	15	33	3	.84	3-4	12-15	19-47	10		

7[15]   a high outside set executed properly to the intended target

⑦[55]   a high weakside set is off the target but playable

~~7~~[51]   a quickset is attempted: setter error

Photo courtesy of UCLA

Chapter 27

RECORDING STATISTICS EASILY:
THE SCHROEDER SYSTEM
Lois Mueller

The importance of accurate volleyball statistics cannot be over-emphasized. They are needed for coaching decisions, match and season evaluations, individual and team rankings and player honors. Yet, recording accurate volleyball statistics can be a very difficult task.

There are a number of factors which contribute to the difficulty of recording statistics. First, some of the moves requiring statistical data occur in rapid succession, such as the set and attack. Second, certain statistics are defined by what occurs afterward. An assist cannot be credited until the result of the attack is known. In these cases, the statistician must remember the players involved while observing the attack, then record both occurrences. Third, keeping statistics requires subjective judgments which must be made quickly and consistently. The difference between an ace for one server and a passing error for an opposing receiver can be very difficult to decipher.

The Problem

Numerous methods of recording match data have been tried in an attempt to keep accurate and consistent volleyball statistics. (Many programs have sufficient funding for courtside computer programs or the necessary crews to collect statistical data; however, a number of high school or smaller college programs are not afforded that luxury.) One possible tack to help overcome this problem is to have one or more persons tally all occurrences on a stat sheet as they occur in each game. A typical stat sheet lists each statistical category in a column across the top of the form while players' names and/or numbers are listed in rows down the left margin. The columns are subdivided into positive and negative outcomes of each statistic, as well as occurrences (e.g., serving attempts, aces and errors).

The difficulty of using this method stems from the time required to find the correct row and column in which to record the tally. The correct player row must first be located and then the statistician must move across the row until arriving at the appropriate stat column to record the tally or vice versa. While doing this searching and recording, subsequent play is often missed. Using more than one statistician can make this method workable, if responsibilities are wisely divided and procedures are clearly understood. However, since skilled statisticians are difficult to find and teams must often limit traveling squads, choosing a method of keeping statistics requiring two or more people may not be possible.

A second method of keeping volleyball statistics requires the statistician to do a verbal play-by-play into a tape recorder. For example, "number 15 passes serve; number 3 sets; 12 attacks for the kill; assist to 3." This enables the statistician to keep his/her eyes on the court while talking into the recorder. Comments regarding assists and other outcome-related information can be added as play progresses. After the match, the tape is transcribed onto a stat sheet.

While this method solves many of the problems

encountered in the first method, it is extremely time-consuming. Transcribing the tape — even without stopping it to record tallies — involves nearly the same amount of time as the match consumed...hours. If the tape must be stopped and restarted while transcribing, even more time is involved. It is difficult to find a statistician who is willing to devote that amount of time. If more than one person is used (e.g., one person records the play-by-play while a second person transcribes the tape, or different people cover different matches), inconsistent judgments and unclear interpretation can result.

A Possible Solution

After struggling with these inefficient methods for many seasons, an alternative was developed. This system will be referred to as the Schroeder System, since it was developed by Susan Schroeder, the Concordia University volleyball statistician. The Schroeder System involves a stat sheet with columns for each major category similar to the first method described (see Figure 1).

However, no player rows are necessary and only the basic statistical occurrence needs a column; no columns are needed for positive or negative outcomes.

As the game progresses, the statistician simply records the player's number anywhere in the appropriate column. This can be done with little attention to the chart since it is not necessary to find a specific row or place in the column. If an error is involved, the number is circled. If a positive result occurs such as an ace or kill, an asterisk is placed beside the number. This method enables one person to keep accurate statistics without spending numerous hours transcribing tapes. Since it is not necessary to locate rows for specific players or columns for positive or negative results, recording statistics is greatly simplified and the statistician is able to keep his/her eyes on the clipboard. Other indicators can be used rather than the circle and the asterisk, if the statistician desires. After the match is completed, the stat sheets can be used to complete totals and percentages just as one would do with the tally stat sheet described in method No. 1 (Figure 1).

Figure 1

Serves	Serve Receptions	Assists	Attacks	Digs	BS	BA	BHE	Other

To simplify the post-match computations, it is recommended that the stat sheets be analyzed twice. The first time, only those numbers without circles or asterisks are crossed out, while a slash is placed through the circled and starred numbers. Then, on the second pass, the slashed numbers are recorded and totally crossed out. For example:

prior to review

15	5	③	12
2	12*	5	11

after first analysis/review

15	5	③	12
2	12*	5	11

after second analysis/review

15	5	⊗	12
2	12*	5	11

Summary

The ease of the Schroeder System is very functional. It can turn a difficult and problematic procedure into a relatively easy task. Using the Schroeder System allows the coach to concentrate on coaching, knowing that accurate statistics are being recorded.

Part 6

SPORTS NUTRITION

Photo by Bob Kalmbach/Courtesy of University of Michigan

Chapter 28

THE DAILY TRAINING DIET:
ENSURING AN ADEQUATE INTAKE FOR PERFORMANCE VOLLEYBALL
Barbara Day, M.S., R.D., C.N.

Research shows that a carbohydrate-rich training diet is the best choice for fueling the volleyball player's muscles. This approach prevents the player from becoming fatigued when following a rigorous day-to-day training schedule. No magic pill or powder can provide the player with all of the high energy nutrients he/she needs. The training diet should include a variety of foods to fuel the growing, active volleyball player. Whether a high school or collegiate athlete, the player needs to know what foods are high in complex and simple carbohydrates and what individual carbohydrate needs are. Complex carbohydrate foods include breads, pasta, rice, cereal, vegetables and dried beans. Simple carbohydrate foods include fruits, sugar, soft drinks and honey.

How much carbohydrate is enough? Simply multiply 3, 4 or 5 (based on the needs of the individual athlete) x pounds of body weight to equal the grams of carbohydrate needed for the daily training diet. The volleyball player needs to know how to plan a training diet that is flexible, with easy-to-prepare meals, and will accommodate a busy schedule.

The Starting Line

Use the *Performance Conditioning for Volleyball* Food Guide Pyramid -- A Guide to Daily Food Choices (Table 1) for specific serving amounts and approximate grams of carbohydrate per serving. The base of the pyramid includes bread, cereal, rice and pasta, the group that contains the highest amount of

complex carbohydrate. Whole grain foods provide the volleyball player with adequate amounts of B vitamins, important to energy metabolism.

Fruits and vegetables offer the player a valuable source of energy, vitamins, minerals, fluid and fiber. Fruits provide a steady supply of energy. They can easily be carried as a snack and used for instant energy. Fruits and vegetables are important to the volleyball player because the nutrients found in these foods are usually the ones lost in sweat during hard work-outs.

Dairy products are also a good source of carbohydrates. They provide protein and are a good source of calcium. Protein is important in growth and tissue repair. Calcium is important in bone development and in muscle contraction. Finally, meat, poultry, fish, dried beans, eggs and nuts round out the volleyball player's diet. While there is very little carbohydrate in most meals, dried beans and nuts provide some carbohydrate. Each serving of lean meat, poultry or fish consists of a 3 oz. portion after cooking and is about the size of a deck of cards.

Fluids play a significant role in the diet. A fluid-deficient player is a tired player. Most volleyball players need at least 10 cups of fluid per day.

Down the Stretch

The best way of determining whether the volleyball player is eating a good training diet is to ask him/her to write down what he/she eats for three days (see sample chart). Then, using as a guide the minimum

**Table 1 — *Performance Conditioning for Volleyball* Food Guide Pyramid
A Guide to Daily Food Choices**

MEAT, POULTRY, FISH, DRY BEANS,
EGGS, NUTS GROUP
minimum 3 serving/day (very little
  carbohydrate)
3 ounces cooked lean meat, fish,
  poultry
1 ounce of lean meat equals: 1/2 cup of
  cooked dried beans (20 grams
  carbohydrate)
1 egg
2 tablespoons peanut butter
  (5 grams carbohydrate)

MILK, YOGURT, CHEESE GROUP
minimum 3 servings/day
(12 grams carbohydrate)
1 cup milk, yogurt
1-1/2 ounces of natural cheese
2 ounces of process cheese

FRUIT GROUP
minimum 4 servings/day
(15 grams carbohydrate)
1 medium piece of fruit
1/2 cup of cooked or
  canned fruit
3/4 cup of fruit juice
1/4 cup of dried fruit

VEGETABLES GROUP
minimum 5 servings/day
(5 grams carbohydrate)
1 cup raw leafy vegetables
1/2 cup of other vegetables,
  cooked, chopped, raw
3/4 cup of vegetable juice

BREAD, CEREAL, RICE, PASTA GROUP
minimum 11 servings/day
(15 grams carbohydrate)
1 slice of bread
1/2 bagel, bun
1 ounce of ready-to-eat cereal
1/2 cup of cooked cereal, rice, pasta

OTHER FOODS Grams Carbohydrate
1 fig bar =11
12 ounce soda =40
1/2 cup nonfat frozen yogurt =24
1 oz. pretzels =22

number of servings from each food group presented in Table 1, have the player check to see if he/she has included all food groups, grams of carbohydrate and fluids needed for the daily training diet.

Over the Finish Line

There are a number of ways to help the volleyball player plan a training diet.

1. Present basic guidelines to the player.
2. Provide brown bag suggestions.
3. For players living at home, notify parents as to what foods should be available.
4. Obtain nutritional information from the school food service concerning the foods served for school lunch.
5. Offer suggestions concerning foods that can be purchased at fast food restaurants or develop guidelines for choosing the right foods at a conventional restaurant.
6. Teach players to read food labels.

For special help, the volleyball player may want to seek the advice of a registered dietitian who understands the complexities of the sport and the player's needs.

Eating the right food each day can positively influence the volleyball player's performance. This strategy can help the player stay healthy and have energy to burn during his/her competitive years. In addition, the volleyball player will develop good eating habits that will last a lifetime.

Reprinted from *Performance Conditioning for Volleyball.*

Food and Activity Record Formula

3 x 130 pounds = 390 grams of carbohydrate (CHO) You can substitute the number 4 or 5 (based on the needs of the individual athlete) and multiply by 130 pounds.

Photo by Eugene Hopkins

Chapter 29

NUTRITION STRATEGIES FOR SURVIVING TWO-A-DAYS

Barbara Day, M.S., R.D., C.N.

Key points to preventing dehydration during two-a-days:

Start drinking upon arising in the morning, as soon as you get up.

Keep a filled water bottle with you at all times and drink from it frequently. (A good swallow is approximately one ounce of fluid).

Sip on a sports electrolyte drink such as Gatorade, Exceed, Powerade, All Sports or diluted juice (one cup water to one cup juice) during extensive practices (more than 90 minutes). Five to eight percent CHO drink is recommended, or 15 to 20 grams of CHO per eight ounces.

Avoid excessive soft drinks. The carbonation in them makes you feel full sooner so you end up drinking less.

Weigh yourself before and after each practice. Then, drink 16 ounces of fluid per pound of weight lost.

Note: Clear urine is a sign of getting enough fluids; dark colored urine denotes dehydration.

Pre-season conditioning means a lot of hard work, but it is critical to condition in order to prevent possible injury during the playing season. A number of nutrition strategies can help you get the most out of this training period. The two most important nutrients to consider during two-a-days are carbohydrates (CHO) and fluids. A CHO-rich diet helps provide the energy needed to complete the heavy work load during this training phase. But this is only part of the story. CHO and fluid work together to help prevent fatigue throughout the day. Therefore, the player needs to consume adequate amounts of fluid during this time, as well.

The Ins and Outs of CHO

There are two forms of CHO: simple and complex. Both provide energy to the working muscle. However, foods high in complex CHOs such as bread, cereal, pasta and rice also contain essential nutrients such as B vitamins and minerals which are important in running energy systems. Fruit and juice, which are simple CHOs, provide the volleyball player with good sources of minerals, vitamins and fluid. Other simple CHO foods such as candy, cookies and soda provide valuable energy, but not much else.

Volleyball players need to consume approximately five grams of carbohydrate per pound of body weight per day during two-a-days to ensure adequate energy levels. Without enough daily carbohydrate during two-a-days, performance and strength slowly dwindle. Read the nutrition facts on the food label to determine the CHO content in foods.

Fluid Facts

Adequate fluid intake is a very important aspect of training and should not be neglected, especially during two-a-days. How much fluid is needed daily? Multiply your normal weight in pounds x 18 for women or 20 for men. Then divide this number by 30. Example, 18 x 125 / 30 = 75 ounces of fluid per day. This gives an idea of how many ounces of fluid are needed per day. Water is not the only fluid that meets this requirement. Lemonade, juice soft drinks (without caffeine) or sport drinks will provide not only fluid, but also CHO and perhaps vitamins and minerals (sport drinks). Do not count caffeinated or alcoholic beverages as part of the fluid requirement since both have a dehydrating effect rather than a rehydrating effect.

What to Eat Before the Morning Workout

Skipping breakfast could result in poor performance and low energy levels throughout the day. Breakfast can be light, less than 300 calories, one to two hours before a strenuous workout. See Table 1 for breakfast ideas.

A two-a-day breakfast/lunch should:

Be high in CHO (>50 grams/breakfast; > 100 grams/lunch)

Be low in fat (<10 grams/breakfast; <20 grams/lunch)

Contain at least 16 ounces of fluid

Contain little dietary fiber

If the practice is very early in the morning, drinking fluids may be more practical than eating solids. Solids take longer to empty from your stomach so they take longer to digest. Something as simple as drinking an instant breakfast made with skim milk may help keep energy levels constant. However, if milk is a problem for the player, several liquid meal replacements are available that do not contain milk but contain ample amounts of calories (250 to 360 per eight ounces).

These are: Gatorpro, Ensure, Ensure Plus, Sustacal, etc. These products can be found in a grocery store or pharmacy.

Table 1 — Breakfast and Lunch Ideas

	Calories	Fat (g)	CHO (g)
English muffin (1)	130	1	26
bagel (1)	163	1	31
toast (1)	60	1	13
CEREAL			
Wheaties 1 cup	100	1	25
Cheerios 1 cup	110	2	21
oatmeal 1 pack	105	0	18
skim milk 1 cup	90	0	13
JUICE			
orange or apple 8 oz.	112	0	27
grape 8 oz.	170	0	42
fat free muffin (1)	120	0	28
FRUITED YOGURT 8 OZ.			
fat free	160	0	33
low fat	250	3	47
Poptart (2)	210	7	34
FRUIT			
banana	105	0	27
raisins (1 1/2 oz.)	130	0	31
honeydew (1 cup)	132	0	23
orange	65	0	16
instant breakfast (1 pk)	130	1	28
cottage cheese			
1% (1/2 oz.)	80	2	4
water-packed tuna			
(3 1/2 oz.)	70	1	<1
PowerBar (2.25 oz.)	225	3	40
FAST FOOD IDEAS			
6 inch sub sandwiches (hold mayonnaise)			
roast beef	345	12	41
turkey	322	10	41
tostada	243	11	27
cheese pizza (1 slice)	153	5	18
grilled chicken			
sandwich (no sauce)	310	3	20
baked potato (plain)	220	0	51
soda (8 oz.)	100	0	27

Lunchtime Options

Choosing the right food at lunch depends on several factors such as when the next practice is, the intensity and length, what type of practice. Small meals containing 500 to 700 calories need approximately three hours to digest. Refer to Table 1. Eating lunch at 12 noon and resuming practice at 3 p.m. should give the player enough time to digest a small meal. Eating a hearty, balanced dinner helps the recharging process. Now is the time to focus on eating enough protein and calories. Fish, chicken, lean meat or low-fat cheese should be included in this meal. Also, don't avoid the fat. You need the calories because you are working so hard. For carbohydrate to be an effective energy source, you first need plenty of calories. So relax a bit. Use the salad dressing, add some margarine to your rolls — you need the energy. Just do not overdo it.

An evening snack rich in both CHOs and fluids provides the player a good start for the next day's worth of energy-expending activities.

Using these simple strategies may help boost the player's level of play and prevent injury.

Reprinted from *Performance Conditioning for Volleyball.*

Chapter 30

EATING ON THE ROAD

Jacqueline R. Berning, Ph. D., R.D.

It is 7 p.m. and you have just finished competing. The team showers, dresses and piles into the bus for the trip home. It is now 8 p.m. The team is starving, you are on a limited budget and you have a two-hour drive home ahead. Where do you eat? Like many traveling teams, you stop at a fast food restaurant. While the athletes' hunger is satisfied, you wonder about their overall nutritional status. Did they eat enough carbohydrates for glycogen resynthesis? Did they consume too much fat? Did they rehydrate? Was a fast food restaurant a good choice?

The Nutrition Factor

Although many athletes and coaches are aware of the importance of nutrition, they do not know how to apply what they know. For example, they know that carbohydrate is the primary fuel for exercising muscles, but when it comes to making food choices, they have no idea what a high carbohydrate food is or how much they should eat. Yet, deficiencies in consumption of energy, nutrients, electrolytes and/or water can hinder performance (American Dietetic Association).

Survey Findings

A survey of elite national swimmers revealed that they, like the typical American, consumed more fat than carbohydrates in their diets (Berning and Troup). Furthermore, when they were given a nutrition knowledge test, they did very well on basic nutrition knowledge but poorly when it came to choosing

foods that were high in specific nutrient.

For example, when asked to name a nutritious carbohydrate, 62 percent chose an apple, but 38 percent chose french fries. When asked which food is a good source of protein, 63 percent chose the correct answer of chicken, but 37 percent chose oatmeal. Overall, 62 percent of the swimmers picked

Table 1	
THE FOUR FOOD GROUPS	
Food Groups	No. Servings
Milk	3-adult/4-child/2-teen
Milk or Yogurt, 1 cup	
Cheese, 1 1/2 slices	
Cottage cheese, 2 cups	
Ice Cream, 1 3/4 cups	
Meat	2 (all ages)
Cooked lean meat, fish, poultry, 2 ounces	
Eggs, 2	
Dried beans or peas, 1 cup	
Peanut Butter, 4 tablespoons	
Cheese, 2 ounces	
Fruits and Vegetables	4 (all ages)
Cooked or juice, 1/2 cup	
Raw — average piece of fruit	
Grain	4 (all ages)
Bread, 1 slice	

the correct answer; however, 38 percent were unable to select the proper balance of foods necessary for the energy demands of their sport.

Determining Nutrient Requirements

An athlete's energy requirements vary depending on weight, height, age, sex and metabolic rate, and on the type, intensity, frequency and duration of the sport. Daily routine training can increase the energy needs of the athlete two to three times the non-training requirements (Van Handel, Calls, Bradley, Troup). Normally, hunger sensations support the need for additional calories. However, the intense emotional stress of training and competition, combined with hectic travel schedules and lack of nutrition knowledge, mean that many athletes fail to consume sufficient calories and essential nutrients (Wilmore and Freund).

The athletes can best meet these higher requirements by increasing the number of servings for each of the four food groups and concentrating on both the bread and cereal group and the fruit and vegetable group (see Table 1).

A suggested distribution of calories for most competitive athletes is 10 percent to 15 percent protein, 25 percent to 30 percent fat and 50 percent to 60 percent carbohydrates (Berning and Troup). Endurance athletes (triathletes, cyclists or marathon runners), however, should consume 60 percent to 70 percent of their calories from carbohydrates, since one of the limiting factors in prolonged human performance is glycogen depletion (Short and Short). Athletes whose diets are chronically deficient in carbohydrates can experience a progressive depletion of glycogen stores (Castill, Sherman, Fink, et. al.). This may cause drops in endurance, precision and speed.

Athletes who eat a normal, mixed diet generally ingest around 300 to 350 grams of carbohydrate (1,200 to 1,450 calories) per day (Castill, Bowers, Brannan, et. al.). Unfortunately, this type of diet does not adequately replace the muscle's glycogen used in exhaustive daily training. Therefore a high carbohydrate diet of around 509 to 600 grams of carbohydrate (2,000 to 2,400 calories) per day is recommended. This higher level can almost completely replace muscle glycogen within 24 hours (Short and Short). Consuming more than 600 grams of carbohydrate (2,400 calories) per day does not necessarily result in proportionately larger amounts of muscle glycogen and the excess can be converted to fat.

Carbohydrate Recommendations

Which carbohydrates should be recommended to the athlete? The research is not clear on this issue. One study compared the effects of simple carbohydrates and complex carbohydrates on muscle glycogen synthesis during a 48-hour period after a glycogen-depleting exercise (Castill, Sherman, Fink, et. al.). During the first 24 hours after exercise, the researcher found no difference in muscle glycogen synthesis between the two types of dietary carbohydrates. But during the second 24 hours, the complex carbohydrate diet resulted in significantly more muscle glycogen synthesis. On the other hand, in a similar comparison of simple and complex carbohydrate intake during both glycogen-depleted and non-depleted states, it was concluded that significant increases in skeletal muscle glycogen content could be achieved with a diet high in simple or complex carbohydrates in that they are more nutrient-dense. They contain more B vitamins necessary for energy metabolism and more fiber and iron, contributing to a nutritionally balanced diet.

Athletes have a high requirement for carbohydrates, yet they may have a difficult time making wise food choices. Trainers, coaches and health professionals should provide practical guidance to athletes on eating a balanced diet, especially when they are competing on the road. To further assure that athletes consume diets high in carbohydrate, commercially available liquid carbohydrate supplements may be helpful.

Practical Applications

The four food groups system offers an easy method for selection of a nutritionally balanced diet. Foods are classified according to their nutrient content: the milk group is high in calcium, riboflavin and protein; the meat group is high in protein, thiamin an iron; the fruit and vegetable group provides vitamins A and C; and the grain groups supply foods high in carbohydrates, iron, niacin and thiamin (see Table 1.)

By eating a variety of foods from each food group every day, athletes will obtain the needed nutrients for a nutritionally sound diet. During heavy training,

---

TABLE 2
EXAMPLES OF HIGH
CARBOHYDRATE MEALS

BREAKFAST
Sample Meal #1
Orange juice
Pancakes with syrup
English muffin
Lowfat yogurt
Sample Meal #2
Apple juice
Raisin bran/oatmeal — large bowl
Lowfat milk
Bran muffin
Banana

LUNCH
Sample Meal #1
Large turkey sandwich on two slices of whole wheat bread
Carrot strips
Lowfat yogurt
Fresh fruit
Sample Meal #2
Baked potato with chili
Cornmeal muffin
Chocolate milkshake

DINNER
Sample Meal #1
Minestrone soup
Spaghetti with tomato sauce
Two rolls
Lowfat yogurt
Lowfat milk
Sample Meal #2
Thick crust cheese-vegetable pizza
Salad bar
Sherbet
When ordering pizza, request toppings such as green peppers, mushrooms and other high-carbohydrate vegetables.

NOTE: Caloric needs depend on age, sex and activity level. In order to determine individual requirements contact a local health professional for assistance.

---

an athlete should consume at least eight servings a day from the fruit and vegetable group and grain group. The increased carbohydrate intake helps minimize the gradual depletion of muscle glycogen and subsequent feeling of fatigue that occur after heavy training.

Another way to make sure your athletes make wise food choices on the road is to determine where you will eat before mealtime. For example, find a suitable restaurant and ask for a pasta meal within your budget. Usually the manager or chef can accommodate you, especially if you make this a regular request. If you stay in a hotel that offers food service, contact the catering manager and ask for high carbohydrate meals within your budget (Table 2).

Remember, as long as you are paying for the meals you can usually demand the type and quality of food desired. Do not be afraid to ask for special foods and make sure your get a reasonable price. The hotel or restaurant wants your business.

If you cannot afford all three meals at a restaurant, choose breakfast for a team meal. With selections like cereal (hot and cold), bagels, English muffins, pancakes, toast, fruit and fruit juices, breakfast can be inexpensive and an easy way to get carbohydrate-rich foods. If your budget does not allow restaurant meals or you must have day trips, remember that a nearby grocery store offers a great variety of foods. They may have a delicatessen or a soup and salad bar and you can pick up fresh fruits and vegetables, fruit juices, low-fat milk and dairy products. Not only are grocery stores easy and fast, they can also be a cheaper source of meals than a restaurant.

Another way to get your athletes to eat more nutrient-dense foods is to offer nutritious snacks on the bus. Usually when athletes have a long bus ride they load up on candy, soda pop and potato chips. To cut down on these foods, offer fruit juices, fresh fruits and vegetables, bagels, muffins, raisins and crackers. Contact your booster club to cut down on cost. Most parents want their children to eat better and they are willing to offer financial help or provide the food for the bus trip. Often the food service manager at your school can help provide wholesome snacks for the road trip.

A few words about fast foods: they are generally high in fat, low in calcium, vitamin C and vitamin A, but you can make wise selections by using the accompanying chart (see Table 3).

Last but not least, coaches and athletic trainers must be role models for their athletes. What good does it do to talk about the importance of good nutrition while the coach is on the sideline or pool deck drinking coffee and eating french fries? Athletes look up to coaches, trainers and other athletic leaders in the community. To change athletes' eating habits, coaches and trainers must give them knowledge to make wise food choices; provide opportunities to practice making good food choices; and, most importantly, set a good example.

Summary

Since athletes have a high requirement for carbohydrates and have a difficult time making wise food choices, they need to be taught how to eat better on the road.

First, it is important for athletes to learn how to use the four food groups as a guide in making wise food choices. Second, athletes need to identify types and amounts of high-carbohydrate foods to eat. Third, athletes should give special consideration to where they eat when traveling to ensure a choice of high-carbohydrate and nutrient-dense foods.

Coaches, trainers and health professionals play an important role in educating athletes on the relationship between nutrition and athletic performance.

References

American Dietetic Association: Nutrition for Physical Fitness and Athletic Performance For Adults. (1989). *Journal of the American Dietetic Association*, 87(7): 933-939.

Berning, J.R. and J.P. Troup. (1984-87). Unpublished data collected from U.S. National and Olympic swim teams. U.S. Swimming, Colorado Springs, Colorado.

Costill, D.L., W.M. Sherman, W.J. Fink et. al. (1981). The role of dietary carbohydrate in muscle glycogen resynthesis after strenuous running. *American Journal of Clinical Nutrition*, 34: 1831-1836, 1981.

Costill, D.L., R. Bowers, G. Branam, et. al. (1971). Muscle glycogen utilization during prolonged exercise on successive days. *Journal of Applied Physiology*, 31: 834-838.

National Dairy Council. *Food Power*. (1983). Rosemont, IL.

Roberts, K.M., E.G. Noble, D.B. Hayden and A.W. Taylor. (1988). Simple and complex carbohydrate-rich diets and muscle glycogen content of marathon runners. *European Journal of Applied Physiology*, 57: 70-74.

Short, S.H.J. and W.R. Short. (1983). Four-year study of university athletes' dietary intake. *Journal of the American Dietetic Association*, 82(6): 632-645.

Van Handel, P.J., K.A. Cells, P.W. Bradley and J.P. Troup. (1984). Nutritional status of elite swimmers. *Journal of Swimming Research*, 1(1): 27-31.

Wilmore, J.H. and B.J. Freund. (1984). Nutritional enhancement of athletic performance. *Nutritional Abstract Review*, 54(1): 1-16.

BREAKFAST

	Calories	Protein	Carbohydrates	Fat

McDONALD'S SAMPLE #1

	747	17%	56%	25%

Plain English muffin (2) with strawberry jam (1 packet)
Scrambled egg (1)
Orange Juice (6 oz.)
2% milk (1 carton)

McDONALD'S SAMPLE #2

	650	11%	66%	25%

Hot Cakes with butter and syrup (1/2 of the packet)
Orange juice (6 oz.)
2% milk (1 carton)
If still hungry, recommend ordering plain English muffin.

FAMILY STYLE RESTAURANT
SAMPLE #1

	761	12%	67%	20%

Buttermilk pancakes 5" (3) with butter (1 pat) and syrup (3 tablespoons)
Egg (1)
Orange juice (6 oz.)

FAMILY STYLE RESTAURANT
SAMPLE #2

	668	5%	58%	26%

Cold cereal with 2% milk (4 oz.)
Egg (1)
English Muffin with butter (1 pat) and jelly (1 packet)
Orange juice (4 oz.)
Breakfast orders usually come with two eggs. Order one instead. Poached, soft- or hard-boiled is recommended.

LUNCH/DINNER

	Calories	Protein	Carbohydrates	Fat

McDONALD'S

	667	23%	51%	25%

Chicken Sandwich with BBQ sauce
Side salad with low-calorie vinegar and oil dressing (1/2 packet)
Orange juice (6 oz.)
2% milk (1 carton)

WENDY'S SAMPLE #1

	719	22%	53%	25%

Chicken breast sandwich on multi-grain bread (no mayonnaise)
Baked potato with sour cream (1 packet)
2% milk (1 carton)

WENDY'S SAMPLE #2

	761	12%	67%	20%

Chili (8 oz.)
Baked potato, plain
Frosty, small
Side salad (3/4 cup lettuce, 3/4 cup fresh veggies, 1/4 cup cottage cheese)

LUNCH/DINNER

	Calories	Protein	Carbohydrates	Fat

ARBY'S SAMPLE #1

	695	22%	51%	27%

Jr. Roast Beef on multigrain bread with lettuce and tomato (no mayonnaise or horseradish)
Side salad*
2% milk (1 carton)

ARBY'S SAMPLE #2

	970	20%	52%	30%

Roast Beef or Ham & Cheese sandwich
Side salad*
Vanilla milkshake
2% milk (1 carton)
*Side salad should consist of the following ingredients: (1/2 cup lettuce, 1 cup fresh veggies, 1/2 cup garbanzo beans, 1/4 cup cottage cheese, 2 tablespoons low-calorie dressing)

TACO BELL SAMPLE #1

	1,040	18%	56%	27%

2 tostadas
1 bean burrito
1 beef burrito
2 plain tortillas
2% milk (1 carton)

TACO BELL SAMPLE #2

	785	19%	53%	28%

3 tostadas
1 plain tortilla
2% milk (1 carton)

TACO BELL SAMPLE #3

	785	19%	53%	28%

1 tostada
2 bean burritos
1 plain tortilla
2% milk (1 carton)
orange juice (4 oz.)
If possible, ask that the tostada shell be plain, not fried.

PIZZA HUT SAMPLE #1

	1,023	19%	61%	20%

Large spaghetti with meat sauce
Breadsticks
2% milk

PIZZA HUT SAMPLE #2

	1,126	20%	55%	25%

1/2 medium onion, green peeper and cheese pizza (thin crust)
2 breadsticks
2% milk (1 carton)

FAMILY STYLE RESTAURANT SAMPLE #1

	1,100	25%	51%	23%

Baked fish
Baked potato with sour cream (1 tablespoon)
1 muffin
Salad bar (1 cup lettuce)
2% milk (8 oz.)
Sherbet (1/2 cup)

Chapter 31

PRE-COMPETITION MEALS

Len Marquart, Ph.D.

The pre-game meal is frequently cited as a means of achieving optimal physical performance. Unfortunately, most volleyball players' concept of the pre-event meal simply includes the few hours before the event. In reality, the foundation of the pre-game meal is built upon a solid training diet leading up to and including the day of competition. What you eat and drink on the days before the event will provide most of the nourishment for competition.

Eating and drinking on the day of an event helps maintain hydration, prevent hunger, light-headedness and fatigue. The pre-event meal consumed a few hours before competition is primarily designed to alleviate hunger, maintain hydration and prepare the athlete psychologically.

Five factors are considered when selecting a precompetition meal: 1) timing, 2) amount, 3) composition, 4) physical and emotional stress and 5) individual variation.

Timing and Amount

In general, schedule the pre-competition meal one to five hours before the event. This allows time for food to move out of the stomach. A full stomach during competition may cause indigestion, nausea and possibly vomiting. The amount consumed is determined by the timing of the pre-event meal. Larger meals (700-1,000 calories) can be eaten four to five hours before; smaller meals (500-700 calories), two to three hours before; liquid meals (blenderized and commercial drinks, carbohydrate loaders) of less than

300-500 calories, one to two hours and small snacks (less than 300 calories) less than one hour before. Liquid meals empty from the stomach faster than solid meals and tend to settle more comfortably when consumed closer to competition. However, "too much" liquid may slosh around in the stomach when taken too close to the event.

Composition of the Meal

The recommended pre-competition meal is primarily composed of carbohydrates (bread, cereals, rice, pastas, potatoes, crackers) with some protein and minimal fat. Carbohydrates readily empty from the stomach, help maintain blood glucose levels and contribute to a light, agile feeling. Fat contained in foods such as hamburgers, hot dogs, french fries and cheese delay gastric emptying and contribute to a sluggish, heavy feeling.

Fluids are the most essential nutrient to the volleyball player during all phases of training, including the pre-game meal. Drink one to two cups of water with the pre-event meal.

Physical and Emotional Stress

During periods of physical and emotional stress, which can occur on the day of competition, blood flow to the stomach is reduced, thus slowing the digestive process. Subsequently, food consumed before competition may take longer to digest than if the athlete were relaxed.

Individual Variations

The optimal time, size and composition of the meal will vary considerably from one athlete to another. Some volleyball players can stuff themselves before competition and perform as well as those who eat nothing. Experimenting with a variety of pre-event meals while simulating actual competitive conditions helps assure that foods settle well during the event. It takes practice to select a pre-event meal that best fits your needs. Never try new foods before competition, especially before major events.

Helpful Hints

Volleyball players who develop food intolerances before the event might consider using liquid meals two to five hours before competition, eating the pre-game meals five to six hours before competition or eating well the day before (particularly the evening meal).

Pre-event Foods to Avoid:

- Too much salt (fluid retention)
- Caffeine (dehydration), i.e., soda, tea and coffee
- High fiber foods, i.e., salad, vegetables, foods with bran
- Gas formers, i.e., broccoli, cabbage, cauliflower, dried beans, onion

Some athletes have "lucky" foods they consume before the big event. If these foods do not interfere with performance, plan to include them even if they do not meet the recommendations for pre-event meals. Be sure to pack your "lucky" foods when traveling.

Drink fluids with the pre-event meal, including four to eight additional cups of fluid the day before the event. Drink three to four cups of fluid up to two hours before and one to two cups within 15 minutes of competition.

Reprinted from *Performance Conditioning for Volleyball*.

Volleyball Players' Guide to Precompetition Meals
What to eat!

FOR EVENTS IN THE MORNING, EAT BREAKFAST!

Breakfast Ideas

Drink fruit juice and water with one of these breakfasts at least two hours before your event:
Bagel, toasted with jelly
Pancakes with syrup or applesauce
Hot or cold cereal with lowfat milk, banana, toast and jelly
Egg, toast with jelly
Muffin or English muffin, lowfat yogurt with fruit slices
If you cannot eat solid foods, use a liquid meal. Blend together:
1 1/2 cups skim milk
1/4 cup nonfat dry milk powder
1/4 cup water
2 tablespoons sugar
1/2 teaspoons vanilla
Instant breakfast drinks mixed with skim milk can also be used. It is quick and easy!

FOR EVENTS IN THE EARLY TO MIDAFTERNOON, EAT BREAKFAST AND LUNCH!

Drink 1 glass of lowfat or skim milk and plenty of water with one of these meals:
Turkey sandwich with lettuce, banana
Tuna sub with lettuce and tomato, orange
Soup made with pasta or rice and crackers, lowfat yogurt with fruit slices

PACKED MEALS

Peanut butter (1 tsp.) and banana sandwich, pudding snack, fruit juice pack
Lowfat yogurt, banana, graham crackers, fruit juice pack
Bagel with thin slice of cheese, orange or grapes

HOME MEALS

Cereal and milk, banana, fruit juice
Chicken or turkey (3 ounces), baked or broiled potato, applesauce, lowfat or skim milk

RESTAURANT/FAST FOOD MEALS

1/2 turkey sub with lettuce and tomato, fruit juice, lowfat or skim milk
Plain baked potato with low fat topping, fruit juice, lowfat or skim milk

FOR EVENTS AFTER 5 PM, EAT BREAKFAST, LUNCH, AND LIGHT DINNER!

Chapter 32

EATING DISORDERS IN ATHLETES

Cheryl Fuller

In the past several decades, the prevalence of eating disorders has increased significantly. Since weight, food intake and physical activity are central to both eating disorders and to sports, it is not surprising to find more and more athletes diagnosed with anorexia nervosa or bulimia. Athletic trainers and team physicians should be familiar with the warning signs of eating disorders and should develop a program for education, prevention, intervention and treatment. Sports should aid the physical and psychological well-being of a participant, not foster or exacerbate eating disorders.

More and more people today suffer from compulsive eating disorders that not only threaten their health, but also threaten their lives (Burckes-Miller and Black, 1988). The increasing prevalence of these conditions has been, in part, blamed on society's standards of physical attractiveness and acceptance (Moore, 1988). It seems that society's preoccupation with weight and thinness has created an unrealistic ideal of appropriate weight which has shaped attitudes of dissatisfaction with body weight and shape even in normal and underweight adolescent girls (Moore, 1988). Other research (Maloney, McGuire, Daniels and Specker, 1989) suggest that these attitudes may even have their roots in early childhood. They found that a high percentage of children 8-13 years old were preoccupied with weight and dieting. A total of 45 percent of the children surveyed wanted to be thinner and 37 percent had already tried to lose weight. It is evident that the stages of childhood through adolescence are not only critical periods for

developing physically and emotionally, but for developing healthy nutritional practices, as well.

Food is an integral part of our lives, fulfilling one of our basic needs. Over the years, food has become very traditional at holidays and special gatherings. It has even come to symbolize feelings such as love and happiness. With eating disorders, however, food has taken on an addictive role, symbolizing feelings of loneliness, anger and frustration. The abuser uses food to obtain numbness from emotional pain or anxiety (Flood, 1989). Food actually becomes a tool which is used for control in one's life.

Eating Behaviors of Athletes

Since athletes place high values on weight and appearance, it is not surprising to find that athletes may have an increased risk for developing eating disorders (Burckes-Miller and Black, 1988). Many sports, including gymnastics, distance running, ballet, figure skating, diving and wrestling impose weight and/or body fat restrictions on athletes. These restrictions or weight limitations are often arbitrary, which sets up an environment conducive to pathogenic weight control. In addition, the athletic personality is a textbook definition of an eating disorder personality: very compulsive, driven and self-motivated (Thornton, 1990). Increased competition and demands from coaches regarding weight limits intensify the pressure for acceptance and success. This, in turn, may encourage many athletes to use unhealthy weight control methods. If the results of these abnormal practices are reinforced by coaches, peers or athletic success, the patterns are likely to continue (Steen and McKinney, 1986) with the potential for them to develop into serious eating disorders.

Many recent studies have shown alarming results that indicate athletes may be at a high risk for developing eating disorders (Burckes-Miller and Black, 1988; Burtis, Davis and Martin, 1988; Humphries and Gruber, 1986; Maloney, 1983; Rosen and Hough, 1988; Rosen, McKeag, Hough and Curley, 1986; Steen and McKinney, 1986; Thornton, 1990; Zucker, Avener, Bayder, Bruman, Moore and Zimmerman, 1985). A study by Rosen, et. al., of 182 female collegiate athletes showed that 32 percent practiced at least one pathogenic weight control behavior such as self-induced vomiting, binges, the use of laxatives, diet pills and/or diuretics (Rosen, McKeag, Hough and Curley, 1986). A similar study by the same author conducted on 42 gymnasts, 17-22 years old, showed that 62 percent were using at least one form of pathogenic weight control (Rosen and Hough, 1986). In a study by Burckes-Miller on 695 male and female athletes, three percent met *The Diagnostic and Statistical Manual of Mental Disorders*, 3rd ed. criteria for anorexia nervosa (4.2 percent female athletes and 1.6 percent male athletes) and 21.5 percent met the DSM III criteria for bulimia (39.2 percent female athletes and 14.3 percent male athletes) (Burckes-Miller and Black, 1988). These studies indicate a higher prevalence of eating disorders in female athletes but also show that both male and female athletes are affected at higher percentages than other populations. This may be due to the fact that athletes lose weight not only for appearance, but also to improve athletic performance. However, many practice weight control behaviors that can adversely affect their performance, along with their health.

Anorexia Nervosa and Bulimia

Anorexia nervosa and bulimia are two eating disorders occurring at alarming rates in adolescent and college-age females. It is estimated that the prevalence of anorexia nervosa is between one percent to five percent in adolescent girls (Shangold and Mirkin, 1988). The prevalence of bulimia is considerably higher with reports of as many as 20 percent of college-age women affected (Burtis, Davis and Martin, 1988). Although these disorders affect

women more than men, at a ratio of 9:1 or 10:1, this trend may be changing (Zucker, Avener, Bayder, Bruman, Moore and Zimmerman, 1985). Men have also been affected by society's standards for physical attractiveness and have responded with an increased obsession with food and fitness (Flood, 1989). Several studies indicate that the incidence of eating disorders in the male population may be increasing significantly, as well (Shangold and Mirkin, 1988; Yager, Kurtzman, Landsverk and Wiesmeier, 1988).

Anorexia nervosa is derived from the Greek word anorexia meaning "want of appetite" and the Latin word nervosa meaning "nervous" (Burtis, Davis and Martin, 1988). It is a condition characterized by self-imposed starvation which results in a substantial weight loss of 25 percent or greater (Burtis, Davis and Martin, 1988; Maloney, 1983; Shangold and Mirkin, 1988). Its victims, however, maintain a distorted body image and though emaciated, have a tremendous fear of being fat. Along with extreme self-imposed dieting, many anorexics have excessive exercise practices. Due to the extreme weight loss from anorexia nervosa, its victims experience conditions such as constipation, hypothermia, insomnia, mood disturbances and depression (Shangold and Mirkin, 1988). Amenorrhea is a classic symptom of the female anorexic.

Bulimia is derived from the Greek word buli, which means "ox hunger" or "to eat like an animal" (Hollis, 1985; Maloney, 1983; Shangold and Mirkin, 1988). The condition is characterized by binges, which are periods of uncontrollable overeating (Burtis, Davis and Martin, 1988). The binges may occur several times a day with intakes ranging from 1,200 to 11,500 Kcal per episode. These binges will often alternate with some form of purging such as self-induced vomiting, fasting, the use of laxatives, enemas, diuretics or excessive exercise (Zucker, Avener, Bayder, Brutman, Moore and Zimmerman, 1985). Bulimia, however, does not mean purging or vomiting, but refers only to the manner in which food is taken in. In fact, some bulimics simply exhaust themselves and resort to sleeping after a binge (Shangold and Mirkin, 1988).

Unlike anorexics, bulimics do not experience a significant weight loss and may even be somewhat overweight (Burtis, Davis and Martin, 1988). In addition, amenorrhea, an essential feature of anorexia nervosa, does not usually occur in bulimia (Gray and Gray, 1989). Both diseases, however, exhibit many of the same characteristics, with victims being obsessive-compulsive, conscientious, achievement-oriented and perfectionists (Burtis, Davis and Martin, 1988; Maloney, 1983; Shangold and Mirkin, 1988). Although they often exhibit ideal behavior, anorexics and bulimics suffer from feelings of inferiority and lack of self-esteem (Burtis, Davis and Martin, 1988). Anorexics and bulimics are also similar in their unnatural use of food to deal with stress in their lives (Hollis, 1985).

Bulimarexia is a term which is used frequently in the lay population. It is often used to designate individuals who binge and purge or restrict food intake, or those who diet and also practice purging. However, the term bulimarexia is not in professional writings since the clinical picture will classify individuals as either anorexic or bulimic (Hollis, 1985).

Health Consequences

The physiological effects that result from anorexia nervosa and bulimia can lead to serious physical and psychological consequences (Palla and Litt, 1988; Patton, 1988; Shangold and Mirkin, 1988; Thornton, 1990; Yager, Landsverk and Edelstein, 1987). Repetitive vomiting can lead to dehydration, esophageal inflammation, electrolyte imbalance, the erosion of tooth enamel and parotid gland swelling and soreness. Malnutrition can lead to mood disturbances, amenorrhea, osteoporosis, impaired renal function, tetany, seizures, cardiac arrhythmias and even death.

What is important to realize is that anorexia nervosa and bulimia are not just illnesses of weight; rather, they are psychological illnesses with weight and diet implications which result in serious medical consequences (Burtis, Davis and Martin, 1988). The common factor in all eating disorders is the obsession with food and control. Food has assumed an unnatural importance in life, dominating both psychologically and physically (Hollis, 1985). Treatment, therefore, requires a comprehensive program to address the psychiatric, nutritional and medical aspects of the disease (Burtis, Davis and Martin, 1988; Gray and Gray, 1989). Eating disorders are serious illnesses which usually run a chronic course requiring long-term therapy. It is estimated that only 30 percent to 40 percent of all patients treated for eating disorders totally recover (Shangold and Mirkin, 1988; Thornton, 1990). Tragically, five to 10 percent of the patients die from direct complications of their disease, which range from cardiac arrest to suicide (Shangold and Mirkin, 1988).

Role of the Athletic Trainer

Athletic trainers and other individuals working with athletes need to be aware of the prevalence of eating disorders among athletes. The athletic trainer is in a good position to observe signs and symptoms of these conditions, often eating in athletic dining halls and traveling with athletic teams. Athletes should be observed for any unusual eating habits. Items to note include types and quantity of food eaten or not eaten, when the athlete eats and behavior and activity following meals. It is not uncommon to hear athletes discuss a teammate's eating behavior or their suspicions of an athlete with an eating disorder. It is also not uncommon for athletes to share their pathogenic weight control behaviors, such as one athlete instructing another on how to induce vomiting.

Proper weight determination for athletes should be the role of the athletic trainer and not arbitrarily set by the coaches. When weight loss or gain is deemed beneficial or appropriate, the trainer should design and monitor the athlete's program. It is important to watch for drastic changes in weight; therefore, routine weighing of the athlete is essential. However, the fragile psychological state of the athlete regarding his or her weight requires that the weigh-ins should be private. Also, the common practice by many coaches of posting athletes' weights should be strongly discouraged.

As a member of the health care team, the athletic trainer should set an appropriate example in terms of health and nutrition, along with providing encouragement and emotional support for the athlete. Another important role which the athletic trainer should assume is development of an educational program for the intervention and prevention of eating disorders among athletes. The program should include education on proper nutrition, stress management techniques, the warning signs of eating disorders, recommendations and guidance for those who suspect they or a teammate may have an eating disorder and the medical complications and risks of the disease. It is important not only to educate the athletes, but also to educate the coaches regarding eating disorders. Because of the influence coaches have on their athletes, pressure or inadvertent remarks about an athlete's weight may exacerbate the disease.

Detection of an athlete with an eating disorder is the first step in providing health care for that athlete. The athletic trainer may be the first professional to become aware of a possible eating disorder with an athlete and it is essential that he or she make a proper referral for evaluation and treatment. If an athlete is suspected of suffering from an eating disorder, it is best to confront the athlete with your observations and concerns regarding his or her health. It will be only natural for the athlete to deny an existing eating disorder since a symptom of the disease is a distorted image of what is normal. However, the trust and rapport established between athletes and athletic trainers provides an ideal relationship in which many athletes are willing to confide and discuss their personal problems and admit their eating disorder.

Due to the psychological and medical aspects of eating disorders, these conditions need to be handled by experienced professionals. Therefore, the athletic trainer must have a referral source, including a medical physician, a psychiatrist or psychologist and a registered dietitian experienced in counseling eating disordered patients. It is also important to get the athlete involved in a support group to provide the understanding and emotional support necessary for a successful recovery.

A plan of action for the athletic trainer in dealing with eating disorders includes the following recommendations: The first step is to develop an educational program for student-athletes and staff members. This may be modeled after or incorporated into the drug education program that many athletic departments now have. Suggestions for the educational program include seminars conducted by local or national organizations, or informal meetings with guest speakers who are professionals in the field, as well as individuals who are recovering from eating disorders. The program should educate the athletic trainers, coaches, administrators and student-athletes about the underlying causes of eating disorders, the effects of nutrition on weight and athletic performance and the steps to take if an athlete shows signs of an eating disorder.

Once the educational program has been established, the athletic trainer must identify the personnel and resources available and develop a referral base. While the athletic trainer may identify symptoms that indicate the risk of an eating disorder, diagnosis and treatment can only be provided by a physician or psychologist who specializes in eating disorders.

Usually, the most difficult aspect of an eating disorder program is the step of confronting the athlete. Rather than to ask the athlete if he/she may have an eating disorder, it is better for the athletic trainer to state his/her observations and concerns and initiate the referral process for proper medical care. It is important for the athletic trainer to provide emotional support during this time. Another important but overlooked responsibility of the athletic trainer is role modeling. Being comfortable with one's own body image and demonstrating sound nutritional practices provides a healthy role model for athletes.

By providing early detection, intervention, proper referral and treatment of an eating disorder, an athlete's life may be saved. It is tragic that due to ignorance of the disease, people often dismiss eating disorders as trivial. But, as health care professionals, athletic trainers must educate athletes, coaches and themselves regarding the prevalence and seriousness of eating disorders and provide the appropriate health care.

References

Burckes-Miller, M.E. and D. Black. (1988). Male and female college athletes: Prevalence of anorexia nervosa and bulimia nervosa. *Athletic Training, JNATA*, 23(2): 137-140.

Burtis, G., J. Davis and S. Martin. (1988). *Applied Nutrition and Diet Therapy*. Philadelphia, PA: W.B Saunders Co., 472-479.

Drummer, G., L.W. Rosen, W.W. Heusner, P.J. Roberts and J.E. Consilman. (1987). Pathogenic weight control behaviors of young competitive swimmers. *Physician and Sportsmedicine*, 15(5): 75-86.

Flood, M. (1989). Addictive eating orders. *Nurs Clin North Am*, 24(1): 45-53.

Gadpaille, W.J., C.F. Sanborn and W.W. Wagner Jr. (1987). Athletic amenorrhea, major affective disorders and eating disorders. *American Journal of Psychiatry*, 144(7): 939-942.

Gray, G.E. and L.K. Gray. (1989). Nutritional aspects of psychiatric disorders. *Journal of American Dietary Association*, 89(10): 1492-1498.

Herzog, D.B., J.F. Borus, P. Hamburgh, I.L. Ott and A. Concus. (1987). Substance use, eating behaviors and social impairment of medical students. *Journal of Medical Education*, 62(8): 651-657.

Hollis, J. (1985). *Fat is a Family Affair*. San Francisco, CA: Harper and Row Publishers.

Humphries, L.L. and J.J. Gruber. (1986). Nutrition behaviors of university majorettes. *Physician and Sportsmedicine*, 14(11): 91-98.

Maloney, M.J. (1983). Anorexia nervosa and bulimia in dancers. *Clinics in Sports Medicine*, 2(3): 549-555.

Maloney, M.J., J. McGuire, S.R. Daniels and B. Specker. (1989). Dieting behavior and eating attitudes in children. *Pediatrics*, 84(3): 482-489.

Moore, D.C. (1988). Body image and eating behavior in adolescent girls. *American Journal of Dis Children*, 142(10): 1114-1118.

Palla, B. and I.F. Litt. (1988). Medical complications of eating disorders in adolescents. *Pediatrics*, 81(5): 613-623.

Patton, G.C. (1988). Mortality in eating disorders. *Psychological Medicine*. 18(4): 947-951.

Rosen, L.W. and D.O. Hough. (1987). Pathogenic weight control behaviors of female college gymnasts. *Physician and Sportsmedicine*, 16(9): 141-146.

Shangold, M. and G. Mirkin. (1988). *Women and Exercise Physiology and Sports Medicine*. Philadelphia, PA: F.A. Davis Co., Publishers, 248-263.

Steen, S.N. and S. McKinney. (1986). Nutrition assessment of college wrestlers. *Physician and Sportsmedicine*, 14(11): 100-116.

Thornton, J.S. (1990). Feast or famine: Eating disorders in athletes. *Physician and Sportsmedicine*, 18(4). 116-122.

Yager, J., F. Kurtzman, J. Landsverk and E. Wiesmeier. (1988). Behaviors and attitudes related to eating disorders in homosexual male college students. *American Journal of Psychiatry*, 145(4), 495-497.

Yager, J., J. Landsverk and C.K. Edelstein. (1987). A 20-month follow-up study of 628 women with eating disorders, I: course and severity. *American Journal of Psychiatry*, 144(9): 1172- 1177.

Zucker, P., J. Avener, S. Bayder, A. Brutman, K. Moore and J. Zimmerman. (1985). Eating disorders in young athletes. *Physician and Sportsmedicine*, 12(11): 88-106.

Part 7

INJURY PREVENTION

Photo by James Stephens

A Player's Guide To Screening For And Preventing Ankle Injury

Reid Elam, Ph.D., L.A.T., C., C.S.C.S.

One of the most common injuries in volleyball is that to the ankle. The type of ankle injury that sidelines more athletes is the plantar-inversion injury. This occurs when the toes are pointed downward and the foot is turned in. This causes undue stress on the ankle joint while it is plantiflexed and inverted, spraining the support ligaments, straining the muscle tendons surround the joint and/or breaking one or more bones of the ankle.

A volleyball athlete may sustain this type of injury by rapid cutting, planting one foot and turning, landing on an irregular surface like a teammate's foot or from a direct blow to the lower body.

To avoid the ankle injuries that take the athlete out of training and participation in practice and competition, consider the athlete's predisposition to ankle injury. This can be done by analyzing the athlete's sports injury history, determining any anatomical factors that make them more susceptible and analyzing the present conditioning program.

Sports Injury History for the Athlete

1. Have you ever injured your ankle?
   a. If yes, how many times?
   b. Have you injured the same ankle more than once?
2. Have you ever injured your foot, knee, hip or back?
   a. If yes, was it the same side as an ankle injury?
3. Are you prone to getting "shin splints?"

4. Have you ever had foot pain along the longitudinal arch or heel?
5. Have you ever worn foot orthotics prescribed by your doctor?
   a. If yes, are you wearing them now?
   b. Has it been over one year since you last had a checkup on your orthotics?
6. Does at least one of your ankles have a tendency to "roll" to the outside when cutting or making a sharp turn?
   a. If yes, is there pain or discomfort when your ankle does this?

If you answered "yes" to four or more of the above, you have a positive sports injury history for susceptibility to ankle injury.

Self-Screening for Anatomical Factors

1. Hold your shoes upside-down and side-by-side and look at the heels: Is there an uneven wear pattern of the heels?
2. Place your shoes side-by-side on a table top and view them from the rear: Does at least one of the heel counters have a significant bow/tilt in or out?

   Perform the following in your bare feet:

3. View your feet as you walk: Do your toes point in or out rather than straight ahead?
4. While standing, bend over and try to slide your fingers under your arches: Were you unable to slide your fingers under far enough to cover the first crease at the far joint of your fingers?

5. View yourself facing a full-length mirror:
   a. Would you consider yourself either "bow-legged" or "knock-kneed?"
   b. Does one shoulder appear higher than the other?
   c. Does one hip appear higher than the other?
6. Lie on your back, bend your knees to 90 degrees and your hips to 45 degrees, keeping your feet and legs together: Does one knee appear higher than the other?

If you answered "yes" to five or more of the above, you are positive for anatomical factors that predispose you to ankle injuries.

Self-Screening for Functional Factors

Perform the following in your bare feet:

1. While standing without any support, press up onto your toes for five repetitions:
   a. Do you favor one leg over the other?
   b. Did you lose your balance?
2. Balance on one foot for 60 seconds and then balance on the other:
   a. Was it more difficult to balance on one foot than the other?
   b. Were you unable to maintain your balance for the entire 60 seconds?
   c. Did you feel you were excessively shaky/wobbly in doing this?
3. Place two objects on the floor 4 feet apart. Hop on one leg in a figure-8 pattern around the markers, then do the same on the other leg. Time yourself:
   a. Did you feel any discomfort at least in one ankle?
   b. Were you significantly (0.5 seconds or more) slower on one leg over the other?

If you answered "yes" to four or more of the above, you are positive for functional factors that could lead to ankle injury.

Conditioning Program Analysis

1. Do you include squats, lunges or step-ups in your strength program?
   a. If yes, do you perform these exercises at least three times per week?
2. Do you include calf or toe raises in your program?
   a. If yes, do you perform these in a standing position?
3. Do you include jump rope drills in your program?

4. Do you incorporate the clean or snatch or variations of these lifts in your training?
5. Do you perform any specific ankle strengthening exercises: inversion (turning in), eversion (turning out), plantar flexion (pointing toes downward) and dorsiflexion (pulling toes backwards) with resistance (i.e., surgical tubing or cable)?
6. Do you perform any bounding drills (plyometric) using one leg?
   a. If yes, do you perform any of these drills moving laterally?
   b. With changes in direction?
7. Do you include any trampoline (mini or regular) work in your program?
8. Do you perform any balancing activities in your program (i.e., walking a balance beam, hop-scotching, use of BAPS board or other balancing apparatus)?
9. Do you perform drills that include quick stops, turns and rapid changes in direction?
10. Do you perform any running or skill drills barefoot?
11. Do you perform any movement drills on sand?
12. Do you regularly (a minimum or three times per week) stretch the lower leg complex?

If you answered "no" to five or more of the above, your conditioning program is deficient in exercises that adequately develop ankle stability.

Program Considerations
Beginner Level

Following are some suggestions for inclusion in your training program to help prevent ankle injuries:

1. Be sure to stretch the calves and Achilles tendons before and after workouts, practices and games.
2. Manually stretch the ankle joint complex by sitting, grabbing the foot in the opposite hand and rolling the foot in all directions.
3. Begin using the squat movement in your strength program. You can even perform squats without a barbell if you do not have access to weight equipment. The movement is more important than resistance at this stage.
4. Include calf or toe raises in your program, performing them with variations of toe-pointing positions (in, out, straight). Do these in a standing position.
5. Have a qualified person teach you the basics of Olympic-style weightlifting. Movements like overhead squat, snatch balance, foot-separation

and reaction drills for power cleans and snatches can be done with a broomstick and will develop total body coordination.

6. Start jumping rope. Perform stationary drills hopping on both feet, one foot and running in place.

7. Add agility drills to your run-conditioning program that include lateral, backward and change of direction movements.

8. Start performing simple bounding drills on a soft surface. These drills include two-legged hops forward and backward, laterally and zig-zagging (slalom-style).

Intermediate Level

Many of the drills suggested for beginners carry over to the intermediate level.

1. Use variations of the squat in training, such as the front squat, hack squat, split squat and overhead squat.

2. Supplement your leg strength program with lunge, lunge walk (forward) and side lunges, with or without weight.

3. Progress into the more complete Olympic-style movements, such as progressions of the power snatch plus front squat and power jerk plus jerk combinations.

4. Begin using dynamic jump rope drills by bounding across a 20-30 foot distance with both legs, forward and backward, laterally and high knee running, forward and backward.

5. Use one-legged drills in bounding forward, backward and laterally.

6. Perform balancing drills by walking on a balance beam or similar device and using hopscotch-like drills and games.

7. If you are positive for factors making you more susceptible to ankle injury or if you had a previous ankle injury, include exercises that are specific to ankle movements. Consult with your sports medicine health practitioner.

Advanced Level

Again, many of the suggestions provided for beginners and the intermediate level are interchangeable with the advanced level.

1. Supplement your squat program with step-ups if using a barbell or with step-thrusts without weight.

2. Consider using the box squat-thrust exercise as a variation in your leg conditioning program. Consult a conditioning specialist for proper instruction in this lift.

3. Incorporate total Olympic-style movements in your program (snatch and clean and jerk).

4. Supplement your Olympic-style lifts with high pulls and other power pull movements using a variation in grip styles for greater facilitation of the ankle complex in generating total body power.

5. When possible, perform running drills and agility drills barefoot or in sand.

6. Use dynamic balancing drills like one-leg hopping on a balance beam.

7. Use a balance device for developing neuromuscular components important in proprioception.

8. Consider using a slide/glide apparatus in your conditioning program, making these drills a regular part of your training regimen.

9. Use one-legged drills in jump rope dynamic exercises in your program, especially if you test positive for predisposing factors.

Reprinted from *Performance Conditioning for Volleyball*.

Courtesy of North Dakota State

Chapter 34

Balancing Injury With Performance Enhancement

Dan McDonough, A.T., C.

When designing a conditioning program, consider your age, conditioning experience, the specific requirements of your sport, time available for training, injury history and strength base plus other factors to be discussed. Some components are a given (age, injury history), while others (conditioning intensity and volume) must be determined. This article will examine how the athlete can stay healthy while increasing performance level.

Time and injuries: never enough of one and always too many of the other. There never seems to be enough time to get into great shape. So, how can you condition for the upcoming season and still look far enough ahead to prevent or reduce injuries? Let's review a few basic principles, then move to a few additional program possibilities.

Program Design Principle No. 1

When to Start Conditioning — Look at the length of the competitive season and the requirements of that level of play. Look at your athletic needs. How much time do you have for conditioning? This time period must be measured in months, not weeks. To assess your weak areas and make improvements while continuing to improve overall performance, you need months. Plan next season at the end of the preceding one. This is a good way to remember team and individual strengths and weaknesses.

After taking a short rest at the end of the season, develop a transition conditioning program. During this transition, you can resolve your injuries and continue rehabilitating until normal, pain-free strength and coordination have been restored. Study your injury history. Do any weak areas stand out?

Rest does not cure injuries. If you have a history of patellar tendonitis (jumper's knee), rest at the end of the season will make the knee feel better. That is, until you resume jumping. A strengthening, stretching and/or proprioception rehabilitation program is needed. Consult the medical staff on continuing a strength and proprioceptive training program during team conditioning.

The late transition period or early pre-season is the time to strength test and develop a plan for pre-season conditioning. Strength test only after you have been lifting for a few weeks and your strength coach has reviewed your technique. A solid aerobic and strength base needs to be developed early in the non competitive season. It is from this base that your athletic performance can be enhanced. Improper strength base development leads to a great number of otherwise avoidable injuries during the late pre-season and in-season.

Program Design Principle No. 2

Evaluations — The first evaluation of your conditioning should be made with an eye toward injury prevention. Only after potential chronic injury sites have been remedied and a conditioning base has been developed can performance conditioning be addressed. Evaluate your flexibility, strength (unilateral strength for each limb and torso strength), proprioception, foot speed and arm and leg power. Additional areas of testing include anthropometric measurements such as girths, percent body fat and lean tissue, and physiological testing including VO2 max (aerobic power) and anaerobic power testing (50-yard dash, Margaria-Kalamen staircase sprint).

The test results, combined with the injury history, will highlight areas of concentration for conditioning and injury prevention. For example, a player with a weak left hamstring (when compared to the right) and an injury history of hamstring strains should start a stretching and strengthening program for that area well before starting sprinting or on-court play. A player who develops rotator cuff strains or shoulder impingement syndrome each season should be evaluated for rotator cuff weakness and poor posture. After the weak areas have been found, a strengthening and stretching program should be performed long before any performance enhancement exercises for the anterior shoulder and chest are begun. Strengthen the weak links in the chain before starting performance conditioning.

Poor flexibility can also be a warning sign for future injuries. The stresses on these muscles will be greater than on the surrounding muscles and also greater as compared to the contralateral muscles (the same muscle on the other side of the body [left vs. right hamstring]). As in our hamstring example, a tight hamstring at the start of the conditioning phase will have a greater chance of strain as the intensity of conditioning increases. A strength or flexibility deficit of 20 percent or more contralateral is an area that needs attention. Remember, treating a muscle strain at the start of the season is a much harder task than increasing flexibility and strength in the pre-season.

Program Design Principle No. 3

Adjustments — Tailor the conditioning program to your needs. Players with a long injury history need an injury prevention program more than performance enhancement. For such a player with knee pain, focusing on leg strength, flexibility and coordination may produce a better and more productive athlete than a plyometric program. Get healthy and strong, then work into low-impact plyometrics. Gradually increase the performance-enhancing portion of your program while reducing the injury prevention portion to its core exercises.

Changes in your health status may mean reverting to injury prevention at some point. Continue injury prevention conditioning for two weeks past the point where you feel healthy. At this point, slowly mix in performance and conditioning with the existing program. Add only one exercise per week. In this way, a problem exercise can be seen and eliminated.

Blending injury prevention and performance conditioning into your own specialized workout is an evolutionary process. A significant amount of time and study needs to be done to evaluate and design your program. Small, incremental changes reflecting your current health and conditioning status must be made. Never hesitate to modify a program if you think you are overtraining. Constantly monitor your conditioning charts and make a step-by-step progression. Remember that rest can be one of the greatest performance enhancers when given at the proper time.

Program design recommendations will give you exercises for injury prevention and performance enhancement in a proper ratio to avoid muscular imbalance and improve performance.

Reprinted from *Performance Conditioning for Volleyball.*

Photo by Dan Houser

Chapter 35

REMEDIAL EXERCISES FOR THE PREVENTION OF SHOULDER INJURIES

Vern Gambetta

Shoulder injuries are common in volleyball due to the repetitive stress placed on the shoulder. Many of the common overuse shoulder injuries in volleyball can be prevented with a multifaceted program of remedial exercises. These exercises are based on the structure and function of the shoulder relative to the demands of volleyball.

In volleyball, the objective is to generate the highest possible velocity at impact. The majority of conditioning activities and technique work is directed toward this objective. Not enough attention is directed toward training the force reduction phase, which is where injuries occur due to the high deceleration forces on the muscles, tendons and ligaments. A remedial exercise program composed of the few simple exercises integrated into the total program can help prevent many shoulder problems.

Due to its structure, with the relatively large head of the humerus in a very shallow cavity, the glenoid fossa (the shoulder) is a very flexible joint. The dynamic stability is controlled directly by the rotator cuff muscles, as well as by the structure of the allied ligaments and tendons. Due to the shoulder's inherent mobility, stability and joint integrity should receive priority over mobility. The stability function is aided by the musculature of the scapulathoracic region. The movement of the scapula controls the movements of the shoulder and the arm, as well as serving as an anchor for the glenohumeral joint. Therefore, it is important to train the muscles that control the movement of the scapula. The key movements at the scapula are protraction and retraction, which are involved in most pushing and pulling movements. In addition to its instability, the shoulder is inherently stronger in internal rotation. This is also due to the structure. The internal rotators, which consist primarily of the pectorals and the latissimus dorsi, are the prime movers during the force production phase.

Shoulder structure and function dictate that the focus in the remedial program should be on the scapulathoracic area. The remedial program is designed to reinforce proportional development between the posterior and anterior areas of the upper extremity. This program is also designed to reinforce the kinetic link principle, enhance joint proprioception and body awareness. These are important considerations throughout an athlete's career, but should be especially emphasized during an athlete's developmental years. This differs from the traditional shoulder exercise routines that focus almost entirely on the shoulder joint itself and virtually ignore the scapula.

None of the exercises are especially new. What makes them unique is their application and sequencing as part of a total conditioning program.

Crawling

When: Use crawling as part of the warm-up for practice. Start with one set of 10 crawls forward and back (see Figure 35.1) and progress to three sets of 10 forward and back. Then add one set of 10 of crawling sideways (see Figure 35.2) right and left, progressing to three sets of 10.

Fig. 35.1

Fig. 35.2

On the crossover crawl (see Figure 35.3) do only one set of 10 in each direction.

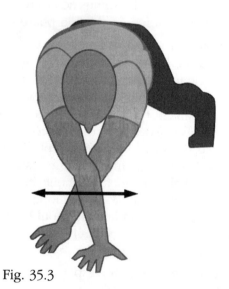

Fig. 35.3

How: Front support position with the weight evenly distributed on the hands and knees. Reach out - stretching out with movement of the arm. See Figure 35.1.

Arm Step-Up

When: It is best to put this exercise at the beginning of a weight training session. Start with one set of 10 of the forward and back movement (see Figure 35.4) and the side-to-side movement (see Figure 35.5) progressing to three sets of 10 of each exercise. One repetition consists of right arm up onto box, left arm up onto box, right arm down off the box, left arm down off the box.

Fig. 35.4

Fig. 35.5

How: Use a 4- to 6-inch high box. Start from a front support position with shoulder directly over the hands and the weight supported on the hands.

Tubing
External rotation

Fig. 35.6

When: Use as a warm-up before practice or as a cool down. Three sets of 10 reps.

How: 90/90 position - upper arm at 90 degrees to the torso and the forearm. Tubing attached in front of the exerciser at shoulder height. Stand back far enough from the attachment of the tubing so that there is tension on the tubing. Stretch the tubing back in a controlled manner into external rotation while maintaining the 90/90 position. Slowly (six seconds) return to the starting position.

External Rotation Flicks

When: Use as a warm-up before practice. Three sets of 10 reps.

How: 90/90 position - upper arm at 90 degrees to the torso and forearm. Attach the tubing in front of the exerciser at shoulder height. Stand back far enough from the attachment of the tubing so that there is tension on the tubing. Extend back into external rotation and rapidly move the tubing forward and back through the last 10 to 15 degrees of movement until fatigue stops the exerciser.

Diagonal Pattern

When: Use as a warm-up before practice. Two sets of 10 reps.

How: Attach the tubing just below waist height. Stand back far enough from the attachment of the tubing with the arm overhead, imitating the position of release. In a controlled manner, let the tubing pull the arm and hand through to a follow-through position.

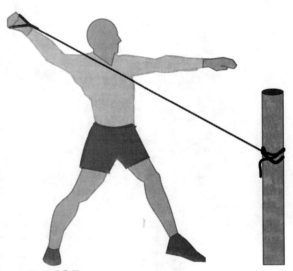

Fig. 35.7

Summary

These exercises are by no means the only exercises for improving shoulder stability. These are the most basic that can be placed within the context of a normal practice and workout routine without a great deal more time or energy expenditure.

Reprinted from *Performance Conditioning for Volleyball.*

REMEDIAL SHOULDER YEARLY DISTRIBUTION			
	OFF-SEASON	PRE-SEASON	IN-SEASON
Crawling	DAILY AS PART OF THE WARM-UP		
Arm Step-up	4 X WEEK	3 X WEEK	2 X WEEK
	USE TO WARM-UP BEFORE WEIGHT TRAINING		
Tubing	EX ROT 3 X WK	EX ROT 4 X WK	EX ROT 2 X WK
	DIAGONAL PATTERN 3 X WK	DIAGONAL PATTERN 3 X WK	DIAGONAL PATTERN 2 X WK

Courtesy of Cal State Northridge

Chapter 36

Low Back And Abdominal Injury Prevention And Performance Enhancement

Dan McDonough, A.T., C.

Volleyball is extremely tough on the lower back. Most players will, at some point in their careers, miss court time due to a low back injury. The sport places athletes in a forward-flexed position (e.g. serve receive and digging) from which they must make very quick movements in all directions as they go for the ball. This places tremendous pressure on the lumbar discs (vertebrae of the low back), ligaments and muscles. A volleyball player repeatedly serve receiving or digging low balls can overwhelm the muscles and ligaments supporting the spine and damage those same structures and/or the vertebral discs.

Prevention is the key. Back injuries can disable athletes for weeks or an entire season. We have heard of keeping the stomach strong to help prevent back injuries. This is true, but only a part of prevention. The entire torso must be stretched and strengthened, in all planes of movement, if low back

Exercises for Performance Enhancement		
Beginner	**Intermediate**	**Advanced**
back extension	same	same
Nautilus or Cybex		single arm
back extension trunk pulleys	same	same
seated row	same	same
one arm db row (lawn mower)	same	same
	bent over row	same
medicine ball-trunk rotation	side throw	same
underhand throw	same	same
overhead throw	same	same
	backward throw	same
	kneeling side throw	same
	cleans	dead lift
	high pulls	good morning
	*CKC power exercises	*same

*Almost any of the closed kinetic chain (CKC) power exercises (feet contacting the ground, pulling or pushing free weights) require controlled pelvic movements and trunk stabilization. Many are used in performance enhancement programs for volleyball. The exercises listed above, plus squats, front squats, snatch, lunges and many variations — hang cleans, snatch pulls, etc., work well and may increase strength in the torso. However, these exercises require supervision and technique analysis by an experienced, qualified conditioning coach. Build a strong conditioning base first and progress slowly in the strength training. Technique is extremely important! Get technique instruction.

Trunk Rotation Ball close to the body. Repeat both directions.

injuries are to be prevented or reduced.

Stretching must include the muscles of the back and the muscles that pull on the pelvis, affecting posture and function of the other torso muscles. Hamstrings, quadriceps, adductors and hip flexors must often need daily stretching. Tightness in any of these areas, or in the specific muscles of the lumbopelvic area, can cause abnormal stress and possible injury to the low back.

The muscles and connective tissue of the back and pelvis, as well as correct lumbopelvic function, should be evaluated at a sports medicine clinic whenever continued pain or dysfunction occur. Then, a specific program addressing problems can be developed and complications can be ruled out.

Underhand Throw Push with legs, drive hips forward.

Overhead Throw Drive arms forward. Accelerate the ball through full range.

Exercises that Combine Prevention and Performance

Back extensions, seated row, high pulls, cleans, medicine ball, all abdominal exercises

Trunk pulley program — can be utilized for performance enhancement as well as injury prevention, depending upon the volume and intensity. Prevention — one to two times per week, two to three sets x eight to 10 reps.

Performance enhancement — three times per week, three to four sets of six to 10 reps, depending on load.

Beginner
one arm row
standing cable row
seated cable row
seated cable row to side

Intermediate
standing two cable rotation pulls
standing two cable rotation pulls chest level
standing cable hip pull
one arm seated cable row to side

Advanced
standing rotation single cable pull low position
seated rotation single cable pull high position
standing rotation single cable pull chest level

Exercises for Injury Prevention

Beginner
crunch sit-up
twisting crunch
reverse sit-up
leg raises
pelvic tilts
bridges
alternating arm leg left
camel backs
press-ups
seated trunk rotations

Intermediate
same as beginner, except add cable abdominal crunch and cable trunk rotations

Advanced
same as beginner/intermediate, except add same single leg bridges, alternating arm left lift with resistance

Side Throw Rotate torso. Accelerate ball.

Backward Throw Keep the back straight, bend knees to start, extend hips, bring ball up overhead.

Kneeling Side Throw Rotate torso. Accelerate ball to side.

Seated Cable Row Keep back straight.

Program Examples

Beginner
back extension
seated row
one arm dumbbell row
crunch
twisting crunch
reverse sit-up
alternating arm leg lift
press ups

Intermediate
trunk pulleys
high pulls
medicine ball underhand throw
side throw
overhead throw
crunch
twisting crunch
reverse sit-up
leg raises
pelvic tilts
camel backs
alternative arm/leg lift

Advanced
weighted back extensions
single arm row
dead lift
cleans
medicine ball kneeling side throw
backward throw
crunch
twisting crunch
reverse sit-up
cable abdominal crunch
single leg bridge
alternating arm/leg lifts with resistance

Reprinted from *Performance Conditioning for Volleyball*.

Beginner Exercises

One Arm Row Keep back flat. No tilt to pelvis.

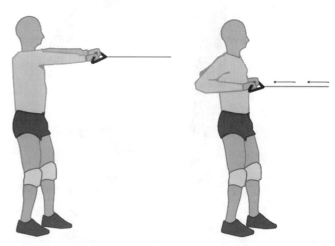

Standing Cable Row One foot forward. No trunk movement.

Intermediate Exercises

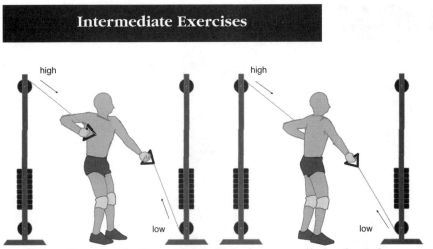

Standing Two Cable Rotation Pull Left arm pulls back, right pushes forward, rotate trunk, then move arms. One foot forward.

Standing Cable Hip Pull Pull down to hips. Torso flexes forward.

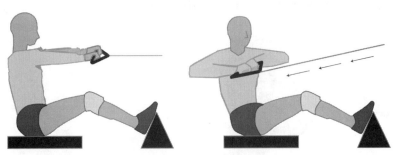

Seated Cable Row to Side Keep back straight. Rotate to either right or left.

Standing Two Cable Rotation Pull, Chest Level Same as above. Use chest level pulleys.

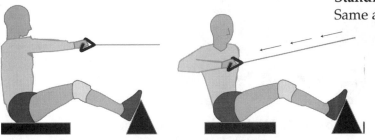

One Arm Seated Cable Row to Side One arm pull to right or left side. Rotate pelvis and torso to same side.

Advanced Exercises

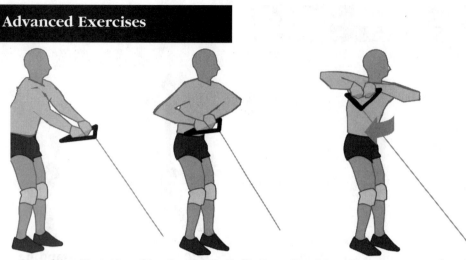

Standing Rotation Single Cable Pull, Low Position Feet face to side of pully, rotate torso to face pulley pull with rotation of torso and extension of legs and flexion of arms. Pull cable up to front of opposite shoulder.

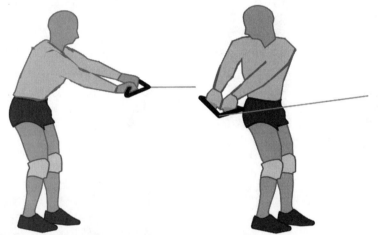

Standing Rotation Single Cable Pull, Chest Level Face pulley with torso bent forward. Feet face to side of pulley. Rotate torso and extend arms to side. Extend torso as rotating.

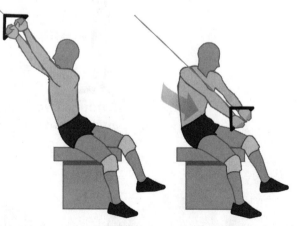

Seated Rotation Single Cable Pull, High Position Pull using trunk rotation then arm extension. Can stabilize back with chair with back support. Contract abdominals as rotating.

Chapter 37

SPINAL STABILIZATION FOR VOLLEYBALL

Reid P. Elam, Ph.D., A.T., C., C.S.C.S.

PROBLEM

The spine is subjected to tremendous amounts of stress during an athletic event. Movements in volleyball such as bending, twisting, lunging, jumping, arching and diving place supernormal stresses on the spine. Forces acting on the vertebral bodies and intervertebral discs are conducted along musculotendinous and ligament structures. These forces are classified as shear and rotational ones due to the undulating of the trunk when the athlete is in motion.

Low back pain often follows vigorous competition, training, or a long, difficult tournament. It can also result from the cumulative stress of repetitive activities.

Acute or sudden low back pain may be caused by an unaccommodating force resulting in trauma to muscular tissues (strain) or ligaments (sprain). The following sequence of events illustrate the pathology of an acute low back injury:

This representation is a simplified view of how low back pain can occur. In addition, it is important to know that the body reacts to injury by causing a muscle spasm as protection. The back muscles naturally tighten when the spine is overloaded. Another important consideration is that reciprocal inhibition of the antagonistic muscles (the abdominals in this case) takes place when back muscles contract strongly to "splint" the injured area.

Continuous bending can also cause undue stress to the longitudinal posterior ligament that runs along the entire back surface of the vertebral column. This ligament is thinner and weaker than its anterior counterpart. Sustained flexion places increased pressure on the posterior ligament due to the tension placed on it by bulging intervertebral discs. This bulging is a natural accommodation to the flexing of the spine and causes a backward shift of the intervertebral discs' nuclear jelly-like material. The low back pain which results often makes an erect, standing position uncomfortable.

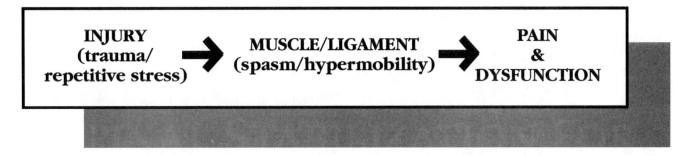

INJURY (trauma/repetitive stress) → MUSCLE/LIGAMENT (spasm/hypermobility) → PAIN & DYSFUNCTION

ACTION

For low back pain emanating from muscle tightness or irritation to the lumbosacral/sacroiliac (small of the back) region, the following exercises are recommended:

Unilateral hip and knee flexion. Raise one kee, holding either on top of the knee or behind the knee (in the crease) with both hands. Slowly pull it to your chest. Keep the other leg extended and relaxed. Perform alternately with right and left legs.

Bilateral hip and knee flexion. Raise both knees to be pulled by each corresponding hand toward the chest in the same manner as in unilateral hip and knee flexion.

Unilateral crossover. Raise one knee (either bent or extended) toward your chest and, with the opposite hand on top of the knee, pull the leg across your body. Alternate with opposite leg.

All the above exercises are held in a comfortable position for a 10 count for three sets each.

For low back pain resulting from prolonged positioning in the bowed or flexed position, the following exercises are often helpful. All exercises are performed prone.

Elbow/full press-up

Unilateral leg raise

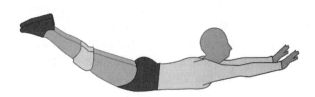

Bilateral leg raise and back hyperextension

Press-ups are held for a 10-count and performed for three to five sets, while the leg raise/back hyperextension is held for a 5-count for five to 10 sets.

For total spinal stabilization, the following exercises are beneficial:

Pelvic tilts. Assume a supine position with knees flexed at 90 degrees and hips at 45 degrees, hands to side of body. Compress stomach so that the low back flattens to the table or floor.

Partial sit-up. Assume a supine position with knees flexed at 90 degrees and hips at 45 degrees, arms folded across chest. Curl up so that the bottom point of you shoulder blades barely touch the table or floor surface.

Partial sit-ups with twist. Same position as partial sit-up. Curl up and twist so that one elbow points to the opposite knee. The elbow-up side will have the shoulder blade off the table or floor, the opposite will remain in slight contact.

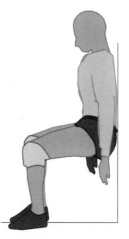

Wall slide. Lean against smooth surface such as a finished door or paneled wall. Set your feet so that the heels are 18 inches from the wall and at shoulder width. Keeping the back in contact with the wall, slide down until the small of the back flattens against the wall, the slide to the erect position.

All exercises are held for a 5-count for five to 10 sets. Continue breathing during these exercises.

These exercises can be combined or used according to their effectiveness for each individual case. If any exercise causes discomfort and/or there is a continuation of symptoms, consult your sports medicine specialist.

In addition to the corrective exercises described here, always maintain good flexibility in the hamstrings, calves and Achilles tendon, and hip flexor and abductor (groin) muscles. Ultimately, conditioning for overall athletic fitness is essential to low back pain prevention.

Reprinted from *Performance Conditioning for Volleyball*.

For all the latest news
regarding volleyball and
conditioning, subscribe to
*Performance Conditioning
for Volleyball.*
For more information,
call 1-800-578-INFO